DUE FOR RETURN

D1576616

MAKING MOCKERY

THE POETICS
OF ANCIENT SATIRE

Ralph M. Rosen

OXFORD
UNIVERSITY PRESS
2007

OXFORD

UNIVERSITY PRESS

Oxford University Press, Inc., publishes works that further
Oxford University's objective of excellence
in research, scholarship, and education.

Oxford   New York
Auckland   Cape Town   Dar es Salaam   Hong Kong   Karachi
Kuala Lumpur   Madrid   Melbourne   Mexico City   Nairobi
New Delhi   Shanghai   Taipei   Toronto

With offices in
Argentina   Austria   Brazil   Chile   Czech Republic   France   Greece
Guatemala   Hungary   Italy   Japan   Poland   Portugal   Singapore
South Korea   Switzerland   Thailand   Turkey   Ukraine   Vietnam

Copyright © 2007 by Oxford University Press, Inc.

Published by Oxford University Press, Inc.
198 Madison Avenue, New York, New York 10016

www.oup.com

Oxford is a registered trademark of Oxford University Press

Library of Congress Cataloging-in-Publication Data
Rosen, Ralph Mark.
Making mockery : the poetics of ancient satire / Ralph M. Rosen.
p. cm.
ISBN 978-0-19-530996-6
1. Verse satire, Classical—History and criticism.   I. Title.
PA3022.S28R67 2007
880.09—dc22   2006023216

1005322861⊤

1 3 5 7 9 8 6 4 2
Printed in the United States of America
on acid-free paper

For Charlotte and Benny
τέκνα φίλτατα

"I" is only a convenient term for somebody who has no real being.

—Virginia Woolf, *A Room of One's Own*

One wonders whether, after painting pictures on the walls of their caves, our primeval ancestors then had to explain them. This might well have marked the birth of aesthetic criticism, a history of negotiation between artist and audience, producers and consumers entangled in a messy web of fictions, truths, and everything in between. As the Greeks figured out early on, *poiêsis*—artistic creation in all its varieties—traffics in the representation of things and ideas, but its representations can never actually be what they purport to represent. As long as our hypothetical cave dwellers painted scenes of woolly mammoths and domestic life, or, in the verbal realm, as long as they told imaginative stories that did not cleave too closely to the lived experiences of their audiences, no one needed to worry much about ontology. Fictions can be entertaining, after all, even if not true.

But things get far more complicated when artists do things that unsettle audiences and force them to pay closer attention to that perennially blurred line between fiction and reality than they might under less troubling circumstances. Such *poiêsis* has taken many forms in the verbal and visual arts, and each plays out differently within its own historical moment, but they all end up forcing a confrontation of sorts with an audience over meaning and intention. Our cave-dwelling audience may smile placidly at depictions of an exciting hunt or a successful battle with hostile neighbors, but what about the painting that caricatures their leader, or the song that uses taboo language or violates other norms of cultural decorum? Why do some people find such representation amusing, others offensive? And for which of these two groups is such art actually intended in the first place? Such questions are notoriously difficult to answer, especially since it is never entirely clear whether we can or should trust the answers given by the artists themselves, or whether these are even meaningful questions to pose. And yet these, and other questions of this sort, always seem to arise when art aggressively and overtly transgresses norms or appears to scandalize at least some portion of a putative audience.

Nowhere, perhaps, is the relationship between artist and audience more fraught than in the case of satirical poetry, where a peculiar mixture of comedy and didactic posturing—what the Greeks came to refer to as *spoudaiogeloion*—

makes for a profoundly elusive artistic form. One of the most distressing tropes for audiences of such literature is satire's predilection for mocking individuals, especially when these are people known to contemporary audiences, and for mocking them with aggressive, often scandalous, language. Somebody is supposed to find this funny; but somebody else is supposed to be harmed by it as well, emotionally, at least, if not physically. The poet claims to have a reason to mock, but how does such self-righteousness interact with an attendant desire to make comedy? Is poetic humor, especially ironic humor, supposed to mitigate the violence of invective and vituperation? And if so, how is an audience supposed to respond to a satirist's relentless insistence, conveyed throughout the work *in propria persona*, that what they hear is incontestably true? Even the most sophisticated, literate audiences wrestle with these questions, and the disarray in which such genres often leave them is ample testimony to the unusual psychological and social power of poetic mockery.

We need not turn very far from our own experiences in the twenty-first century to see that satire has lost little of its power to alarm as well as entertain, and the great divide between what satirists claim to be doing and how audiences receive their work is as vast and complicated as it has ever been. Satirists form alliances with their audiences or rouse hostilities in them as unpredictably today as they did in antiquity, and even literary scholars, for all their analytical powers, often cannot quite extricate themselves from the snares that satirical genres carefully lay out. This is, of course, a triumph for the satirist, but something of a dilemma for the scholar, especially for those who study satire in cultures and historical periods not their own. For in such cases—that is, when we have only limited access to how a satirical work was actually experienced by its various contemporary audiences—the satirist's already strident voice takes on even greater force. Satirists tend towards a soapbox rhetoric, and have little interest in entertaining opposing points of view, so it often takes considerable effort for an audience not to take their ranting at face value, or, more precisely, to convince themselves that they *ought* not to do so. For all the generic cues that seek to complicate a naïve reception of their work, satirists simultaneously construct an "I" that claims an opposite agenda, namely to dissuade us from too much analysis and convince us that the experience of satire, unlike other forms of literature, should be direct and unmediated.

Satire engenders such tensions and paradoxes in any era, and they become particularly urgent literary problems when satirists foreground their vituperative side. Audiences have always found it difficult to retain their composure in the face of poets who represent and claim to endorse all the negative behaviors—violence, narcissism, obscenity, to name only a few—typically associated with mockery and abuse. Vigorous invective or mockery may elicit in some audiences a nervous laughter, while others are driven to repudiation and even censorship; but any audience confronted by such poetry must at some point come to terms with the satirist's persistent desire to drag them into his (occasionally her) orbit, even when they would prefer to keep their distance.

This book is concerned with precisely such dilemmas as they arise in Greek and Roman poets of satire, and attempts to understand the complex literary dynamics at work when such poets—usually in a voice they claim to be their own—attack individuals through mockery, invective or other modes of abuse. This is not, therefore, a comprehensive study of ancient satire, but rather an examination of a relatively circumscribed poetic phenomenon. Ancient satire had plenty to offer beyond personal mockery, but it was its aggressive postures that drew the most attention and concern from audiences and critics. The fundamental argument of this book is that the Greco-Roman poets working in such genres composed their attacks on targets, and constructed their relationships with audiences, in accordance with a set of common poetic principles, protocols, and tropes. I am hoping to encourage, therefore, a synoptic view of such poetry, from archaic iambus through Roman satire, and to suggest that an appreciation of an abstracted poetics of mockery can help us better understand how individual instances of such poetry functioned in their own historical contexts.

In recent decades, classicists have become attuned to the forces of irony, persona-construction, rhetorical posturing, and other devices by which satirists complicate and destabilize their poetry. But they have generally trained their eye on one poet at a time, or a cluster of poets working in the same tradition, and when all is said and done, despite a toolkit of sophisticated critical methodologies, they have often found it difficult—claims to the contrary notwithstanding—to resist treating a satirical work as anything other than thinly veiled autobiography. I have long felt, therefore, that a more synchronic analysis of poetic mockery is called for, and that such an approach would allow for a deeper and more nuanced understanding of satirical genres more broadly conceived in classical antiquity.

A book on such a topic could clearly be written in a variety of ways. The chronology spans close to a millennium, across two cultures and their two languages, and over such a long period of time there are far more satirical poets than could possibly be contained within the scope of a single book. Someone else writing this book might focus on different poets or different works than those I examine here; but I would like to think, at least, that a different selection of authors and texts would not make my arguments necessarily substantively much different or any better. This is another way of expressing my hope that what I have to say about the satirical poets who do appear in this book will, mutatis mutandis, be applicable to those who do not. The omission of satirical prose authors, notably Lucian, is perhaps worthy of brief comment. While there were some purely practical reasons for limiting this study to poetry, differences in the mimetic procedures and formal qualities of prose and poetry also led me to conceptualize them as distinct literary realms. The satirical "I" of the prose author will have much in common with the satirical poet's "I," but there are differences, too, especially in how each type of author goes about constructing relationships with audiences, which are better left for future study.

This book has been written over a number of years, and many friends, colleagues, and students have helped me keep my focus and refine my thinking along the way. Many have generously read individual parts of the book as it took shape and I have benefited incalculably from their expertise and critical acumen. Among the first to see versions of the early chapters were Stephen Halliwell and Deborah Steiner, and their enthusiasm for the project in its formative stages, as well as their criticisms and suggestions, were invaluable. Others who read and offered comments on various chapters include Peter Bing, Erwin Cook, Thomas Hawkins, Catherine Keane, Elfriede Knauer, James Porter, Andrea Rotstein, Ineke Sluiter, and Bryce Walker. The combined intellectual gravitas of this list is formidable indeed, and I thank them all profoundly for the various ways in which they engaged with my work. S. Douglas Olson and Eric Casey deserve special thanks for reading nearly the entire manuscript in its penultimate form, and offering not only penetrating and sober comments on substantive matters, but many stylistic and bibliographical suggestions as well. Many thanks also to Seth Bernard for compiling the Index Locorum, and to Jeremy Leftt for assistance in proofreading during the final stages of production. It remains for me, finally, to thank profusely the Press's referees, both of whom clearly read the manuscript with extraordinary care and thoughtfulness. Every aspect of the book has been improved by their suggestions, challenges, disagreements, and encouragement. Even in cases where I chose not to follow their advice, I did so, at least, with a heightened sense of peril.

In recent years I have presented some of the material in this book in departmental colloquia at the University of Pennsylvania, and have always learned much from the lively discussions that occurred on these occasions. I thank all my colleagues and graduate students in the Department of Classical Studies at Penn—it is a great privilege to work with such a stimulating and distinguished group of scholars. A few colleagues deserve individual thanks: Joseph Farrell, for the kind of intellectual tenacity and frankness that is only possible in a friendship as long and close as ours; Rita Copeland, for her endlessly creative mind and her ability to find something interesting and profound to say about just about anything; Sheila Murnaghan, for her uncanny ability to see right to the heart of a problem, and her continual encouragement of this project over the years; and Emily Wilson, who generously read a draft of the entire manuscript and brought to it her uncommonly refined literary sensibilities. I also thank the Deans of the School of Arts and Sciences at the University of Pennsylvania, whose enlightened support of the Humanities has allowed Classical Studies to thrive at this institution. In particular, I am grateful to the School for a research leave during the spring 2005 semester, which enabled me to complete this book.

Finally, many thanks to my editors at the Oxford University Press—Shannon McLachlan, who worked with the manuscript in its early forms; Stefan Vranka, who shepherded it to publication; and my production editor, Gwendolyn Colvin, whose efficiency and patience were always remarkable. All three have made every stage of production a real pleasure.

In the spirit of mockery, I had told my wife, Ellen, that there was no way I would mention her in this preface. She probably would not lose too much sleep over it if, in fact, I had not. But I am not myself an especially good satirist, and I can no longer maintain the conceit. It is true that neither of us can quite put a finger on what exactly she did to help in the writing or production of this book, but her contribution is no less significant or appreciated for being intangible.

A note on translations: I have used available English translations of the Greek and Latin texts I cite throughout the book if I found them to be satisfactory. Uncredited translations are my own.

CONTENTS

MAKING MOCKERY

1

The Dynamics of Ancient
Satirical Poetry

1. Questions and Methods

Comic poetry can be found in one form or another in classical antiquity for as long as we have a literary record. For every poet who sought to entertain audiences with sober and earnest perspectives on the world, it seems that there was always another just as happy to ridicule or ironize traditional pieties, or test the limits of decorum, all in the service of drawing laughter from an audience. Such poets achieved their comic goals through a variety of methods, and they worked in diverse forms and performance contexts across antiquity, but one of the most pervasive and enduring practices, and indeed often one of the most puzzling to ancient and modern audiences alike, was to compose poetry that mocked, abused, or otherwise satirized other people. In some cases verbal abuse and vituperative satire became for ancient audiences the hallmark of a poet's style even if that poet's work, taken as a whole, was in fact much more varied. This was certainly true, for example, of the archaic Greek poet Archilochus and the fifth-century poet of Athenian Old Comedy, Aristophanes. Their poetry offered much more than personal attack, but so powerful was the effect of this particular aspect of their work, that throughout antiquity they were regarded—and not always approvingly—as paragons of mockery and unbridled aggression. Although such poets composed in radically different forms and within different social settings, their shared interest in the trope of mockery suggests that they were similarly inspired by the comic possibilities inherent in a stance of interpersonal confrontation.

The same situation holds later on for Roman traditions of poetry that have roots in comedy. Horace and Juvenal, for example, although culturally, linguistically and generically distinct from Greek comic poets (and even quite distinct from one another), at various points in their work adopted very similar authorial postures in the service of personal attack. It is fair to say, in fact, as we shall see in greater detail in the course of this book, that all Classical poets of satire—from Archilochus to the Roman satirists—who assumed a personalized comic voice, a poetic *ego* girded for verbal battle against a target, shared a common desire to portray themselves as morally self-righteous, indignant at

3

the behavior of others, and eager to capture the allegiance of their audience through their poetry. Despite the commonalities of ethos, attitude, and poetic technique among ancient poets of mockery, however, there has never been a sustained attempt to conceptualize all such poets as participants in a literary activity that transcends the boundaries of single authors, genres, and temporalities. It is not so much that Classical scholars have expended much effort in trying to repudiate a more synoptic approach to ancient forms of poetic mockery and satire, as that they have simply been uneasy making comparisons among what appear on first glance to be unlikely literary bedfellows. It is easy enough, perhaps, to see that when Hipponax ridicules his bête-noire, Bupalus, in the sixth century BCE, or, centuries later, when Juvenal satirizes the crass host Virro, each is seeking a laugh from his audience at the expense of a target. But precisely because such satirical gestures are so often directed against specific, historically attested, individuals, it can be rather more difficult to think of them independently of an author's putative temperament or the circumstances surrounding the composition of a given poem. The fact, moreover, that the aggressive posture underlying personal attack will often appear to an audience as socially problematic, and that the poet will often deploy potentially transgressive tactics such as obscenity or lurid innuendo, further complicates the attempt to understand poetic mockery as a broad literary phenomenon. Such poets, after all, will always strive to leave the impression, however disingenuously or ironically, that they are driven to transgress social norms by the depth of indignation they feel against their targets; and indignation will always *seem*, at any rate, to be rooted in the highly contingent and personalized historical moment.

This study, by contrast, tries to avoid the seduction of the poet's indignant personal voice—a constructed *ego* that would be pleased, after all, to have the reader conclude that the world revolved solely around itself—if only long enough to explore the dynamics of personal ridicule and vituperative satire across the entire continuum of Greek and Latin comic poetry, before allowing ourselves to return to the marked fictive world in which such poets routinely dwell. Such a perspective, I believe, will allow us to articulate a specific poetics of mockery underlying and affiliating its various forms, and will deepen our understanding of a perennially elusive, often paradoxical and contradictory, literary phenomenon.

There has been an abundance of excellent critical work on such poets, whether in the area of formal and generic analysis, or in the interpretation of textual meaning. Classical scholars have never hesitated to assume that individual, historically localized examples of comic abuse and satire bear some relation to one another. Hence, for example, Greek iambography will routinely be invoked in considering the generic provenance of Catullus's scurrilous lyrics or Horace's *Epodes*.[1] This connection is relatively easy to make,

---

1. See, e.g., Freudenburg 1993, 96–108, Mankin 1995, 6–9, Cucchiarelli 2001, 125–52.

since these two Roman poets suggest it explicitly themselves. Even in cases where two poets who engaged in comic abuse seem quite unlike each other in terms of genre, performance context or the like—Juvenal and Aristophanes, let us say—critics have often noted, if vaguely and fleetingly, that their mocking, ad hominem satires are somehow interrelated. For the most part, however, literary criticism in Classics has focused primarily on specific texts, authors or genres, and the relationship between disparate works, particularly when they are separated by a great expanse of time, is traditionally articulated in strictly diachronic terms: What, for example, can Aristophanes tell us about Juvenal? What more can we say about Catullus, once we know that he was familiar with the Greek iambus? Such an approach will typically consider only those elements in antecedent texts that have explicit bearing on the later text, and little attention is paid to a set of logically prior questions surrounding the very nature and legitimacy of positing an affiliation between two literary phenomena in the first place. What does it really mean to say, for example, that Juvenal's mockery of targets is somehow "like" Aristophanes', and how might the comic mockery found in the *later* poet illuminate its deployment in a poet centuries earlier? To put the question in its simplest form: Why do apparently analogous manifestations of comic mockery persist throughout antiquity (or, for that matter, transhistorically and cross-culturally) in otherwise disparate forms of poetry?

Classical poets themselves often confronted this question in a conscious, if occasionally oblique, way. Horace's famous declaration at the opening of *Sermones* 1.4, for example, that this very Roman satirical work had deep connections with the comic drama of fifth-century Athens certainly suggests that poets of Greco-Roman antiquity could situate themselves comfortably within a literary tradition that crossed many genres and cultural boundaries:

> Eupolis atque Cratinus Aristophanesque poetae,
> atque alii quorum comoedia prisca virorum est,
> si quis erat dignus describi quod malus ac fur,
> quod moechus foret aut sicarius aut alioqui
> famosus, multa cum libertate notabunt.
> hinc omnis pendet Lucilius, hosce secutus
> mutatis tantum pedibus numerisque;

> The poets Eupolis, Cratinus, and Aristophanes, and the other men who constitute the Old Comedy, used to brand with great freedom anyone who deserved to be portrayed as a blackguard and a thief, a lecher or a cut-throat, or as notorious in any other way. Lucilius derives entirely from them, having followed them in every respect except rhythm and metre. (trans. Rudd 1966, 88)

5

But what exactly does it mean for Horace to claim Athenian comedy as a crucial poetic exemplar?[2] The aspect of Greek comedy that he specifically highlights is its abusive elements, its notorious attacks on public malefactors, its unrestrained license to mock. Yet, as is often noted, Horace's *Sermones* can hardly be characterized along these lines: They are, by comparison with Old Comedy, restrained and tame, with only the very occasional hint of genuine vituperation.[3] If Horace's *Sermones* have any generic affiliation with Greek comedy, it is the gentler New Comedy of Menander that comes to mind, with its character studies and comic types, rather than the relentless *onomasti kômôidein* of Old Comedy.[4] To add to the confusion, Horace's *Sermones* 1.4 (as well as 1.10) proceeds to contrast explicitly his own brand of satire with that of his early predecessor, Lucilius, a poet much closer to Greek Old Comedy in his aggressive language and posturing than to Horace.[5] Why then, would Horace single out Old Comedy as an antecedent for his own work, which bore virtually no formal resemblance to Aristophanes or Eupolis?[6]

2. In fact, Horace's exact claim is not clear: The first five lines of *Satire* 1.4 describe Old Comedy as a poetry of attack; line 6 states that *Lucilius* depended entirely on Old Comedy as a literary model, not Horace himself. But as many have pointed out, despite Horace's stylistic criticisms of Lucilius, he too wanted to maintain the relationship with Lucilius that linked him with Old Comedy. See, e.g., Rudd 1966, 90–92; Freudenburg 1993, 92–108, and 2001, 23–71; and Cucchiarelli 2001, passim, but esp. 15–83.

3. See Freudenburg 2001, 18: "The lines are fraught with misinformation that caricatures not only the poets of Greek Old Comedy, but Lucilius as well. For Lucilius's dependence on these poets is hardly what it is made out to seem here, so utterly direct and all-encompassing that Lucilius has 'merely' to adjust their rhythms and meter." Clearly, as most scholars realize, the lines are ironic in the sense that Horace cannot possibly believe that he is offering a historically accurate assessment of his work's literary provenance. At the same time, however, he is certainly interested in recovering the fundamental satirical mode that distinguished these earlier poets. Much of the *Sermones*, as Freudenburg 2001 and Cucchiarelli 2001 have most recently shown, are concerned to work out Horace's attempts at simultaneously modeling himself on, and distancing himself from, these exemplars of explicit, aggressive satire.

4. Cf. Dickie 1981; Hunter 1985, 486–87; and Freudenburg 1993, 100–102. Cucchiarelli 2001, 45–46, argues that Horace finds Terence a more appealing model than Plautus for the "new comic" strains of his *Sermones*.

5. Freudenburg 1993, 97–103, rightly emphasizes that Horace in 1.4 does not repudiate Lucilius's notorious *libertas*, his freedom of speech (a point also made by Rudd 1966, 91), and in many ways sees himself as an heir to the earlier poet, but it remains a fact that Horace had not adopted the vituperative attitude that characterizes Lucilius (and Old Comedy). For the influence of Callimachean iambus, New Comedy, and Cynic diatribe on Horace, see Freudenburg's discussion, with bibliography ad loc. On Callimachus and Horace, see also Cucchiarelli 2001, 168–79.

6. As Rudd 1966, 89, put it: "The problem here is not that Lucilius is compared to Aristophanes and the rest, or even that some general influence is discerned, but rather that he is said to 'derive entirely from' Old Comedy. . . . This, of course, is an absurd over-simplification, ignoring as it does not only the various Hellenistic influences on Lucilius's work, but also its characteristic Roman flavor." Horace, of course, (as Rudd well realized) was perfectly aware of these areas of influence on his *Sermones*, as has been well shown in recent years by Freudenburg 1993 and 2001, and Cucchiarelli 2001.

Scholars have proposed a variety of answers to this question, nearly all of which focus on the status of Old Comedy in Horace's time as a literary and rhetorical marker. Leo, for example, suggested that in first-century BCE Rome ancient theories of Old Comedy began to be applied to Roman satire,[7] and many since then have assumed the influence of such theorizing on Horace's claims at the beginning of 1.4.[8] In the same vein, Freudenburg has attempted to explain Horace's programmatic *Sermones* as a synthesis of two competing approaches to satire, the "Aristotelian" and "iambographic."[9] These approaches have gone far to clarify the interplay of contemporary literary discourses in Horace's *Sermones*, but they rarely ask what it was specifically in Old Comedy that encouraged Roman critics and poets to derive their own satire from it, or how meaningful the theoretical connection posited between the two genres was for understanding the dynamics of a work such as Horace's *Sermones*. Did Aristophanes' infamous attacks on Cleon, for example, function in a qualitatively similar way to Horace's attacks on boorish hosts or arrogant poetasters? After all, even though Horace's literary world was highly mediated by philosophical and poetic trends subsequent to Old Comedy, at some point he, like Aristophanes, had to decide to work in a form that prominently featured comic mockery. What factors, then, would have influenced their respective decisions to compose this kind of poetry in the first place?

In the case of Horace, scholars have often been content to argue that Horace wrote satire essentially because he wanted to emulate the poets of Old Comedy and Lucilius, doing what they did, only better and more appropriately to his own age. But this explanation helps us little with the more fundamental question of *why* this might have been so: What was it about Old Comedy or Lucilius that allowed him to consider them as appropriate analogues to his own satiric proclivities? If Horace felt that what he was doing in the *Sermones* was in a fundamental sense similar to what poets of Old Comedy did, even when his poetry looked nothing like theirs, we may assume that the affiliation he sensed between his *Sermones* and Greek comedy—the polemical, aggressive, yet comic, impulse—transcended all aspects of form, time, and place, and offered an abstract paradigm against which he could gauge his own compositions.[10] Only by achiev-

---

7. Leo 1889. Leo suspected that Varro may have proposed the connection between Greek comedy and Satire. See also Brink 1962 and Dickie 1981, 185–86.

8. See Hendrickson 1900; Rudd 1966, 86–90; Heldmann 1987, 122–39; Freudenburg 1993, 96–99.

9. "Certainly Horace is a good Aristotelian, subscribing to the theory of the liberal jest in creating the distinctly New Comic world of his *Satires*. At the same time, however, he is a writer in the iambographic tradition: the Old Comic poet, the writer of iambs, and the Cynic who vaunts his right to name and abuse enemies. The combination is impossible and absurd . . . [y]et this is exactly what Horace has done." Freudenburg 1993, 107.

10. On Horace's relationship to Old Comedy in particular, see Müller 1992, and Cucchiarelli 2001, 47–55. "Lucilio ha saputo riprendere dalla commedia antica lo spirito 'giambico', la forza

ing a clearer sense of what such a paradigm might have meant for Horace can we begin to understand the poetics of the *Sermones*. For once we articulate the more abstract structures and systems that affiliate various poets or types of poetry, the essentially metahistorical relationships that emerge can significantly augment our understanding of how individual poets and their genres were instantiated in their particularized historical and cultural milieux.

In the *Sermones*, of course, Horace's unabashed self-consciousness makes it easier to chart a literary genealogy for his work and a sense of substantive linkages with its antecedents.[11] Even so, many of the forces that gave rise to comic mockery in Greek and Roman poetry operated well beyond the awareness of any poet, and, as we shall see in later chapters, these often reveal more about such poetry than any authorial disquisition could. Besides, the traditional emphasis within classical scholarship on literary antecedents ends up begging the question of where the antecedents themselves came from. Horace, for example, can depict Aristophanes and his colleagues as foundational authors for his own work, but the reverse is obviously not possible—Aristophanes did not have the benefit of knowing the subsequent history of comic mockery. And yet it is also obvious that the mockery of Old Comedy had its own history, and this history must, by implication, have some relevance to the formation of a work such as the *Sermones*, even if Horace would have little awareness of the mechanisms at work.

To put the matter concisely, one of the most common methodological dilemmas in assessing comic mockery (and, indeed, any number of literary phenomena) is how to explain two phenomena that appear strikingly similar or even homologous, yet seem otherwise disconnected, whether in terms of history, genre, or place of origin. To illustrate this dilemma, we may consider a familiar topos from a work by another Roman satirist, Juvenal. Like most satirists of any age, Juvenal's poetry is simultaneously topical and abstract: In its details it is suffused with the culture of Imperial Rome, though most of its recurrent themes—hypocrisy, greed, sexual behavior, to name a few—would be more or less intelligible to audiences of any time or place. This tension between contemporaneity and universality creates a set of critical problems especially idiosyncratic to satirical literature. For just as the satirist may insist that he tells a certain historically rooted truth about his situation, the generalizing purport of this truth tends to deflect the audience from taking it at face

---

censoria che opera *multa cum libertate* (*sat.* 1, 4, 5), ma non ha saputo riprenderne le altre qualità; ed è questa ragione che impedisce ad Orazio di ripetere per lui quanto Aristofane, pur con qualche malizia, aveva detto di Cratino . . ." (Cucchiarelli 2001, 51).

11. Freudenburg 2001 and Cucchiarelli 2001 are excellent recent attempts at explaining Horace's relationship to his literary antecedents, both of which stress the ways in which politics and social considerations intersected with Horace's poetic choices.

value, and in fact steers it in the direction of comedy.[12] Juvenal's complaints about his poverty are an excellent case in point. In the famously programmatic first satire of Book 1, Juvenal's fundamental problem is that because the rest of Rome is so corrupt, and he, by contrast, so self-righteous, he ends up literally impoverished. The vivid exemplary scenes Juvenal conjures up are well known: wealthy patrons hoarding money, desperate clients (such as the poet) vying for a paltry allotment (the famous *sportula*) from the patron, undeserving foreigners posing as citizens, and so on. The effects on the oppressed satirist are summed up at lines 1.132–34:

> vestibulis abeunt veteres lassique clientes
> votaque deponunt, quamquam longissima cenae
> spes homini; caulis miseris atque ignis emendus.

> The old and weary clients leave the porches, abandoning their wishes—
> although the hope of a dinner is the one that lasts longest. The poor souls have got to buy their cabbage and firewood.
> (trans. Braund 2004)

The poor client, frustrated in his attempt to extract from his patron enough to rise above the poverty line, gives up for another day on the possibility of an extravagant feast and retires to his humble meal of cabbage. Now, poverty is perennially associated with poets, presumably because poetry so often tends to be perceived as a profession of marginal status. But in his first *Satire*, Juvenal hardly wants his audience to be thinking of poverty as a mere literary cliché, applicable to anyone who chooses a literary profession. *His* poverty, so he claims, is a result of the sordid, real-life socioeconomic conditions of Rome, and the poetry itself is alleged to have been inspired almost exclusively by the poet's anger and indignation. But the motif of poverty recurs so frequently in Juvenal's work, and in so many peculiar contexts, that one soon becomes suspicious of the seriousness of his complaints.[13]

In *Satire* 7, for example, Juvenal focuses on how the contemporary poet in particular suffers from inadequate material security. Despite his "incurable itch for writing" (*insanabile . . . scribendi cacoethes*, 50–51), a poet can never hope to rise to an exalted level because he is plagued by constant anxiety. By con-

---

12. See the remarks of Branham 1989, 189–90, on Lucian's *Alexander*, where he describes Lucian's "seriocomic strategy, in which wit supplants argument, using laughter to shape our considered perceptions of the grounds for admiration [of Alexander]. . . ."

13. See Rudd 1976, 102–4, who says of lines 147–51 (against any number of scholars at the time who took Juvenal's complaints against poverty seriously): "whatever social complaint it may entail, it must also be seen as a splendid piece of comic writing. After saying that the poor man's clothes look as if they'd been in a battle, Juvenal then protests that poverty makes a man look ridiculous!"

trast, he argues, poets of an earlier age who were well supported had at least the bare necessities of life that the Juvenalian poet lacks: Horace had plenty of food and wine, and so could compose the *Odes*; Vergil had enough to buy a blanket, and he had a slave and a place to live, so that he could compose the *Aeneid* (see lines 59–62; 66–71). The irony here is, of course, transparent: Juvenal (following, no doubt, the lead of Horace in his *Sermones* 1.4.39) maintained in his programmatic first *Satire* that his poems sometimes struggle to be considered poetry at all, that they are rather the rantings of a person who just cannot take it any more.[14] This attitude makes it all the more comical when, as in *Satire* 7, he laments the fact that he will never be able to compose poetry removed from the *publica vena* (53) because he is too poor. The stance of the satirist as a mere spontaneous ranter is simultaneously exposed as disingenuous and programmatically reinforced within the work.

The theme of poverty is replayed in *Satire* 9, only this time the complaints come from the mouth of a disreputable gigolo named Naevolus, whom Juvenal purports to be satirizing. Recent scholars have seen Naevolus's tirade against his own stingy patron as rhetorically analogous to the tirades Juvenal delivers elsewhere in his own voice, and as we will see in detail later in this study (chapter 6), an identification between Naevolus and the poet further ironizes the moral stance of the allegedly moralistic satirist. For now, we may simply note that the opening lines (27–33) of Naevolus's harangue sound as if they could have been lifted from the programmatic first *Satire*:

> utile et hoc multis vitae genus, at mihi nullum
> inde operae pretium. pingues aliquando lacernas,
> munimenta togae, duri crassique coloris
> et male percussas textoris pectine Galli
> accipimus, tenue argentum venaeque secundae.

> Many people find even this way of life profitable, but I get no reward
> for my efforts. From time to time I get a coarse overcloak loosely made
> by a Gallic weaver's comb, or some thin silver plate of inferior quality.
> (trans. Braund)

Naevolus, like Juvenal himself in the other examples quoted above, indignantly maintains that inequitable social conditions, combined with the immoral behavior of others, have made him poor and oppressed. Even a pass-

---

14. See *Sat.* 1.79–80, where Juvenal famously associates his poetry with that of the hack poet Cluvienus, and claims that indignation alone will be enough to drive his verses if native talent (*natura*) fails him. The claims are of course disingenuous, as was Horace's position that his *Sermones* were closer to speech than poetry (1.4.39). See Braund 1996, 94 ad loc., for additional parallels in Roman poetry.

ing glance across the works of various other classical poets, however, reveals that complaints of poverty and general beleaguerment are typical of those who deploy their subjective voices to mock, criticize or satirize. What are we to make, for example, of the fact that the iambographic Greek poet, Hipponax, composed verses that foreshadow uncannily the motifs of poverty and material destitution so characteristic of Juvenal some six centuries later? Hipponax's Ionian Greek world bore little resemblance to Juvenal's Rome. His complaints were directed at various gods whom he held responsible for his condition, rather than at boorish Roman patrons or bisexual aristocrats; but even so, as the following fragments illustrate, Hipponax's stance as an indignant, disempowered but deserving poet is essentially identical to that adopted by Juvenal:

Fr. 42 Dg. (= 32 W)
a) Ἑρμῆ, φίλ᾽ Ἑρμῆ, Μαιαδεῦ, Κυλλήνιε,
  ἐπεύχομαί τοι, κάρτα γὰρ κακῶς ῥιγῶ
  καὶ βαμβαλύζω . . .
b) δὸς χλαῖναν Ἱππώνακτι καὶ κυπασσίσκον
  καὶ σαμβαλίσκα κἀσκερίσκα καὶ χρυσοῦ
  στατῆρας ἑξήκοντα τοὐτέρου τοίχου

Fr. 43 Dg. (= 34 W)
ἐμοὶ γὰρ οὐκ ἔδωκας οὔτε κω χλαῖναν
δασεῖαν ἐν χειμῶνι φάρμακον ῥίγεος,
οὔτ᾽ ἀσκέρηισι τοὺς πόδας δασείηισιν
ἔκρυψας, ὥς μοι μὴ χίμετλα ῥήγνυται.

Fr. 44 Dg. (= 36 W)
ἐμοὶ δὲ Πλοῦτος—ἔστι γὰρ λίην τυφλός—
ἐς τὠικί᾽ ἐλθὼν οὐδάμ᾽ εἶπεν· "Ἱππῶναξ,
δίδωμί τοι μνέας ἀργύρου τριήκοντα
καὶ πόλλ᾽ ἔτ᾽ ἄλλα"· δείλαιος γὰρ τὰς φρένας.

Fr. 42 Dg. (= 32 W)
a) Hermes, dear Hermes, Maia's son, Cyllenian,—
  hear thou my prayer, for I am bloody frozen,
  my teeth are chattering . . .
b) Grant Hipponax a cloak and a nice tunic
  and some nice sandals and nice fur boots,
  and sixty gold sovereigns to balance me up. . . . (trans. West)

Fr. 43 Dg. (= 34 W)
For thou has never granted me a cloak
thick in the winter to cure me of the shivers,

nor hast thou wrapped my feet in thick fur boots
to stop my chilblains bursting. (trans. West)

Fr. 44 Dg. (= 36 W)
And Wealth—he's all too blind—he's never come
to my house, never said, "Hipponax, here's
three thousand silver drachmas, and a heap
of other stuff besides." No, he's a dimwit. (trans. West)

Many other examples of such complaints could be cited throughout Greek and
Latin literature, but I juxtapose these two poets at chronological extremes in
order to illustrate the fundamental problems of analysis and interpretation that
have inspired this book. Is it a mere coincidence that Hipponax and Juvenal
have constructed such similar subjective personae for themselves? If not, and
if we posit some sort of connection between the two, what is the nature of such
a connection? Whereas Horace, at least, left us some clue that he situated his
satirical project in an old and varied tradition, Juvenal's explicit acknowledgement of his antecedents is much more muted and is limited to Roman poets
who also composed satire. We may never know whether Juvenal had Hipponax,
or any other specific Greek poet, in mind when composing his tirades against
injustice, but our aporia on this question should not overshadow the far more
remarkable fact that Hipponax and Juvenal were engaged in a common literary pursuit, a pursuit shared, as I argue in the course of this book, in various
degrees and through manifold permutations, by all poets who engaged in comic
mockery, satire or, other forms of stylized confrontation and complaint.

Problems arise, however, as soon as we entertain the possibility that poets
in superficially unaffiliated genres, separated by time and culture, may be
enmeshed in an analogous poetic enterprise. Of what explanatory value, for
example, is it to articulate elements of poetic composition that transcend not
only an author's conscious intention, but even the formal constraints of genre
and historical contingency? If, that is, we begin to think of a set of rules gov-
erning the production of poetic mockery in classical antiquity, what questions
does this actually help us to answer? Classicists have traditionally been suspicious of attempts to map formal and abstract connections among diverse types
of comic poetry, in particular, since such poetry so often appears, as we have
just noted, to be historically localized and contingent upon the individual personality that produced it. When Hipponax and Juvenal, for example, make
claims about their own poverty and abjection, our first instinct is to take these
at face value: The subjective "I" that orchestrates their respective satires virtually insists that we do so. Even the most savvy critics, who may acknowledge the satirist's many masks and his playfully deceptive rhetoric, usually
conclude that, when all is said and done, his decision to compose satirical poetry must reflect at least some fundamental aspects of his actual life. When we

view each poet's self-presentation, however, as a function not primarily of actual autobiography, but of a matrix of poetic structures common to all classical instantiations of comic mockery, any historical model for the interpretation of each poet is thrown into a different light. For in this case, the highly specific and idiosyncratic details of each poet's work—chilblains in Hipponax, for example, or Juvenal's *sportula*—must be seen to have a more complicated etiology than is commonly supposed for such genres. This is not to say that auto-biographical contingencies, for example, have no influence on a given work. Rather, a satiric poetics will be conceptually prior to such factors, insofar as a poet, if he did in fact want to draw on personal experience, would first have to make certain decisions about *how* to represent them in poetry. Hipponax, to return to our example, may indeed have suffered from chilblains, but that fact alone would tell us nothing about why and how autobiographical features found their way into his poetry; *that* question, I believe, is more meaningfully answered by invoking an abstractly conceived poetics that generates and structures individual cases of poetic satire.

The notion of an abstraction that helps account for poetry of various kinds is hardly novel. It is not uncommon for critics to conceive of literary genre or tradition in this way, or to allude to even vaguer principles, such as "the comic" or "the tragic." Such conceptual modes allow, for example, Amy Richlin to see in Lucilius aspects that are not only idiosyncratic to him, but which seem to belong to a more broadly conceived *ars satirica*.[15] Very few of those who use such terms, however, have cared to articulate systematically what they mean by them and what their exegetical force is for the study of literature.[16] One reason for this is doubtless because extrapolating a general explanatory system from particulars appears reductive and imprecise, like arguing for the existence of a Platonic form: If a, b, c, and d share certain elements that we speak of abstractly as X, how can we know that some heretofore unseen e, f, or, g will not call into question our newly established abstraction?[17] So while

15. Richlin 1992, 171, referring to Lucilius, lines 1022–23, *hic ut muscipulae tentae atque ut scorpios cauda || sublata* ["here like mousetraps stretched tight and like a scorpion with its tail || raised . . ."] states that the "authorial boasting probably exemplified by the image of the mousetrap and the scorpion's tail . . . amounts to an *ars satirica* valid not only for sexual satire but for all satire."

16. In the case of Greek literature, the problem of how to approach "Greek satire"—or even whether we may legitimately use such a term—has long vexed scholars. See Geffcken's (1911) and Korus's (1991) attempts to conceptualize Greek satire as a literary *genos* of sorts. See also van Rooy 1965, 90–91.

17. The question of whether genres are conceived of inductively (from particular instances to a general theory) or deductively (from a posited premise to individual texts) has been central to the history of genre theory. The inductive-deductive dichotomy has often been seen to underlie the common distinction between a "historical genre" (established inductively, by observing texts) and a "theoretical" one (a generalized premise from which individual manifestations are deduced). Rosmarin 1985, 23–51, offers a useful historical survey of these and related questions. She herself (33) describes the "procedures of genre criticism as ineluctably deductive—always, in however

classical scholars still like to think in terms of unifying abstractions—genre, tradition, tropes, poetics, etc.—they often hesitate to confront the logical consequences: Where do these abstractions come from? How do they work? And, perhaps most pointedly, how do they, once constructed by critical discourse, augment our understanding of the ways in which poetry operates in all its contingent circumstances?

Genre theorists perennially wrestle with questions such as these, though one critic, Adena Rosmarin, has suggested an approach that will be useful for this study. In *The Power of Genre*, Rosmarin confronts the tension between the generalizing force of genre and the particularizing demands of an individual text, and she describes the common fear that a preponderant focus on genre bleaches texts of their "literariness." Rosmarin argues, however, that texts become literary at precisely the moment in which it becomes clear that no genre can ever completely describe them: "[W]hen the genre's trace and incompletion are acknowledged, their discovery 'in' the text does not so much impugn the genre as create an impression of a distinctly *literary* text, one that seems infinitely particular and heuristically powerful precisely because it eludes our generalizing grasp."[18] This view of genre injects a certain pragmatic power into the literary abstractions that are continually constructed to explain individual works: We need not think of genre, that is, as only a historical artifact for it to illuminate actual texts in historical time.[19]

---

concealed a fashion, moving from general to particular," and in constant tension with a "representational" procedure that operates in the reverse (by assuming that particulars will validate—can be *represented* by—an inherent truth about the nature of a genre). Because of their traditionally historical orientation, most classicists would probably regard their procedure for establishing ancient genres as inductive and rooted in individual texts. Inductive reasoning may be the first step in constructing a theory, but once new texts are considered in the light of this theory, the process becomes deductive, i.e., evaluating a new text as a corroborative or inadequate manifestation of a general premise. On the philosophical problems of inductive reasoning, and the ways in which induction transforms itself into deduction, see Popper 1959 and 1962, 54–55.

18. Rosmarin, 1985, 46–47. She continues this thought with an important defense of the deductive method of establishing genres (see previous note): "[B]y starting with the general we can deduce the most minute and numerous particulars, whereas when we purportedly start with those particulars we commit ourselves to moving away from them, to reducing them to the general. Thus does the very direction of explicitly deductive argument encourage 'discovery' of an *irreducible* text, one capable of being indefinitely because never conclusively unfolded" (47). This approach is particularly appealing in that it acknowledges the importance of a given text's historical and cultural contingencies in any act of interpretation, without denying that antecedent *and* subsequent texts can be equally illuminating.

19. This is not, of course, to say that concepts of genre cannot be construed historically: Most authors in fact are profoundly self-conscious about their position within a generic tradition. An author's avowed generic affiliations, however, need not coincide with the ways in which *we* configure them, especially since our vantage point is by definition synoptic, encompassing literary traditions subsequent to his own production. But an author's placement of his own work within a generic tradition is itself a revealing factor in any attempt to articulate his genre more theoretically.

Even when we feel comfortable with our generic taxonomies, however, it remains to explain why genres configure themselves in the ways they do. Furthermore, even the most accommodating concepts of genre do not always explain every instance of similarity between works. We may easily agree, for example, that Hipponax and Juvenal share certain attitudes toward obscenity and satire, and we may even call this a generic affinity, despite the great gulf of time and culture (not to mention poetic form) that separates them.[20] But when, as in such cases, it becomes difficult to imagine a direct, conscious and diachronic direction of influence from the earlier author to the later, we must explain their similarities by invoking forces that go well beyond their respective biographies or intentions. We must, in short, inquire into the very nature of their poeticizing: What, in other words, were Hipponax or Aristophanes or Juvenal, or any poet engaged in comic mockery, *representing* in the first place?

One of the premises of this book is that an understanding of what constitutes a poeticized act of mockery or satire—how real mockery is transformed into fictionalized mockery and represented as comic *form*—is essential to a full appreciation of its specific, historically-bound manifestations. Anthropologists and psychologists have often discussed the complexity of laughter as an emotional reflex, and the difficulties in accounting for the many conceptions of humor throughout history, but it is even more confounding when a culture's sense of the laughable becomes aestheticized or ritualized so as to become a distinct mimetic activity in its own right—when laughter is represented rather than lived. This is the moment when "things that are perceived as funny" become *comedy*. When the laughable is represented in comic *forms*, whether in performance or literature, its production and reception are mediated by a new set of rules that frequently operate independently of the ways in which humor is regulated among individuals in real life.

Like all mimetic activity, comic poetry is fundamentally artificial and symbolic. But it also tends to be more personal than other mimetic forms: Jokes, comic scenes, mocking or satirical discourse, etc., tend to represent the activity of an individual directed *against* another or at another's expense. These personal, intersubjective tendencies of comic mimesis raise a variety of questions when we try to understand how such mimesis functions both within its immediate poetic vehicle and in its broader cultural context. How is it, for example, that an audience can be simultaneously amused and offended by certain forms of comedy? How can artistic form transform locker-room jokes from vulgar to high humor? Why do people bother to attack individuals, often

20. Note in this regard, Fowler's insistence (1982, 73) that "almost any feature, however minor, however elusive, may become genre-linked . . . any relatively infrequent or noticeable feature may be regarded for a time as generic." He cautions, however, that this need not imply an infinity of generic characteristics: "Every characteristic feature, as a means of communication, must be recognizable, and this limits the relevant possibilities at any particular time."

breaching standards of social and dictional decorum along the way, when the medium itself so often undermines the very possibility of being taken seriously? While the answers to such questions will vary in detail with individual cases and contexts, I shall argue in this study that at a more fundamental level they also show remarkable consistency across culture and genre, allowing us, in turn, to articulate a system of poetic structures that undergirds Greco-Roman comic mockery and satire.

The mention of underlying poetic "structures" will require further elaboration, since the term has a number of very distinct, and often polemical, associations within the history of literary criticism. While this is not a book of high theory itself, and it never strays terribly far away from ancient texts, I have tried as much as possible to keep an eye on the theoretical models and assumptions that have shaped my thinking about the topic. To begin with, I follow a general principle originating in semiotics and developed in various forms of anthropology and psychology, which views language as a complex system of communication governed by abstract laws that generate specific utterances or modes of behavior. Saussure's often-cited distinction between *langue* (a socially constructed, abstractly conceived system of language) and *parole* (the actual verbal utterances of individuals) has provided a useful conceptual framework for this study. In a sense, I am interested in this book in articulating a language (or *langue*) of ancient comic mockery as a communicative system that helps explain the particular expression of individual subjects. Some of the theoretical premises and strategies I draw on in the service of this endeavor might be described as structuralist in orientation, in that they attempt to explain texts (and manifestations of culture) in terms of the underlying, synchronically conceived, symbolic systems that produce them. But my interest in structuralist methodology remains ultimately grounded in my desire to answer a number of distinctly diachronic questions concerning the relationship between ancient poets of abuse, on the one hand, and their targets and audiences on the other.

This task, however, requires a preliminary agreement about the nature of the phenomena under discussion. Much of the time, such phenomena—verbal abuse, personal ridicule, aggressive posturing—seem easily distinguished from other poetic tropes, and the risk of plunging directly into a diachronic analysis of a work may seem minimal. We can all agree, for example, that some lines in Aristophanes can be regarded as political mockery, and we can proceed from there to address any number of historically based questions about them. But how do we know whether or not to take this mockery at face value— biographically, metaphorically, or ironically, to name only a few options? In fact, we decide such questions at least in part by situating each instance of mockery in a relationship with some other: To say that Aristophanes engages in political mockery is to say that the poet does something that we have observed in other poets as well, and in so doing we presuppose the existence of a structuring system that transcends historical localization.[21] Aristophanes' political mockery may take a different form from Juvenal's centuries later, but we are still able to identify both as examples of a similar phenomenon.[22] And by organizing such abstracted structuring principles into a synchronic poetics, a poetics of satire, and then applying them to other individual instances of poetic mockery, we end up better equipped to understand an author's idiosyncratic engagement with such comic forms within his own literary and historical microclimate.[23]

2. A Taxonomy of Poetic Mockery

So far I have been using terms such as "mockery," "satire" and "abuse" somewhat freely and often interchangeably, and before proceeding we must clarify the parameters of this study and the terminology it employs. We always run some risk of anachronizing on this score, since our own terminology can never fully capture the cultural valence of the ancient phenomena to which we apply it, but we can only hope that a heightened consciousness of this danger will prevent gross misrepresentation and unreflective hypostasizing. To take one clear example of the problem: Our own word "satire" derives ultimately from the Latin term *satura*, as it was applied technically to the poetic genre we know as Roman satire, that is, a Latin hexameter tradition, associated with identifiable authors within a period of about a few centuries at most (essentially from Lucilius to Juvenal).[24] No Roman, in other words, would apply the term *satura* to the production of, say, an archaic Greek poet, even though *we* might comfortably speak of "satirical elements" in the latter, or even refer to

---

21. Cf. Jameson 1972, 188–89, summarizing the views of Greimas: "It follows [from Greimas's structuralist approach to historical understanding] that insofar as we can 'apprehend' history at all conceptually, such apprehension must have taken the form of a translation of genuine diachrony into synchronic terms. Real diachrony, therefore, real history, falls outside the mind of a kind of *Ding-an-sich*, unattainable directly: time becomes an unknowable." Ultimate historical knowledge may always elude our grasp, but we continue to construct accounts of history as best we can. As Jameson makes clear, however, we make progress in these attempts only by first adopting synchronic modeling.

22. As Jonathan Culler has put it (1975, 11), "the notion of relational identity is crucial to the semiotic or structural analysis of all kinds of social and cultural phenomena, because in formulating the rules of the system one must identify the units on which the rules operate and thus must discover when two objects or actions count as instances of the same unit."

23. Rigorous structuralism has often been criticized for its neglect of historical particulars (cf., e.g., Bremmer's [1983] critique of Lévi-Strauss on the Oedipus myth). As Jameson 1972, 214, has said in a critique of the structuralist concept of "homology" or "isomorphism," "... there remains the danger that the identity [of two given phenomena] holds good, not for the concrete realities themselves, but merely for the conceptual abstractions that have been derived from them."

24. On ancient definitions of Roman satire, see van Rooy 1965, 1–29; and Coffey 1989 [1976], 3–10.

one of his works as a *bona fide* satire. We think of satire, that is, as a form of literature featuring a certain range of topics, a certain stance by the poet, a certain store of idiosyncratic dictional strategies, etc. I hope to show, however, that despite the obvious gulf between the ancient and modern terminology, both the questions that frame this study and the critical concepts invoked in this book to answer them would be equally intelligible to the ancient poets themselves, once articulated in terms of the literary-critical modes available to them.

Scores of books have been written about the definition of satire, both in its broadest, generic sense, and as it is applied to specific periods and writers.[25] We need not ourselves, therefore, rehearse the entire history of this elusive and diffuse subject,[26] but a few remarks about the scope of this study are in order. A recent scholar of English literary satire, Frederic Bogel, has laid out some principles for conceptualizing satire in his book, *The Difference Satire Makes: Rhetoric and Reading from Jonson to Byron*, which will also be useful for the ancient authors we discuss here. His formulation (2004, 1–2) summarizes many decades of scholarship on literary satire:

> [S]atire is a full-fledged artistic mode ("literary"), not merely a symptom of ill humor or personal spite or something else. Though it is often, undeniably, an intervention in personal or literary or political quarrels, as a literary mode it cannot simply be reduced to those quarrels or their motives. . . . Second, the originating moment of satire is the satirist's perception of an object that exists anterior to the satiric attack. This object is often assumed to belong to the real world . . . [b]ut it may also be an imaginary object constructed by the satirist . . . This dual insistence on the artistry of the satirist rather than on a mere propensity to attack, and on the extratextual reality and temporal priority of the repellent satiric object goes a long way toward establishing the traditional view of the rhetorical situation of satire. This situation can be figured as a triangle with the satirist at one point, the satiric object at another, and the reader or dramatic audience at the third. In this scheme, the satirist aims a certain combination of attack and artifice

25. Griffin 1994 and Bogel 2004, both contain useful overviews of the history of satire criticism, although they are oriented around English literature. Still classic is Kernan 1959, esp., for the ancient material, chapter 1. As will become clear, Kernan's emphasis on the paradoxical nature of the satirist informs many aspects of this study. Within classical scholarship Kernan's approach has had a particularly marked influence on studies of Roman satire; see, for example, Anderson 1964, and most recently, Plaza 2006, esp. 1–37. On satiric irony in particular, see Dane 1991 and Hutcheon 1994 (esp. 37–56), with further bibliography.

26. Griffin 1994, 5: ". . . satire is problematic, open-ended, essayistic, ambiguous in its relation to history, uncertain in its political effect, resistant to formal closure, more inclined to ask questions than to provide answers, and ambivalent about the pleasures it offers."

(including, in different formulations, wit, humor, exaggeration, fictionality) at the satiric object that has attracted his or her notice.

This book is not a comprehensive study of satire, but rather concerns a specific area to which Bogel alludes in his last point, namely, those moments when a poet situates himself in an antagonistic relationship with some character marked out as a target of righteous indignation. This relationship can manifest itself in many ways—straightforward, vituperative, blaming, for example, or milder off-color innuendo, irony or sarcasm—but the antagonism itself is always explicit, for it is in the poet's interest to clarify who is the blamer and who the target. This is a far more complex relationship, as I hope to show in this study, than classical scholars have generally cared to entertain, despite the considerable progress made in other areas of literary history toward understanding its dynamics.

Next, it must be said, at the risk of stating the obvious, that I understand satire as a species of comedy, or more generally "the comic," and that when a poet mocks someone in a satirical work, that mockery invariably can be seen as a comic strategy, that is, it exists in order to make an audience laugh, whether that laughter is of the raucous physical sort or a mere intellectual appreciation of a humorous conceit.[27] Indeed, I regard comedy (in the sense of "performed humor") as one of the few unassailable defining qualities of satire, and by extension, of mockery, ridicule and invective. This is not to say that every work in which satire (or mockery) occurs is a work of comedy, only that wherever there is satire, there exists some measure of comedy at that moment, however fleeting that moment may be within the work as a whole. Nor would I say that every instance of satire or mockery will succeed in drawing a laugh from every listener or reader every time; but there is usually little doubt that satirical passages, especially those that feature personal ridicule, are crafted with the intention of amusing at least some portion of a hypothetical audience, even if the poet may misjudge how his work will play among the audience's diverse constituencies.

One more preliminary point: The presence of an audience imagined to be sympathetic to the poet's complaints is essential for the success of satirical

27. A note about how I use the terms "mockery" and "satire": While they are not exactly synonymous, they each imply the other, at least when confined to the realm of poetry. In general, I use "satire" to refer to a literary form or structure, and "mockery" to refer to an element within that form. A "satirist" is a poet who engages in mockery, although this is obviously not the only thing he does. Not everything that constitutes "satire" (conceptualized as a literary form or genre) will be mockery, although anything to which we apply the adjective "satirical" will typically imply its presence. Certainly, however, as I note above, not all mockery (if by "all" we include "real" mockery between "real" people outside of literature) is "satirical," which is why our emphasis on "*poetic* mockery" is critical. While all mockery strives to effect humor in some capacity, however cruel it might be, it is not satire until it assumes literary form.

mockery, for if the poet is trying to make a case against a target, the justice of his cause must be convincing. We will have much more to say about this in later chapters, but for now it is enough to remember that satire is always a self-consciously literary and essentially performative mode that cannot exist without an audience.[28] Laughter, however, and an ability to assess the mockery (that is, to consider the merits of the attack, both in terms of form and content), becomes possible as soon as a third party is present to witness the event and the act of mockery suddenly becomes a performance. In an actual conflict in real life, a mocker may attempt to ignore such an outsider, but he cannot alter the fact that his mockery now has an audience, and that the instance of mockery can now be seen and judged. Once mockers becomes conscious of an audience, and aware that they and their targets are orchestrating a performance, they may want to consider ways by which they can make their audiences complicit in their mockery; that is, to persuade them to share in whatever indignation gave rise to their verbal attack in the first place.

It is at this point, it seems, where comic strategies have the potential to emerge. Although in real-life situations of verbal aggression, a third-party audience might really want the skirmish to end as soon as possible, the verbal aggressor at least has an option to craft his invective so as to become as much a showpiece to be contemplated by this third party as a vehicle of harm against his target. At such a moment a witness to actual mockery might say that the one party is "satirizing" the other with his verbal abuse, if, that is, the abuse can be said to be in some sense "comic." This is an intermediate stage between simple, unmediated verbal aggression and its formalized representation in what we would regard as literary satire; another way we might put this is to say that the audience of an actual confrontation may find such a performance satirical, without necessarily considering it, strictly speaking, satire. I shall have more to say on this topic in a moment, but for now I reiterate concisely the three main points that inform this study: (1) Satire is a comedic, literary form, implying a "performance" and an "audience"; (2) As such, a work of satire is a fictionalized, mimetic representation of aggressive human behavior, but is not in itself a "real" instance of that behavior; (3) Verbal abuse and mockery, insofar as they are deployed in the service of satire, are also mimetic *comic* forms.

It should be clear by now, then, but is worth emphasizing, that we will be concerned specifically with mockery as a performance, and as it is deployed in *poetry*, not as it may have occurred in real life, nor even as it occurred in other

---

28. Even private mocking banter between two people, where we do not have a third party present to serve as an audience, may well be considered a type of "satire," if we consider that the recipient of mockery in such cases functions also as its "audience." Bantering mockery exists as a kind of performance, in other words, even if the "audience" is simply the target. For more on this topic, see below pp. 23–27. For laughter (both literary and nonliterary) in Greek culture in particular, see the excellent study by Halliwell, 1991. López Eire's study (2000) of the Greek expressions for laughter is also useful.

nonfictional literary genres such as rhetoric or philosophy.[29] To be sure, we occasionally find mockery embedded in those genres as well, where it can certainly retain a satirical, and hence comic, edge. But I exempt such forms of mockery from this study because they are qualitatively very different from poetic forms and operate according to entirely different dynamics. The most critical difference between poetic and non-poetic mockery lies in the nature of the relationship that authors in each form are interested in establishing. This is chiefly a generic question, it should be said, not one of probing an author's intention: A rhetorical writer such as Demosthenes or Aeschines will often resort to invective and personal mockery of putative enemies, but whether or not they actually despise their targets, an audience will assume that their rhetorical performance is intended to do actual harm.[30] Orators may fictionalize and exaggerate beyond all credibility their portraits of their enemies, spicing their mockery with traditional satirical elements such as obscenity and lurid accusations, but in the audience's mind there is never any question (a) that the characters and situations addressed in the speech are all real, (b) that every aspect of the speech is ultimately directed at persuading them to side with the speaker's point of view, and (c) that whether the speaker is successful at persuading them or not, the *consequences* for the person inveighed against are real and potentially substantial (especially in the case of juridical speeches). An audience may laugh heartily at Demosthenes' ridicule of Aeschines' mother or his profession as an actor, but they will always be aware that there is nothing fictional about the reality of the personalities involved or the issues at stake, and the orator will construct his speech with this understanding in mind. Insofar as an instance of mockery within a written speech is a representation of a moment in an oratorical performance, it shares with poetic mockery some mimetic qualities. But the mimetic object in each case is acutely different: In the case of a court speech, the confrontation between two antagonists that it represents is always real and unmediated; humor and entertainment are rarely, if ever, ultimate goals of the speech. In the case of a poem, mediated by poetic form and freed from the necessity of representing a real situation accurately, the audience knows (or should know, at any rate)[31] that the mockery repre-

29. For a useful survey of "invective" across the entire spectrum of Greek and Roman authors up through the Empire, see Koster 1980.

30. Corbeill 1996 has taken a strong stand on this point in his study of humor and invective in Roman oratory. See his programmatic remark: ". . . aggressive humor exercises real power of persuasion over a late Republican audience and . . . as a cultural product, this humor also helped shape the ethical standards current during the politically convulsive period of the late Republic" (5). See also Corbeill 2002 on Ciceronian invective as a serious didactic rhetorical mode.

31. Audiences may of course misunderstand the nature a performance they are witnessing, whether through mere ignorance or misconstrual of generic cues, as satirical poets routinely complain about; see for example, Aristophanes' complaints about Athenian audiences in several of his parabases (e.g., *Clouds* 524–27), or Horace's concern that people often misunderstand the nature of satire (e.g., *Serm.* 1.4.78–105).

sented in the poem is essentially a confection, interacting, perhaps, with real people and things, but ultimately existing apart from them.[32]

I focus in this book, therefore, on the peculiar dynamic that arises between a poet and an audience when fictional modes and marked language (such as verse forms) are used to represent moments of satirical mockery. This dynamic becomes especially elusive and complex when, as so often happens, the poet represents *himself* as the mocking agent, for in such cases, as we shall see in later chapters, the poet disingenuously insists that behind his mockery of a target lies a "real" antipathy toward his target, and a genuine relationship with him. By *poeticizing* this reality, and so removing it to a fictional realm, the poet playfully calls into question the credibility of his self-representation, as well as of any claims to historical truth that may be embedded in the narrative.

At this point, a few further points of terminology are in order. I assume that "poetry" implies "fictionality." By "fictionality," I mean that what an author represents in words does not necessarily bear a direct, one-to-one correspondence to a lived external reality[33] and an author writing "fiction" would never presume that it should. As a form of marked speech,[34] poetry differs from prose in its particular set of self-conscious formal artifices. Prose employs its own artifices, of course, and may obviously be used also for fiction, but insofar as poetry formally distances itself from everyday speech—the speech we associate with our lived realities—it creates an ontologically distinct world from that of prose. While prose may or may not be fictional, purely formal devices

---

32. This is not to say that it is always easy to distinguish between "real" mockery, with its ramifications for real people and historical events, and poetic mockery, which operates in a mimetic zone marked off from everyday reality, however much its content flirts with that reality. Indeed, the history of satirical genres is a history of a literature constantly under threat by those who fail to make this distinction (and see chapter 3 for a paradigmatic example of this from Greek myth). Corbeill's discussion of political mockery in republican Rome (see esp. 1996, 174–217) reveals a complicated dynamics in which jokes often carried real and intended consequences for joker and target alike, but this only confirms the distinction I would maintain between mockery where poetic form is at least prior to content and intention, and mockery as a form of speech-act, where the speaker and audience alike are primarily interested in actual aggression against a target. The lines between these two types of mockery are often blurry, as we shall see throughout this book, especially since the very act of mockery practically by definition implies that the mocker is interested in having a "real" effect against a target, no matter how disingenuous this might turn out to be.

33. Bakhtin might refer to the contrast I am after as one between "monologic" and "polyphonic" discourse, although he applied these terms to different literary discourses (the latter especially applicable to the novel) rather than to fictional versus non-fictional writing. Still, the kind of poetry that interests me in this book is, in Bakhtinian terms, decidedly polyphonic, incorporating a multiplicity of "voices" while rendering the author's own voice elusive, if not ultimately irrelevant. See e.g. Bakhtin 1984b, 32–36, 79–85. The perennial problem with satire and mockery, however, is that the speaking *ego* often tries to characterize his voice as monologic—mapped on to a single, stable reality—when in fact performance context, poetic medium, and generic conventions often argue against this. Political and forensic mockery written in prose (see above p. 21) is in fact monologic, whereas poetic mockery only pretends to be.

34. See, e.g., Nagy 1991, 29–34.

alone rarely allow us distinguish between the two; with poetry, on the other hand, its marked forms of speech instantly problematize any relationship it may appear to have with reality. To bring things back to a more concrete level, it may be helpful to imagine challenging a satirical poet at the moment he claims to be representing a real conflict with another by asking: "Why have you chosen to attack your enemy with poetry in the first place?—for poetry is so mediated by form, and so marked from daily speech, that you'll distract your audience from the aggressive cause your work claims for itself." The truthful response from the poet, I should think, would be for him to admit that with his chosen poetics he aims for an aesthetic and intellectual effect on the audience that at least parallels, if it does not always transcend, the work's claims to record a literal autobiographical encounter.

By contrast, orators who mock their enemies, as we have just noted, must always strive to produce actual results in a real, historical context, whether it be winning a court case or, at the very least, ensuring a bad name for their targets after the case is over. Thus, their relationship with an audience is far less mediated than a poet's, who, as an entertainer, need not be guided by the demands of historical accuracy or credibility, even though he might want to pretend that he is. Poets of mockery, therefore, are constantly engaged in a kind of game in which the audience never quite knows when to give themselves over to the fiction of the poet's constructed enmities or when to take them at their word; and the poet can never be quite sure, in turn, whether he has succeeded in getting the audience to experience the comic pleasures of a fictional attack, or whether he has left them with the impression that the poet's performance is merely playing out aspects of his autobiography.

In the light of the complex interplay between and among the mimesis of mockery, autobiography, poetic form, and audience expectation laid out above, it will perhaps be useful before we proceed to present in more schematic form the mimetic structures that inform genres of poetic mockery, and to describe the relationships between poet and audience that arise within them. I have arranged these in order of mimetic complexity, from the simplest, most unmediated form of interpersonal confrontation to the most nuanced and ironized.

The Mimetic Object: The Originary Moment of Mockery

When a poem represents the mockery of another person, its mimetic object is the interpersonal conflict—whether real, imagined, or deliberately feigned—between two people. In its simplex form, this event takes place in real time, in a real historical moment, with no witnesses present:

Person A attacks → Person B

This event is essentially the material, which at some point may become poeticized, but which is in its purest form hypothetically real. Most people have themselves played the role of one or the other of these participants at some point in their lives, and there is usually nothing humorous or pleasant in the experience for target or abuser. (I do not include in this category bantering mockery between acquaintances, which can certainly be pleasant for each party, since this is already a form of representation and is not "real" aggression.) Poetry of abuse will attempt to replicate this moment, and so inevitably transform it into something other than it was originally; but at the beginning, we are to imagine nothing more than aggression of one person against another.

1. Mimetic Mode 1: Protodramatic Stage

Person A attacks → Person B ← Person C witnesses the event

When a third party is present to witness the moment of abuse, we have the first potential step toward a mimesis of the event. Person C now functions as an "audience," except that this audience knows that the event is in fact "real," and not a dramatized version of a real event. At a later time, Person C could describe the event to another party, and the act of representation begins. In its plainest form, however, the representation of the original event will attempt to narrate the details as accurately as possible.

2. Mimetic Mode 2: Dramatized Mockery

When a *poet* imagines a real-life moment of conflict as in (1), he acts as *Person C* in (1), that is, the one who witnessed the event. He can now recount the event in a mimetic gesture, but he does so according to the requisite generic and formal conventions. This becomes a moment of intersection (and tension) between content (conflict between individuals known to an audience) and form (conventions of the poeticized mockery). The poeticization of the event assures that it will be comic and that the audience's experience of it will be qualitatively different from how they would experience real acts of interpersonal aggression (which are not mediated by poetic form). A poet may represent the mockery between individuals in real time, that is, as a theatrical performance with actors playing the parts in the conflict, in which case the audience views directly what purports to be a reenactment of the original event. (One thinks of the plays of Old Comedy, for example, where countless examples of mockery are played out on the stage.) Our schema would now look like this:

Hypothetical original event of abuse →
→ transformed into mockery, and hence, into comic poetry by poet

→ performed on a stage in real time with actors
→ audience watches a poeticized variation of original

3. Mimetic Mode 3: Third-Person Poetic Narratives of Mockery

Alternatively, the poet may recount within the poem the story of the original event, as told in the third person by the poet. This mode is ubiquitous across all ancient satirical genres, but is especially prevalent, as we will see throughout this book, in the Greek iambographers and Roman satirists. With this category we are one step further removed from the reality of the hypothetical original event; the event is dramatized only in the poet's mind, and then in his text; it is as if the poet imagines himself in the role of the audience (mimetic mode 2, above) witnessing a dramatization of the event, but now recounting the details himself to an audience of his own.

Hypothetical original event of mockery→
→ transformed into comic poetry by poet
→ performed by the poet in front of an audience
→ embedded in written narrative genres for future audience

4. Mimetic Mode 4: The Poet as Mocker

This category of mockery is perhaps the richest and most complex, and also one of the most common in antiquity. There are two variants:

(a) The poet implicates himself directly in the narrative, and assumes the role of the mocker himself. Whereas in the other categories above the poet relates a narrative of abuse about parties in the third person ("He—[mocks]—him), the relationship with the target is now "I—[mock]—him." In each case, the poet speaks either directly or implicitly to the audience. Examples can be found in many of Aristophanes' parabases, where the chorus leader, claiming to speak on behalf of the poet, will often mock various targets. Here the "poet" (that is, the chorus leader impersonating the poet) may recount his antagonism (sometimes ongoing, sometimes fleeting) against a target in front of the audience as a means of inducing them to share in his indignation. Aristophanes' infamous quarrel with Cleon is presented across several parabases in this mode.[35] One thinks also of the Cologne Archilochus (fr. 196aW), in which the speaker—presumably the poet's persona—inveighs against one of

---

35. On Cleon, see below, chapter 3, pp. 78–91.

the daughters of Lycambes *indirectly* through a narrative ("I—mock—her") told to an assumed audience.[36]

(b) This variation is the most playful, open to irony, and, therefore, the most problematic, as we shall see throughout this book. Here the poet addresses his target directly in the work, and the mockery exists within an "I—[mock]—you" relationship. The audience in effect "listens in" on an event of mockery, as the poet pretends that he is ridiculing his target in the here-and-now. This variant has clear affiliations with category (2) above, in that in each case the audience witnesses what purports to be the dramatic re-enactment of a scene of mockery. There are two differences, however: First, the poet is now himself the central actor in the drama, and second, the target is not present in the flesh, but exists only as character in the narrative. When the poem is actually *performed* in front of an audience, and the poet addresses his target in the second person, we see essentially a form of (1), where the audience serves as a witness to an event of abuse and mockery in real-time (the poet pretends the target is present and rants against him in the second person). This mode has a particular immediacy about it that can draw the audience deeply into the poet's constructed, often picaresque, world of personal enmities. It is an especially common stance among iambographic poets and Roman satirists, who frequently vent their *indignatio* directly against targets as if present themselves at the moment of abuse. There is much dramatic potential in this mode, as the poet works to conjure up a convincing relationship with a target who may or may not be actually present,[37] and it is easy to see why scholars have often speculated that in the case of the early iambus, at least, poets might have used props and masks to assist them in their performances.[38]

The preceding discussion outlines the basic relationships that the satirical poet, engaged in mockery, could construct with his audience and targets. Most individual poets settled into one mode or another, with their choice usually determined by the specific genre they chose to work in, but all of them worked in one way or another at the nebulous crossroads of fiction and reality.

36. On the narrative structure of the Cologne Archilochus, see Stoessl 1976, and Nagy 1979, 246–48.

37. It has been suggested that many iambographic *psogoi* were composed to be performed in the presence of the targets themselves, and not always for the purpose of actually injuring them. This notion imagines that the audience, poet, and target alike formed a relatively closed group of *philoi*, who enjoyed the comic entertainment of creative mutual banter. See Nagy 1979, 244–45, who finds support for this in Archilochus fr. 168W.

38. See West 1974, 29 (on Hipponax: "If it is not [reported speech], we must envisage the speaker of the iambus as dressed for a character part and as doing a little acting too."), Lasserre 1979, and West 1981, 86–87. Bartol (1992 and 1993), however, remains skeptical that the evidence allows us to speak with any confidence of the literary iambus as in any real sense a dramatic form in the manner of a bona fide theatrical production.

As *poets*, they were fictionmakers, but as *satirists*, their fictions were supposed to represent a veridical reality familiar to the audience. Indeed, as I maintain in this study, it is this persistent tension between fiction and reality that distinguishes poetic from non-poetic forms of mockery, and allows us to consider such forms as a fundamentally separate human activity from such non-poetic forms as we find either in the ancient law courts or on the streets.

3. Conceptualizing Mockery in Antiquity

This book will make several principal points: that ancient poets and at least some critics and audiences understood as well as any modern critic the dynamics of satire, that they were well attuned to the problems of fictionality and reception so idiosyncratic to such poetry, and, in general, that they were able to understand satirical mockery in a much more sophisticated way than the evidence might lead us to believe at first glance. Indeed, as we will consider in detail later on (chapter 7), we are often left with the impression that ancient critics and audiences found the poeticizing of mockery unilaterally disturbing, and as modern critics we may find ourselves in the odd position of imagining that *we* are better able to understand ancient satirical poetry than the culture that produced it. But there are other—often less explicit but nevertheless informative—entrées to the question of how ancient audiences conceptualized mockery and satire, which it will be useful to set out here.

The search for underlying structures and patterns in Greek comic drama, in particular, has periodically occupied modern scholars, although this has generally taken the form of an inquiry into "origins"; what was the prehistory of Attic comedy, for example, or what would explain its predilection for mockery and obscenity? At the end of the nineteenth century, comparative work in the then nascent field of anthropology inspired classicists to answer such questions with recourse to the presumed ritual and mythicoreligious background of Greek comedy. This trend began with a focus on the origins of Greek tragedy, but was soon applied to comedy as well. Both genres were tailor-made for such analysis, given their institutional association with Dionysus, and Aristotle's monumentally influential account of Attic drama in his *Poetics*, which stressed its specifically Dionysian provenance.

Unfortunately, early scholars of the religious background of Greek drama are usually remembered more for their eccentric theories and immoderate universalizing than for their foundational aetiological project.[39] More recently,

---

39. Taking a cue from the work of Sir James Frazer, scholars such as Jane Harrison, Gilbert Murray, and Francis Cornford (and others of the so-called Cambridge ritualist school) located the origins of Greek religion and myth in agrarian rituals closely associated with seasonal rhythms. The concept of a single, paradigmatic divinity, the *eniautos daimon* or year-god, whose celebration would

however, scholars have at least come to appreciate the significance of the Cambridge ritualists' interest in the organizing patterns or structures that underlay the extant forms of tragedy and comedy. Richard Seaford, for example, has argued forcefully that Greek tragedy arose specifically from the rites of Dionysus, and that the genre continued to celebrate throughout the fifth century the god's particular resonance for Athenians as a force encouraging the formation and consolidation of the polis. While some have found Seaford's argument improbably monolithic,[40] his approach has been useful in showing how the abstract patterns that emerge from an analysis of myth and ritual can help us formulate a poetics of Athenian tragedy.

Attempts to locate the origins of the mockery emblematic of Old Comedy in religious rituals such as the well-documented celebrations of Demeter and Dionysus, and so to extrapolate from such hypothetical connections abstract structures or typologies of poetic satire, have been much more frustrating.[41]

---

explain the nature of Greek myth and ritual, was ridiculed as naive and excessively primitivist in subsequent decades. See Versnel 1990, 28–44, on the reception of the Cambridge ritualists. See also Friedrich 1996, 259–68. It was even easier to repudiate Murray's and Cornford's attempts to apply the theory to Greek tragedy and comedy, respectively, which found in dramatic texts evidence at every turn for cosmic agones, New Year rituals, divine death and resurrection. The collective mistake of these scholars was a tendency to suppose that Attic drama not only exploited its ritual antecedents for poetic purposes, but actually *enacted* them. See Easterling 1988 and Friedrich's modifications of her argument, 1996, 269–271. See also Henderson's remarks in his new preface to the 1993 reprint of Cornford (1934 [1993] xi–xxvii). Several scholars since Cornford have attempted to refine his search for the origins of Greek comedy, by abandoning the notion that ritual can offer a "a single nucleus" (Adrados's term, 1975, 247) for the genre, and concentrating instead on the prehistory of various constituent elements, many of them with demonstrable ritual origins that somehow developed into the forms we now know through our texts. This has proven to be a more productive approach, especially in its recognition that ritual activity need not be associated exclusively with a single god for it to have an influence on comedy. See Reckford 1987, 450–55. Reckford's own interest in broader categories of the comic has its roots in the Cambridge ritualists, but has been mediated by Bakhtin's formulation of the "carnivalesque" in his study of Rabelais (1984a) and Dostoevsky (1984b, cf. esp. 122–37). For a reading of Aristophanes through the lens of Bakhtinian dialogism and "festive play" see von Möllendorff 1995 (esp. 39–109, on methodology). See also Carrière 1979 and Gelzer 1991; Rösler 1986 on Bakhtin and Old Comedy; Nagy 1991, 397–99 on Bakhtin and Greek iambus, esp. Archilochus.

40. In an otherwise sympathetic review of Seaford 1994, Murnaghan 1996, 318, finds that Seaford underestimates the contributions of individual poets to the development of the genre. Seaford 1996 revisits the argument of his 1994 book in a response to Friedrich 1996, and concludes with his own definition of tragedy: ". . . the dramatization of aetiological myth shaped by the vital need to create and sustain the *polis*" (293). While the inadequacies of such a sweeping definition are clear enough, it characterizes well Seaford's view that powerful abstract forces guided the developmental trajectory of the genre.

41. For recent work on the origins of Greek comedy, see Fehr 1990 (on a class of beggars in the archaic period, *aklêtoi*, whose performances at symposia may be related to the padded dancers found on fourth century vases); Leonhardt 1991 and Flashar 1994 (on Aristotle's account of the origins of tragedy and comedy); and Stark 1993, 1995, and 2004 (who downplays a cultic origin of comedy in favor of social roots, in line with Fehr). Also Cottone 2005, 42–51.

Aristotle famously claimed that Attic comedy originated in ithyphallic dances for Dionysus, and Aristophanes' syncretistic chorus of mystic initiates in *Frogs*, who explicitly link religious mockery with comic drama, have left little doubt that comic abuse has some affiliation with ritual abuse. But because we have so few textual antecedents to Old Comedy, there seems to be a vast, unbridgeable lacuna between religious rituals and comic drama. Even Adrados (1975), in his exhaustive study of the ritual background of Greek theater, had to concede the enormity of the problem. After setting forth his intention to investigate the origins of Greek drama in agricultural religious practice, he notes: "There is a big distance between such ritual, only partially mimetic, to a great extent symbolic, and Theatre, almost wholly mimetic and anthropomorphic, wholly verbalized" (1975, 14). It is even more confusing to locate mockery, in particular, within an evolutionary scenario from ritual to theater. For while it is reasonable enough to suppose that both tragedy and comedy arose in some fashion from choral songs that celebrated gods or heroes, the cultic evidence we have for ritual insults seems to indicate a decidedly prose, nonlyric origin.[42] Even if we accept a connection between the mockery of ancient comedy and religious rituals, it is less clear that such a connection reveals anything about the development of its *poeticized* comic forms. The fact of the matter is that there is little in Attic comedy to suggest any *self-conscious* interaction with religious rituals of abuse.[43]

There is one important passage in Old Comedy, however, that *does* draw attention to such an interaction, the parodos of mystic initiates in Aristophanes' *Frogs*. This passage can lead us toward a more productive approach to the question of comic mockery precisely because Aristophanes here articulates meaningful analogies between comedy and ritual without himself worrying about the exact process by which the two phenomena came to be related. Scholars in recent decades have analyzed the parodos of the play in great detail and have detected numerous elements of Dionysian and Eleusinian ritual.[44] They have shown that the references to *aiskhrologia* and mockery have demonstrable cultic associations, and, as such, that the chorus behaves in character as religious initiates engaged in ritual *aiskhrologia*. But Aristophanes never lets us forget that the chorus's identity specifically as a *chorus* of a *comedy*, and in this role their specifically poeticized mockery advances the project of comic theater. Their mockery now takes a *form* the audience associates more with theater than ritual; the parodos, that is, taunts and mocks according to a by-then conventional, well-delineated system of meter, diction and epirrhematic song. Aristophanes interweaves allusions to this dual role of the chorus throughout

42. See Adrados 1975.
43. See the remarks in Carey 1986, 65.
44. E.g., Segal 1961; Graf 1974, 40–50; Rosen 1988, 24–25; Hubbard 1991, 203–4; Bowie 1993, 229–38; Lada-Richards 1999, 45–51; and Riu 1999, 115–41.

the parodos, but lines 368–76 emblematically reflect his unabashed synthesis of religious and literary mockery. Completing a long list of people whom they forbid to witness their comico-ritual mockery, the chorus arrives at the orator who has worked to decrease funding for poets:

κωμῳδηθεὶς ἐν ταῖς πατρίοις τελεταῖς ταῖς τοῦ Διονύσου.
τούτοις αὐδῶ καὖθις ἀπαυδῶ καὖθις τὸ τρίτον μάλ᾽ ἀπαυδῶ
ἐξίστασθαι μύσταισι χοροῖς· ὑμεῖς δ᾽ ἀνεγείρετε μολπὴν   370
καὶ παννυχίδας τὰς ἡμετέρας αἳ τῇδε πρέπουσιν ἑορτῇ.

χώρει νυν πᾶς ἀνδρείως
εἰς τοὺς εὐανθεῖς κόλπους
λειμώνων ἐγκρούων
κἀπισκώπτων   375
καὶ παίζων καὶ χλευάζων.

. . . on the grounds that he has been satirized (kômôidêtheis) in our
   ancestral celebrations of Dionysus.
To such as these, I say it once, twice, and even a third time, that
they should stand back from our mystic dances. Now wake up our song
and our all-night dances, which are fitting for this festival.

Now, everyone, come forth boldly
into the flowery folds
of the meadows, dancing,
and mocking
and joking and taunting . . . .

It is uncertain whether this association between cultic and comic mockery was already a trope by this time, or whether it was an original conceit of Aristophanes, but in any event he does seem to have understood that, however prosaic the rituals of insult were in his day, however far removed they were from the poetic conventions that made Attic comedy a recognizable genre, ritual and comic mockery were fundamentally analogous. The formal, and even contextual, discontinuities between ritual and comedy, which have led so many scholars to a state of agnosticism about their connection, were clearly of no concern to Aristophanes. For him, comic poets were simply doing something very much like what was happening when initiates were greeted by indecent insults as they crossed the Cephisus River on their way to Eleusis (a ritual known as the gephyrismos).[45]

45. On the gephyrismos, see Fluck 1931; Graf 1974, 45–46; and Rusten 1977.

Aristophanes himself might not have been able to articulate much more than this, but his basic insight is more profound than might at first appear. For what aligns comic and ritual mockery is not merely their shared vituperative activity, but also the fact that they are two forms of confrontational expression intrinsically removed from a lived reality. Both comic poetry and religious ritual can *represent* mockery, but neither one actually *is* the mockery one might experience in a real-life situation. Comic and ritual mockery are, rather, symbolic enactments of, but qualitatively different from, a lived, social experience. Furthermore, both are fundamentally *performed* mimetic phenomena, however different their respective venues and audiences may be. Each type of mockery will display different mimetic qualities. Comic drama, for instance, represents for a passive audience the verbal aggression between two fictionalized characters in a more or less unique plot. The situation with Greek religious mockery, on the other hand, is more complicated: The verbal assaults here are supposed to be directed *at* its intended audience, thereby practically cajoling them into believing that the abuse is in fact what it represents itself to be, namely, real abuse. Still, the ritual context in which this occurs (a procession to Eleusis, a celebration of Dionysus) ensures that, however intense the assault, it is perceived as a symbolic representation of a form of interpersonal behavior well-known to its audience.[46]

Despite the fact that Greek comic and ritual mockery displayed substantial contextual and morphological differences, it was not lost on Aristophanes that they were also affiliated as performances of the same type of interpersonal discourse. Nor was Aristophanes unaware, as the *Frogs* parodos makes clear, that comic drama itself was part of a religious ceremony for a god (Dionysus) who himself was associated with rituals of mockery. Indeed, the parodos specifically encourages the audience to view comic and religious mockery as phenomena that require a special understanding, precisely because they are *not* what they seem to be. The orator referred to at l. 367, who withholds funding from poets because he has been satirized in a comedy, simply does not understand what motivates comic abuse in the first place (or so, at least, Aristophanes represents him, whether or not it was actually true). The chorus of initiates blurs the line between comedy and religious ritual, treating that orator as if he were sacrilegious and unworthy of participation in a sacred moment. Through this conceit, of course, Aristophanes assumes an ironically sanctimonious attitude toward his work—to clearly humorous effect—yet beneath the humor of the passage lies an apologia for comedy as a symbolic performance governed by a set of rules that make it look more like ritualized activity than lived experience.

---

46. As Catherine Bell 1992, 220, puts it: "[r]itualization is fundamentally a way of doing things to trigger the perception that these practices are distinct and the associations that they engender are special."

A symbol attempts to communicate meaning about something besides itself, and a symbolic ritual simultaneously universalizes and particularizes the meanings encoded within it.[47] Aristophanes' conflation of comic and ritual mockery in the *Frogs* parodos suggests that for him the meaning(s) of their respective symbolic performances intersected at a level that transcended their particularized form: For him, it seems, comic mockery, perhaps even all poetry, was very much like ritualized performative behavior, whether or not one could draw direct genealogical lines between them. As such, our passage from the parodos of *Frogs* seems like a first step toward acknowledging that comic mockery can be conceptualized as an abstract phenomenon that continually resists its own particularizing impulses, like other forms of ritualized behavior.

4. Aristotle on Poetic Structures and the "Origins" of Comedy

Not everyone in antiquity was, in Aristophanes' terms, "initiated" into the "mysteries" of comedy. Plato and Aristotle, for example, stand at the beginning of an ancient critical tradition that problematized comic mockery and tended to analyze *all* comic poetry according to a calculus of vituperation,[48] and bear a good deal of responsibility for the impression that satire was not particularly well understood in antiquity.[49] They were responding, in a manner that anticipated Freud's discussion of hostility in jokes, specifically to the fact that so many forms of humor depend on the denigration or demeaning of a third party. At one level, both philosophers found what Freud called "tendentious joking" (jokes that attempt to make a—usually hostile—point) beneath the dignity of any person aspiring to an aristocratic, "liberal" way of life.[50]

---

47. Cf. Geertz's working definition of the symbol (1973, 91): ". . . any object, act, event, quality or relation which serves as a vehicle for a conception—the conception is the symbol's 'meaning' . . . ."

48. Aristotle, for example, in his well-known discussion of the history of Attic comedy in chapters 4–5 of the *Poetics* (1448b4–1449b20), located its origin in the composition of invective by "lighter" poets (Halliwell's translation [1987, 34] of *eutelesteroi* 1448b26), imitating "the actions of base men."

49. But see our discussion of Plato on comic mockery in chapter 7.

50. As in many areas, Aristotle favored a middle course in humor. In the *Nicomachean Ethics* he sketches a theory of joking appropriate for the *eleutheros* (the "free", "aristocratic" man), and distinguished such humor from that of the *bômolochos* ("buffoon"), 1128a34:

"The buffoon can't restrain himself from joking, and he spares neither himself nor others if he'll get a laugh from it; and he does this by saying the sorts of things that no refined man would say, and some things that he wouldn't even hear." [ὁ δὲ βωμολόχος ἥττων ἐστὶ τοῦ γελοίου, καὶ οὔτε ἑαυτοῦ οὔτε τῶν ἄλλων ἀπεχόμενος εἰ γέλωτα ποιήσει, καὶ τοιαῦτα λέγων ὧν οὐδὲν ἂν εἴποι ὁ χαρίεις, ἔνια δ᾽ οὐδ᾽ ἂν ἀκούσαι].

For discussion of Aristotle's theories of humor (and his influence on later ancient critics), see Freudenburg 1993, 55–72. See also Cullyer 2006 and Rosen 2006.

But behind the issue of decorum lay deeper concerns that the representation of such humor could disrupt the psychic equilibrium of an audience and, by consequence, the social equilibrium of the polis.[51] This fear that aggressive humor could lead to aggressive behavior in a listener influenced Plato's and Aristotle's assessment of iambographic poetry and Old Comedy to such an extreme that they seem almost oblivious to any aspects in these genres that were not abusive. It seemed to matter little to them that, in Aristophanes, for example, direct personal attack was merely one among many comic modes, most of which rely on what Freud would call "innocent jokes."[52]

Plato's attitude to comic and satiric poetry is complex and will receive a fuller discussion later in this book (chapter 7), but it is worth considering here Aristotle's remarks about comedy in the *Poetics*, because despite his fundamental animosity toward comedy's more transgressive forms, he anticipates—albeit in sketchy form—the guiding questions and methodological premises of this study. For here we can clearly see Aristotle's own attempts to understand the mechanisms by which poetry takes on a particular morphological cast and the abstract categories that allow us to speak of poetic "types" or "genres" that can be conceptualized as operating independently of individual authors and their works.

Aristotle was mainly concerned in the *Poetics* with tragedy rather than comedy, but his intention to turn to comedy in the second, now lost, book of the work is well known,[53] and one of the first tasks he faces in the extant first book is to confront the differences between these two large poetic groupings. While he certainly cannot claim the last word on defining comedy, it is remarkable that merely within several paragraphs, he manages not only to assert (even if implicitly) the legitimacy of thinking about poetry in terms of generic

---

51. Plato is the more explicit about the potentially detrimental social effects of comedy. His dissatisfaction with most forms of contemporary dramatic representation presupposes that the arts in fact have the power to alter human behavior. See *R.* 377–99.

52. See Freud [1912] 1960, 90–96: "It is easy to divine the characteristic of jokes on which the difference in their hearers' reactions to them depends. In the one case the joke is an end in itself and serves no particular aim, in the other case it does serve such an aim—it becomes *tendentious*. Only jokes that have a purpose run the risk of meeting with people who do not want to listen to them" (90). Freud's distinction between two categories of joking is artificially schematic and vague, since his criterion—the presence of absence of "purpose" or "aim" in a joke—seems incomplete. The aim of all jokes is, after all, to elicit laughter from an audience, and it is thus difficult to conceive of a joke that "serves no particular aim." Further, because Freud was concerned primarily with individual cases of joke-telling, and less so with larger literary works that employed them, he did not consider how even jokes that *appear* benign or purposeless in themselves may, in the appropriate context, function tendentiously as part of a attack on a target, however obliquely (see 181–236). Nor was Freud especially interested in the ways in which literature as a mimetic phenomenon mediated, and could manipulate, the relationship between the joker, the target and the intended audience. But Freud's observation that the audience's reaction to a joke is crucial for determining its character remains fundamental.

53. See Janko 1984.

abstractions—epistemological constructs rather than material artifacts—but also to lay out a critical framework for articulating the comic which essentially guided all subsequent discourse about comic poetry in antiquity.

The importance of Aristotle's contribution to our understanding of comic poetry, as I see it, is twofold: First, he conceptualized the comic in a relationship with what was non-comic, and made this relationship an evaluative, moral one. Comedy was to be distinguished from what was serious; "serious" meant "good" (or at least "better"), and so comedy becomes, by association with serious genres, inferior. Second, in working out his notion of poetic mimesis, or representation, Aristotle (unlike his predecessor Plato) was profoundly sensitive to the ontological distinctions between the representation (the poetic work itself) and what was represented (the content of the work), and was more sanguine than Plato about an audience's ability to make a similar distinction. Aristotle was well aware that an audience, at least in ideal circumstances, can be emotionally moved by a poetic performance at the same time as they are intellectually detached from it and reflective about its form and content. Aristotle was also attuned to, and I think a little puzzled by, the fact that such poetry could be considered morally inferior, and often transgressive, yet could give pleasure to an audience. This dilemma, as we shall see later on, characterized thinking about comic poetry throughout antiquity, not only by critics but by poets themselves, who, as we might expect, reveled in exploiting the culturally problematic status of their chosen genre.

Aristotle's struggle to understand the challenges posed by comic poetry begin early in the *Poetics*. In one of the boldest theoretical chapters of the work, chapter 4, Aristotle famously declared that poetry had two main causes: first, a human being's inborn inclination to engage in mimesis—that is, in the representation of an objective reality—and second, the pleasure that all humans take in contemplating the artifacts of such a representation.[54] It remains as problematic today as it was then to speak of the origins of poetry in such categorical terms, and it is easy to dismiss Aristotle's theorizing as simplistic, if not arrogant. But as he proceeds to explain what led him to this fundamental insight, we can see that he was troubled by an apparent paradox of literary aesthetics that is still familiar to us. Aristotle takes as a sign (σημεῖον) of a human being's capacity for mimetic pleasure the fact that we take pleasure in viewing the representations of painful things: ἃ γὰρ αὐτὰ λυπηρῶς ὁρῶμεν, τούτων τὰς εἰκόνας τὰς μάλιστα ἠκριβωμένας χαίρομεν θεωροῦντες, οἷον θηρίων

54. ... αἰτίαι δύο τινὲς καὶ αὗται φυσικαί. τό τε γὰρ μιμεῖσθαι σύμφυτον τοῖς ἀνθρώποις ἐκ παίδων ἐστὶ καὶ τούτῳ διαφέρουσι τῶν ἄλλων ζῴων ὅτι μιμητικώτατόν ἐστι καὶ τὰς μαθήσεις ποιεῖται διὰ μιμήσεως τὰς πρώτας, καὶ τὸ χαίρειν τοῖς μιμήμασι πάντας. [... poetry arose from two causes, which are both 'natural.' For it is an inherent trait in humans from childhood to imitate/represent (on this point they are they differ from the other animals as being the most 'mimetic'; and he forms his first understandings from mimesis), and for all to take pleasure in mimesis.] (1448b4–9).

τε μορφὰς τῶν ἀτιμοτάτων καὶ νεκρῶν ("for of the things which we find in themselves painful to look at, we enjoy images that are represented with particular accuracy, such as the shapes of the basest animals and corpses." 1448b10-12) Aristotle speaks specifically here of the attitude an audience (θεωροῦντες = "watching as a passive observer") has toward the mimesis of objects that are distressing to them. One might think that the more accurate a painful representation appears to be, the quicker one would recoil from it, as one might from a painful scene in real life. The reverse seems to be true, as Aristotle perceived, and as the history of art and literature continually bears out.

Aristotle's own explanation for *why* humans feel this odd pleasure at seeing painful representations is another simple, but bold, insight—for him it was the intellectual pleasure derived from the ability to correlate mimetic images with familiar objects.[55] We may see a poet's or an artist's depiction of a "base animal" or a "corpse" (to use his examples), but our consciousness that this aesthetic experience is mimetic rather than real allows the intellectual pleasures to mediate whatever emotional response we may also be feeling. Even if, as Aristotle continues, a person has no previous knowledge of the mimetic object, he can at least take a kind of intellectual pleasure in the formal aspects of the representation: ἐπεὶ ἐὰν μὴ τύχῃ προεωρακώς, οὐχ ᾗ μίμημα ποιήσει τὴν ἡδονὴν ἀλλὰ διὰ τὴν ἀπεργασίαν ἢ τὴν χροιὰν ἢ διὰ τοιαύτην τινὰ ἄλλην αἰτίαν ("for if someone happens not to have seen the thing before, it will not give pleasure in its capacity as a *mimêsis*, but by virtue of its execution or its color, or some other cause," 1448b17). In short, for Aristotle, artistic mimesis in general, and poetic mimesis in particular, had a different experiential, even ontological, status from lived reality; and he came to this conclusion, it seems, simply because he could observe, as we can in our own culture, that people enjoy watching or hearing the sorts of "bad" or "painful" things—characters, behavior, images, situations, etc.—which, if experienced as part of their actual lives, could potentially cause extreme displeasure. As long as a mimesis was well executed, in terms not only of form but also of intellectual engagement,[56] even the most painful objects and subjects of the real world could be rendered pleasurable.

Aristotle's heady and abstract preamble to his own historical sketch of Greek poetry is, like most of the *Poetics*, frustratingly truncated, but it is clear that what was driving his analysis of mimesis was an aesthetic moral dilemma:

---

55. διὰ γὰρ τοῦτο χαίρουσι τὰς εἰκόνας ὁρῶντες, ὅτι συμβαίνει θεωροῦντας μανθάνειν καὶ συλλογίζεσθαι τί ἕκαστον, οἷον ὅτι οὗτος ἐκεῖνος· ("So for this reason people enjoy looking at images, because it happens that as they contemplate them they learn and form a conclusion about what each thing is, for example that 'this [image of a] person represents that person'") (1448b15–17).

56. For further discussion of this topic, see below, chapter 7, pp. 260–62.

How could an audience of "good" people take pleasure in poetry that represented "bad things?" Put another way, if someone did take pleasure in such morally compromised representations, did that reflect badly on the viewer/auditor? Did one's enjoyment of such poetry constitute an illicit pleasure? Aristotle himself does not phrase the question in quite this way, but his insistence on the disjunction between a mimetic object (such as a poetic work) and the thing it represents, as well as the need to evaluate each according to different criteria, makes it clear that for him mimetic pleasure is morally neutral.

This attitude is almost certainly at least a partial response to Plato's hardline approach to the poetic mimesis of morally suspect topics, well known from the *Republic*; although even Plato, as we shall see later on, may have harbored some sympathies for scandalous comic poets. But even Aristotle would not deny that there was a moral hierarchy to poetry, and that some types of poetry were more ennobling or enlightening than others. This much, at any rate, becomes clear in *Poetics* 4 once Aristotle begins his brief history of poetry; for here, in a radical move, Aristotle claims that, after a very early period of undifferentiated improvisations, poetry developed along one of two distinct lines, each one reflecting the "character" of their respective practitioners (διεσπάσθη δὲ κατὰ τὰ οἰκεῖα ἤθη ἡ ποίησις). The language used to describe both types of poets and their work is essentially moral: "Serious" or "dignified" poets (σεμνότεροι) represented "fine" or "beautiful" actions, while "less serious" (εὐτελέστεροι) ones concerned themselves with the actions of "base" or "vulgar" men (*Poetics* 1448b26–27).[57] The two specific types of poetry that Aristotle here opposes to one another are well known—serious poets composed such things as hymns and encomia, while more low-brow poets wrote invectives (*psogoi*)—but the significance of this formulation has not been fully appreciated. Once again, Aristotle's analysis falls far short of offering anything like a rigorous, or even particularly accurate, literary history, and it is obvious that, in the absence of any real evidence for the earliest periods of Greek poetry, he had little choice but to extrapolate backward from his own conceptualization of how poetry worked in his own time.[58] Yet this historical retrojection is highly revealing in itself for several reasons. First, it shows Aristotle thinking of poetry in terms of broadly conceived structures that transcend identification with individual poets and even specific genres. This is itself iconoclastic for an age used to thinking of poetry in terms of well-delineated genres and their poets,

57. οἱ μὲν γὰρ σεμνότεροι τὰς καλὰς ἐμιμοῦντο πράξεις καὶ τὰς τῶν τοιούτων, οἱ δὲ εὐτελέστεροι τὰς τῶν φαύλων, πρῶτον ψόγους ποιοῦντες, ὥσπερ ἔτεροι ὕμνους καὶ ἐγκώμια. (*Poet.* 1448b25–27).

58. As Halliwell 1987, 81 says: "the factual data of literary history, in so far as we take Ar. to have had access to them, are subordinated or even sacrificed to a theoretical view of the direction of change and development within what we might term poetry's 'natural history'."

but even more startling, it seems, is the specific content of the two major branches of early poetry that Aristotle posits.

Since, again, Aristotle was primarily concerned in *Poetics* with the development of tragedy, and for all intents and purposes the knowable history of tragedy for him began with Homer, it makes sense that one of Aristotle's two basic branches of poetry would involve the mimesis of "serious" (τὰ σπουδαῖα) subjects (Homer's great hallmark, 1448b34). But why did he characterize the second branch, which was the functional opposite to the "serious" poetry of the first, as a *psogos*, that is, the mimesis of interpersonal invective? Aristotle's phrasing on this point is unusual, for it juxtaposes a generalized type of poetry —the mimesis of "base" characters (οἱ δὲ εὐτελέστεροι τὰς τῶν φαύλων)— with a particular *manifestation* of that activity—the composition of invectives (πρῶτον ψόγους ποιοῦντες). He proceeds in a famous passage to associate such invective with iambographic poetry in particular, and from there he traces a crude and unnuanced development, once again via Homer (and the allegedly Homeric *Margites*), to the comic drama of his own day. As Aristotle sums up:

παραφανείσης δὲ τῆς τραγῳδίας καὶ κωμῳδίας οἱ ἐφ᾽ ἑκατέραν τὴν ποίησιν ὁρμῶντες κατὰ τὴν οἰκείαν φύσιν οἱ μὲν ἀντὶ τῶν ἰάμβων κωμῳδοποιοὶ ἐγένοντο, οἱ δὲ ἀντὶ τῶν ἐπῶν τραγῳδοδιδάσκαλοι, διὰ τὸ μείζω καὶ ἐντιμότερα τὰ σχήματα εἶναι ταῦτα ἐκείνων. (1449a2-6)

And when the potential of tragedy and comedy became evident, men gravitated toward one or the other type of poetry according to their particular nature; some became comic instead of iambic poets, while others became tragic instead of epic poets, since the forms of tragedy were greater and more esteemed than those of epic. (1449a2–6)

The literary trajectory here parallels a moral one: Just as epic and iambic invective represent "superior" and "inferior" forms of poetry, respectively, so do they each metamorphose into genres—tragedy and comedy—that retain analogous moral qualities. The *psogos* seems for Aristotle to lie at some level at the heart of all poetry that can be considered "comic," and such poetry will always have a compromised moral status because the objects of their mimesis are by definition "base."[59]

59. For discussion, see Nagy 1979, 253–59. I would differ from Nagy only in his conclusion that for Aristotle the *psogos* ("blame poetry") only had the *potential* for comedy rather than that it was intrinsically comic. In Nagy's reading of Aristotle, "comedy formalizes" this comic potential in blame poetry, "[b]ut blame poetry itself is more inclusive and thus cannot be equated with comedy. Blame poetry can be serious as well as comic; it can condemn as well as ridicule" (256). Nagy is correct to note that Aristotle explicitly says (at *Poet.* 1448b37–38) that "'*to geloion* 'the laughable' rather than *psogos* 'blame' is the function of comedy," but this need not imply that the *psogos* can be anything other than comic at some fundamental level. Aristotle would certainly hold that comedy

When we consider that Aristotle was working back from the relatively tame New Comedy of his own day in an attempt to trace its literary history, it is curious that he would locate the origins of this genre in invective. Invective poetry seems to us, at any rate, like a specific and limited form; we know how such poets as Archilochus, Hipponax and Aristophanes, for example, deployed lampoons, mockery, and personal attack in their work, but one can think of many other elements within the works of such poets that were *not* explicitly invective, yet also "represented base things." Why, then, would Aristotle posit something as specific as a *psogos* at the base of the one branch of poetry that eventually developed into a non-invective form of comedy? His discussion is vague and rushed to be sure, but he seems to be struggling to make several critical methodological and substantive points at once. On the one hand, as Aristotle asserts at *Poetics* 1449b7, the comedy of his own day had long abandoned the "iambic form" (ἰαμβικὴ ἰδέα) of earlier times, having taken its cue, he says, from Homer himself, who "was the first one to show the form of comedy (τὸ τῆς κωμῳδίας σχῆμα), by dramatizing the laughable (τὸ γελοῖον) rather than invective (ψόγον)" (*Poet.* 1448b36–37). As such, comedy seems to have become something different from its earlier invective antecedents.[60] On the other hand, Aristotle still regarded comedy, even in his own time, as mimeses of characters and situations morally inferior to those in tragedy or epic. When he says, in the passage quoted above, that poets gravitated to the one or the other type of poetry, tragedy or comedy, depending on their individual character, he maintains a moral opposition between these two types of contemporary poetry that he had articulated for their earliest, pre-Homeric forms. Just as Aristotle considered early epic poets more "dignified" (*semnoteroi*) than those hypothetical early poets of the *psogos* (who were *eutelesteroi*, "less serious"), so did he regard their successors in tragedy and comedy in similar moral terms. The "laughable" (*to geloion*) that was the hallmark of comedy in Aristotle's mind, may have lost its iambic, "psogic" edge, but both *psogos* and *geloion* remained affiliated by virtue of their opposition to the "serious" (*spoudaia*), morally superior content of tragedy, epic, and other related poetic genres.

(by which he probably has in mind comic drama, as opposed to tragedy), and more abstractly, *to geloion*, need not always be "psogic," and he would likely find that at the root of the *psogos* one could always find comic elements. See my discussion below.

60. Aristotle was surely over-schematizing, since it is hardly the case that obscenity disappeared entirely from Greek comic drama in the fourth century, though his general view of the development of Greek comedy from "old" to "new" as a movement away from explicit vituperation is corroborated in the main by the textual evidence. He was far less nuanced (in the *Poetics*, at any rate, where, to be fair, he was only tangentially concerned with comedy) about what we have come to call "Middle Comedy," i.e., fourth-century comic drama that still displayed many of the features we associate with Old Comedy. On Middle Comedy, see Hunter 1983, 20–30, Nesselrath 1990, and Rosen 1995.

What is most striking about Aristotle's discussion of comedy is his implicit attempt to articulate fundamental or constituent elements of "the comic" that would have some explanatory value for all its specific manifestations. This seems to be the force of Aristotle's own term σχῆμα ("structure") when he notes that "the *skhêma* of comedy" was the "ridiculous"; even though Aristotle is here thinking specifically of comic drama (*kômôidia*), the notion of a *skhêma* that informs this genre implies that any work of poetry that has *ta geloia* as its mimetic objects can be said to be constructed in accord with a more broadly conceived notion of "the comic."[61] Aristotle was differentiating "the *skhêma* of comedy" from invective proper, but, as we have seen, there was a direct developmental line in his mind from the *psogos* to comic drama, and the common thread all through was their shared imitation of base objects. Put in more concrete terms, Aristotle regarded "the comic," conceived of as a broad, unspecified poetic category and contrasted to tragedy, as a verbal mimesis derived ultimately from an essentially invective impulse of personal attack and mockery.[62] It is easy to quibble at such a reductive formulation of a complex phenomenon, but as we shall see, it reveals an attitude toward comic poetry and poets that was culturally entrenched throughout Greco-Roman antiquity.

61. See also the discussion at Branham 1989, 49–50.

62. I should mention that Aristotle's notion of the mimesis of comic objects would have been limited to third-person, dramatic or quasi-dramatic (as in epic) narratives. There was essentially no place in his conception of poetry, at least as he articulated it in the *Poetics*, for the poet himself to perform the mimesis speaking in his own person. As he states at 1460a7 (chapter 24), "It is necessary for the poet himself to speak as little as possible; for in speaking himself, he is not an imitator." (αὐτὸν γὰρ δεῖ τὸν ποιητὴν ἐλάχιστα λέγειν· οὐ γάρ ἐστι κατὰ ταῦτα μιμητής.) See Halliwell 1987, 172–174 and Clay, 1998, 25–27. Halliwell, 172, sums up the dilemma: "Indirectly and paradoxically, chapter 24 remains a testimony to the tenacious traditional idea of first-person utterance as equivalent to the poet's own voice; it is just because of this assumption that Ar. wishes to minimise such utterance, rather than attempting through some conception of a poetic persona, to fictionalise even the 'I' of poetic texts." As Halliwell notes (173), it is impossible to say what Aristotle might have said about the poetic-mimetic qualities of the vast swathe of ancient poetry that employed the personal "I" as its main voice; but there is no reason why we cannot extend his own theories of mimesis to poetic structures that did not particularly interest him, or which (in the case of first-person narratives) he actually seems to have misunderstood. It may be true, as Clay (27) writes, that ". . . in its beginnings in the fourth century, Greek *theory* [my italics] had no real conception of the *literary* persona," but there is ample evidence to show that even much earlier than this poets themselves (usually working in the comic genres) could routinely (and self-consciously) deploy sophisticated strategies of fictional, essentially mimetic, "self-construction." It is, of course, the central claim of this book that, *pace* Aristotle, virtually all poets using first-person narratives would at some level construe their methods as mimetic and fictional, and that they worked on the assumption that their ideal audience would understand this. Indeed, I would argue that any time a poet portrayed himself in an obviously *comic* narrative, this (i.e., the fact of comedy itself) is a generic cue to the audience that the plot was more likely than not fictional. It is always difficult to prove in every instance that a poet was fully aware of his own self-fashioning, but the existence alone of such texts as Cratinus's *Pytine*, in which the poet himself was the play's main character in an obviously fictionalized account of his troubled marriage to an allegorized "Kômôidia," ought to serve as an emblematic example of the possibilities open to comic poets in pre-Aristotelian periods. For discussion and bibliography, see below, pp. 252–53.

Of all the ways in which Aristotle might have accounted for comedy, then, he chose the most negative, socially problematic, and indecorous point of origin, locating at the root of such genres not, for example, the charms of a therapeutic laughter, but rather the cruel laughter and mean-spiritedness arising from ridicule. If nothing else, this seems to imply a deep-seated anxiety on Aristotle's part about mockery and satire, as well as a fundamental fear that comedy brought pleasures that were morally suspect as if by definition. But such anxieties were not merely the product of a philosopher's idiosyncratic rumination: Time and again throughout this book, we will see comic poets of mockery portray themselves as if they too agreed with Aristotle that poets of their sort were by turns abject, mean-spirited, morally transgressive and quick to anger. Aristotle astutely sensed, it seems, that despite the obvious differences among poets of comedy broadly conceived, they shared many similar qualities, including a sense of self-marginalization (however contrived or disingenuous), a moral edginess, and a perennial desire to flirt with the scandalous, whether in diction or subject matter. As far as we can tell, Aristotle was the first to attempt to analyze the perceptible affiliations among otherwise unrelated poets of mockery and satire, and to suggest that the forces determining the character of such poetry and the portrayal of such poets within their works could profitably be conceived of as abstract epistemological categories, logically prior to the textual or performative manifestations of the works themselves.

5. Myth and the Structures of Mockery

Aristotle had little actual evidence on which to base his theories of the pre-historical origins of poetry, but his experiments in thinking abstractly about literary phenomena anticipated in many respects critical methods that have emerged only over the course of the last century. We have already touched upon one of these, genre theory, which concerns itself with such questions as how we conceptualize relationships among literary works and the benefits or drawbacks of categorizing them according to apparently shared characteristics. Following in the footsteps of Aristotle, arguably our first genre theorist, we too will often have occasion in this study to conceptualize abstractly the various elements that urge us to affiliate otherwise diverse literary works with one another. But another window into the morphology of ancient comedy and satire is revealed, I believe, in the analysis of myth, perhaps the most explicitly symbolic and fictive realm in antiquity. Some of the most trenchant commentary on ancient mockery comes from Greek mythology, as we shall explore over the course of the next two chapters. Myth provides another productive portal to our subject because it exists prior to any of its expressions in verbal or visual forms. Before myths find their way into individual narratives they carry sufficient symbolic signposting to enable a culture to derive meaning (or multiple meanings) from them. This is not the same as saying that the meaning of a myth is a strictly delimited, immanent constant waiting to be decoded in a monolithic fashion. Obviously, the same myth could be deployed and interpreted in many ways in different historical contexts and narrative forms. At the same time a myth can only be interpreted if there is something to interpret, and that "something" can be seen as the raw symbolic data that emerge when a myth is analyzed in its most abstract form. One principle that underlies my attempts to address the question of how mockery in antiquity became poetic mockery, and from there, specifically comic mockery, has been well established by anthropologists and historians of religion, namely (to put it most simply) that myths tend to reflect a culture's basic values, beliefs, or ideologies. There are several representations of comic mockery in Greek mythology that hint at its cultural origins in more fundamental ways than most social or institutional practices ever can, and I discuss these in detail in the next chapter. My contention there will be that, while we generally think of Plato and Aristotle as our first systematic theorists of comedy, long before they appeared, a rudimentary theory of comedy was evolving in Greek culture through poetry, iconography, myth, and ritual. I mean by this that before the advent of analytical discourse about art and literature, a discourse about the nature and parameters of comedic expression can be inferred from various paradigmatic texts. Some of these works address the problem of humor and the comic more or less directly, even if not explicitly in terms of literary history. This material is largely mythical and religious, and offers useful exempla of what was considered humorous and comedic at the moments of their production, and by the subsequent communities that valued them. This type of evidence substantially enriches our understanding of the structures, dynamics and poetic typologies that governed the literary texts to which we will turn in later chapters.

The evidence from myth, moreover, may also be regarded as a corrective counterpoint to the ancient philosophical commentary about comedy, which is often taken as a starting point in traditional literary histories. To be sure, Plato and Aristotle were the first in Western culture to investigate the nature and origins of comedy. In analyzing the comic forms they knew best and evaluating their desirability or utility for the polis, they attempted at various points what almost looks like a taxonomy of comedy.

Both philosophers, however, framed their discussions of comedy in terms of the prevailing codes of social propriety and nearly always registered some embarrassment, as we have seen, at having to confront a representational form, which for them was doomed to remain essentially vulgar and indecorous. For them, comedy was largely a problem to be explained and domesticated; it implied a popular, if marginal, poetic arena that demanded a certain amount of special pleading for it to become philosophically integrated into the social equilibrium. If they can be said to have sanctioned comic poetry at all, their attitude was usually one of grudging tolerance. Even when we might detect some genuine interest in, and sympathy for, comedy in Plato and Aristotle, neither can be said to have offered a philosophical *endorsement* of comedy as a poetic form with any redeeming aesthetic, if not moral, value. They were not interested in the social or psychological needs comedy fulfilled in an audience, and they regarded the most aggressive, vituperative forms as categorically perverse and objectionable.

As we shall see toward the end of this book, the philosophical tradition provides indispensable insight into the reception of comic forms in particular historical contexts, and in some cases even influenced poetic trends, but ancient philosophical theories of "the comic" were, almost by definition, parochial. They had recourse to none of the comparative data that we do, and their analysis and evaluation of literature, as far as we can judge, primarily served their respective moral positions. Obscene language, aggressive and confrontational stances of a poet against a target, fictionalized moments of cruelty and violence, and other such elements of ancient comedy, were largely repudiated by the prescriptive and protreptic rhetoric of Plato and Aristotle, and they never asked what motivated poets to engage in such literary forms,[63] or what audiences were responding to in them. Because the explicitly exegetical tradition about comic poetry, therefore, will not take us much beyond its own circumscribed parameters of analysis, we must also look to the more philosophically ingenuous body of evidence about mockery and satire that we find in mythography, before turning to the evidence of the poets themselves.

---

63. Beyond, at any rate, the most obvious conclusion that people who enjoyed or engaged in this sort of comedy were morally dysfunctional. See discussion below, chapter 7, pp. 255–62.

2

Two Paradigms of Mockery
in Greek Myth

Iambe and Demeter, Heracles and the Cercopes

It is commonly noted that humans create myths in order to account for complex, often problematic aspects of their own humanity, and to explain the various practices and institutions inherited from their ancestors. Like many other cultures throughout history, the ancient Greeks were eager to know the origins of the things in their world, and their mythical record preserves a variety of aetiological narratives intended to make sense in the present of a distant, chronologically indistinct past. Generally speaking, this was necessarily what we might consider a fictionalizing endeavor: The content of their myths—the stories they told to explain monuments or cults, or even human behavior—tended to be ahistorical and unencumbered by our own obsessions with chronological specificity or verifiable historical "truths."[1] *We* may want to know, for example, in what year exactly the Trojan War broke out, but in mythical accounts of the war chronological exactitude (if it was a concern at all) needed to satisfy no other criteria than what was consistent with the particular narrative at hand. By contrast, the specific literary instantiations of myths, the actual means by which a myth was told, can often be situated historically and so can reflect the cultural forces that generated them. This distinction between the content and the vehicle of myths is never as clear-cut as one would like it to be, but since I propose in this chapter to use myth as at least a species of

---

1. In recent years scholars have become increasingly skeptical about whether the analysis of Greek myths can tell us anything "new" or "universal" about Greek history and culture, and have articulated the pitfalls of extrapolating too broadly from mythical variants idiosyncratic to specific times and places. But even the most cautious scholars of mythology recognize that even the most localized version of a myth exists in an intertextual relationship with all others. As Dowden (1992, 56) puts it: "without reuse, there are no myths, only one-off fictions." What we make of the "reuse" of myth is the big question. As soon as we posit an intertextual relationship among mythic variants across time and place, however, we are in fact in a position to make claims both about particular historical contexts that may have informed such variants, and about those very aspects of the myth that seem to migrate from one variant to another. Analyzing narratological substrata that survive localizing tendencies *does* allow us, I would suggest, to make some synchronic claims about Greek culture.

evidence in an essentially historical enterprise, I would like to be clear from the beginning about what I think we can legitimately extrapolate from it.[2]

This chapter will focus on two Greek myths which in one form or another recount the effects of comic mockery on an individual, the myths of Iambe and Demeter, and of Heracles and the Cercopes. While comic mockery can be found here and there in any number of other Greek myths, whether as a rhetorical mode or a marker of a particular personality type, these two myths are distinguished by the fact that their respective denouements are themselves acts of comic mockery, acts which, in short, serve as the point of the narrative that leads up to them. The story of Iambe's obscene language and comic mockery of Demeter became embedded within the larger myth of the goddess's grief over her abducted daughter precisely *because* it accounted for her eventual change of mood.[3] Similarly, most of the accounts of Heracles and the Cercopes brothers end with them making obscene fun of the hero, and effecting in him a change from anger to mirth.

But such a simplified description of these myths, however unobjectionable, raises a host of methodological questions. Quite apart from the obvious problem of how variants on each myth, scattered across the broad span of ancient Greek culture, might relate to one another, we are left wondering whether the questions these myths seem *to us* to be addressing were the same ones that generated the myths in the first place. Was the society that produced either of these myths, for example, trying to answer through them questions such as: "Where does comic mockery come from?" "Is there a difference between 'actual' mockery, originating in real anger and malevolence, and 'comic' mockery, which is benign and even potentially restorative?" Did these myths serve to explain behavior and practices within their own culture that they found alarming when judged according to the values that ordered their actual lives?[4] Did these myths, for example, make it less troubling for an audience to take pleasure in hearing obscenity in poetic performances, or in finding humor in representations of men abusing each other or behaving in other obviously antisocial ways? Finally, did such myths implicitly make an almost philosophical claim for the didactic function of a mimetic mode traditionally regarded as vulgar and morally bankrupt?

2. All such questions imply enormous methodological premises about how myth actually worked in antiquity, its relation to "history" and its explanatory potential of symbolic discourse. While we cannot here enter into the details of such controversies, the issues are well laid out in Edmunds 1990, 1–20, Brillante 1990, 91–138, and Graf 1993, 121–41.

3. See Foley 1994, 45–46.

4. On myths that appear to explain problematic aspects of human life, see, e.g., Kirk 1970, 234–36, 258–59. In Greek mythology, any number of examples leap to mind: Pandora, to account for the ills of the world (and the fraught question of hope in adversity), or Tithonus as an explanation of the inevitability of aging.

From a strictly historical perspective, these questions cannot be answered: We are never privy to the exact moment when myths become instantiated in literary form, and we have no way of knowing what motivated one author to privilege some details over others. We cannot, that is, judge whether the story of Iambe recounted in the *Homeric Hymn to Demeter* had any particular resonance either for some hypothetical first author or for the generations of rhapsodes who performed it at various festivals. Iambe "came with" the story of Demeter, just as the Cercopes formed part of the larger saga of Heracles' travails; so the question remains, can we legitimately look to traditional stories for evidence about the culture in which these stories were retold or re-performed as *mythos*, when one of the powerful principles driving their transmission was the preservation of details generated in an earlier period?[5] Put another way: If we decide that the story of Iambe or the Cercopes must reflect, in origin at least, a concern for the role of humor and mockery in society, what can these stories tell us about, say, the way comic mockery was deployed in Athenian Old Comedy? A skeptic might worry, after all, that we have very little direct evidence of a relationship between these myths and contemporary theorizing about the actual practice of Greek comic poetry.[6] But once we probe beneath a society's *conscious* knowledge of its cultural practices, and recognize that modes of behavior and discourse are just as often generated by forces operating well beyond a society's ability to conceive of, or articulate, them, we remain well-positioned to consider ways in which even anachronistic phenomena such as myth can help explain historically-situated phenomena such as literature.

In this chapter, therefore, our examination of how the Iambe and Cercopes myths conceptualize the dynamics of mockery and satire will be essentially atemporal; that is, I approach both myths as narratives with a point to make about interpersonal humor and abuse, whether or not we are able to pinpoint their origin to a specific place or time. While it may be anachronistic to speak of these myths as reflecting certain inchoate notions of comedy as a literary genre (as this chapter will suggest) when the myths themselves almost certainly antedate any ancient genre known as comedy, viewing the myths through the lens of chronologically later constructs offers us an illuminating escape from the limitations of a strict historicism. This is especially true for mythical material, which by its very nature is not necessarily interested in providing systematically historical signposts. Jean-Pierre Vernant has described well how

---

5. Cf. Graf 1993, 2–8; Nagy 1996, 113–46; Csapo 2005, 1–9.
6. We are in a slightly better position with the myth of Iambe and its relation to Aristophanes, since, as we noted in the preceding chapter [pp. 29–32, q.v., with bibliography], the parodos of *Frogs*, with its chorus of Eleusinian initiates, alludes to the ritual *aiskhrologia* for which the Iambe-Demeter story is the *aition*.

this ahistorical aspect of myth is precisely what allows it to resonate across time and culture: ". . . what matters is not the way the story is told, which can vary from one account to another, but rather the mental categories conveyed by the stories as a whole and by the intellectual organization that underlies all the various versions."[7] Vernant urges a move from the

> ". . . surface text to the bases that provide its structural organization, and guide us through the many different variants of the myth to the structural framework that provides the overall key we can use to decipher a veritable system of thought not, at every level, immediately accessible to the habitual working of our minds."[8]

We shall analyze our myths of mockery in this chapter guided by such general principles, and attempt to identify the underlying thematic and structural elements that would remain even were we to change the details of the story. As I hope to show, the myths of Iambe and the Cercopes share many such elements, which seem to point to a "veritable system of thought" about what it means to represent, and perform a representation of, mockery. For these myths ultimately address not only the problem of aggressive humor (as we might put it in our post-Freudian age), but also its *poeticization* within specific generic parameters. It may be too optimistic to think, following Vernant's lead, that we can use these myths as a "key" to reveal all the hidden mysteries of poetic mockery as it comes to manifest itself in Greco-Roman literature, but I will be suggesting in this chapter that they do articulate a system for aestheticizing mockery that in the historical period helps process the mockery and abuse of everyday life into what we would recognize as satire. Satirists were known in antiquity by many names[9] and adopted diverse poetic styles, but they all shared the common goal of generating comedy from a discourse of complaint and abuse that took on a life of its own within the fictionalizing world in which it operated as a mimetic phenomenon, despite whatever claims they might make for a connection with reality. It may not always be easy to find this goal clearly stated by the poets themselves, but the myths we will examine in this chapter

---

7. Vernant 1990, 224–25.

8. Vernant proceeds in this chapter ("The Reason of Myth," 1990, 203–60) to discuss and critique various forms of radical structuralism, especially Lévi-Strauss, whose interest in "decoding" myths guides Vernant's own. Vernant has often been criticized for being too synchronic in his approach (as has Lévi-Strauss), but in this essay at least he remains very sensitive to the necessary interaction between diachronic and synchronic analysis; see esp. 258–60.

9. Greek literature offers an array of terms for poets engaged in satirical writing, *kômôidoi*, *iambistai*, *iambographoi*, to name only a few; Latin seems to have lacked nominal forms, but tended to refer to poets of mockery and satire periphrastically (e.g., Hor. *Serm.* 1.4.41–42, . . . *qui scribat . . . sermoni propiora . . .* , 2.1.1, *sunt quibus in satira videar nimis acer . . .* ; or Juvenal *Sat.* 1.30: *difficile est saturam non scribere.*

go far to suggest that it was culturally available to them to conceptualize a poetics of mockery and satire along these lines. While the main questions that interest me in this study are historical—how did poetic mockery function within the genre that deployed it? What relationship between poet and audience is presupposed by the specific forms of mockery a poet might adopt? How might an audience interpret and respond to the representation of mockery in performance?—we will find in this chapter that the various structures of mockery embedded in the mythical material provide a template that helps explain the morphology and dynamics of subsequent representations of mockery in attested poetic forms.[10]

1. The Mockery of Demeter

The myth of Demeter wandering the earth as she mourns for her daughter Persephone, who had recently been abducted by Hades, is best known to us from the *Homeric Hymn to Demeter*. After learning the identity of her daughter's abductor from Helios, Demeter disguises herself as a mortal named Dôsô and arrives at the house of king Celeus in Eleusis. She asks for work in the royal house and the queen Metaneira gives her charge of her infant son Demophoon. Nearly all versions of the myth focus on Demeter's attempt to make Demophoon immortal by anointing him with ambrosia by day, and burying him in the fire at night, although the immortalizing process was thwarted when Metaneira witnessed Demeter's alarming treatment of her son (242–49). Immediately preceding this episode in the hymn, however, we are told how a servant named Iambe was able to cheer up the grieving Demeter with verbal abuse and obscenity:

τὴν δ' αἰδώς τε σέβας τε ἰδὲ χλωρὸν δέος εἷλεν·   190
εἶξε δέ οἱ κλισμοῖο καὶ ἑδριάασθαι ἄνωγεν.
ἀλλ' οὐ Δημήτηρ ὡρηφόρος ἀγλαόδωρος
ἤθελεν ἑδριάασθαι ἐπὶ κλισμοῖο φαεινοῦ,
ἀλλ' ἀκέουσα ἔμιμνε κατ' ὄμματα καλὰ βαλοῦσα,   195
πρίν γ' ὅτε δή οἱ ἔθηκεν Ἰάμβη κέδν' εἰδυῖα
πηκτὸν ἕδος, καθύπερθε δ' ἐπ' ἀργύφεον βάλε κῶας.

10. In speaking of a "grammar" of mockery reflected in myth, I do not mean that all myths form a strict system analogous to a linguistic grammar, only that in analyzing the structures of myths of mockery, we can begin to postulate a cultural system with principles that could, if not directly generate (like a "generative grammar"), then surely help us analyze (like a "descriptive grammar") forms of representational mockery. See Detienne, 1979, 10–11, and Segal 1986 [1983] 50: ". . . [m]yth is a narrative structure whose sign- and symbol-systems are closely related with the central values of a culture, especially those values which express a supernatural validation, extension, or explanation of cultural norms."

ἔνθα καθεζομένη προκατέσχετο χερσὶ καλύπτρην·
δηρὸν δ᾽ ἄφθογγος τετιημένη ἧστ᾽ ἐπὶ δίφρου,
οὐδέ τιν᾽ οὔτ᾽ ἔπεϊ προσπτύσσετο οὔτε τι ἔργῳ,   200
ἀλλ᾽ ἀγέλαστος ἄπαστος ἐδητύος ἠδὲ ποτῆτος
ἧστο πόθῳ μινύθουσα βαθυζώνοιο θυγατρός,
πρίν γ᾽ ὅτε δὴ χλεύης μιν Ἰάμβη κέδν᾽ εἰδυῖα
πολλὰ παρασκώπτουσ᾽ ἐτρέψατο πότνιαν ἁγνὴν
μειδῆσαι γελάσαι τε καὶ ἵλαον σχεῖν θυμόν·   205
ἣ δή οἱ καὶ ἔπειτα μεθύστερον εὔαδεν ὀργαῖς.
τῇ δὲ δέπας Μετάνειρα δίδου μελιηδέος οἴνου
πλήσασ᾽, ἣ δ᾽ ἀνένευσ᾽· οὐ γὰρ θεμιτόν οἱ ἔφασκε
πίνειν οἶνον ἐρυθρόν, ἄνωγε δ᾽ ἄρ᾽ ἄλφι καὶ ὕδωρ
δοῦναι μίξασαν πιέμεν γλήχωνι τερείνῃ.   210
ἣ δὲ κυκεῶ τεύξασα θεᾷ πόρεν ὡς ἐκέλευε·
δεξαμένη δ᾽ ὁσίης ἕνεκεν πολυπότνια Δηὼ

Reverence, awe, and pale fear seized Metaneira.   190
She gave up her chair and bade the goddess sit down.
But Demeter, bringer of seasons and giver of rich gifts,
did not wish to be seated on the shining seat.
She waited resistant, her lovely eyes cast down,
until knowing Iambe set out a well-built stool   195
for her and cast over it a silvery fleece.
Seated there, the goddess drew the veil before her face.
For a long time she sat voiceless with grief on the stool
and responded to no one with word or gesture.
Unsmiling, tasting neither food nor drink,   200
She sat wasting with desire for her deep-girt daughter,
Until knowing Iambe jested with her and
Mocking with many a joke moved the holy goddess
To smile and laugh and keep a gracious heart—
Iambe, who later pleased her moods as well.   205
Metaneira offered a cup filled with honey-sweet wine,
But Demeter refused it. It was not right, she said,
for her to drink red wine; then she bid them mix barley
and water with soft mint and give her to drink.
Metaneira made and gave the drink to the goddess as she bid.   210
Almighty Deo received it for the sake of the rite.
(trans. Foley, 1994)

Although a minor episode in the Demeter story, this little scene was regarded
as significant enough to be ritually reenacted every year at the Eleusinian

mysteries in honor of Demeter.[11] Obscenity figured in the ritual, such as when (possibly) masked figures mocked initiates from a bridge as they crossed the river Cephisus on their formal procession to Eleusis, or during the *pannykhis*, the night-long festival preceding the day of the actual initiation. Further, the detail recorded in the hymn of the *kykeôn* barley-drink offered to Demeter was also reenacted by the initiates, who evidently drank a similar concoction as part of the secret final rites (*teletai*).[12]

It is impossible to determine whether the hymn's clearly aetiological narrative influenced the details of the festival, or whether it simply referred to an already well-established institution,[13] but it is certainly clear that the confrontation with Iambe resonated broadly across Greco-Roman culture and was regarded as an essential ingredient of the story. One of the more curious aspects of this episode, especially given its subordinate status within the myth of Demeter as a whole, is that in different versions the role played by Iambe in the *Homeric Hymn* was taken by a figure named Baubo. Iambe and Baubo performed the same function in the myth, namely to cheer up Demeter, but used a different method, Iambe preferring verbal abuse, Baubo choosing to expose herself to raise a laugh from the goddess. This gesture has come to be known as an *anasyrma*, from the verb *anasurô*, which is used to describe it in some of the ancient sources.[14] Although our evidence is not extensive, it seems that across the entire tradition Baubo was always associated with sexual obscenity and the kind of laughter that arises from the unexpected display of sexual body parts. It certainly seems appropriate that the word *Baubon* came to mean "dildo" at least by the Hellenistic period, if not earlier.[15] The evidence for Baubo's

11. For details, see Richardson 1974, 13–30; and Foley 1994, 84–97, 169–75.
12. On the *kykeôn*, see Delatte, 1955; Richardson 1974, 344–48; Rosen 1987; Foley 1994, 46–47; and O'Higgins 2003, 56–57.
13. Cf. Richardson 1974, 5–12; Foley 1994, 169–75.
14. Baubo is generally associated with "Orphic" versions of the myth, i.e., versions that were ascribed in antiquity to Orpheus, Musaeus, or Eumolpus. Details about the so-called "Orphic" tradition can be found in Richardson 1974, 77–86, who emphasizes that the tradition is far from monolithic. For further details about Baubo, see Scarpi 1976, 151–58 (esp. 152, for further references and bibliography on the *anasyrma*); Devereux 1983 (psychoanalytical in its orientation); Olender 1990; and Foley 1994, 46–47. See also J. Clay 1998, 224; and O'Higgins 2003, 52. The *locus classicus* of ancient evidence for Baubo is Clement of Alexandria (second century CE), *Protrepticus* 2.20, who describes the *anasyrma* as motivated by the fact that Baubo was indignant that Demeter refused to drink the proffered *kykeôn*:

... περιαλγὴς ἡ Βαυβὼ γενομένη, ὡς ὑπερορραθεῖσα δῆθεν, ἀναστέλλεται τὰ αἰδοῖα καὶ ἐπιδεικνύει τῇ θεῷ· ἡ δὲ τέρπεται τῇ ὄψει ἡ Δηὼ καὶ μόλις ποτὲ δέχεται τὸ ποτόν, (Baubo is annoyed, since she really feels disdained; so she uncovers her private parts and shows them to the goddess. Demeter is pleased by the sight and at length receives the drink").

For examples of the *anasyrma* in Asian mythological traditions, see Dexter and Mair 2005.
15. E.g., Herodas 6.19; for discussion see Olender 1990, 84, 103.

explicit association with Demeter is early,[16] but our most substantial accounts of her role in the story occur much later in the early Christian writers, Clement and Arnobius, to whose accounts we will soon turn. In considering these texts, I would like to ask: What is the significance of bifurcating the character who mocks Demeter into Iambe and Baubo, and what does this detail tell us about how the myth conceptualizes the dynamics of mockery?

Of the many scholars who have traced the textual and historical evidence for Iambe and Baubo,[17] Maurice Olender also calls attention to the ways in which Iambe and Baubo represent different approaches to mockery, although his focus is more on what Baubo (and the so-called "Baubo" terracotta statuettes of fourth-century Priene, small female figurines in which the face, vulva and belly are grotesquely fused)[18] can tell us about ancient representations of the female body and female sexuality. In particular, Olender sees Baubo as a visually obscene version of Iambe: "Iambe had proffered from the mouth above, things that cannot be said without obscenity, while Baubo in her gesticulations . . . had displayed her lower mouth" (1990, 104). The origin or point of this verbal or visual obscenity has been debated for more than a century, and various theories have been invoked, some looking to religious practice, some to psychological or ethological conditions, and others (such as Olender) to sociological and cultural factors. None of these approaches, however, has shown much interest in the fact that Iambe and Baubo are participants in a *relationship* with another individual. Their respective acts of mockery, that is, are directed *against* someone, namely Demeter, and as such we ought to consider how their behavior is received, and why their confrontation has the effect on the goddess that it has. I do not mean by this that we should begin ascribing to a fictional character—a character not especially well developed in this scene in any case—a subjective interiority that is nowhere to be found in our texts. Rather we should ask what the myth implies about how both mocker and target

16. Hesychius (c. fifth-century CE, s.v. Βαυβώ 1.318 Latte) claims that Empedocles (fifth-century BCE) mentions her, although his note is too laconic to tell whether Empedocles himself connected her with Demeter: "Baubo: Demeter's nurse; and it also means 'hollow/stomach(?)' as it does in Empedocles." (= Emped. DK 31, fr. 153).

17. See Olender 1990, 88 n.25, and *passim*, for a survey of scholarship on Baubo. See now also O'Higgins 2003, 51–53.

18. See Karaghiorga-Stathacopoulou 1986; and Pfisterer-Haas 1989, 71–73. We should remember, however, that there is in fact no direct evidence to connect these statuettes with the mythical Baubo, however eager we are to do so. Olender (1990, 84) notes how these nameless figures were first associated with Baubo by Hermann Diels in 1901, and then later more extensively in 1907, when he was trying to make sense of the term *Baubo* for his edition of Empedocles (see n. 16 above). There are also a number of figurines discovered in the nineteenth century in Egypt that were identified early on as Baubos, although scholars have long been skeptical of the connection. Bibliography on the controversy can be found in Dunand 1984; and Olender 1990, 93, n. 52. At the end of his study Olender (103) quietly notes that "the Alexandrian terracottas representing women in obscene poses are no longer considered Baubos."

viewed what was happening in the episode. Why, for example, was Demeter's reaction one of mirth and not of anger? Certainly Iambe herself would have no guarantee that Demeter would be gladdened, since in many other contexts in life insult and mockery, not to mention obscenity, are construed as "fighting words." Somehow Iambe managed to make it clear that her words were humorous and, above all, *ironic*. They were not, in short, intended to be taken literally as an insult, and Iambe had to calculate that Demeter would understand this as well. Several unarticulated premises, then, underlie Iambe's decision to use verbal mockery to cheer up Demeter, or Baubo's decision to expose her private parts. These premises, I suggest, constitute within the myth itself an inchoate theory of comic abuse that anticipates the particular reflexes of mockery and satire in ancient literary genres.

Our analysis of the encounter between Iambe/Baubo and Demeter begins with Iambe's name and its obviously literary associations. It is often noted that "Iambe" is etymologically related to *iambos*, the term applied in antiquity to invective, abusive poetry. *Iambos* also became the technical term for the metrical foot that seemed to be favored by this type of poetry, the short + long syllable metron that we still know as the "iamb."[19] The particular poetic associations of *iambos* in turn generated verbal forms such as ἰαμβίζειν, "to 'iambize,' that is, to hurl insult at someone, to mock." We cannot know the developmental vector of these associations—whether iambographic poetry was actually named *for* the figure of Iambe in the myth, or whether the figure of Iambe herself was inspired by a preexisting form of poetry in which the poet played a vituperative role analogous to Iambe in the myth—but in either case it is clear that the myth came to be commonly connected with a poetic form in the minds of ancient audiences. Indeed the inverse may also be true, namely that whenever the term *iambos* was used in antiquity to refer to a poetic genre, the myth of Iambe and Demeter was never far below the surface.[20] Whereas the myth of Demeter as a whole served to account for Eleusinian ritual practice, the episode with Iambe had an aetiological layer that pointed beyond religion toward the realm of poetry.

This poetic connection is profoundly significant because it allows an audience already familiar with the poetic iambus to ask the myth, retrospectively,

19. On the history of the term *iambos*, see West 1974, 22–24; Bartol 1992, 30–41; Kantzios 2005, 1–33; and Rotstein 2007 (forthcoming). For an idiosyncratic account of the iambus, especially concerning its originally intended audience, see Steinrück 2002.

20. Rotstein 2007 (forthcoming). Rotstein argues, however, that *iambos* became inaccurately associated already in antiquity with mockery and abuse, and that we should conceptualize the genre as far more varied than mere invective poetry. This seems reasonable enough—iambus is, in fact, a highly variegated genre, containing much that is not specifically abusive—but its ancient associations with mockery and abuse (however inadequate), and, by extension, with the aetiological myth of Iambe, are persistent. See also Heath 1990, Degani 1991, and E. Bowie 2001 for varied approaches to the evidence.

a different set of questions than they would if its point were solely to account for a religious ritual. As an explanation of religious ritual, the episode answers a simple hypothetical question: How did it come about that initiates drink the *kykeôn* or engage in *aiskhrologia* at the Eleusinian mysteries? But once the episode becomes implicated in the history of a poetic form, as the name Iambe undeniably indicates, any subsequent audience is set up to ask what relationship this form would have with the details of the story. Someone familiar with the iambus as a genre of mockery could see easily enough that the poetic iambus has formal and substantive affinities with Iambe's mockery of Demeter; but it is less transparent *why* this particular myth would serve as an appropriate *aition* for a poetic genre. After all, in the myth itself Iambe is not explicitly behaving as a poet,[21] nor is there any indication that her mockery of the goddess is anything other than a spontaneous gesture. However, since Iambe herself is emblematic of the iambus, one might appropriately look to the episode for commentary on the ways in which literary genres of this sort, genres of abuse and mockery, behave. The Iambe/iambus connection, in short, allows us (and ancient audiences likewise) to read the episode as programmatic of the entire genre, and to analyze the mockery of Iambe in terms of the poetic performance to which she was to lend her name. Furthermore, an awareness of the connection encourages an audience to consider *how* the details of the myth function as a paradigm for iambographic poetry, to ask why, for example, mockery had the particular effect on Demeter described in the story, or whether Iambe knew in advance that she would be successful in her abusive designs. What steps must she, or any mocking character, take to ensure that her abuse is received in the appropriate, intended spirit of jocularity? It is not, of course, the duty of the myth itself to provide the answers to such questions (nor does ancient mythography generally contain its own explicit self-exegesis). But a rigorous analysis of the scene in the *Homeric Hymn to Demeter*[22] shows that it is constructed so as to allow its audience to reflect on the dynamics of a performance of mockery in the light of existing forms of abusive poetry.

I begin with the last point: The Greek iambus was a *performed* poetry which became infamous for its deployment of *aiskhrologia* and other varieties of unelevated diction in the service of personalized, often satirical, attacks.[23] Like any performance it required an author and an audience, but poetry of mockery and invective, such as the iambus, also requires a recipient of the mockery, a target of abuse. As such, the iambus generally highlighted a relationship be-

---

21. The same issue arises, as we shall see in the next chapter, when scholars want to see Thersites in Homer, *Iliad* 2 as a "poet" of mockery and blame. For discussion, see esp. pp. 67–78.

22. I use this text for convenience, since it provides the most detail, although other renditions of the myth corroborate the points made here.

23. On the question of performance practices of the archaic iambus, see Bartol 1992, and 1993, 61–74.

tween an author, identifying himself throughout by means of a subjective "I," and the target. As we have discussed in the first chapter, it is precisely the presence of the authorial "I" that complicates the ways in which an audience can respond to the performed work, since the author personalizes the mockery and strives to convince the audience that his relationship with the target is "real," despite the fact that this relationship is mediated by a poeticized performance. An awareness of the mediating force of representation, however, mitigates the aggressiveness of the mockery and transforms the target into an accomplice for the sake of the audience's pleasure. In the Homeric hymn, Iambe and Demeter play out precisely this sort of relationship. First, it is clear that Iambe's mockery of the goddess is contrived for motives that have nothing to do with a desire for abuse: She sees that it would take extraordinary measures to cheer Demeter and release her from her catatonic state, and decides that the best course of action will be to try to shock her out of it. Her self-consciousness about this decision is emphasized by the epithet *eiduia* in line 202 (πρίν γ᾽ ὅτε δὴ χλεύης μιν Ἰάμβη κέδν᾽ εἰδυῖα). While κέδν᾽ εἰδυῖα is a formulaic phrase, its position here seems particularly resonant, implying as it does that the decision to mock Demeter was based on a rational assessment of the situation: Her mockery is a mere stratagem, in other words, which will proceed in accordance with her calculation as to how she might succeed in changing Demeter's mood. We might legitimately say, therefore, that she does not so much mock Demeter as she *assumes the role of a mocker*, which is to say that she *represents mockery* in a mimetic performance.

Iambe's act of mockery will only achieve its goal, however, if Demeter understands that it is a performance rather than a sincerely hostile gesture, that she is as much an audience for this performance as the target of insult. How does Iambe know that Demeter will not perceive her raillery as a genuine threat? The poem does not penetrate Iambe's inner thoughts, but we may perhaps answer the question by focusing on her decision to use *aiskhrologia*. Although the hymn does not specify the nature of Iambe's obscenity, it leaves no doubt that she adopted a diction marked off from ordinary usage (χλεύης. . . || πολλὰ παρασκώπτουσ᾽ . . . , 202–3).[24] To be more precise, the context in which Iambe and Demeter found themselves would have made any utterance of *aiskhrologia* unexpected and extraordinary: Nothing about their interaction would motivate it, and the social norms of guest-friendship would have rendered verbal insult scandalous. The very fact that Iambe chose words that could be regarded as insulting presupposes a concept of transgression and scandal. If a word is regarded as obscene or shameful it will not matter whether anyone is actually scandalized by it, only that within its own cultural context it comes to be *classified* as scandalous diction, and so is differentiated from other forms

24. On the verbal form (χλευάζω) of nominal χλεύη, see Rosen 1988, 54–55.

of speech.[25] Now, truly insulting diction and malevolent mockery, where the intention is actually to provoke a target into verbal or physical conflict, occurs when what is classified as offensive speech is also *interpreted* as such by the target. Clearly this does not happen in the case of Demeter; rather than take offense at Iambe's "attack," she finds it so unexpected and amusing that she is able, at least temporarily, to put aside her intense grief for her daughter.

But what allows Demeter to find Iambe humorous and not offensive? I trust that an answer to this question will clarify my analysis of the myth as an emblem of ancient comic genres. In essence, I would like to suggest, the Iambe-Demeter encounter plays as comedy because Demeter perceives a discontinuity between what she expects of Iambe and what her scurrilous behavior might otherwise imply about her if she were to take it at face value.[26] Similarly, we must assume that Iambe is able to undertake her abusive strategy with full confidence that Demeter is attuned to this discontinuity. The episode, therefore, illustrates just how self-conscious and artificial comic mockery actually is. In order for the comedy of mockery to work, each actor in the drama must be conscious that the mocking speech at hand will immediately become something other than what it purports to be. It is *not* literal speech, but rather *pretends* to be so, and the mocker, the target and the audience are all bound together by the knowledge that they are in the midst of a mimetic performance. One of the lessons we may draw from Iambe-Demeter episode, therefore, is that genres of mockery and satire become comic precisely when their potential for scandal and transgression is deflected by various factors that call attention to the work as a fictive representation. Such factors, as we shall see throughout this book, emerge from the subtle interplay of generic markers embedded within a given text and extratextual, cultural cues that suffuse the performative context.

In the case of Iambe and Demeter, there can be no doubt that a character in Demeter's situation would be conscious that Iambe was trying to cheer her up, and this in itself would reassure her that no harm can come from Iambe's verbal assault. Yet for the external audience, the listener or reader of the account, there exists an exhilarating moment of uncertainty when Demeter might very well misunderstand Iambe's motives. As we shall see later on in other

25. Many of us, for example, might freely use expletives and obscenities in our everyday speech without necessarily intending or creating offense, but we choose to use them for rhetorical purposes precisely because they are regarded as marked off from "acceptable" speech.

26. I infer this from Demeter's reaction to Iambe's mockery, not because I claim special knowledge of the goddess's inner thoughts. If Demeter took Iambe's mockery seriously and at face value she would have presumably found her conduct a genuine breach of social order (see below n. 50). Simply put, servant girls do not under normal circumstances abuse the people they are serving (let alone goddesses). If Demeter really thought Iambe was serious in her ridicule, she would hardly have taken it lightly. It seems, therefore, that Demeter's laughter occurs because she realizes at some level that Iambe's behavior simply does not, so to speak, compute.

examples, this is a tension peculiar to transgressive genres, because unlike other forms of poetic representation that do not depend on the pretense of attack, there are genuine consequences when poeticized mockery is mistaken for unmediated hostility.

At this point it is worth asking whether the figure of Baubo functions analogously to her counterpart Iambe. If the interplay between Iambe and Demeter can be regarded as a paradigm for poetic mockery, how would Baubo, a figure who cheers up Demeter with a gesture rather than with words, figure into this analysis? Baubo is an extraordinarily complex figure with peculiar associations that take her far from her relationship with Demeter, but all the versions of Baubo's *anasyrma* suggest a commentary about the nature of fictive transgression similar to that which we found in the Iambe episode. Like Iambe, Baubo calculates that she might make Demeter laugh by shocking her with indecorous and shameful behavior; unlike Iambe, however, who uses *words* of personal abuse, Baubo does not actually direct her gestures *at* Demeter, but instead *performs* for her.[27] Demeter, already sitting down in a posture of ritual grief,[28] remains passive like an audience taking in a show. Once again, a paradox arises: If Baubo's indecent exposure, akin as it is to Iambe's *aiskhrologia*,[29] is "shameful" according to prevailing social codes (which it must be, if it is thought to contain things that are *aiskhra*), what prevents Demeter from being truly scandalized by such a gesture? Does the fact that she rather takes pleasure in the sight make her in some sense shameless herself? Or if not, can it be that Baubo's obscene gestures are not after all to be considered shameless in their particular instantiating moment? But this is an absurdity, since without the consciousness that exposing one's genitalia is "shameful," there would be no story to be told in the first place! Such questions again point to the distinction between a lived reality and a fictional reality, a distinction Demeter must implicitly internalize for her laughter to make sense.

The Baubo variant, therefore, highlights the performative dimension that we already discerned in Iambe's verbal mockery of Demeter, while delineat-

---

27. It is often claimed (e.g., Olender 1990, 89; Foley 1994, 46) that the historian Philochorus (fourth–third centuries BCE), mentioned an Iambe (i.e., not only Baubo) who cajoled Demeter with both words *and* gestures (i.e., an *anasyrma*), although this is hardly explicit in the fragment usually cited, Philochorus *FGrH* 328 F 103, from Natal. Com. *Myth* . 3.16 p. 245: *erat Iambe muliercula quaedam, Metaneirae ancilla, ut tradidit Philochorus . . . quae . . . ridiculas narratiunculas et sales iambico metro ad commovendam deam ad risum et ad sedandum dolorem interponebat.* ("There was a certain little woman, the servant of Metaneira, as Philochorus related . . . who . . . put on little comic narratives and witticisms in the iambic meter so as to make the goddess laugh and calm her down.")

28. For sitting down as a ritualized posture of grief, see. Richardson 1974, 218–20.

29. Olender 1990, 90, notes that despite the focus on Baubo's sexual gesture, she is "also a creature of words . . . [B]efore proceeding to her silent action, Baubo *greets* Demeter, *offers* her the *kykeôn*, *cajoles* her, *begs* her and *encourages* her to give up her mourning. What remains is the failure of language along with her insistent care and concern for the goddess."

ing even more clearly the relationship between the figure who generates the transgressive material and the audience. Baubo, in fact, appears distinctly in this episode as an actor on a stage, deploying games of costuming and identity, surprise and shock, which we come to associate with later comic drama. In the end, what prevents her behavior from creating the true scandal, which *de facto* it *ought* to create, are the same factors that mitigated the scandalous discourse of Iambe, namely, a tacit understanding on the part of both mocker and target that the transgressive act belongs to a mimetic rather than an actual realm. In such a case, then, humor arises precisely from the artificiality of the context and a consciousness that, however aggressive or transgressive a mimetic act may be, the participants and bystanders remain safe from physical or emotional harm.

This reading of the mockery of Demeter suggests, therefore, that the myth offers its audiences a guide to differentiating between the mockery that exists in quotidian interpersonal relations and that which becomes marked as artifice by a kind of collusion between the mocker and his audience (which sometimes will include the target).[30] Beyond the myth's undisputed function as an *aition* for certain rituals at the Eleusinian mysteries, it is not difficult to regard its episode of poeticized mockery as an *aition* of Greek comic genres in particular. For even within its brief compass it manages, as we have seen, to lay out emblematically the fundamental elements of comedy: fictionality, the nature of humor, the mimesis of transgression, and the complex relationships that the "poet" (the "maker" of the comic mockery) has with others. Indeed, the myth's very association with Eleusis supports the argument that beneath its tale of what was to become ritual abuse lies an even deeper commentary on the nature of poetic abuse generally. For as an *aition* for Eleusinian ritual, the story of Iambe/Baubo explicitly calls attention to a kind of mockery that was so highly stylized, constrained as it was by the religious context and ritual form, as to leave no doubt that it was marked off from actual mockery.[31] An ancient audience listening to the myth of Iambe and Demeter would already know that it offered an account of a familiar ritual, and they would presumably be able to retroject onto that first story of mockery the festive and fictionalized ripostes and banter they knew firsthand from cultic practices. Nothing about the behavior of Iambe or Baubo, in short, could have been construed as genuine or serious mockery of Demeter by an ancient audience.

Even the many parallels to the Iambe/Baubo-Demeter episode which scholars have often noted in other literatures all seem to make a similar dis-

---

30. I adapt here sociologist Erving Goffman's (1974, 83–84) useful term, "collusion," which he uses to describe aspects of interpersonal behavior in "everyday life." For further discussion of this term as I apply it to poetic satire, see chapter 4, p. 117, n. 1.

31. On the ritualized *aiskhrologia* of the Eleusinian mysteries, see Richardson 1974, 216–17; and Rösler 1993.

tinction between real and poeticized mockery, and to account for the paradoxically transformative power of humor when deployed under the right conditions and with the proper relationship between the mocker and an audience. Many of the parallels involve (like the Demeter myth) scenes of grief, or are specifically associated with funeral customs.[32] In his classic study of such scenes, Karl Meuli described many cases in which ritual mockery at funerals became the province of professional jesters, pointing even more distinctly to the performative, fictionalizing aspects of such activity that I have attributed to the Greek examples.[33] Most of the many cross-cultural variants of the story serve aitiological purposes which scholars typically locate in an existing ritual. I am suggesting for Iambe-Baubo and Demeter, however, an aitiological layer that takes us even deeper than the religious or ritual explanation.

To be sure, these myths urge their audiences to ask, "What actual practice does this story explain?" But as I have argued above, they seem also to urge them to ask questions such as: "*Why* is the story told the way it is? "*Why* does obscenity or nudity generate laughter?" "Under what circumstances does aggression become harmless?" In the case of Iambe-Baubo the poetic associations of her name itself implicitly address these questions. Our next illustration, however—Heracles and the twin rogue Cercopes—probes these questions further, and offers an even more detailed paradigm for the nature of Greek comedic practices.

2. Heracles and the Cercopes

There are few figures in Greek mythology with as rich and varied a tradition as Heracles. An elaborate literary and iconographic tradition survives, which casts this hero in a remarkable number of diverse roles and reveals a broad spectrum of cultural responses to his character and exploits. Indeed, there are so many stories about Heracles, and so many representations of him in art and literature, that a veritable canon of his activities has emerged over the centuries, ever since the mythographers of the Hellenistic period began categorizing his "twelve labors." One consequence of all this attention in antiquity is that many of Heracles' adventures were devalued and relegated by commentators to the status of *parerga*, which tended to suggest that these episodes were mere diversions in a mythological narrative that otherwise offered coherence and a sense of teleology. Beyond the world of ancient scholarship, however, some of these minor adventures exercised considerable influence on the popular imagination and maintained a life of their own independent of any role they played in a more formally constructed narrative.

32. Richardson 1974, 216.
33. Meuli 1975, 2.1035–81.

The story of Heracles' encounter with the scoundrel Cercopes is a particularly rich example of one such *parergon*, and although it traditionally receives barely a notice in both ancient and modern handbook accounts of Heracles' exploits, it represents an important stage in the evolution of the hero as an explicitly comic figure. In fact, this episode became a motif of considerable popularity in Greek art and literature from the sixth- to the fourth-centuries BCE during which period it appears in monumental sculpture, vase painting and literature.[34] In this section I consider this evidence and argue that the story of Heracles and the Cercopes reflects at the mythic level a cultural and literary paradigm of the comic fundamentally analogous to, but broader and more refined than, the paradigm implicit in the Iambe-Baubo myth.

The story is recounted or alluded to in various sources across antiquity, although the fullest accounts are the latest. We know, for example, that the poets of Old and Middle Comedy were attracted to the story (plays entitled *Cercopes* are attested for Hermippus, Platon and Eubulus, and Cratinus mentioned them in his *Archilokhoi*),[35] but next to nothing of substance has survived among the fragments. Nevertheless, most of the details missing from the earliest literary sources appear in the early iconographic record, showing that the essential elements of the myth coalesced early on.[36] The fullest literary account is found in the pseudo-Nonnus (fifth-century CE) scholia to Gregory of Nazianzus's *Invectiva adversus Iulianum* 39 (fourth-century CE),[37] which recounts what happened when the twin-brother Cercopes one day came upon Heracles asleep under a tree, presumably after one of his labors. When they tried to steal his armor, he caught them and bound them by the feet to either end of a pole, slung the pole over his shoulder and set off with them hanging upside-down on either side of him. The Cercopes had been warned early on by their mother "not to encounter the one with the black buttocks," and when they noticed that Heracles' profuse hair made his buttocks appear black, they

34. See Zancani Montuoro and Zanotti-Bianco 1954; and Woodford 1992 for the iconography of the Cercopes; Kirkpatrick and Dunn 2002, 51–54, for discussion and further bibliography. For the literary evidence, see K. Seeliger, s.v."Cercopes, " in Roscher 1884–1937, 1166–73.

35. Cf. Cratinus 13 K-A, Platon 95–97 K-A (an alternate title for *Xantai*), Hermippus frr. 36–41 K-A, Eubulus fr. 52 K-A. See further on the dramatic tradition in Kirkpatrick and Dunn 2002, 36n18. They argue plausibly that Euripides *Her.* 1380–81, where Heracles imagines his weapons chastising him for murdering his wife and children, alludes parodically to the story of the Cercopes. Aristophanes seems to have the Cercopes in mind at *Ach.* 945, when he refers to the way in which the character Nicharchus is carried off ("upside-down," κατωκάρα); see Olson 2002, lxiii, and ad loc. 306.

36. The earliest pictorial representation of the story comes from an early sixth-century Middle Corinthian cup from Perachora; see Gantz 1993, 441; and Woodford 1992, for other visual evidence for the myth.

37. Text in Westermann 1843, 375. See also Brock 1971, 100–101; and Kirkpatrick and Dunn 2002, 36–38.

began to mock this apparition. Heracles was so amused that he untied them and set them free.[38]

The story is a remarkable comic version of the typical revenge-through-punishment motif that characterizes so many of Heracles' adventures. Whereas Heracles almost invariably resorts to violence in resolving conflicts with opponents who act unjustly, and is usually cast in the role of moral castigator when doing so,[39] in this story the expected violent punishment is suddenly averted, and the expected moral of the story frustrated; the πονηρία of the Cercopes is not so much endorsed in the end as "paid for" by the currency of laughter. The story, then, ceases in midstream to function as an object lesson about the punishment of antisocial behavior as embodied by the Cercopes, and focuses instead on the role of laughter and the comic in transforming human emotions from anger to mirth.

This motif will easily remind us of the story of Iambe-Baubo and Demeter, in which, as we have seen, the grieving Demeter regains her cheer as a direct result of the servant Iambe's scurrilous verbal abuse or Baubo's obscene gestures. Scholars have at times suspected, even if conclusive evidence is lacking, that the myth of Iambe and Demeter ultimately helps to explain the origins of the *aiskhrologia* and generally abusive quality of both the iambographic poets, such as Archilochus and Hipponax, and the poets of Old Comedy. Aristotle certainly abetted this view, when he referred to the abusive element of Old Comedy at *Poetics* 1449b7 as an *iambikê idea*,[40] and we saw in the first chapter

38. For the comedy that arises from viewing buttocks, see also Archil. frr. 185–87, and Aristoph. *Ach.* 119–20; on the comedy of hairy buttocks in particular, see Aristoph. *Lys.* 802–803

39. Among many examples, one may cite his murder of the following (for details, cf. Gantz 1993, 432–40): the Centaur Eurytion, who tried forcibly to marry the daughter of Dexamenus (either Azan or Deianeira, depending on the version); another Centaur, Nessus, who tried to rape his wife; and the rogue Syleus, who forced captors into working the land, but undid their work at the same time. It is noteworthy as well that there existed also a different version of the Cercopes myth that followed a more traditional pattern of crime and punishment. Diodorus Siculus (4.31.7) and Apollodorus (2.6.3) have Heracles capture the Cercopes as part of his servitude to Omphale; Diodorus mentions that Heracles brought them back to Omphale as prisoners. While pseudo-Nonnus and the Suda—our only *explicit* sources for the version in which Heracles sets the Cercopes free as a result of their joking—are late, the earliest iconographic representations suggest that the comic ending of the story lay behind them. (See above n. 33). Furthermore, writing still in the classical period, Plutarch (*Mor.* 60c) clearly alludes to the comic version of the Cercopes, if obliquely. In this passage, Plutarch is concerned with the "frankness" (*parrhêsia*) of the "flatterer" (*kolax*), and, in particular, his use of insulting jest for amusement. He tells a story of how the Spartan king Agis once berated Alexander (note that this anecdote is set several centuries earlier than when Plutarch was writing in the late first- to early second-century CE) for rewarding flatterers and jokesters (*katagelastoi*). Agis explains: ". . . For Heracles took delight in certain Cercopes, and Dionysus in Sileni, and one can see that you think well of such people." (καὶ γὰρ Ἡρακλῆς Κέρκωψί τισι, καὶ Σειληνοῖς ὁ Διόνυσος ἐτέρπετο, καὶ παρὰ σοὶ τοιούτους ἰδεῖν ἔστιν εὐδοκιμοῦντας). There can be little question that this alludes to a comic version of the Cercopes myth which focused on the mocking speech of the bound rogues.

40. *Pace* E. Bowie 2002, 42, who argues tendentiously against the idea that fifth-century Athenians would have associated the practices of Old Comedy with the iambus.

how Aristophanes teases us in the *Frogs* with a chorus of Eleusinian initiates who explicitly link the trademark abuse of comedy with that of the Eleusinian mysteries. But the evidence from Aristophanes must be handled delicately; no real explanation is given about how comic abuse as it was performed on the Athenian stage actually derived, either formally or functionally, from a hypothetical religious context. There can be little doubt that what Aristophanes really had on his mind was to "sanctify" (albeit half-seriously) his own tradition of abuse by aligning it with a well-known contemporary religious ritual with similar invective features.[41]

There is little to encourage us to believe that people in the fifth century understood much more about any original links between comic abuse and Eleusinian *aiskhrologia* than we do.[42] Scholars have often noted that in the myth of Iambe and Demeter, the goddess's reconstituted good cheer, brief as it is, and her willingness to drink the *kykeôn* has association with fertility.[43] This supports the widely held assumption, inspired by comparative anthropology and folklore, that the *aiskhrologia* found in Greek poetry had its origins in apotropaic and fertility rituals. Such an assumption even led Geoffrey Kirk (1974, 199) to connect the myth of Iambe and Demeter, if somewhat loosely, with the Cercopes. Commenting on the obscenity they hurl at Heracles buttocks, he concludes: "Obscenity, of course, was common ritual practice, useful for keeping away evil spirits or for promoting fertility. Iambe, one remembers, had made Demeter laugh when the goddess was mourning for Persephone . . . So the Cercopes may not always have been figures of fun, nor Heracles' hairy bottom an unimportant detail. . ."

Although Kirk does not explain this implicit disjunction between a "fun" and "serious" function of a myth, he implies that, like the myth of Demeter, the Cercopes myth ultimately had some ritual origin. Folklorists have provided numerous examples of stories and myths that associate laughter with the generation or regeneration of life in many cultures,[44] and even in the case of the

---

41. See the discussion in chapter 1, pp. 28–32; also Riu 1999, 136–40; and Lada-Richards 1999, 224–26.

42. Carey 1986, 65, claims, reasonably enough, that by the time we get to Archilochus, "iambos had broken free of its connection with ritual to become an independent poetic genre." This need not mean, however, that poets and audiences lost all consciousness of a ritual prehistory of the iambus.

43. As Richardson 1974, 217, puts it, speaking of the initiates at Eleusis who reenacted ritually the events narrated in the *Hymn to Demeter*:

"At Eleusis, the initiates who joined in the fasting, and the *aischrologia* and dancing which ended it . . . were sharing in the sorrow of Demeter, and its relief by laughter, song, and dance. At the same time, the return of life to the fields and the growth of the crops formed an essential background. Thus, in the version of Euripides (*Hel.* 1301 ff.), Demeter has already caused famine over the earth (*Dem.* 305 ff.) when she is appeased by the music and gaiety of the Graces, Muses, and Aphrodite."

44. See Richardson 1974, 216–17; di Nola, 1974, 55–57; and Reckford 1987, 46–52.

Cercopes, a myth that seems to have nothing to do with agriculture or fertility *per se*, the laughter of Heracles has the result of returning life to a pair of thieves otherwise destined for a certain punitive death at the hero's hands. Clearly this notion of laughter as a life-affirming force is important for explaining the social and psychological substrata of humor and comedy in many societies, including ancient Greece. But by fixating on what "original" or "essential" impulses may underlie the laughter of Demeter and Heracles, there is a danger of ignoring the particularized reflexes of laughter in the myths themselves, and their significance for the culture that produced them. I concentrate here, therefore, not on what the myth of the Cercopes tells us about a prehistorical stage of Greek society, but rather on how it embodied conceptions of humor, verbal abuse, and comic role-playing implicit in the forms of comic literature that developed in the historical period. In short, it is more revealing to focus on the fact alone that laughter was able to transform so drastically and suddenly the mood of a sad or angry individual, and that in each myth such a transformation became symbolic of averting a potential catastrophe: a murder in the case of the Cercopes, and agricultural blight in the case of Demeter.[45]

In spite of the fact that the Iambe-Baubo and Cercopes myths share a central motif, namely the transformative power of laughter, only the former is usually regarded as an *aition* for the invective strains of the iambus and Old Comedy, presumably because of the connections made early on between Iambe, the name of the iambic genre, and the so-called iambic elements of comedy. I would like to suggest in this discussion, however, that the myth of the Cercopes anticipates much more closely the actual dynamics of such genres and the presumptions and premises about comic praxis inherent in them. I am interested, in particular, not only in how the myth enacts the kind of personal abuse (ψόγος) we find in Greek comedy, but also in how this abuse can be seen to mediate and resolve interpersonal and, on a broader scale, societal tensions.

One difficulty in viewing the Iambe-Baubo myth as ultimately explanatory of Greek comedy is that the context of the myth is so specifically religious (recounted as part of a hymn celebrating the goddess), so enmeshed itself in the aetiology of a nonliterary phenomenon. Iambe engages in comedy, but she is not herself a comic figure in any sense, nor is Demeter the kind of character we would expect to find in any of the comic genres (except perhaps by way of parody). The myth exists, at least superficially, to explain a ritual activity, *aiskhrologia* at the Eleusinian mysteries, and within this context, as I have argued above, it offers an inchoate theory of comedy; but its characters and plot

---

45. In the narrative offered by the *Hymn to Demeter*, the goddess's laughter does not, it is true, avert the famine that she ends up inflicting on humankind (305–13). That famine is only relieved when Persephone has been returned to Demeter (453–56). But as Richardson notes (see above, n. 42), Demeter's breaking of her fast after Iambe's jesting became symbolic of fertility and rebirth when ritualized at the Eleusinian mysteries.

line are not themselves comic. The myth of the Cercopes, on the other hand, which, like the Iambe myth, illustrates the therapeutic powers of laughter, never leaves a comic world. To begin with, the relationship between the Cercopes and Heracles prefigures the characteristic relationship between mocker (Cercopes as κωμῳδοῦντες) and target (Heracles as κωμῳδούμενος),[46] in which the mocker reacts to something that he finds either ludicrous or offensive in his target. The sight that elicits the Cercopes' ridicule and laughter, according to the pseudo-Nonnus scholiast, is the extraordinary hairiness of Heracles' posterior, recalling to them the "black buttocks" their mother warned them about in the past. Heracles becomes the target of their jokes ("they discussed this sight with each other and made a great joke out of it at Heracles"). As if to foreshadow the unexpected outcome of the story, this dialogue takes place while the brothers are rather ridiculously hanging upside down, strapped by their feet onto a pole that rests on Heracles' shoulder.

There is some variation in the portrayal of this scene in the many pictorial representations of the myth—some depict Heracles in a frontal pose, with the Cercopes hanging upside down on his left and right; others show the two Cercopes slung over Heracles with the one in front of him facing backward, the other over his back facing forward.[47] This last pose would provide the best vantage point for the one in back to notice Heracles' buttocks. Regardless of the variations, the point of suspending the Cercopes upside down over Heracles' shoulder is that their faces are compelled to come into unusually close contact with zones of the body that are normally considered private, not only the buttocks, but also the genitals, which are in clear view to the brother in front in some representations. Extensive documentation of the prevalence in Greek comic literature of genital and anal humor is hardly necessary here. As Jeffrey Henderson states about the word *prôktos* ("anus"/"asshole") in Old Comedy: "its low tone assured that even in the absence of a joke its mere mention could be counted on to raise a laugh,"[48] and the same could surely be said for the numerous examples of jokes involving *peos* ("penis"), and related words. It is not insignificant, therefore, that the very name of the Cercopes can be etymologized to embody the kind of humor that they generate: *kerkos + ops* transparently means "tail-face/head," formed along the lines of *Kyklops* or *kynôpis*, and the obscene meaning of "tail" as "penis" is well documented in Greek.[49] The pseudo-Nonnus scholiast ascribes to another commentator named Dios the

46. The category of "comic target," or κωμῳδούμενος, was evidently articulated early in the Greek critical tradition, probably, as Halliwell argues, as early as the fifth-century BCE, and formalized as lists in the Hellenistic period. See Halliwell 1984; also Steinhausen 1910.

47. Further description and iconography, in Woodford 1992 and Fitzpatrick and Dunn 2002, 52–54, and 58–61 (plates).

48. Cf. Henderson [1975] 1991, 201.

49. As it is in Latin literature, cf. Adams 1982, 35–36; and Richlin 1992, 116–43. For *kerkos* as an obscenity in Greek, see Henderson [1975] 1991, 20, 87, 128, and 177.

information that the individual names of the Cercopes were *Passalos* and *Aklêmon*. While the latter is uncertain, and has been corrected by others to *Akmôn*, *passalos/pattalos* ("nail" or "peg") is a well-attested phallic obscenity in comedy.[50] A scholiast on Lucian has their names as Sillos ("mocker") and Triballos (perhaps exploiting the known phonological affinity between *phallos* and *ballos*), and even though this last set of names is probably late and inauthentic, they clearly continue a tradition that viewed the Cercopes as figures whose names reflected their association with obscene humor. A Lucanian red-figure vase from the early fourth century[51] goes out of its way to exaggerate the genitals of a simian-looking pair of Cercopes, in contrast to Heracles' heroically-sized (that is, small) member, thereby emphasizing their puckish, low-life character.

The reaction of the Cercopes to Heracles' buttocks and genitals, therefore, implies a type of humor thoroughly in keeping with the explicitly obscene strands in iambographic poetry and Old Comedy,[52] as does the fact that the Cercopes themselves essentially emblematize the scandalous objects they find so amusing. The obscene associations of the Cercopes in the episode (their off-color names, their exaggerated genitals), in fact, are remarkably similar to those of Baubo, a figure who, as we have seen, not only deployed her genitals for comic effect with Demeter, but whose very name came to be synonymous with the dildo. The ancient tradition about Baubo's sexual associations is clearly unstable and ambivalent: At times she seems to represent, in Devereux's term, "la vulve mythique,"[53] at other times (especially in her association with the dildo) Greek male-centered culture seems to have appropriated her as a phallic surrogate. Olender cautions (1990, 103) about assuming a fixed nature for Baubo: "Baubo is the mother of the androgynous Misê, and Priapos is the brother of Hermaphroditos, but there is no ancient link between Priapos and Baubo. The best we can do is to cast fragile lines from one to the other, using Greek vocabulary and the Greek repertory of images." To this "repertory of vocabulary and images," however, I would add a motival connection between the vulvate Baubo and the phallic Cercopes, namely the fact that both play analogous roles in tales of obscene comic mockery. Both characters, that is, rely on assumptions about what their "audience" will find transgressive, and both implicitly conclude that calling attention to traditionally unmentionable body parts will cause the greatest scandal and result in laughter.

---

50. Henderson [1975] 1991, 123.
51. Getty Museum 81.AE.189.
52. On obscenity in Old Comedy, see Henderson 1991 [1975]; and Halliwell 2004. On the iambographic associations of obscenity in Old Comedy, see Rosen 1988, 1–35.
53. The title of his idiosyncratic psychoanalytic study (1983); he opens his book by referring to Baubo as "une véritable personnification du sexe de la femme, tout comme Phales est une personnification de la verge" (11).

At the most fundamental level, then, Iambe-Baubo and the Cercopes myth tell a similar story of obscenity and mockery in the service of humor. A closer comparison of the two myths, however, shows that the two stories diverge in critical areas and offer different, though complementary, perspectives on the dynamics of comic mockery. The first point to emphasize is that the contexts in which the mockery is embedded in each story point to different aspects of the relationship between mocker and target. In the case of the Cercopes, the mockery is spontaneous, unexpected, and gratuitous, while in the case of Iambe-Baubo her rude, confrontational behavior is a gesture calculated to produce a specific effect, namely Demeter's laughter. Her mockery, that is, exists not intrinsically for the sake of the joke, but in the service of a higher goal which, in its origin at least, cannot be said to be comic.

We concluded earlier that Iambe-Baubo appears to be playing a role, as if borrowing from an already known repertoire of histrionics that she knows will get the reaction she is looking for. As such, therefore, Iambe-Baubo can be seen to function as the paradigm of a self-conscious comic actor. The Cercopes, on the other hand, initially respond to something that *they* think is humorous, the sight of Heracles' nether regions, and as such respond as members of an audience moved to laughter by a comic spectacle. Their laughter, in a sense, is not far removed from Demeter's laughter: Both instances of laughter arise when each figure is suddenly confronted with something *aiskhron*, some putative affront to cultural norms. By finding humor in the obscene, the myths make what perhaps seems to be a simple point, but as an example of self-conscious theorizing about the comic, a striking one. As I noted earlier, this myth is atypical of the Heracles saga in its avoidance of violence and murder, and it is humor in particular that takes the story in this different direction. I have little doubt, therefore, that ancient audiences responded to, and continued to generate versions of, the myth of the Cercopes, inter alia, as a means of contemplating the central questions about comedy and humor I am addressing throughout this study. They especially addressed the question of how confrontational and transgressive speech and action can at times be destructive and sociopathic, and at other times—especially when poeticized—humorous and benignly entertaining.

The Cercopes story walks this fine line between "real" and "represented" aggression more ambiguously than the myth of Iambe-Baubo, especially since in their real-life occupations, the Cercopes were known as transgressive, counter-cultural figures (whereas Iambe and Baubo were legitimately employed servants!)[54] This is the reason, in fact, why we would ordinarily expect Heracles

54. Despite the differences in the social acceptability of Iambe-Baubo and the Cercopes, it is worth noting that each figure is involved in a similar power relationship with their targets. In each case the socially inferior character breaks rank to rise up, mockingly, against the socially superior. The transgression is even more apparent in these myths, which pit mortals against divinities. As we shall see throughout this book, satire replays this relationship time and again, with the mocker daring to confront targets who have (or are imagined to have) at least the potential to repress them with brute force.

to deal with them as he usually deals with such villainous, antisocial characters—by killing them. Why, then, does Heracles not become offended at their mockery of his body parts? Why does he soften, laugh, and then set them free? With Iambe-Baubo and Demeter, we remarked how the context made it clear to Demeter that the mockery directed at her was artificial and staged; that is, the discontinuity between what Demeter would expect of Iambe's behavior and what she actually heard from her was a recipe for comedy, and also made it clear to her that there was no real threat from her "attacker." What is it about the context in which Heracles finds himself mocked by the Cercopes that changes his mood from vengeful wrath to amusement?

The answer to this question, I suggest, lies in the relationship between mocker and target which Heracles—the target himself—initiated at the moment when he decided to sling the Cercopes over his shoulder. With this gesture, the myth has made Heracles perform an act emblematically comic: He inverts the normal human stance, transporting two figures upside-down, enabling them to contemplate all that is low, literally and figuratively (the ground, the lower body parts) from an inverted perspective. The tableau of the Cercopes slung across Heracles' shoulder is intrinsically comic for Greek culture, as the iconographic and literary evidence makes clear. By striking this pose, then, Heracles himself essentially establishes that the entire narrative is to be comic, and so played out in a fictionalized, nonliteral, domain. When the Cercopes catch sight of Heracles' lower body parts, they act in keeping with the newly created comic context by calling attention to unmentionable things, and so offending against standards of decorum by joking about *aiskhra*. This act of buffoonish scurrility, however, which can best be described by the Greek term πονηρία,[55] instead of angering the target as one might expect, has the opposite effect of gladdening him, and hence of defusing a potentially explosive situation. Heracles, in the end, actually *rewards* the kind of behavior in the Cercopes that he originally set out to punish. He ends up liberating the Cercopes because he responds to their particular sense of the comic; but in order for this to occur, Heracles too must situate himself, like his assailants, in a context where *ponêria* prevails, where he cannot invoke concepts of justice or injustice and expect them to have any real force. The Cercopes may well behave as if they intended their verbal attacks to cause actual psychic or emotional distress in Heracles (they are, after all, in a desperate and defenseless position), but, as we noted, Heracles' own act of carrying the brothers upside-down guarantees that the mockery will be benign and itself comedic. Since,

---

55. The term πονηρία, when used subjectively (i.e., by characters to describe their own condition) often has a meaning akin to "abjection" (referring to their own wretchedness or misery); when applied objectively to characters by others, it tends to take on a moral cast, and is often translated as "baseness," "wickedness," "rogueishness," *vel sim.* See further below, pp. 244–45.

then, Heracles cannot help but find their mockery humorous, the laughter it elicits from him ultimately turns into self-laughter: *He* has become the butt of the joke (as it were), and *he* now finds this highly amusing. Now complicit in the Cercopes' ridicule, Heracles cheerfully acknowledges his own suitability as a target of transgressive humor, and as such adopts, if only for the duration of the episode, their own stance of *ponêria* and the comic abjection it gives rise to.[56] We see, therefore, that what promises to be a typical myth of heroic vengeance and justifiable homicide soon becomes a story that offers a completely different reality, a comic world that transforms the menacing pretense of mockery into a harmless representation of that pretense. This is the fictional world we come to know more fully in the comic genres of Greek literature, a world where physical and verbal aggression somehow do no damage, where *ponêria* can be temporarily celebrated for its comic, if not therapeutic, effect rather than repudiated, as it usually is in the real world, for its disruptive and anarchic tendencies.

It should not be difficult to see at this point how the myth of the Cercopes serves as a revealing *aition* for the Greek literary *psogos*, in which the mocker and the target are similarly implicated in each other's abjection. Whether we are considering Greek iambographic poetry, Athenian Old Comedy, or Roman satire, neither the mocker nor his target is ever devoid for long of some measure of *ponêria*, despite the mocker's usual pretense of moral self-righteousness. One thinks, for example, of the persona adopted by Archilochus or Hipponax and their targets: each iambographer, in his own idiosyncratic way, attacked a variety of targets for alleged violations of trust and other injustices, though each also portrays himself as vindictive, abusive and roguish, as equally obedient to his own lusts and passions as those he self-righteously rebukes. And such a relationship is replicated dozens of times in Aristophanes, as we will have occasion to see in detail in the next chapter when we examine the interaction between the Sausage-seller and the Paphlagonian in *Knights*.[57]

56. Although the term "abjection" is perhaps self-explanatory, it has taken on a quasi-technical aspect in recent literary criticism. My use of it here, and throughout this book, owes much to the ways in which literary scholars in nonclassical fields have been applying it to comic and satirical figures. See, for example, Bernstein 1992, 1–35 (and *passim*) on the notion of the "Abject Hero"; and Limon 2000 on "abjection" in contemporary American stand-up comedy.

57. Given the ways in which the myth of the Cercopes illustrates the fundamental impulses and premises that undergird Greek psogic comedy, it should hardly surprise us to find that it made its way into various forms of Greek comic literature. A παίγνιον (an informal term generally applied, often pejoratively, to "light," whimsical works) entitled Κέρκωπες is attributed to Homer by Harpocration and various Homeric *vitae* (*Vita Herod*, line 333 Allen; *Vita Proc.* p. 102.6 Allen; *Vita Sudae* line 102 Allen), and as we noted above [n. 35] the story was evidently popular in Old and Middle Comedy.

3

Where the Blame Lies

The Question of Thersites

The myths we examined in the preceding chapter begin to suggest how Greek culture could conceptualize the fundamental mechanisms by which mockery might be formalized, ultimately poeticized, and so transformed into comedy.[1] As such, they serve as a guide to the dynamics that energized actual poetic genres of mockery and abuse, offering implicit commentary on both the relationship between the poet and his target, and the generic signposting in performances of mockery that help a knowing audience distinguish the fictionality of the work from the reality it alleges to represent. In this chapter, we will proceed to examine several ancient texts that can be interpreted as similarly programmatic and theoretical, and which reflect an even more detailed and nuanced understanding of comic mockery than the myths of the preceding chapter. Whereas the myths of Iambe and the Cercopes seem to be concerned at one level with the most basic aetiological elements of the *psogos* as a comic phenomenon, the texts we will discuss in this chapter play out at considerable length the complex, often unstable, triangulated relationships among mocker, target, and audience that we associate with the *psogos*. I will focus in the next two chapters on two famous Homeric characters, who participate in dramas of abuse, invective, and satire: Thersites and the Cyclops Polyphemus. Odysseus's relationship with both characters in the *Iliad* and *Odyssey*, respectively, is antagonistic and abusive, yet he plays a substantially different role in each, and a careful analysis of his behavior in each scene will reveal much about the ways in which ancient poets and audiences construed the mechanisms of the *psogos*. As we will see, Odysseus is cast sometimes as the blamer, sometimes as the target; sometimes he seems to have just cause for his taunting, and at other times his abuse is portrayed as gratuitous and unjust. Similarly, the figures he attacks sometimes appear blameworthy, sometimes not. If we sort through the various ways in which blame is assigned to targets, and in which comedy is

---

1. An abbreviated version of this chapter appeared as Rosen 2003.

generated from verbal abuse, we will end up with a much clearer sense of the generic protocols that governed ancient forms of satire and mockery.

Homer composes in an essentially third-person narrative mode, and only extremely rarely does his personal voice intrude,[2] so all the instances of Homeric mockery we examine here will concern characters other than the poet himself.[3] Dramatized mockery of this sort, in which the poet does not figure himself as one of the antagonists, raises a particularly complex set of questions for the audience, namely how to determine who of two antagonists is *justified* in his attack or counterattack. Does the moral vantage point of the poet who relates the scene coincide with that articulated by the characters in that scene? How does a poet go about representing a *psogos* within a poetic genre such as epic, which is not itself comic or satirical? Does the poet himself lead the audience to believe that he *agrees* with the character he portrays as having the *just* cause for blame? Does he, in short, configure such scenes of mockery as analogues to the activity of a *psogos*-poet, or can they equally serve as foils to the *psogos*, thus actually distinguishing the poetic *psogos* from the versions of mockery he portrays in his narratives? I am interested in this chapter, then, in the relationship between the instances of mockery embedded in a third-person narrative such as Homer's and the forms of first-person mockery in which the poet portrays himself as the instigator of blame, what we might refer to as "primary" satire or mockery. We might say that even a poet such as Homer, using dramatic, impersonal narrative, can engage in satire of certain people or things. But it is important to acknowledge that as soon as we apply the term "satire" to the work of such a poet, we are tacitly assuming that, in our capacity as *audience*, we have constructed an essentially personal relationship with the poet, at least at those moments when we believe he is trying to convey to us his *disapproval* of whatever it is that he satirizes. Satire always implies a personal voice, even when the form of presentation is oblique and appears distanced from an authorial *ego*. While the Homeric scenes we will examine in this chapter offer a type of dramatized mockery (see chapter 1, above p. 25), the antagonists do not themselves generate satire until they are perceived by an audience as part of a fiction orchestrated by an author, that is, not until the scenes are regarded as poeticized. Odysseus himself does not *satirize* the characters he is made to mock in epic—Thersites, Irus, or Polyphemus, for example—but rather our consciousness of Homer as the one who gives literary form to these Odyssean scenes of mockery, and so poeticizes them, transforms them from mere mockery to bona fide satire. Once we understand this process, I believe, we are in a better position to treat embedded scenes of mockery and *psogos* in epic as emblematic of the procedures of poetic mockery and satire, rather than simply as

---

2. As Plato was first to notice; see discussion below, chapter 7, pp. 255–58.
3. See end of chapter 1 for my taxonomy of different psogic modes, pp. 17–27.

events within an epic narrative otherwise disconnected from the poet's arsenal of literary strategies.[4]

1. Thersites the Satirist?

Nowhere is the problem of treating embedded scenes of mockery more pronounced than in the Thersites episode of *Iliad* 2.211-78, for here one finds both technical terminology and narrative structures that clearly associate the entire scene with, as Nagy has put it, the poetry of "blame":[5]

> ἄλλοι μέν ῥ᾽ ἕζοντο, ἐρήτυθεν δὲ καθ᾽ ἕδρας·
> Θερσίτης δ᾽ ἔτι μοῦνος ἀμετροεπὴς ἐκολῴα,
> ὃς ἔπεα φρεσὶ ᾗσιν ἄκοσμά τε πολλά τε ᾔδη,
> μάψ, ἀτὰρ οὐ κατὰ κόσμον, ἐριζέμεναι βασιλεῦσιν,
> ἀλλ᾽ ὅ τι οἱ εἴσαιτο γελοίϊον Ἀργείοισιν   215
> ἔμμεναι· αἴσχιστος δὲ ἀνὴρ ὑπὸ Ἴλιον ἦλθε·
> φολκὸς ἔην, χωλὸς δ᾽ ἕτερον πόδα· τὼ δέ οἱ ὤμω
> κυρτώ, ἐπὶ στῆθος συνοχωκότε· αὐτὰρ ὕπερθε
> φοξὸς ἔην κεφαλήν, ψεδνὴ δ᾽ ἐπενήνοθε λάχνη.
> ἔχθιστος δ᾽ Ἀχιλῆϊ μάλιστ᾽ ἦν ἠδ᾽ Ὀδυσῆϊ·   220
> τὼ γὰρ νεικείεσκε· τότ᾽ αὖτ᾽ Ἀγαμέμνονι δίῳ
> ὀξέα κεκλήγων λέγ᾽ ὀνείδεα· τῷ δ᾽ ἄρ᾽ Ἀχαιοὶ
> ἐκπάγλως κοτέοντο νεμέσσηθέν τ᾽ ἐνὶ θυμῷ.
> αὐτὰρ ὃ μακρὰ βοῶν Ἀγαμέμνονα νείκεε μύθῳ·

Now the rest had sat down, and were orderly in their places,
but one man, Thersites of the endless speech, still scolded,
who knew within his head many words, but disorderly;

---

4. Nagy 1979, 226 (and *passim* chapter 12), discusses the way in which epic "quotes the language of blame within the framework of narrating quarrels" (see also 43n1), and from this point he assumes, as we will see below, that characters using this sort of language are behaving as "blame poets." As I hope to have made clear, merely using the language of blame poetry does not in itself necessarily turn a character into a blame poet. My central contention throughout this study is that true blame poetry (and I would not hesitate to substitute the term "satire" here) can exist only as a function of a relationship between the poet and his audience, and that, in particular, if the poet has not succeeded in capturing the audience's sympathy he fails as a blamer/satirist. Nagy is correct, I think, to suspect that behind many scenes of "blame" embedded in epic, there lie structures (dictional, thematic, etc.) that we associate with discretely *poetic* performances of the *psogos*, but these will always be mediated by the narrating poet himself (e.g., Homer), and it is only by analyzing the nature of this mediation that we can ascertain whether these embedded *psogoi* tell us anything about the dynamics of a specifically *poetic* satire and mockery. For further discussion, see below in this chapter on Thersites.

5. Nagy 1979, 263: "[T]he story of Thersites in the *Iliad* surely stands out as the one epic passage with by far the most overt representation of blame poetry."

vain, and without decency, to quarrel with the princes
with any word he thought might be amusing to the Argives.
This was the ugliest man who came beneath Ilion. He was
bandy-legged and went lame of one foot, with shoulders
stooped and drawn together over his chest, and above this
his skull went up to a point with the wool grown sparsely upon it.
Beyond all others Achilleus hated him, and Odysseus.
These two he was forever abusing, but now at brilliant
Agamemnon he clashed the shrill noise of his abuse. The Achaeans
were furiously angry with him, their minds resentful.
But he, crying the words aloud, scolded Agamemnon . . . .
(2.211–24, trans. Lattimore 1951)

Nagy's pioneering study of Thersites concludes that he functions as the paradigmatic blame poet, not unlike an Archilochus or Hipponax—poets conspicuously involved throughout their work in quarrels (*neikê*) with prominent individuals in which they employ the rhetoric of reproach and blame (*oneidos*, *elenkhos*).[6] Nagy's most enduring contribution has been to situate Thersites within the ancient polarity of praise and blame, where everything about his behavior as a blamer, even his very demeanor, places him in stark opposition to the realm of praise and praisers. Nagy's analysis of the terminology of praise and blame found in Greek poets such as Pindar and Bacchylides (praise poets), or the iambographers (blame poets), has been crucial for our understanding of the generic forces that shaped such poetic traditions.[7] Further, his notion of the *psogos* as a type of poetry that existed as a foil to the *ainos*, or praise poetry, has helped overcome the tendencies of earlier criticism to treat the iambus and other forms of mocking poetry as idiosyncratically autobiographical and disconnected from more mainstream generic currents within Greek poetry.

One of Nagy's insights in this regard was to realize that several characters in Homer, notably Irus in the *Odyssey* and Thersites in the *Iliad*, are portrayed in a manner that recalls blame poetry quite explicitly: Not only do they engage in mockery and use satirical techniques in front of a putative audience, but the narrator (Homer) has also described these characters with terminology that Nagy has identified as specifically associated with the *psogos*. Nagy gleans this quasi-technical vocabulary of praise and blame largely from Pindar, who will often contrast his own epinician poetry of praise with its functional opposite, the *psogos*, which exists in a world characterized by such negative

6. See Nagy 1979, 263–64, who details the "striking concentration of words indicating blame as a foil for Epos."
7. Nagy 1979, 222, credits Dumézil 1943 and Detienne 1973 with etablishing a praise-blame opposition as a fundamental principle of archaic Indo-European (Dumézil) and Greek society (Detienne). See more recently, Cottone 2005, 91–170.

forces as *phthonos, oneidos, eris*, and *neikos*.[8] Pindar is himself a praise poet, and when he speaks programmatically of his activity he uses terms that evidently distinguish it from poetry of abuse. But very often when he warns against the dangers of strife and reproach, blame and envy, Pindar does not seem to have poetic forms as such in mind at all, but rather the insidious types of interpersonal behavior that lead to social disharmony or human destruction.[9] This raises a crucial methodological question, namely whether it is legitimate for us to assume that every time an archaic Greek poet portrays characters who engage in mockery or abuse, such scenes must be taken to reflect a poetic tradition of blame. I think that Nagy has made this assumption rather too readily in his discussion of how non-iambographic poets went about representing the poet of mockery or blame, and I argue in this chapter that, while Nagy has isolated the language of blame in archaic poetry, his conception of what constituted blame poetry *per se* requires some adjustment. My central contention here will be that we may only identify a character as behaving like a satirical poet within a given narrative when that character can be said to have established the sort of triangular relationship with a target and putative audience that was associated with the actual practice of satire. In other words, just because a character may ridicule someone within a narrative does not necessarily mean that the audience of the work in which the scene is embedded would regard this ridicule in the same light as they would ridicule by an actual satirist in an actual performance of that genre.

As we have seen in chapter 1, the satirist wants to establish himself in an intimately collusive relationship with the audience, enlisting their sympathies for his cause and his stance of self-righteousness, and entertaining them with his humorous tropes. In third-person narratives that represent *psogoi* between characters other than the poet, it is often difficult to determine exactly who is the satirist, who the target, and who the audience. One of the main differences between first-person and embedded third-person satire is that in the former we normally do not have access to the target's point of view, whereas in the

---

8. See Nagy 1979, 223–28. *Pythian* 2.52–56 are justly famous for their programmatic repudiation of the Archilochean *psogos*, and certainly indicate that Pindar conceptualized his own enterprise as distinct from abusive genres such as the iambus:

ἐμὲ δὲ χρεών ‖ φεύγειν δάκος ἀδινὸν κακαγοριᾶν. ‖ εἶδον γὰρ ἑκὰς ἐὼν τὰ πόλλ᾽ ἐν ἀμαχανίᾳ ‖ ψογερὸν Ἀρχίλοχον βαρυλόγοις ἔχθεσιν ‖ πιαινόμενον. ["... but I must flee the unrelenting bite of malediction. For I have often seen Archilochus, a man full of *psogos*, standing far off, helpless, fattening himself on heavy-worded enmities."]

9. It is unclear to me, for example, whether Nagy's example of Pindar *Nemean* 8.32–33 (with 50–51), discussed at 1979, 227, really indicates that Pindar is speaking of blame poetry as a foil for praise poetry:

ἐχθρὰ δ᾽ ἄρα πάρφασις ἦν καὶ πάλαι, ‖ αἱμύλων μύθων ὁμόφοι-‖ τος, δολόφραδής, κακοποιὸν ὄνειδος: ["Hateful misrepresentation has existed for a long time, ‖ companion of wily words, deviser of deceit, ‖ maleficent *oneidos* (reproach)" tr. Nagy].

latter, the author has the luxury of offering a full account of an encounter between mocker and target. Understandably, scholars are often thrown off when confronted with not only a mocker but also his target—each of whom may be afforded equal time for his respective attack and counterattack—since it can be confusing for them to decide where their sympathies (as a putative audience) "should" lie.[10] This confusion, I believe, accounts for a persistent misidentification of Thersites himself as a "blame poet" figure in *Iliad* 2, rather than as the *target* of a blame poet's abuse. In this passage, therefore, Homer offers an extraordinarily subtle commentary on the complex dynamics of poetic mockery, and in particular on the mechanisms by which mocking speech generates comedy. In the end, I suggest, Homer implicitly makes it clear that we can identify the specific roles of the players in any poetic *psogos* only as a function of (1) the relationship they have with an actual or implied audience, and (2) the degree to which the audience of the *psogos* finds comedy in the drama of mockery it witnesses. These scenes reveal, therefore, just how sensitive ancient audiences could be to the formal and thematic subtleties operative within the various forms of literary mockery, and allow us to pinpoint with even greater precision the taxonomy of satire and abuse that underlay ancient conceptualizations of this type of poetry.

We turn at this point, then, to the Thersites episode itself and begin our discussion with a fundamental question inspired by Nagy's analysis of the passage: If the scene employs the discourse of blame poetry, what cues does it offer to enable a reader/auditor to distinguish who is blaming whom, and which character in the Homeric narrative replicates which role in a hypothetical confrontation between blame poet/satirist and target? The answer is far from straightforward, for the simple reason that, as many scholars have noted,[11] it is not clear what attitude Homer's audiences would have had toward the behavior of Thersites and Odysseus, nor whether we can even suppose that the poet himself would have expected a monolithic response from his audiences. We can, however, compare the details of the scene to what we know about poetic

---

10. That is, if two characters are engaged in mutual mockery, and the entire scene plays out as comedy, the issue of whose case is the more justified is often confused. Ultimately, deciding who is the more justified may be irrelevant to an enjoyment of the scene, but I would maintain that the author constructs nearly all cases of third-person *psogoi* with at least the *pretense* that one of the sparring parties is "in the right," and that the other is the aggressor who must be verbally (or even physically) put in his place. What is often forgotten about first-person satire is that the satirist's attacks are reactive in that they respond to an initial perceived affront, whether it be another person's action (a politician's behavior, a rival's accusations) or simply the state of the world (too many foreigners in the city, hypocritical moralists, etc.). Certainly a figure who represents a mocking poet must by definition be made to adopt a stance of self-righteousness about his verbal aggression, and also (and this is crucial) his self-righteousness must be endorsed by the author's hypothetical, or real, audience. I discuss this dynamic below in detail as it operates in the Thersites episode.

11. See Ebert 1969; Rankin 1972; and Thalmann 1988, 2–3, 14–15; and Marks 2005.

psogoi from other texts, and from there articulate the specific morphology of mockery as it is played out between Thersites and Odysseus.

It is actually only by chance that Thersites ends up in an altercation with Odysseus; in fact, Thersites began by reviling Agamemnon for what he regards as his ill treatment of Achilles and his desire to press the attack on Troy for his own material gains (226–43). Homer tells us at 220–22 that Thersites already had a history of friction with Achilles and Odysseus (ἔχθιστος δ᾽ Ἀχιλῆϊ μάλιστ᾽ ἦν ἠδ᾽ Ὀδυσῆϊ· ‖ τὼ γὰρ <u>νεικείεσκε</u>), and one senses that he cultivated his relationships with these leaders at least in part as a gesture of deliberate comedy, since as Homer tells us, he routinely made it a point to say things that would make the Argives laugh (215–16): ἀλλ᾽ ὅ τι οἱ εἴσαιτο <u>γελοίϊον</u> Ἀργείοισιν ‖ ἔμμεναι.[12] Indeed, it is all the more curious that his quarrel now is initially with Agamemnon—almost as if the actual confrontation needed to be deflected from Agamemnon toward Odysseus in order to satisfy the audience's (both the Argives in the narrative and Homer's flesh-and-blood audiences) expectations of comedy from the scene. If, that is, the audience would be able to recall, or would think they were supposed to be able to recall,[13] other episodes in which Odysseus and Thersites had had comic encounters, they would be all the more inclined to understand this scene as they might any other exercise in a poetic *psogos*, with each party playing a more or less predictable role in the drama. But what exactly are these roles?

To answer this question, we must sort through a number of factors left obscure by the manner in which the episode is constructed as part of an epic narrative. First, the question of "blame." There is no doubt that Thersites "blames" Agamemnon for poor judgment and venality, mocking him with sarcasm and insinuations of effeminacy, and this leads Nagy to think of him as behaving like a "blame poet." But Nagy correctly senses a critical problem in the fact that Thersites is himself portrayed as a repulsive "object of ridicule" in the passage as a whole, and this is hardly the way a satirical poet would want to portray himself—certainly not the way he would want to appear in an ac-

---

12. Thalmann 1988, 16, has described Thersites as a thoroughly comic figure: "His ugliness and the anti-heroic realism with which his appearance is described, his pretensions, his skill at imitation and parody . . . these traits mark him as a comic figure. He represents the the comic type of the *alazon*, or imposter, in the particular form of the *miles gloriosus*." See his n. 14 for earlier bibliography on humor in the passage; also Nagy 1979, 262; and Koster 1980, 45, who notes that the word γελοίϊον is a hapax in the *Iliad* "im Sinne von schadenfrohem Lachen." At *R.* 620c, the famous "Myth of Er" scene, Plato referred to Thersites as a γελωτοποιός. In this scene in which Er witnesses a variety of famous, largely mythological, characters choosing their souls for subsequent incarnations, he sees the soul of Thersites appropriately taking the form of a monkey.

13. Whether or not there existed an independent tradition of *neikē* between Thersites and Odysseus is immaterial: It is sufficient for Homer to mention that they routinely "used to quarrel" (νεικείεσκε), to imply—for the sake of the immediate fiction—the existence of other, presumably comic, episodes involving the two of them.

tual performance. We will see later that that satirists will in fact often adopt a stance of abjection and inferiority, but this is invariably done in order to assert an ironic superiority over their targets and in the face of an otherwise oppressive world. In the case of Thersites, the narrative offers only a singular, unironized portrait of his physical appearance,[14] and, more significantly, he is resoundingly *defeated* in the end by his antagonist. As Nagy says, "the combined physical and verbal abuse of Thersites results in pain and tears for the victim…but laughter for the rest of the Achaeans."[15] How, we might ask, can such a humiliated figure represent a satirist/blame poet, who almost by definition needs to be able to claim at least a fiction of self-righteousness about his attacks, and, even more significantly, who is himself supposed to be the one to elicit laughter from an audience? The satirist, after all, who ends up debased in the eyes of an audience and their object of ridicule and scorn has failed at what he set out to accomplish.[16]

Nagy does not quite articulate the question like this, but suggests implicitly how he might answer it. Insofar as Thersites is said to be ἔχθιστος, "most hateful," to the Achaean leaders, Nagy sees him as emblematic of blame poetry in explicit contrast to praise poetry, which privileges φιλία instead.[17] As Nagy puts it: "Epos is here actually presenting itself as a parallel to praise poetry by being an institutional opposite of blame poetry." So Nagy seems to regard the incidents of "blame" embedded in Homer as in some sense anathema to, or at least working against, the nature of epic as a fundamentally "encomiastic" genre. If I understand Nagy on this point, he would hold that within epic, blame poetry can only be judged to be a "negative" phenomenon, and the blame poet is always characterized as Thersites is in *Iliad* 2, or Irus is in *Odyssey* 18. The comedy that normally arises from blame poetry,[18] moreover, is turned on

14. Thalmann 1988, 17, perceptively notes Thersites' "detached, ironic perspective," which, he adds, aligns him with other "marginal, comic figures," but any irony that might momentarily protrude from within the narrative seems overshadowed by the final outcome of the altercation with Odysseus. I would add that I detect no irony in the physical description of Thersites; the irony we so often find in self-portraits of comic satirists (one thinks Aristophanes' baldness [cf. *Kn.* 560, *P.* 767–74], Cratinus's alcoholism [in *Pytine*], or Horace's eye infection [*Serm.* 1.5.30]) is more difficult to convey when the description is left to a third-person narrator rather than the poet's subjective "I."

15. Nagy 1979, 262.

16. Thersites at first seems to be a figure of buffoonery, who intends to draw a laugh from his audience (cf. line 217, cited above), but there is nothing about the way Homer presents his complaints that would lead us (or his audience of fellow soldiers) to suspect that he was engaging in a comic performance of any sort, i.e., a performance replete with generic cues indicating that the content of his *psogos* was mediated by marked poetic language and so not necessarily to be taken at face value.

17. Nagy 1979, 260.

18. As one might suspect from our discussion in chapter 1, I am uneasy with Nagy's claim that "blame poetry has a potential for the comic element . . . [b]ut blame poetry itself is more inclusive and thus cannot be equated with comedy. Blame poetry can be serious as well as comic; it can condemn as well as ridicule." Technically speaking, Nagy is probably right that some poetry that engages in "blaming" may not be explicitly comic. But the fact is that nearly all the genres that

itself because epic seems incapable of allowing blame poetry any legitimacy. As Nagy says (1979, 262): "Homeric Epos can indeed reflect the comic aspect of blame poetry, but . . . it does so at the expense of the blame poet. In the Thersites episode . . . it is Epos that gets the last laugh on the blame poet rather than the other way around." I infer from this that for Nagy, epic would never be able to represent a "righteous" blame poet, but must always ridicule the institution of blame poetry itself. Certainly this is what leads him to say of Irus in the *Odyssey* (1979, 230) that his story "in effect ridicules the stereotype of an unrighteous blame poet. Like the unrighteous blamers, who are righteously blamed by praise poetry, Irus has *eris* 'strife' with a good man . . . and makes *neikos* 'quarreling' against him. . . ." Similarly, concerning Thersites, Nagy concludes (263) that his "base appearance . . . serves to mirror in form and content . . . his blame poetry." In short, Nagy sees epic and forms of blame poetry (such as iambos) as generically antagonistic to one another, to the point where the laughter elicited by such scenes is not a function of the comedy of blame poetry, but rather of epic asserting, after a fashion, its generic superiority.

Nagy's formulation here, however, raises further questions, to which we must now turn. First, Nagy seems to be extrapolating a definition of blame poetry from the Homeric passages that deploy the discourse of blame, rather than asking whether Homer is representing manifestations of blame poetry that existed prior to his appropriation of this discourse. It seems to me, however, that before concluding that Thersites must be acting as a blame poet, we would first want to set out how we would expect a blame poet to behave independent

---

Nagy would characterize as poetry of "blame" (e.g., iambus, Old Comedy) are highly comic, and even in cases where "blaming" is embedded in other genres (e.g., the attacks on Perses in Hesiod's *Works and Days*; and the Thersites episode in Homer), one can usually detect a comic tinge to the moments of blame. Blame poetry is, after all, different from the prosaic "blaming" humans engage in as a part of everyday life; "real" blaming need not be comic, especially when it occurs privately and so has no audience. Once the blaming is poeticized, however, an audience (real or imagined) comes into existence, and comedy (which, as a kind of performance, requires an audience) becomes a viable strategy for the poet pursuing his audience's sympathies over against his target. What complicates the matter is that a pretense of "seriousness" is so often a generic characteristic of poetry that deploys strategies such as mockery, ridicule, sarcasm, etc., which are all at root "comic." They may not be "nice" or "pleasant"—their humor may be vindictive and cruel—but they are intended to make some audience laugh in some way. It may be that the real problem is terminology. I find "blame" to be an extremely broad, often imprecise, term, inadequate for describing what is going on in poetry of abuse and satire. I have discussed my reservations about this term elsewhere (Rosen 1990, 19n25), but reiterate here only that what we call "blame" need not in itself be abusive or emotionally charged, nor, for that matter, "satirical." Moreover, although the notion of attack in a poem does imply that the attacker is "blaming" the target for something, in this type of poetry the content of the blame is so often subordinated to the poet's apparent desire for literary effect (such as satire and comedy) that it becomes irrelevant. For example, when Hipponax takes an opponent (almost certainly his favorite target Bupalus) to task in fr. 69 Dg. for "plundering his mother's blind sea-urchin while she sleeps," (ὃς κατευδούσης ‖ τῆς μητρὸς ἐσκύλευε τὸν βρύσσον ‖ τυφλόν . . .), the term "blame," with its almost juridical, serious connotation, hardly seems to capture the comic ribaldry of the passage.

of Homer's representation of him. I have shown in the first two chapters of this book that by examining extant genres of blame, mockery, and satire, such as iambus or comedy, as well as the mythical commentary about them, we may say that these poetic forms and their practitioners can be delineated with a good deal of precision. When we turn to the Homeric scenes of embedded mockery, then, we must look carefully at the roles assigned by the poet to the various players in the drama and see how they map onto the known structures and dynamics of the *non-Homeric* genres of satire and mockery. As we have discussed earlier, "blaming" (mockery, ridicule, etc.) virtually by definition involves two (or more) parties; but while many characters may engage in blame, there can be only one playing the role of the blame *poet* in a given context, and the criterion for identifying him as such is the level of "righteousness" he can persuade an audience that he has on his side.

In the case of the Thersites episode, as Nagy and others have pointed out, Thersites himself is not portrayed as having a just cause,[19] and for this reason especially I would maintain that it is inaccurate to consider him analogous to a blame poet. A blamer he is, to be sure, but not one who behaves as a blame *poet* should, that is, as one who must create at least the pretense of having an intimate relationship with an audience, which, in its turn, must find his cause convincing.[20] At the very least, the poet of mockery must operate on the *assumption* that the audience for whom he ideally creates his performance will be convinced of his cause; and in embedded scenes of mockery, the audience of the larger work will need to find the case made by the figure representing such a poet similarly convincing.[21] Plenty of mockery and abuse may emanate from both parties involved in a poetic *psogos*, but only one of them can be re-

---

19. We may in fact sympathize with Thersites, and even find the content of his speech compellingly "serious," but the fact remains that within the narrative he is not portrayed as anything other than at best buffoonish (witness the Achaeans's laughter, 271), and at worst seditious (evident from Odysseus violent reaction to him, 247–65). See Martin 1989, 109–13, for a discussion of how Thersites' speech is "overdetermined to look bad." Martin argues that the style of Thersites' language marks him as a "flawed" performer, in contrast to other more explicitly heroic speakers, such as Menelaus or Nestor.

20. It has often been assumed that Thersites represents something of a *vox populi*, echoing the genuine conerns of the rank and file of the Greek army. If so, one might want to imagine that *they* would be his audience, and his relationship with them would be close and sympathetic. But Thersites' social status, as has periodically been noticed (see most recently, Marks 2005) is actually high and not well-suited to serve as a voice of the "common people." We shall return to this point below (pp. 104–16). Moreover, the Greek army end up laughing at him when Odysseus rebukes and beats him (*Il.* 2.270). Thalmann 1988, 18, sees this scene as further evidence for a "distance" between Thersites and the army; distance is not what a blame poet is looking for in an audience.

21. This is a complicated issue: I do not mean to imply that the audience of an embedded scene of mockery must "agree with" or "endorse" the content of a character's mockery, only that if one of two quarreling characters in a scene is going to be construed by the audience as behaving like a poet who works in a genre of mockery, he must be seen within the context of that scene as having the "higher" moral ground, however ironized or comic his moral stance might be.

garded as justified; this is the role that an actual blame poet will always assume in an actual performance of mockery and satire, and any figure within a psogic narrative supposed to be functioning analogously to a blame poet—but not explicitly a poet himself—must play a similar role. In general, the blame poet will present himself as a figure who would just as soon *not* be involved in any confrontation; he would claim to be a relatively passive individual, incited to action only by his inability to endure the behavior of his target (or if he is attacking institutions or ideas, his inability to accept these without a principled fight). Juvenal's famous phrase, *difficile est saturam non scribere* (1.30), rounding off a litany of complaints about contemporary degenerates (in the face of whom, ". . . it's impossible *not* to write satire"), reflects an attitude that all Greek and Roman blame poets would hold toward their work.[22] Such poets routinely present themselves as reacting to someone or something that they assume the audience will also find offensive. The attitude of the audience here is crucial, for if they do not find the content of the poet's blame and satire legitimate, or at least if he does not act as if they will find it so, then he will never succeed as a blame poet.

If we apply this principle to the Thersites episode, we see that Thersites does not emulate the prototypical blame poet. Certainly he takes a self-righteous and indignant stance against Agamemnon's behavior; and one could likewise also say that he is reacting to a state of affairs that he regards as unendurable. But in any given confrontation between two antagonists, it is easy to assume that even the figure presented as the poet's target would believe he has a just cause. Thersites, too, then, from *his* perspective, believes his cause is just. If we accept, however, that what distinguishes the poet from the target is largely the audience's point of view (and here I refer to *Homer's* audience, not to whatever audience we think Thersites was playing to), Thersites can really only be regarded as the *target* within a *psogos*. Even though he makes the first move in the altercation and so gives an initial impression that the target of the narrative will be Agamemnon, or his stand-in here, Odysseus, he is still just the target.[23] The narrator, Homer, makes the audience ill-disposed toward Thersites from the opening of the episode (220), where he describes Thersites as "most hate-

---

22. I want to make it clear, however, that this dictum—that the poet felt compelled to attack his targets out of extreme indignation—does not necessarily have any bearing on the poet's personal attitudes or feelings. This is a generically generated pose first and foremost, even if a poet happens to agree with the sentiments he expresses in his work.

23. There is a temptation, perhaps, to see Thersites in *Iliad* 2 as something of a "failed satirist," i.e., someone whose cause can be construed as "just" (certainly *he* thinks it is), but who is not allowed by the narrative to succeed. We will see below (pp. 91–98) that outside of the *Iliad*, Thersites is portrayed as a bona fide satirist, who fails to be understood as such; that narrative makes it clear that his cause was just, even though he has had to suffer for it with his death. But in the case of *Iliad* 2, we may want to *imagine* that Thersites' dissent was justified, but Homer's narrative will not sustain such a notion (*pace* Cottone 2005, 116, n. 40), and without the perception in an audience's mind that the mocker has a just cause, he can never be accurately construed as a satirist.

ful" (ἔχθιστος) to Achilles and Odysseus, in particular for his continual quarreling with them:

> ἔχθιστος δ᾽ Ἀχιλῆϊ μάλιστ᾽ ἦν ἠδ᾽ Ὀδυσῆϊ·   220
> τὼ γὰρ νεικείεσκε·

Beyond all others Achilleus hated him, and Odysseus.
These two he was forever abusing, (2.220–21; trans. Lattimore)

Of course, in the context of any antagonistic relationship, each party will usually be considered ἔχθιστος to the other, so *in itself* this negative portrayal of Thersites need not imply that he could only play the role of target. But Achilles and Odysseus are not just any antagonists: They are two of the most favored heroes of the entire epic, and Homer's audience (again, the audience of the larger work in which the Thersites *psogos* is embedded), expecting to experience a serious poetic treatment of heroic figures, cannot be supposed to find anything just in Thersites' attacks.[24]

2. Thersites and "Paphlagonian" in Aristophanes' *Knights*

A clearer illustration of the dynamics at work within the Thersites episode may be found in an analysis of the well known "feud" between Aristophanes and the demagogue Cleon, as it is related in Aristophanes' play *Knights*. As in the case of Thersites, *Knights* can portray an extended *psogos* between two characters—here between a "Sausage-seller" and a figure named Paphlagonian, who serves as a transparent cipher for Cleon—but Aristophanes can add an important dimension that Homer cannot. By means of the self-referential parabasis, in which the poet of Athenian Old Comedy could make the chorus leader speak on his own behalf, Aristophanes is able to interject a first-person *psogos* into a genre not otherwise explicitly concerned to dramatize the poet's subjectivity. In *Knights*, it so happens that the character alleged more or less transparently[25]

24. It is not so much that Homer is incapable of being critical of his heroes, or that, in the specific case of Thersites, he could not have left his audience with at least a soupçon of criticism against Agamemnon; rather it is that only from the point of view of the narrative's premises and structures, Thersites can only be seen as a negative, illegitimate figure. Thalmann's remarks (1988, 27) on the conflict of ideologies within this passage are apposite here; the episode may seem to us to present conflicting ideologies of class and authority (for further bibliography, see Thalmann 27n78), and we may even want to imagine that Homer himself was sensitive this sort of problematization. But the narrative is constructed so that the heroic ethos always maintains a position of privilege and legitimacy over against forces that challenge it.

25. Cleon is never mentioned by name in the parabasis, but he is clearly referred to at 511 as a "Typhoon" (Τυφῶ) and a "hurricane" (ἐριώλη). In a play concerned almost solely with Cleon, it is a mark of Aristophanes' gamesmanship that his name occurs only once, at line 976. Even the

in the parabasis (507–50) to be the poet's target, namely Cleon, coincides with one of the two antagonists of the *psogos* represented within the plot of the play. That is, we have the parallelism, Parabasis: poet vs. Paphlagonian/Cleon; Plot: Sausage-seller vs. Paphlagonian/Cleon. We are encouraged, therefore, to read the fictional *psogos* between the Sausage-seller and Paphlagonian as a variation on the poet's own feud with the same target, Paphlagonian (*qua* Cleon)— a relationship that alleges to be factual even though embedded itself within a fictional plot. The "autobiographical" information about the poet and Cleon provided by the parabasis thus functions as a kind of commentary on how the audience is to determine which of the two antagonists, Sausage-seller or Paplagonian/Cleon, has the just cause, which is the target, and which plays the role of "legitimate" blame poet. A closer look at the Aristophanic text will show in greater detail how these pieces fit together, and how they illuminate the poetics of the Thersites passage.

At the opening of the parabasis, Aristophanes makes it no secret that he expects his audience to be sympathetic to his cause, and we soon find out, albeit obliquely, that this cause is the repudiation of Cleon:

> ὑμεῖς δ' ἡμῖν προσέχετε τὸν νοῦν
> τοῖς ἀναπαίστοις,
> ὦ παντοίας ἤδη μούσης   505
> πειραθέντες καθ' ἑαυτούς.
> εἰ μέν τις ἀνὴρ τῶν ἀρχαίων κωμῳδοδιδάσκαλος ἡμᾶς
> ἠνάγκαζεν λέξοντας ἔπη πρὸς τὸ θέατρον παραβῆναι,
> οὐκ ἂν φαύλως ἔτυχεν τούτου· νῦν δ' ἄξιός ἐσθ' ὁ ποιητής,
> ὅτι τοὺς αὐτοὺς ἡμῖν μισεῖ τολμᾷ τε λέγειν τὰ δίκαια,   510
> καὶ γενναίως πρὸς τὸν Τυφῶ χωρεῖ καὶ τὴν ἐριώλην.

> . . . And now draw your attention to our anapaests, you who have personal experience in all sorts of the arts. If any of the old producers of comedies tried to compel us to step out in front of an audience and deliver a speech, he would not have had much success with this. But now our poet is worthy of it, because he hates the same people we do, dares to say just things, and nobly advances against Typho and the whirlwind. . . .
> (*Kn.* 503–11)

The chorus leader begins with a traditional parabatic appeal for the audience to heed the "anapaests,"[26] simultaneously warning them that a full under-

---

central target of the play, the Paphlagonian, is never explicitly equated with Cleon. There are enough indications, however, throughout the play to make the identification secure; see Sommerstein 1981, 3; and MacDowell 1995, 86–87.

26. On the structural components of the parabasis, see Sifakis 1971, 53–70.

standing of his play will require considerable poetic experience, and flattering them that they already have it (ὦ παντοίας ἤδη μούσης ‖ πειραθέντες καθ' ἑαυτούς, "[you who have had] personal experience with all sorts of the arts" [lit. = "every sort of Muse"]).[27] This *captatio benevolentiae* is addressed to a knowing, ideal audience, one that will be able to understand the play's generic cues, and so to establish a framework for the "appropriate" interpretation of the plot and its characters. In the ensuing lines, the chorus leader's explanation for why they come forward to speak to the audience in the parabasis is a variation on the Juvenalian principle we mentioned earlier (that is, the poet's claim to be so indignant that he has no choice but to write satire): In the old days, they say, it would have taken a lot to rouse them to speak (507–9); but now they feel compelled to support the poet because he has a just cause (νῦν δ' ἄξιός ἐσθ' ὁ ποιητής . . . τολμᾷ τε λέγειν τὰ δίκαια), because he hates the same people as they do (ὅτι τοὺς αὐτοὺς ἡμῖν μισεῖ), and, to be more specific, because they heartily endorse his attacks on Cleon (γενναίως πρὸς τὸν Τυφῶ χωρεῖ καὶ τὴν ἐριώλην). These lines serve to guide the audience's understanding of the formalized *psogoi* between the Sausage-seller and Paphlagonian that both precede and immediately follow the parabasis. Neither of these antagonists turns out to be particularly savory, but there will never be any question as to how the poet intends the audience to view them. Within the drama of the *psogos* itself, each character would no doubt view the other as his "target," but from the vantage point of the poet (who controls the proceedings) and the audience (whom the poet humorously cajoles into taking his point of view) there is only one real satirist (the Sausage-seller) and one real target (Paphlagonian/Cleon). As the parabasis makes clear, if the poet were hypothetically to assume a role within the *psogoi* he has dramatized, constructing them, that is, as a *first-person* attack on a putative enemy, he would play the part of the rakish Sausage-seller. It is thus easy to see that the Sausage-seller behaves analogously to the blame poet—indignant, self-righteous, and aligned with the audience's sentiments.

In the Thersites episode there are fewer explicit clues to reveal the poet's putative attitude toward the antagonists in the passage. But if we read the passage in terms of the typical structures of a poetic *psogos*, it becomes easier for the audience to get a sense of where their sympathies should lie, and of how to decide which of the antagonists—Thersites or Odysseus—plays a role analogous to that of a "blame poet," and which to the prototypical "target." In this regard, it will be illuminating to compare the *psogos* between the Sausage-seller and the Paphlagonian in *Knights* with that between Thersites and Odysseus; both episodes depict an altercation involving two characters other than the composing poet himself, and both show the reciprocal nature of a *psogos*. This

27. Such flattery is also traditional for the parabasis; Sifakis 1971, 38–39; see for example, *Clouds* 521 and 535, or *Frogs* 676–77.

means that each character has a chance to inveigh against the other, and it is left up to the audience to decide which one to sympathize with. Each character is convinced of the rectitude of his case: In the *Iliad* passage, Thersites thinks Agamemnon has dragged his feet long enough, and remains in Troy for his own material benefit. Odysseus, in fact, counters with little in the way of substance—he takes Thersites to task for daring to accuse his superiors of poor behavior and general ignorance about the Greek officers's military strategies—but his response is little more than a prolonged *ad hominem* insult followed by a physical blow. By any measure, Thersites' argument has more legitimate "content" than Odysseus's; so how does the audience decide whether to take Thersites' side in this debate or to sympathize with Odysseus in his reactive vituperation?[28] Put another way, how can the audience distinguish between the *legitimate* "blamer" and the "blamed," between the figure who behaves like a blame poet, and the target?[29] The *psogos* in *Knights*, as we will see, poses a similar dilemma for the audience, made all the more complex by the fact that that neither character is, at least initially, morally attractive. But in the case of Aristophanes we have the luxury of knowing from the parabasis, where the poet identified his "personal" target as Cleon, how we are "supposed" to view the cause of each antagonist. If we attend closely to the diction and tropes of the full Aristophanic *psogos* in *Knights*, therefore, we will be in a better position to evaluate the poetic dynamics and morphology of the Iliadic *psogos*, and so to understand more accurately the deployment of poetic mockery within epic.

As the *Knights* parabasis eventually makes clear, the play's chorus of Athenian cavalry is sympathetic to the poet's hatred of Cleon, so when they first enter the stage chasing after the Paphlagonian at line 247, they represent a point of view that the audience will be urged in the parabasis to identify with the poet's, and so to endorse. To prepare us for the chorus's entrance, one of the household slaves describes the Knights as "a thousand good men who hate him [Cleon]," (ἄνδρες ἀγαθοὶ χίλιοι ‖ μισοῦντες αὐτόν), and he associates them

28. Scholars have often noted parallels between Thersites' attack on Agamemnon in *Iliad* 2 and Achilles' attack on him in *Iliad* 1, with Thersites "recapitulating the very points Achilles has made in Book I," (Martin 1989, 109, with further bibliography in n. 50). Why, then, should an audience feel differently, as they clearly do, about Thersites' censure of Agamemnon in Book 2 than they do about Achilles' in Book 1?

29. Thersites and Odysseus, of course, both in their turn engage in active blaming and each also receives it (although Odysseus only obliquely as a kind of surrogate for Agamemnon, who is not present during Thersites' attack). But, as I have argued above, this will be the case in any *psogos*, and it is critical for the audience to evaluate the legitimacy of each antagonist's motivations for blaming and to attempt to determine the poet's vantage point on the question. It may be theoretically possible for there to be a *psogos* in which neither side's attack has any merit whatsoever; but this would result in pure farce, without the possibility of satire. Satire, by definition, requires claims of legitimacy on one side, and imputations of illegitimacy on the other; the lines may be blurred while two characters are attacking one another, but in the end, one of the two must be portrayed by the poet, however jocularly or disingenuously, as the moral "victor."

with all upstanding citizens, all spectators who are "clever," himself, and even "the god" (227–29). By setting up an antagonism between people who are καλοί τε κἀγαθοί and a figure regarded as a threat to this group and the status quo they represent, the poet prepares the audience to disapprove of the Paphlagonian when he appears, and to regard him as the proper "target" of the *psogoi* that follow. Yet it is interesting that the Paphlagonian's first speech, at 235, takes a raucous stance not unlike that of Thersites when he first speaks. Like Thersites, the Paphlagonian claims to be protecting an unspecified group of putatively powerless people (he calls them "the demos") against a sinister conspiracy of political leaders. On seeing the Sausage-seller with a Chalcidian cup, he leaps to the comically absurd conclusion that his antagonist must have been involved in a Chalcidian plot against Athens:[30]

οὗτοι μὰ τοὺς δώδεκα θεοὺς χαιρήσετον,
ὁτιὴ 'πὶ τῷ δήμῳ ξυνόμνυτον πάλαι.
τουτὶ τί δρᾷ τὸ Χαλκιδικὸν ποτήριον:
οὐκ ἔσθ᾽ ὅπως οὐ Χαλκιδέας ἀφίστατον.

No way, by the twelve gods, will you be happy, since the two of you've been plotting against the people for so long. What's this Chalcidian cup mean? You two must be driving the Chalcidians to revolt. (235–38)

Some lines later in the scene, when the chorus has caught up with the Paphlagonian and begins attacking him, he likewise invokes the "polis" and "demos" as his allies against what he presents as the oppressive constraints of an arbitrary authority:

ὦ πόλις καὶ δῆμ᾽, ὑφ᾽ οἵων θηρίων γαστρίζομαι

O polis! O demos! What beasts are kicking me in the stomach! (273)

Thersites too claims to be protecting a group of people, in this case his fellow soldiers, in the face of what he portrays as Agamemnon's princely greed. He implies that he alone is giving voice to the frustrations of all the Achaeans, whose wartime efforts produce benefits only for their leaders. It is hardly fitting, he says in line 234, for a Greek leader to bring evil on the rank and file:

ἦ ἔτι καὶ χρυσοῦ ἐπιδεύεαι, ὅν κέ τις οἴσει
Τρώων ἱπποδάμων ἐξ Ἰλίου υἷος ἄποινα,
ὅν κεν ἐγὼ δήσας ἀγάγω ἢ ἄλλος Ἀχαιῶν,
ἠὲ γυναῖκα νέην, ἵνα μίσγεαι ἐν φιλότητι,

30. On these lines, see Sommerstein 1981, 155 ad loc.

ἦν τ᾽ αὐτὸς ἀπονόσφι κατίσχεαι; <u>οὐ μὲν ἔοικεν</u>
<u>ἀρχὸν ἐόντα κακῶν ἐπιβασκέμεν υἷας Ἀχαιῶν.</u>

Or is it still more gold you will be wanting, that some
son of the Trojans, breakers of horses, brings as ransom out of Ilion,
one that I, or some other Achaian, capture and bring in?
Is it some young woman to lie with in love and keep her
all to yourself apart from the others? It is not right for
you, their leader, to lead in sorrow the sons of the Achaians.
(2.229–34, trans. Lattimore)

On the surface, then, both Thersites and the Paphlagonian express what appears at first glance to be genuine indignation by a beleaguered party within a classic power struggle between leaders and "little guys," and as such, they would presumably each claim that their cause was just. Aristophanes, however, never allows the audience to take any of the Paphlagonian's indignation seriously, because he has made sure to contrast early on the Paphlagonian's character to that of the καλοί τε κἀγαθοί. With Thersites the situation is complicated by the fact that the scene is not supported by a comic framework which could provide cues to the audience about how they should respond to its various players. But precisely because the Thersites episode is embedded within the context of epic, there can be no question that the audience will be disposed toward that genre's version of the καλοί τε κἀγαθοί, namely its heroic personalities. Hence, when Thersites rails against a member of this élite group, Agamemnon, the poet clearly constructs him as an unwelcome outsider, who threatens the established social order. The final words of the episode immediately following Odysseus's excoriation of Thersites confirm that, whatever group of people Thersites thought he was supporting against Agamemnon, the Achaean soldiers prefer to distance themselves from him, as is clear from their unqualified approval of Odysseus's behavior:

ὧδε δέ τις εἴπεσκεν ἰδὼν ἐς πλησίον ἄλλον·
ὢ πόποι ἦ δὴ μυρί᾽ Ὀδυσσεὺς ἐσθλὰ ἔοργε
βουλάς τ᾽ ἐξάρχων ἀγαθὰς πόλεμόν τε κορύσσων·
νῦν δὲ τόδε μέγ᾽ ἄριστον ἐν Ἀργείοισιν ἔρεξεν,
ὃς τὸν λωβητῆρα ἐπεσβόλον ἔσχ᾽ ἀγοράων

. . . and thus they would speak to each other, each looking at the man
    next to him:
"Come now: Odysseus has done excellent things by thousands,
bringing forward good counsels and ordering armed encounters;
but now this is far the best thing he ever has accomplished
among the Argives, to keep this thrower of words, this braggart
out of assembly." (2.271–75, trans. Lattimore)

This is as close as one can get within an epic context to the role played by the chorus in Aristophanes' *Knights*. Both the hypothetical Achaean soldier[31] and the Aristophanic chorus function as commentators on the *psogos* at hand, and guide the audience in their proper understanding of how blame is to be apportioned and conceptualized.

A further indication that Thersites plays the role of the "target" within a *psogos* emerges from Homer's portrayal of him as unscrupulous and opportunistic, and thus deserving of the blame and violence he receives from Odysseus. Once again, comparison with Aristophanes is instructive. When the chorus in *Knights* finally appears on the stage, they repeatedly characterize their target the Paphlagonian as a "scoundrel" (πανοῦργον), who ought to be beaten, and the epithet ταραξιππόστρατον implies a Thersites-like antipathy toward military authority in the service of what amounts to demagoguery:

παῖε παῖε τὸν πανοῦργον καὶ ταραξιππόστρατον
καὶ τελώνην καὶ φάραγγα καὶ Χάρυβδιν ἁρπαγῆς,
καὶ πανοῦργον καὶ πανοῦργον· πολλάκις γὰρ αὖτ᾿ ἐρῶ.
καὶ γὰρ οὗτος ἦν πανοῦργος πολλάκις τῆς ἡμέρας.
ἀλλὰ παῖε καὶ δίωκε καὶ τάραττε καὶ κύκα
καὶ βδελύττου, καὶ γὰρ ἡμεῖς, κἀπικείμενος βόα·
εὐλαβοῦ δὲ μὴ ᾿κφύγῃ σε·

Hit, hit the rogue, the cavalry-annoyer, the tax-collector, the deep chasm and Charybdis of theft, the rogue, the rogue! For I say it over and over: this guy was a rogue many times a day. But hit him and chase him and annoy him, and confuse him and hate him—for that's what we're doing—and shout at him as you attack! But take care that he doesn't get away from you. . . . (247–53)

The Paphlagonian's description of himself immediately following these lines is reminiscent of the way in which Thersites is introduced in the Iliadic passage, for just as Thersites will say anything to get a laugh from the Greek soldiers (215), so does the Paphlagonian imply that he will do anything to re-

---

31. This oblique way of offering commentary on a scene of comic abuse (and of adding an extra measure of mockery to it) by imagining what a hypothetical by-stander might say may have been a bona fide literary trope by Aristophanes' time. He uses it to good effect elsewhere, for example, at *Peace* 44–50, where a hypothetical Ionian is imagined to explain to a young self-styled intellectual in the audience (τῶν θεατῶν τις . . . νεανίας δοκησίσοφος) what the significance of the dung beetle on the stage is. As he explains, the beetle is an allegory for the recently deceased Cleon, who now eats excrement in the underworld. (. . . ἐς Κλέωνα τοῦτ᾿ αἰνίσσεται, ‖ ὡς κεῖνος ἐν Ἅιδεω τὴν σπατίλην ἐσθίει). See Rosen 1984; and Olson 1998, 76 (ad loc.), who cites Cratinus fr. 342 K-A as another example. On *tis*-speeches in the *Iliad*, see de Jong 1987.

tain the allegiance of citizens in their capacity as jurors, even if he has to make unjust accusations:

ὦ γέροντες ἡλιασταί, φράτερες τριωβόλου,
οὓς ἐγὼ βόσκω <u>κεκραγὼς καὶ δίκαια κἄδικα</u>,
παραβοηθεῖθ᾽, ὡς ὑπ᾽ ἀνδρῶν τύπτομαι ξυνωμοτῶν.

O old men of the jury, brothers of the Three Obols [the pay for jury service], whom I nourish with my shouting, whether about just or unjust things, come help me, since I am being beaten up by conspirators! (255–57)

To this appeal for help against the attacks of the Sausage-seller and one of the slaves, the chorus responds that in fact the attackers are justified (ἐν δίκῃ γ᾽, ἐπεὶ τὰ κοινὰ πρὶν λαχεῖν κατεσθίεις . . . "[yes, and they're beating you] justly, since you consume public funds, even before the lot [of holding office] falls to you"). The chorus sees the attackers's sense of indignation, in other words, as grounded in an implicit claim of unwavering justice, in contrast to the Paphlagonian's questionable moral sensibility. He too wants to claim that he acts justly and on behalf of the chorus (even if, as he lets slip at 256, he must stoop to unjust behavior at times!), but the chorus sees through his flattery. When he claims that he was about to propose that "it is *just* that a monument be set up in the city" to honor the chorus's courage (267–68), they call him a "bull-shitter and a scoundrel" (269: ἀλαζών . . . μάσθλης), and proceed to set upon him violently.

Another characteristic that affiliates Thersites with the Paphlagonian in *Knights*, thus constructing them both as quintessential targets of blame, is their proclivity for loud shouting in their response to the situation that they complain about. Thersites' reproaches against Agamemnon are evidently piercing and loud (ὀξέα κεκλήγων λέγ᾽ ὀνείδεα . . . αὐτὰρ ὃ μακρὰ βοῶν Ἀγαμέμνονα νείκεε μύθῳ, 223–24), which may well lie behind Odysseus's characterization of Thersites' speech as ἀκριτόμυθος "undisciplined, indiscriminate."[32] Aristophanes' putative "target," the Paphlagonian, is described by the Sausage-seller in exactly the same way, with the implication that such a trait is indecorous and boorish: καὶ κέκραγας, ὥσπερ ἀεὶ τὴν πόλιν καταστρέφει (274). Note that the second clause belongs to the discourse of the blame poet, in its self-righteous complaint that the Paphlagonian routinely bullies the polis with his shouting. The Sausage-seller, that is, assumes that the polis had been heretofore stable until the target came along to disrupt it;

32. See Martin 1989, 110–12 on this epithet as a stylistic marker of Thersites' speech in this passage. On Cleon's (i.e., the Paphlagonian's) loud, disruptive character in *Knights*, see Edmunds 1987, 5–9.

like many a satirist, he fears a perceived threat to the sociopolitical status quo. And like many a target, the Paphlagonian reinforces the fears of the satirist by redoubling his loud threats: ἀλλ' ἐγώ σε τῇ βοῇ ταύτῃ γε πρῶτα τρέψομαι (275). All of the Paphlagonian's pernicious qualities come together in the chorus's summation in a strophe at 304, which notes his shouting and brazenness (κρᾶκτα, θράσους, 304)[33] and his political subversiveness (ὦ βορβοροτάραξι καὶ τὴν πόλιν ἅπασαν ἡμῶν ἀνατετυρβακώς, 309–10):

ὦ μιαρὲ καὶ βδελυρὲ κρᾶκτα, τοῦ σοῦ θράσους
πᾶσα μὲν γῆ πλέα, πᾶσα δ' ἐκκλησία,   305
καὶ τέλη καὶ γραφαὶ καὶ δικαστήρι', ὦ
βορβοροτάραξι καὶ τὴν πόλιν ἅπασαν ἡ-
μῶν ἀνατετυρβακώς,   310
ὅστις ἡμῶν τὰς Ἀθήνας ἐκκεκώφωκας βοῶν
κἀπὸ τῶν πετρῶν ἄνωθεν τοὺς φόρους θυννοσκοπῶν.

O you vile and disgusting screamer! The whole world is full of your audacity, the whole Assembly, and all taxes and indictments and courts, O you mud-swirler, who have thrown the entire polis into confusion, you who have made our Athens deaf with shouting, as you keep a watch for tribute like a fisherman from the rocks on high. (304–13)

Odysseus and Thersites play out a similar relationship in the *Iliad*, particularly evident when Odysseus chastises Thersites for his presumptuous attacks on the current military leadership:

Θερσῖτ' ἀκριτόμυθε, λιγύς περ ἐὼν ἀγορητής,
ἴσχεο, μηδ' ἔθελ' οἶος ἐριζέμεναι βασιλεῦσιν·

---

33. Nagy 1979, 260–61, notes that the element of "boldness" is etymologically built into Thersites' name, and maintains that the "boldness conveyed by the element *thersi-*. . . is akin to the *thersos*/*tharsos* 'boldness' of the blame poet." But while the semantics of *thersi-* in Thersites' name are surely operative, it does not seem to follow that this must conjure up the boldness specifically of the "blame poet." Nagy has put his finger on "boldness" as a characteristic element of the *psogos*, but the target can have it as well as the poet. Indeed, several of the Homeric examples that Nagy cites to support his claim that Thersites' *thersos* is that of the "blame poet," indicate rather that they are considered legitimate targets of abuse themselves. At *Odyssey* 22.287, for example, the suitor Ktesippos (who had earlier insulted Odysseus when disguised as a beggar, 20.287–319) is called Πολυθερσεΐδη φιλοκέρτομε by Philoitios as he kills him. Nagy (261) would explain this epithet as a reproach by Philoitios for "improper speech at the time of the physical attack on Odysseus . . . In sum, a man who had reproached Odysseus is now getting a taste of his own medicine." If we can say, however, that in the context of a *psogos* between Philoitios and Ktesippos, one plays the role of a blame poet and the other a target, it should be clear that the dying Ktesippos has always been regarded by the poet and his imagined, "ideal" audience as the illegitimate, immoral, upstart, whose boldness is, like that of the Paphlagonian in *Knights*, something the blame poet must strive to fight against with his own, *legitimized, tharsos*.

Thersites, you of undisciplined speech, though you're a shrill orator,
hold back: don't quarrel alone against kings. (246–47)

. . . τὼ οὐκ ἂν βασιλῆας ἀνὰ στόμ᾽ ἔχων ἀγορεύοις
καί σφιν ὀνείδεά τε προφέροις, νόστόν τε φυλάσσοις.

You should not take up the two kings in your mouth and address them,
and you should not reproach them or maintain the idea of a return from
war. (250–51)

Like the Sausage-seller, then, Odysseus responds with indignation at a
situation that has the potential to change radically an otherwise generally stable
social order.[34]

This is not to say that the figure who acts like a blame poet cannot match
the behavior of the target. In the case of *Knights*, there follows a rambunctious
exchange between the Sausage-seller and the Paphlagonian in which each
claims that he will out-shout the other:

ΠΑ. καταβοήσομαι βοῶν σε.
ΑΛ. κατακεκράξομαί σε κράζων.
ΠΑ. διαβαλῶ σ᾽, ἐὰν στρατηγῇς.
ΑΛ. κυνοκοπήσω σου τὸ νῶτον . . .

P.: I'll shout you down by shouting! SS: I'll yell you down by yelling!
P: I'll slander you, if you act as a general! SS: I'll whup your backside
like a dog's! (286–89)

Each figure proceeds, as well, to threaten the other with physical violence, but the balance of power is stacked against the Paphlagonian, who has
to contend all alone against the combined force of the Sausage-seller, the
slave, and the twenty-four members of the chorus. The slave exclaims in his
valediction to the Sausage-seller, as he and the Paphlagonian exit just before the parabasis:

---

34. Nagy 1979, 262, 262n4, also notes that Thersites' quarrels with the kings were a threat to
the "established order of things," as Homer makes clear himself in line 213–14: ὃς ἔπεα φρεσὶ ἦσιν
ἄκοσμά τε πολλά τε ᾔδη ‖ μάψ, ἀτὰρ οὐ κατὰ κόσμον, ἐριζέμεναι βασιλεῦσιν. But I do not agree
that "the expression *kata kosmon* 'according to the established order of things' . . . implies that blame
poetry, when justified, has a positive social function." This view holds that Thersites is somehow a
blame poet "gone bad" or the like, and that there can be blame poetry that would somehow work
"against the established order" and still be beneficial. More often than not, blame poets prefer to see
the established order (or what they perceive as the established order) preserved rather than overturned—another reason not to think of Thersites as analogous to a "blame poet."

μέμνησό νυν
δάκνειν, διαβάλλειν, τοὺς λόφους κατεσθίειν,
χὦπως τὰ κάλλαι᾿ ἀποφαγὼν ἥξεις πάλιν.

Now remember to bite him, slander him, devour his comb, and make
sure you come back again having eaten up his wattles. (495–97)

Likewise, Odysseus exercises his physical superiority over Thersites at the
end of the episode, where he first threatens him with frightening severity, and
then strikes him on the forehead and back:

εἰ μὴ ἐγώ σε λαβὼν ἀπὸ μὲν φίλα εἵματα δύσω
χλαῖνάν τ᾿ ἠδὲ χιτῶνα, τά τ᾿ αἰδῶ ἀμφικαλύπτει,
αὐτὸν δὲ κλαίοντα θοὰς ἐπὶ νῆας ἀφήσω
πεπλήγων ἀγορῆθεν ἀεικέσσι πληγῇσιν.
ὣς ἄρ᾿ ἔφη, σκήπτρῳ δὲ μετάφρενον ἠδὲ καὶ ὤμω
πλῆξεν·

. . . if I do not take you and strip away your personal clothing,
your mantle and your tunic that cover over your nakedness,
and send you thus bare and howling back to the fast ships,
whipping you out of the assembly place with the strokes of indignity."
So he spoke and dashed the sceptre against his back and shoulders. . . .
(2.261–66; trans. Lattimore)

The quarrel between Odysseus and Thersites, therefore, dramatizes a full-
blown *psogos*, reflecting the behavior not just of the party who initiates the
blaming, but of both antagonists, who play roles that must be judged in different ways by the audience, as one would expect in the case of a genuine performance of a blame poet, where the distinction between target and poet was
clear. It is easy enough to see why scholars have typically seen Thersites as
analogous to the blame poet within a *psogos*, since the poet is typically the one
who portrays himself as the initial aggressor. But as our comparison with
Aristophanes' *Knights* made clear, a full *psogos* will always include aggression
and blaming from two sides, and it is not always immediately apparent in a
given narrative who plays which role. We have seen that the activity of blaming alone is an insufficient criterion for determining which antagonist is the
poet-figure and which the target. Rather, the blame poet will normally need
to be portrayed as *justified* in the eyes of the audience in his attempt to right a
perceived wrong on their behalf, however jocularly or ironically. What makes
the Thersites episode so confusing is that Homer's narrative is constructed
essentially as a "reverse" *psogos*, in which we are treated *first* to the base behavior (Thersites') that inspires the righteous indignation of the figure

(Odysseus) who reacts as a blame poet would if he were to compose a first-person version of the occasion.

Once again, it is illuminating to compare the Homeric scene with the *psogos* in Aristophanes' *Knights*, which has a far more typical structure. The play establishes in the opening scenes the putative threat to society, namely Cleon (well established before the Paphlagonian/Cleon even appears on stage at 235, and confirmed as the poet's own point of view in the parabasis, 509–11). The play's opening, that is, allows the audience to answer the hypothetical question implicit in all *psogoi*, namely "Why am I, the poet who composes this work, so upset that I am driven to mockery in this particular case?" By the time the Cleon-figure is brought on to respond to the poet's attacks, his status as target and his reprehensible behavior have been well identified for the audience (even the first five lines of the play leave no doubt about this). The Thersites episode works similarly, in that the audience here too first encounters a subversive buffoonish character (Thersites), who is then dressed down by an indignant mocker (Odysseus).

The parallel structure of these episodes highlights a crucial feature of *psogoi*: Whatever the target did to motivate the blamer's mockery was done in the *past*, and the poet's mockery will always *respond* to such a past deed. Typically in satire, the audience enters into the narrative well after the target's alleged misbehavior, with the result that the poet *seems* to be the one initiating the *psogos*. One might say, for example, that when Juvenal attacks hypocritical philosophers and same-sex marriages in Satire 2, he is the one picking a fight without any real provocation. But the pretense of such a satire is actually reactive, implying as it does that something horrible has already happened "out there" in society that must be corrected through the poet's efforts. Where the Thersites episode differs is only at what point in the history of this *psogos* that the narrative begins. Homer begins the episode not from the vantage point of the justified satirist, but from that of the figure who will function, by the end of the passage, as the satirist's legitimate target.

Nagy sensed that something was reversed in this passage, since Thersites himself ends up being laughed at as an object of ridicule, despite the fact that Homer noted in line 215 that the laughter he normally sought from his audiences seems not to have been at his own expense.[35] But this would only seem

---

35. In point of fact this is very difficult to determine from the text. If we think of Thersites, as some have done, as fundamentally a "clown" figure (Freidenberg 1930), a deformed buffoon, distinguished for his "shame-causing" speech and appearance, as Lowry puts it (1991; cf. esp. 93–189), then the element of comedy (the *geloiion* of line 215) that he routinely strives for in his public speaking may well come at at his own expense. On the other hand, the passage implies that, despite the comic elements of Thersites' mockery of Agamemnon, he had intended to make a serious point of criticism; and in any case, he certainly had not anticipated that he would be physically beaten by Odysseus in response. From his point of view, that was an undesired and unanticipated humiliation, whereas in the hypothetical context of other past "comic" performances (when he would say

unusual if one assumes that Thersites must represent the figure of a blame poet.[36] Indeed, such an assumption, which, as I have argued in this chapter, seems misguided, led Nagy to infer that "Homeric Epos can . . . reflect the comic aspect of blame poetry, but that it does so at the expense of the blame poet. In the Thersites episode . . . it is Epos that gets the last laugh on the blame poet, not the other way around."[37] If my argument is correct, however, epic remains perfectly capable of representing a poetic *psogos* and of distinguishing with reasonable precision the different roles within it, and there is no reason to think that blame poetry as such is generically anathema to epic.

On the other hand, Nagy is right to raise the question of the relationship between epic and comedy, for if the Thersites episode dramatizes a bona fide poetic *psogos*, a certain amount of tension is inevitable between the inherently comic undercurrents of this genre and the more elevated, serious concerns of the epic in which it is embedded. Is there anything comic, after all, about Odysseus's verbal and physical attack on Thersites? Within the context of the narrative, Thersites is portrayed as offering a serious critique of Agamemnon's behavior (by which I mean that the narrative had set him up to respond to a serious issue of morale among the rank and file), and there is no question that Odysseus's response is motivated by genuine anger. At this point in the narrative, in other words, and within this generic framework, we are far removed from a performance context that might be considered comic; the epic audience is hardly prepared for anything like an Aristophanic play, or an iambographic vaudeville routine. The fact that, as we have already noted, Thersites is depicted from the outset as concerned with *geloia*, both in his thoughts and in his very physiognomy, problematizes the pretense of seriousness that the episode (*qua* epic) initially presumes. The same can be said of Odysseus's language at 2.257–64, quoted above, and his behavior in the ensuing verses (265–70):

ὣς ἄρ' ἔφη, σκήπτρῳ δὲ μετάφρενον ἠδὲ καὶ ὤμω
πλῆξεν· ὃ δ' ἰδνώθη, θαλερὸν δέ οἱ ἔκπεσε δάκρυ·
σμῶδιξ δ' αἱματόεσσα μεταφρένου ἐξυπανέστη
σκήπτρου ὕπο χρυσέου· ὃ δ' ἄρ' ἕζετο τάρβησέν τε,

---

things that were *geloiia*), he might very well have set himself up to be ridiculed as a buffoon or fool. From the point of view of the audience, and the narrating poet, however, the laughter they are steered toward is the laughter associated with the satirist's victory over his target.

36. Another useful way to look at this is in terms of Halliwell's (1991) distinction between "playful" and "consequential" laughter. Under normal circumstances, Thersites would be known as a jocular figure, who made people laugh without incurring any animosity against himself. But in the *Iliad*, he has produced laughter of the "consquential" sort, where the consequences are directed against him in the form of Odysseus's punishment." See Halliwell 1991, 283, with 281 and 291 on Thersites in particular.

37. Nagy 1979, 262.

ἀλγήσας δ' ἀχρεῖον ἰδὼν ἀπομόρξατο δάκρυ.
οἳ δὲ καὶ ἀχνύμενοί περ ἐπ' αὐτῷ ἡδὺ γέλασσαν·

So he spoke and dashed the sceptre against his back and
shoulders, and he doubled over, and a round tear dropped from him,
and a bloody welt stood up between his shoulders under
the golden sceptre's stroke, and he sat down again, frightened,
in pain, and looking helplessly about wiped off the tear-drops.
Sorry though the men were, they laughed over him happily. . . .
(2.265–70, trans. Lattimore)

Odysseus is here responding to what he regarded, within the context of
the epic plot, as a serious threat (in fact he had been charged by Athena at 2.179–
81 specifically to ensure that the Greeks did not flee to the ships), but this sense
of genuine urgency soon resolves itself into comedy. While it is difficult to judge
what the tone of Odysseus's oath against Thersites is, Homer makes it clear
that the Greek soldiers, who function as the audience of their "performance,"
were amused by the outcome of the altercation (line 270). Indeed, the manner
in which the scene is recounted is reminiscent of the Iambe-Demeter myth
that we discussed in the preceding chapter. For just as Iambe elicits laughter
from the grieving Demeter by hurling obscenity at her (and Baubo, in the alternate traditions, by exposing herself to her), here too a causal relationship is
noted between obscenity and laughter: The culmination of Odysseus's oath
against Thersites is that he will strip him of all his clothes, and he adds the
particular detail that he will even strip off those clothes that *cover his genitalia*
(τά τ' αἰδῶ ἀμφικαλύπτει, 262). This threat, combined with the physical blows
that Odysseus delivers, reduces Thersites to a position of extreme humiliation,
but it has the effect of making the Greeks "laugh sweetly" (ἐπ' αὐτῷ ἡδὺ
γέλασσαν) even though up to that point they have been very "upset" (οἳ δὲ
καὶ ἀχνύμενοί περ, 270). Just as we saw in the *Homeric Hymn to Demeter*,
where it was Iambe's obscene jesting (or Baubo's obscene *anasyrma*) that brought
a smile to the grieving goddess, here too, it is a Odysseus's comically obscene
image of a stark-naked Thersites that contributes to the altered mood of the
Greek soldiers at the end of the scene. Whereas the scene opened at a moment
of crisis and tension for the Greeks, it closes on a note of calm and respite, which
finds the potentially rebellious troops siding with Odysseus and the established
order that he represents.

3. Thersites as "True" Satirist in the *Aethiopis*

As in the stories of Iambe-Demeter and Heracles-Cercopes, the sense of comedy generated by transgressive speech and behavior in the Thersites episode

likewise transforms sadness into mirth, and potential danger into social harmony. But there is a crucial difference as well, which highlights the uneasy integration of comedy into epic. Unlike Demeter and Heracles in their roles as targets of abuse, Thersites suffers *real* violence at the hands of Odysseus within the narrative and sheds real tears. The beneficiaries of the scene's comedy, therefore, are the superior mocker (Odysseus) and his audience (the Greek soldiers), who renew their sense of purpose by humiliating the subversive Thersites. It would seem as if epic, generically more hospitable to the sarcastic humor typical of battlefield invective and vaunting than to the ironic, often self-undermining, stances of comic and satirical poets, needed to find a way actually to fulfil the threats made by the abuser within the narrative itself. It even seems as if in an epic context such as the *Iliad*, any comic drama must operate according to the dynamics of the heroic ethos that suffuses the work as a whole. As in the story of a real war, there are aggressors and enemies, and, like the barbs of real weapons, the verbal barbs found in epic—even wildly humorous ones—must have real consequences. Thersites suffers on both counts, reduced as he is to a state of emotional abjection by Odysseus's taunts, and physically subdued by his blows. How different the flavor of this comedy from that of the Paphlagonian on the Aristophanic stage, who is repeatedly chased and physically attacked throughout *Knights*, yet is always ready for a sharp rejoinder, up to his very last appearance (1248–52), where in a humorous burst of paratragedy he concedes defeat to the Sausage-seller and asks to be carried off on the *ekkyklema* like a dead tragic hero! The Paphlagonian's departure from the play is quick and painless, and his suffering more symbolic than real. At the end of the Thersites episode, audiences may or may not share in the laughter of the Greek soldiers, but his pain is palpably real, and whatever comedy can be said to remain in the passage is, like other Homeric passages involving comic derision, cruel and polarizing rather than playful.[38]

It has often been pointed out, in fact, that Thersites functions as a *pharmakos*, or "scapegoat," figure, onto whom, as Thalmann puts it, "all the emotion and potential violence that have accumulated in the first two books, and . . . over the ten years of war, are unloaded . . ."[39] Indeed, even outside of the *Iliad*, Thersites seems to be ineluctably marked as a sacrificial victim of sorts, for in the *Aithiopis*, as we will see, he is killed after abusing another of the Greek generals, this time Achilles. Whether or not these episodes imply

---

38. See Halliwell 1991, 279–81.

39. Thalmann 1988, 21. That Thersites bears some resemblance to a ritual scapegoat was noticed as long ago as Usener 1897, 42–63. For further bibliography and discussion, see Nagy 1979, 279–80; and Thalmann 1988, 21–28 (for an interesting Girardian reading of the passage). On the use of the term *pharmakos* by ancient iambographers and comic poets as a metaphor for their targets, see Rosen 1988, 21–24. On the Girardian *pharmakos*-model (see Girard 1986) applied more generally and theoretically to satire, see Seidel 1979, 16–21; and Bogel 2004, 44–47.

that Thersites behaves like a ritual scapegoat, may remain for the moment an open question, to which we will return in due course. First, however, it is worth comparing the stories of Thersites' death in the *Aithiopis* (as recorded by a variety of ancient sources) to his treatment in *Iliad* 2.[40] As I argue, these stories show Thersites in a different light, emphasizing a side of him that looks more like what we expect of a bona fide satirist, that is, one who displays an attitude of comic self-righteousness *endorsed by the narrative in which it is embedded*. The ancient anecdotes about his death at the hands of Achilles and the events that immediately follow, assume a narrative in which at least some of the Greek army understood that when Thersites behaved as a satirist rather than as a subversive, he did not deserve the sufferings that always seemed to dog him. The differences between the two Thersites stories will, in the end, confirm that ancient Greek audiences in virtually all periods were well-attuned to the distinction between true satirists, who blamed according to certain generic and occasional protocols, and genuine threats to social stability.

In Proclus's summary of the *Aithiopis*, which began where the *Iliad* left off, we find the following outline of a story about the death of Thersites:

καὶ Ἀχιλλεὺς Θερσίτην ἀναιρεῖ λοιδορηθεὶς πρὸς αὐτοῦ καὶ ὀνειδισθεὶς τὸν ἐπὶ τῇ Πενθεσιλείᾳ λεγόμενον ἔρωτα· καὶ ἐκ τούτου στάσις γίνεται τοῖς Ἀχαιοῖς περὶ τοῦ Θερσίτου φόνου. μετὰ δὲ ταῦτα Ἀχιλλεὺς εἰς Λέσβον πλεῖ, καὶ θύσας Ἀπόλλωνι καὶ Ἀρτέμιδι καὶ Λητοῖ καθαίρεται τοῦ φόνου ὑπ' Ὀδυσσέως.

Achilles killed Thersites after having been reviled by him and reproached for the love he allegedly felt for Penthesileia. As a result, *stasis* arose among the Achaeans over the death of Thersites. After this, Achilles sailed to Lesbos, and after making a sacrifice to Apollo, Artemis, and Leto, he was purified of the murder by Odysseus.

(Proclus, *Chrestomathia* p. 67.25–26 Bernabé 1987 = p. 47.7–12 Davies 1988)

Evidently the *Aithiopis* opened with the story of the Amazonian warrior, Penthesileia, who had come to fight for the Trojans, but was killed by Achilles after fighting heroically.[41] It seems as if a report had been circulating that Achilles had fallen in love with Penthesileia (τὸν . . . λεγόμενον ἔρωτα), and

---

40. See now Marks 2005, esp. 15–23. Marks adduces parallels from Indic epic to emphasize the importance of Thersites' high social status, an argument with which I am sympathetic; see above n21, and further discussion below p. 97.

41. For a full account of the sources of the myth and iconography of Penthesileia, see Kossatz-Deissmann 1981 and Kauffmann-Samaras 1981.

certainly later writers often assumed that he had,[42] although is uncertain whether the veracity of the report was confirmed or denied in the *Aithiopis*. In any case, Thersites ridicules Achilles for something that others had already been talking about, whether or not it was actually true. In itself, this depicts a situation different from that in *Iliad* 2, for there Thersites' opposition to Agamemnon was cast by the narrator as a self-generated minority view, whereas in the *Aithiopis* Thersites evidently takes up the popular critical opinion on a preexisting controversial issue of the day—the report that Achilles had fallen in love with an enemy—and repackages it as a form of comic mockery against him. In each narrative Thersites attacks a superior, but each narrative characterizes the justification for each attack very differently: In the *Iliad*, Thersites' complaint against Agamemnon threatens to upset the order of events (and to undermine the *Dios boulê*, "Zeus' plan," which governs the entire action of the poem), and receives no endorsement from the Greek soldiers; but in the *Aithiopis*, Thersites reproaches Achilles for behavior that actually threatens to undermine the Greek cause against Troy.

Quintus Smyrnaeus, writing late (fourth-century CE) and no doubt with considerable embellishment, gives us an idea of what Thersites might have said to Achilles in an early *Aithiopis*, and even though Quintus's Greek soldiers (like those in the Iliadic episode) reveal no sympathy for Thersites,[43] it is clear that his taunting of Achilles has at least some measure of legitimacy. Like all good satirists, after all, Thersites here ridicules a conspicuous lapse of a prominent figure, pointing out that Achilles, smitten with an erotic attraction to the dead Penthesileia, came close to compromising his heroic stature, and so jeopardizing the entire Greek mission:

"ὦ Ἀχιλεῦ φρένας αἰνέ, τί ‹ἢ› νύ σε‹υ› ἤπαφε δαίμων
θυμὸν ἐνὶ στέρνοισιν Ἀμαζόνος εἵνεκα λυγρῆς
ἢ νῶιν κακὰ πολλὰ λιλαίετο μητίσασθαι;   725
καί τοι ἐνὶ φρεσὶ σῇσι γυναιμανὲς ἦτορ ἔχοντι
μέμβλεται ὡς ἀλόχοιο πολύφρονος ἥν τ' ἐπὶ ἕδνοις
κουριδίην μνήστευσας ἐελδόμενος γαμέεσθαι.
ὥς ‹σ'› ὄφελον κατὰ δῆριν ὑποφθαμένη βάλε δουρί,
οὕνεκα θηλυτέρῃσιν ἄδην ἐπιτέρπεαι ἦτορ,   730
οὐδέ νυ σοί τι μέμηλεν ἐνὶ φρεσὶν οὐλομένῃσιν

---

42. See [Apollodorus] *Epit.* 5.1–2, and Propertius 3.11.15 (part of a catalogue of famous women, who exerted extraordinary power over men). Quintus Smyrnaeus offers an extended, highly romanticized version of the story, *Posthomerica* 1.538–722, although it is impossible to know how much, if any, of the details derive from the version in the epic cycle.

43. In Quintus's version, the Greeks are said to have taken pleasure in Thersites' death; they hated him because he had quarreled with all of them at some point or other in the past (1.747–49). As in the *Iliad*, Thersites is treated here more as a target than a satirist, but as we will see shortly, the myth itself calls into question the legitimacy of Thersites' death.

ἀμφ᾽ ἀρετῆς κλυτὸν ἔργον, ἐπὴν ἐσίδησθα γυναῖκα.
σχέτλιε, ποῦ νύ τοί ἐστι †περὶ† σθένος ἠδὲ νόημα;
πῇ δὲ βίη βασιλῆος ἀμύμονος; οὐδέ τι οἶσθα
ὅσσον ἄχος Τρώεσσι γυναιμανέουσι τέτυκται;   735
οὐ γὰρ τερπωλῆς ὀλοώτερον ἄλλο βροτοῖσιν
ἐς λέχος ἱεμένης, ἥ τ᾽ ἄφρονα φῶτα τίθησι
καὶ πινυτόν περ ἐόντα. πόνῳ δ᾽ ἄρα κῦδος ὀπηδεῖ·
ἀνδρὶ γὰρ αἰχμητῇ νίκη‹ς› κλέος ἔργα τ᾽ Ἄρηος
τερπνά, φυγοπτολέμῳ ‹δὲ› γυναικῶν εὔαδεν εὐνή."   740
Φῆ μέγα νεικείων· ὁ δέ οἱ περιχώσατο θυμῷ
Πηλείδης ἐρίθυμος. Ἄφαρ δέ ἑ χειρὶ κραταιῇ
τύψε κατὰ γναθμοῖο καὶ οὔατος· οἳ δ᾽ ἅμα πάντες
ἐξεχύθησαν ὀδόντες ἐπὶ χθόνα, κάππεσε δ᾽ αὐτὸς
πρηνής· ἐκ δέ οἱ αἷμα διὰ στόματος πεφόρητο   745
ἀθρόον· αἶψα δ᾽ ἄναλκις ἀπὸ μελέων φύγε θυμὸς
ἀνέρος οὐτιδανοῖο.

"Wretched Achilles, what—has a spirit beguiled your heart for the pitiful Amazonian woman, who was bent on contriving evil things for us? Ah, your woman-crazed heart is after her as if she's a respectable wife whom one desires to woo with gifts and marry. Oh, I wish she had struck you first with her spear on the battlefield, since your heart takes such utter pleasure in women, and the moment you see a woman, you have no more care in your wretched soul for the glorious work of *aretê*! You fool!—what's become of your strength and your brains now? Where's the power we expect from a distinguished king? Don't you realize the misery the Trojans have suffered because of their own madness for women? There's nothing more destructive for mortals than the lust for sex, which makes sane men witless. But glory comes from hard work: For the fame that comes from victory and the deeds of Ares are the soldier's pleasures, while a woman's bed pleases the war-deserter." So he spoke in his wrangling; but the high-spirited son of Peleus became exceedingly angry. Immediately he struck him with his strong hand on his cheek and ear, and all his teeth flew out on to the ground, and he fell to the ground himself on his face. The blood poured forth from his mouth with a gush. And swiftly the cowardly soul of that worthless man fled from his limbs. . . . (Quintus Smyrnaeus *Posthom.* 1.723–47)

It is noteworthy that in the final lines of this passage Thersites articulates the most traditional values of heroic epos, (κῦδος; νίκη‹ς› κλέος; ἔργα Ἄρηος), which he sees threatened by erotic interests (γυναικῶν . . . εὐνή). Particularly poignant is the reminder in line 732–35 that it was precisely a weakness for women that brought ruin to the Trojans to begin with (οὐδέ τι οἶσθα ‖ ὅσσον ἄχος Τρώεσσι γυναιμανέουσι τέτυκται). Though critical of Achilles, this nevertheless implicitly upholds the notion of Greek superiority over Troy, and the legitimacy of the Greek war effort against them. In short, there is nothing *intrinsically* subversive about what Thersites says in the *Aithiopis* against Achilles, and in fact his satire amounts to a lament for lost virtue and nostalgia for a *status quo ante*—both stock satirical themes.

Rather, what clearly goads Achilles into a murderous rage at Thersites is his insubordination and presumption of a right to criticize his superiors. The Greek soldiers in Quintus's version echo what Odysseus said to Thersites in *Iliad* 2, namely, "quarrel with kings at your own peril!":

καί ῥά τις ὧδ᾽ εἴπεσκεν ἀρηιθόων Ἀργείων·
"οὐκ ἀγαθὸν βασιλῆας ὑβριζέμεν ἀνδρὶ χέρηι
ἀμφαδὸν οὔτε κρυφηδόν, ἐπεὶ χόλος αἰνὸς ὀπηδεῖ·
ἔστι θέμις, καὶ γλῶσσαν ἀναιδέα τίνυται Ἄτη,
ἥ τ᾽ αἰεὶ μερόπεσσιν ἐπ᾽ ἄλγεσιν ἄλγος ἀέξει"

Then someone spoke from among the warlike Argives: "It is not a good thing for a base man to wrangle with kings openly or in secret, since dire anger follows. It is the divine law, and Atê avenges a shameless tongue, she who produces pain upon pains for humans." (Quintus Smyrnaeus *Posthom.* 1.750–54)

ἴσχεο, μηδ᾽ ἔθελ᾽ οἶος ἐριζέμεναι βασιλεῦσιν·
οὐ γὰρ ἐγὼ σέο φημὶ χερειότερον βροτὸν ἄλλον
ἔμμεναι

. . . Stop, nor stand up alone against princes,.
Out of those who came beneath Ilion with Atreides
I assert that there is no worse man than you are.
(Homer, *Iliad* 2.247–49; trans. Lattimore)

Once again, we see how epic cannot comfortably accommodate a comic figure whose particular métier is satire. Despite the fact that, as Nagy has pointed out, all dictional and physical signs point to Thersites as a mythical figure of comedy, epic seems unable to deploy him as a comic genre might have, whether he serves there as a target or satirist. We have seen Thersites by now playing both roles, first that of the comic target in the *Iliad*, and then of the satirist in the *Aithiopis*, but in each case the framing narrative gives only the impression that the comedy he represents is, at best, a mere distraction from its own seriousness of purpose.

The story of Thersites' death (referred to in antiquity as the *Thersitoktonos*, cf. n. 67 below) however, contains curious details that suggest that within the narrative his role among the Greeks was misunderstood and his death considered, in the end, unjustified. Proclus's summary (above, p. 93) notes that after Achilles killed Thersites, he had to sail to Lesbos in order to propitiate Apollo, Artemis and Leto and then receive ritual purification from Odysseus.[44] This offers us little more than a summary, but it implies that the homicide was problematic enough to merit a complex purification ritual.[45] Something about Thersites' death did not sit well with all the Greeks, and "strife" arose among them (καὶ ἐκ τούτου <u>στάσις</u> γίνεται τοῖς Ἀχαιοῖς περὶ τοῦ Θερσίτου φόνου, "As a result, *stasis* arose among the Achaeans over the death of Thersites"). One explanation for this *stasis* is Thersites' unexpectedly distinguished provenance. He turns out to be related to Diomedes (Thersites' father, Agrios, was the brother of Diomedes' grandfather, Oineus),[46] and in Quintus, Diomedes raises angry objections to Achilles' slaying of his relative:

Τυδείδης δ᾽ ἄρα μοῦνος ἐν Ἀργείοις Ἀχιλῆι
χώετο Θερσίταο δεδουπότος, οὕνεκ᾽ ἄρ᾽ αὐτοῦ
εὔχετ᾽ ἀφ᾽ αἵματος εἶναι, ...   767–69

τοὔνεκα Θερσίταο περὶ κταμένοιο χαλέφθη.
καί νύ κε Πηλείωνος ἐναντίον ἤρατο χεῖρας,
εἰ μή μιν κατέρυξαν Ἀχαιῶν φέρτατοι υἷες

44. μετὰ δὲ ταῦτα Ἀχιλλεὺς εἰς Λέσβον πλεῖ, καὶ θύσας Ἀπόλλωνι καὶ Ἀρτέμιδι καὶ Λητοῖ καθαίρεται τοῦ φόνου ὑπ᾽ Ὀδυσσέως. ("After this, Achilles sails to Lesbos, and after having offered a sacrifice to Apollo, Artemis and Leto, is purified of the murder by Odysseus.")

45. Achilles' trip for ritual purification seems unusual and significant. As Gagarin 1981, 17–18, has noted, in all of the Homeric (and cyclic) evidence only one instance of homicide (out of the 31 he collects) other than Achilles' slaying of Thersites leads to a ritual purification, and he concludes that there is almost "no hint in the epics that religious pollution was one of the consequences of homicide." As Parker 1983, 130–31 has noted, Homer's silence about purification for bloodshed was noticed even in antiquity, and variously explained. Parker (133–43) argued that, although "purification" is never mentioned in Homer, the concept of pollution was still operative throughout the poems, if itself never explicitly articulated. Nevertheless, the purification of Achilles in the *Aithiopis* remains our first example of the phenomenon, and the fact that Proclus's brief summary of the episode makes mention of it implies that the ritual was anything but routine, and that the murder of Thersites was a particularly transgressive act that merited a particularly scrupulous atonement. This may be what led Moulinier 1952, 42–43, to describe Achilles' purification at Lesbos as "un nettoyage . . . non plus matériel . . . plutôt un nettoyage . . . morale."

46. For further discussion of Thersites' parentage, see Kullman 1960, 148; Gantz 1993, 621–22; Spina 2001, 3; and Marks 2005, 2n3. Marks emphasizes, rightly, I think, that it is precisely Thersites' high social status that gives him the "right" to quarrel with kings: "repeated public confrontations between 'men of standing' and 'men of the people' simply are not an established feature of Homeric society" (24).

πολλὰ παρηγορέοντες ὁμιλαδόν· ὡς δὲ καὶ αὐτὸν
Πηλείδην ἑτέρωθεν ἐρήτυον.   774–78

But only the son of Tydeus among the Argives was angry at Achilles
over the death of Thersites, since he claimed to share the same
blood-line . . .

So he was distressed over Thersites' death, and he would have raised
his hands against the son of Peleus, if the noblest sons of the
Achaeans had not crowded round him to urge him against it; so too
they restrained the son of Peleus from the other side.

It is difficult to know how to understand this aspect of the story. On the
one hand, Quintus's version implies that the dispute over Thersites' death was
a private matter between Achilles and Diomedes, soon resolved by the intervention of mediators. On the other, Proclus's summary suggests that the issue
divided the Greek army into factions (στάσις γίνεται τοῖς Ἀχαιοῖς).[47] Proclus
makes no mention of Diomedes in a short passage otherwise replete with proper
names (note his specificity about the gods to whom Achilles must sacrifice:
θύσας Ἀπόλλωνι καὶ Ἀρτέμιδι καὶ Λητοῖ), and the implied causal link between the dispute over Thersites' death and Achilles' trip to Lesbos for ritual
purification is painfully tantalizing (μετὰ δὲ ταῦτα Ἀχιλλεὺς εἰς Λέσβον
πλεῖ): What happened in the narrative to motivate the trip to Lesbos? Was it
felt to be the only way to assuage indignation over what was perceived to be an
unjustified homicide? Was Achilles' sacrifice demanded by the gods, indicating that the death of Thersites was felt, at least by some, to be cosmically
offensive?

4. Thersites and Aesop

Some answers to these questions suggest themselves when we consider the
parallels that scholars have drawn between the death of Thersites and the tradition about the death of Aesop.[48] According to the Aesopic *vita*, Aesop offended the Delphians with his pointed moralistic storytelling, to the point
where the rulers (ἄρχοντες) began to worry that he would damage their reputation (Vitae G + W 127). They decided, therefore, (with the encouragement

47. It is possible that Proclus's phrasing is loose here; to say that "stasis arose among the
Greeks," may be an imprecise way of representing a feud between Achilles and Diomedes alone. It
is hard, however, to overlook the fact that stasis tends to imply strife on a civic scale, and Proclus's
phrase leaves the impression that, if the dispute began between Achilles and Diomedes, it esca-
lated to the level of genuine factionalism among the Greeks.
48. Nagy 1979, 280–88.

of Apollo, who himself was angry at Aesop for an earlier slight) to execute him by planting a sacred cup in his bags and then accusing him of theft. On the point of being tossed from a cliff by the Delphians, Aesop cursed his accusers for their unjust act and threw himself to his death.[49] *Vita* G concludes tersely that the Delphians were subsequently afflicted by a plague, which could only be alleviated by expiating the death of Aesop (λοιμῷ δὲ κατασχεθέντες οἱ Δέλφιοι χρησμὸν ἔλαβον παρὰ τοῦ Διὸς ἐξιλάσκεσθαι‹τὸν› τοῦ Αἰσώπου μόρον, 142 Perry). A papyrus version of the vita (P.Oxy. 1800 fr. 2 ii.32–63 = Testim. Perry 25) notes that, in response to the oracle, the Delphians honored Aesop with a hero cult. Wiechers analyzed these stories in great detail, and showed that Aesop functions in them as a *pharmakos*-figure, that is, as the marginalized figure cast out by a society as a means of ritual purification.[50] As early as 1897, Usener suggested that Thersites seems to function as a *pharmakos*, and more recent scholars have found it instructive to compare Thersites with Aesop in this regard.[51] The similarities between the figures are compelling. To name only a few: Both are described as ugly and deformed,[52] and both are ultimately killed for insulting men of status and power.[53] For our purposes, it is worth noting that both are killed, in essence, because they are satirists.[54]

49. Αἴσωπος καταρασάμενος αὐτούς, καὶ τὸν προστάτην τῶν Μουσῶν μάρτυρα προσκαλούμενος, ὅπως ἐπακούσῃ αὐτοῦ ἀδίκως ἀπολλυμένου, ἔρριψεν ἑαυτὸν ἀπὸ τοῦ κρημνοῦ κάτω, *Vita* G, 142 Perry.

50. Wiechers 1961, 31–42. See also Nagy 1979, 28–88; and Parker 1983, 260–62. On the evidence for historical scapegoat rituals, see Bremmer 1983.

51. On Thersites as a *pharmakos*, see Usener, 1897, 244; on the connection between Thersites and Aesop, see the discussions in Nagy and Parker, cited in the previous note.

52. The opening sentences of the G + W *vitae* of Aesop sum up his unattractive qualities:

ὁ πάντα βιωφελέστατος Αἴσωπος, ὁ λογοποιός, τῇ μὲν τύχῃ ἦν δοῦλος, τῷ δὲ γένει Φρὺξ τῆς Φρυγίας· κακοπινὴς τὸ ἰδέσθαι, εἰς ὑπηρεσίαν σαπρός, προγάστωρ, προκέφαλος, σιμός, σόρδος, μέλας, κολοβός, βλαισός, γαλιάγκων, στρεβλός, μυστάκων, προσημαῖνον ἁμάρτημα . . . ("Aesop, the teller of fables, useful for all things in life, happened to be a slave, but was originally a Phrygian from Phrygia, disgusting to look at, useless as a servant, potbellied, with a distorted head, snub-nosed, mute, dark-colored, dwarfish, bent-legged, short-armed, twisted, big-lipped, a public aberration. . . ." *Vita* G, 1 Perry)

53. Aesop's social status is clearly low in contrast to those whom he routinely rebukes. On Thersites' social status, see above n. 21; while his genealogy makes it clear that he has "kingly" status, Homer nowhere alludes to this in *Iliad* 2, and describes him in terms that would easily lead one to align him with low-born commoners. See Marks 2005, 4–5.

54. See Nagy 1979, 286–87, who notes that Aesop's hero cult is "based on his death as a poet." I do not see, however, as Nagy proceeds to argue (287) how Aesop can be construed in a meaningful way as a "praise poet" in addition to his more apparent role as a "blame poet." There is no reason why a *psogos* may not include "praise" if it is contextually motivated (such as if a satirist wishes to contrast his target to someone or something that he would himself endorse and so praise). People may be targeted for blame from within the genre of praise poetry (such as Pindar's famous complaint about Archilochus [*Pyth.* 2.55–56]), but this does not transform Pindar into a "blame poet" himself.

Even allowing for the fact, however, that in myth and ritual *pharmakoi* could take many forms,[55] in at least one crucial respect Thersites and Aesop do not seem to follow a conventional *pharmakos* pattern: Their respective deaths require atonement from their killers.[56] Under normal circumstances, ritual *pharmakoi* were undesirable and expendable, whether morally or aesthetically,[57]

55. Actual *pharmakoi* such as those chosen to be expelled from the city during the Thargelia festival seem to have been criminals (see Bremmer 1983, 305), although in literature and myth there was a parallel tradition in which individuals of high social standing would be expelled as a pollution on the land. Bremmer (303) notes the remarkable range of categories from which scapegoats could be (at least hypothetically) drawn—"criminals, slaves, ugly persons, strangers, young men and women, and a king"—and finds in them a common element of social marginality. The "scapegoat-king" may be an exclusively literary construct, but has provided a useful model for understanding such well known tragic figures as Oedipus (whose incestuous past had brought the plague upon Thebes) or Pentheus (whose blindness to the power of Dionysus is responsible for the murderous rampage of the Theban women). See Parker 259–60, with bibliography. Dodds (1960, ad loc. p. 196) saw a hint of the *pharmakos* ritual in Euripides *Bacchae* 963 (Dionysus speaking of Pentheus): μόνος σὺ πόλεως τῆσδ᾽ ὑπερκάμνεις, "you alone toil on behalf of the city." For discussion of the "scapegoat-king" see Parker 1983, 265–71.

56. It is difficult to find other instances of a bona fide *pharmakos* (that is, a figure explicitly identified as a *pharmakos*, not just one who may exhibit certain characteristics associated with *pharmakoi*) whose exile or execution was regarded as unjustly administered. The aitiological myth of the primal Pharmakos, as preserved by the historian Istros (via Harpocration = *FGrH* 334 F 50) makes him a simple thief, stoned to death by Achilles' men for having stolen a sacred bowl of Apollo, and the excerpt tells us nothing about his guilt or innocence: ὅτι δὲ ὄνομα κύριόν ἐστιν ὁ Φαρμακός, ἱερὰς δὲ φιάλας τοῦ Ἀπόλλωνος κλέψας ἁλοὺς ὑπὸ τῶν περὶ τὸν Ἀχιλλέα κατελεύσθη, καὶ τὰ τοῖς Θαργηλίοις ἀγόμενα τούτων ἀπομιμήματά ἐστιν, Ἴστρος ἐν α΄ τῶν Ἀπόλλωνος Ἐπιφανειῶν εἴρηκεν. It seems clear that the detail of his crime influenced the tradition of Aesop's "crime," except that in Aesop's case the charge of stealing the bowl is known to the audience of the narrative to be false from the start. It is easy to see why Nagy 1979, 280, would assume that Pharmakos was unjustly accused of theft and unjustly stoned to death by Achilles' men, given the parallels with the Aesop story. But the aorist participle κλέψας implies, at least, that the narrator thought Pharmakos was, in fact, guilty as charged. In any case, there is no mention in Istros' testimony about the necessity for the Greeks to atone for Pharmakos's death. We are on firmer ground, however, with a similar aition attributed to Helladios by Photius (*Bibl.* 279, 534a3–4 Bekker) about a Cretan named Androgeos, which accounts for the Athenian scapegoat ritual: . . . λαβὸν τὴν ἀρχὴν ἀπὸ Ἀνδρόγεω τοῦ Κρητός, οὗ τεθνηκότος ἐν ταῖς Ἀθήναις παρανόμως τὴν λοιμικὴν ἐνόσησαν οἱ Ἀθηναῖοι νόσον, καὶ ἐκράτει τὸ ἔθος ἀεὶ καθαίρειν τὴν πόλιν τοῖς φαρμάκοις. Here it is clear that the unjust death of Androgeos causes a plague, which will only go away with the establishment of a ritual that reenacts the original injustice. See Wiechers 1961, 41–42; and Nagy 1979, 280.

57. Parker 1983, 258: "In practice [the *pharmakos*] was some miserable creature—physically repulsive, a condemned criminal, a beggar—who could be forced into the role or would even accept it voluntarily in return for the preliminary feeding that it brought with it . . . Aetiologically, however, the *pharmakos* is not merely a wretch but also a villain. . . ." This is certainly the case with Aristophanes' final send-off to Cleon/Paphlagonian in the final lines of *Knights*, 1395–1408, where he is banished to the outskirts of the city, and even referred to as (1405) as a *pharmakos*. In myth, it is worth remembering that the abjection of the *pharmakos* is often a state to which an ostensibly noble character descends, when it is discovered that he harbors some form of polluting guilt. Oedipus is an obvious example of this, as discussed in Vernant, 1990 [1972], 131–33; Burkert 1979, 65–66; Parker 1983, 260–80; Bremmer 1983, 304; and Foley 1993, 525–38 (with further bibliography, 525n4). Indeed, the scapegoat ritual itself, as it was practiced at the Thargelia and other related

and as such it is difficult to imagine them being welcomed back into the very society which had expelled them earlier in the name of the communal good. Walter Burkert describes the culmination of the *pharmakos* ritual as "rites of contact and separation to establish the polar opposition, those active and safe on the one side, the passive victim on the other. . . . The unquestioned effect of the procedure is salvation of the community from evil and anxiety, *which disappears with the doomed victim*" (my emphasis).[58] In the cases of Thersites and Aesop, however, precisely the opposite occurs: Their deaths bring only trouble to their respective communities—*stasis* to the Greeks at Troy, a plague on the Delphians who executed Aesop—which with hindsight seems to be a mistake.

Clearly both stories reflect a very specific aitiology for a *pharmakos*-ritual, namely an event that demands the expiation of communal guilt for a past crime by reenacting the original crime itself. Wiechers pointed out in his discussion of the death of Aesop that in this regard the story seems analogous to the aition of the *Bouphonia* ritual, which celebrated the primordial blood sacrifice of a bull, but which viewed the sacrifice itself as a crime that demanded atonement in the form of an annual ritual reenactment of the original ox-murder.[59] Wiechers also noted the parallels between Aesop and Androgeos (see above, n. 56), whose unjust death, according to Helladios, caused a plague and motivated the institution of scapegoating at Athens. If, however, Thersites and Aesop function within their narratives as figures who *motivate* ritual reenactments of a primordial crime, their status as *aitiological* forces is fundamentally different from the status of those figures who merely *reenact* the ritual. It seems misleading, therefore, to regard Thersites and Aesop as themselves *pharmakoi*, since the *pharmakoi* of actual ritual were by and large regarded as expendable embodiments of pollution, even if the rituals had their origins in the celebration of individuals who had attained a kind of heroic status.

It is hard to tell whether ritual *pharmakoi* played out some sort of scripted narrative of the original aitiological story,[60] or whether they remained more or less in character as the reprobates that they presumably were in real life. In

---

occasions throughout Greece, required that the victim be treated like a person of significance before being driven from the city. Usually this involved feeding the intended victim well at public expense, and dressing him in fine clothes preliminary to his expulsion. For examples, see Bremmer 1983, 305.

58. Burkert 1979, 67.

59. Wiechers 1961, 38–52; for a detailed discussion of the Bouphonia, and the Athenian Dipolieia, where it was practiced, see Burkert 1983 [1972], 136–43.

60. Possibly this is what lies behind Istros's ἀπομιμήματα, which he uses to describe what occurred at the Thargelia. Nagy 1979, 280, speculates that the word might refer to the ritual deaths of *pharmakoi* "stylized in song and dance," but it is not clear whether he would conceive of such performances as retelling an unchanging primordial tale, or describing the death of a contemporary chosen as a *pharmakos* and known to the participants in the ritual.

any case, the difference between Thersites (in the *Thersitoktonos* tradition) and Aesop on the one hand, and actual *pharmakoi* on the other, is that with the former, despite whatever negative qualities they may have (physical appearance, speech patterns, etc.) that lead to their destruction, they are in the end posthumously reintegrated into the community through rites of expiation and atonement, while real *pharmakoi* are simply expelled, and along with them, ideally, a community's problems and anxieties.[61] The audience of the Aesopic *vitae*, for example, never loses sight of Aesop's "real" nature, his moral superiority that contrasts with the folly of his targets. They share in his indignation when he is abused, and are privy all along to the trumped-up nature of the charges that lead to his execution. Ultimately, readers of the *vitae* may understand *why* Aesop suffered as he did, and they can easily infer from his demise an object lesson about the perennial dangers of satirical modes. But from the narrator's point of view, Aesop is a righteous man, innocent of the charges laid against him and undeserving of his death.[62] Needless to say, this seems a long way from the ritual *pharmakos* attested for the celebration of the Thargelia, who, as far as we can tell, retained his disreputable status throughout the ritual.

The deaths of Thersites and Aesop, then, may well be related as stories that aitiologically account for subsequent *pharmakos*-rituals, but the most profound aspect of their affiliation has to do with why they must die in the first place. We have already noted that both deaths require expiation of some sort, and that this implies disapproval of their deaths at the divine level. If we ask what exactly the gods might disapprove of about the way in which they were

---

61. Burkert 1979, 67–68.

62. Presumably, an actual ritual scapegoat, even if he was chosen because of a reputation for criminality, was also, technically speaking "innocent" of the charges that a community laid upon him as an excuse for exile. In this sense, the various *pharmakos*-aitia that we have examined here illustrate how the actual "guilt" of a scapegoat is less relevant than the communal presumption of it. In the ritual, that is, scapegoats are made "guilty" by the simple fact of being chosen, as if in compensation for an originary moment when a community had to find someone to sacrifice for the greater good. Burkert (1979, 71–72) tried to imagine such a moment when a community is desperate to save itself by handing over one of its members to a certain death, whether to "hungry carnivores" or enemy humans, but remains uncomfortable with the decision. Hence the victim is "termed subhuman, particularly guilty" or "raised to the superhuman level, to be honored forever." The situation is different, however, in the case of those we may consider specifically "aetiological" (as opposed to "ritual") *pharmakoi*, such as Thersites or Aesop, for neither can be said to be "blameless" insofar as they actually did provoke someone to the point of killing them. From the point of view of the narratives in which their stories are told, they may be "innocent" in a legal sense, and their capital "punishment" may appear disproportionate to their alleged "crimes," but they are not innocent in the same way as the victim in Burkert's hypothetically primordial scenario, where a desperate community has to find someone to sacrifice in order to avert imminent disaster. Even if that community had to rationalize their choice by assigning some sort of guilt to the victim, such guilt would have been fabricated in response to a situation for which they could themselves bear no responsibility; in the case of Thersites and Aesop, by contrast, their behavior (Thersites' mockery of Achilles, Aesop's satirical pronouncements to the Delphians) is directly implicated in the situation that leads—however unfairly—to their deaths.

treated, the answer would be this: Both Thersites and Aesop were satirists, ridiculing, as satirists always have, anyone who might seem morally compromised, foolish, or hypocritical. Both died, in short, as a result of their mockery. The gods evidently found this a great injustice, and they saw to it that the community suffered for it until proper measures of atonement were taken. Both stories, therefore, embed a commentary on the nature of satirical blaming (not unlike what we discovered in the myth of the Cercopes in the previous chapter) and, in particular, on the relationship the satirist should have with his audience and targets. In the *Thersitoktonos* story these relationships are subtly, yet forcefully, articulated: Thersites ridicules his target Achilles for his love of Penthesileia and for failing to behave according to the principles of heroic *andreia*. Given Thersites' reputation elsewhere in epic (for example, *Iliad* 2) as a stylized buffoon and incorrigible mocker, one might well wonder why Achilles here responds to his mockery with murderous fury rather than simple irritation, or even mild amusement. As we have noted, the putative audience of his performance, the Greek army, also seems to share Achilles' outrage, so it is all the more revealing that the story did not end with an uncomplicated portrayal of Thersites' death. Instead, it shows that the punishment was inappropriate to the crime, that a *verbally* aggressive attack—especially one delivered by a character known by all to be a comedian—does not call for a *physically* aggressive response. The target and audience have, in other words, misread the generic markers of satire, which ought to have been apparent in any performance in which Thersites was involved, and, like the Delphians responding to Aesop's mockery, they have excluded the comedy of blame from their social experience.

Thersites functions, therefore, differently in the *Aithiopis* than he does in *Iliad* 2. In the latter, when Odysseus dresses him down and literally beats him bloody, all the Greeks approve and, as we have seen, consider the altercation a kind of comic performance in which the target (here Thersites) is bested by the successful mocker (here Odysseus). His criticism of Agamemnon is presented as out of line, and the narrating poet makes it clear that his readers should conclude that Thersites got what he deserved. The *Thersitoktonos*, on the other hand, seems to turn Thersites into the justified mocker, who ultimately suffers for his art rather than for any truly actionable villainy. We have already noted how Thersites' mockery of Achilles (and Achilles' murder of Thersites in response) ultimately led to some sort of *stasis* among the Greeks, indicating that at least some of them did not think he deserved to die; and the fact that his death requires atonement from Achilles implies that his mockery has, at some level, a divine sanction. The Aesop story operates analogously, and if either story can be said to convey a message to its audience, it would be that legitimate satire has its place in society, however unsettling to its targets, and that the the satirist should be immune from retaliation. At the same time, as the stories also indicate—echoing the anxieties of satirists throughout history—

mockery and ridicule, performed even within a well-defined generic and occasional context, are inherently dangerous because they constantly risk being misunderstood by an audience all too willing to be convinced by the poet's own claims of ingenuousness.

5. The Boston "Thersitoktonos" Vase

It is unfortunate that we have so little ancient testimony about the death of Thersites. The brief summaries of Apollodorus and Proclus are relatively late, and leave many questions of detail unanswered, and Quintus's account seems idiosyncratically romanticized. Nevertheless, there is some literary and pictorial evidence indicating that the story captured people's imagination quite early. The fourth-century tragedian Chaeremon composed a play entitled either *Achilleus Thersitoktonos*, or simply *Thersites*,[63] and it is possible that in the previous century, an unassigned fragment of the comic poet Pherecrates refers to Achilles' slaying of Thersites:[64]

†ὸ δ' Ἀχιλεὺς εὖ πως ἐπὶ κόρρης αὐτὸν
ἐπάταξεν, ὥστε πῦρ ἀπέλαμψ' ἐκ τῶν γνάθων.

Achilles gave him a good blow to the jaw, so that fire shone forth
from his mouth (?)

Certainly, punching someone so hard in the jaw that the teeth fall out of one's mouth was a popular conceit of ancient comic hyperbole,[65] and it is easy to suspect, along with several early scholars,[66] that Chaeremon's drama was a satyr play rather than a tragedy. When distanced from the generic constraints of an epic narrative, it seems, the comic potential of Thersites could be developed more consistently, and the rather dark epic versions of his treatment at the hands of Odysseus and Achilles could be transformed into lighter fare, where an audience might witness the violence directed against him without feeling that any of the blood was real. Whether Chaeremon's play was tragic

63. *TrGF* I, 71 F 1a-3, p. 217–18. The two extant lines, one by Stobaeus, the other by the *Suda*, tell us virtually nothing about the plot of the play. For a full treatment of the evidence for Chaeremon's play, see now Morelli 2001, esp. pp. 73–168.

64. Pherecrates fr. 165 KA; as Paton 1908, 413 notes, if the fragment does refer to this episode, it would be the earliest reference we have.

65. Hipponax seems to be the recipient of such a blow at fr. 132 Dg: †οἵ δέ μεο ὀδόντες ἐν τοῖσι γνάθοισι πάντες κεκινέαται† and Degani 1991a (ad loc. p. 142) collects many other examples of this kind of scene.

66. E.g., Crusius, 1883, 152; Nauck in *TGF* 1.782. Morelli 2001, regards the play as a tragedy; for bibliography and discussion, see 90n25.

or satyric (and hence comedic), there would have been plenty of opportunity for the character Thersites to come into his own. It is easy to imagine the poet giving him ample space to defend his behavior at Troy, and to articulate his own understanding of the role he played as a satirist intent upon keeping the commanders honest. Beyond this it is difficult to speculate about what the plot of such plays might have looked like, but it would not surprise me to find that the comedic Thersites took as his starting point the controversial aspects of the epic episodes, and recounted them from an idiosyncratic and comically self-righteous perspective.

In the absence of more detail about the *Thersitoktonos* episode of the *Aithiopis*, we cannot say how much of an explicit commentary on Thersites' predicament the epic version itself would have offered, or what a comic version may have assimilated from it or parodied. There remains, however, one tantalizing piece of evidence which may put a little more flesh on the bare bones of the episode as we have come to understand it, and which, I think, may support my argument that the scene must have addressed the larger issue of Thersites' role as satirist at some point in the course of the narrative. I refer here to a fourth-century Apulian volute krater, housed in the Boston Museum of Fine Arts (figure 3.1), which evidently depicts the version of the *Thersitoktonos* ascribed by our later sources to the *Aithiopis*.[67] This large funereal vase offers an extraordinary, and virtually unique, rendition of the episode, and conveys a remarkable amount of narrative detail, even if a good deal of it remains obscure to us. The episode is painted on the front of the vase and its identification is assured by the names inscribed beneath each of the mythological characters. In the center of the scene Achilles and Phoinix are seated on a couch within a small building no doubt representing Achilles' hut (figure. 3.2). They gaze out at the action taking place toward the right of the building, where Menelaus seems to be restraining Diomedes from drawing his knife and attacking Achilles (figure 3.3). It is likely that Achilles is shown at the moment when he is springing up from his couch in order to meet Diomedes' challenge. To the left of the building, Agamemnon can be seen approaching, with arm outstretched as if to importune Achilles. Above Agamemnon and Menelaus on either side of the building are two pairs of gods: On the right Athena sits and Hermes stands facing her; on the left,

---

67. Boston 03.804. The fullest discussion of the vase is one of the earliest, Paton 1908, who collects the early bibliography on this type of vase and its iconography. The vase has been most recently published in Padgett, et al. 1993, 99–106, with detailed bibliography, 106. See also Ebert 1969; and Trendall and Cambitoglou 1982, 472. Morelli 2001, 135–68 maps the details of the vase on to Chaeremon's *Achilles Thersitoktonos* ("Un'analisi più approfondita del cratere di Boston viene pertanto a confermare che tutti i personaggi raffigurati sul vaso, ad eccezione di Pan, dovevano avere una parte più o meno rilevante nell' *Akhilleus Thersitoktonos* di Cheremone," 147). See his reconstruction of the action, 153–68.

FIGURE 3.1. Fourth–century BCE Apulian Krater from the Boston Museum of Fine Arts (03.804) depicting the death of Thersites (*Thersitoktonos*). Reproduced with permission from the Boston Museum of Fine Arts.

FIGURE 3.2. Boston *Thersitoktonos* vase, detail: Achilles and Phoinix inside.

positioned symmetrically with the pair on the right, a winged Poina, represented as an avenging Erinnys,[68] sits while Pan stands and looks at her. The
members within each divine pair seem to be conversing with one other. The
reason for the hubbub is obvious from the scene just below Achilles' hut, for
there we see Thersites gruesomely decapitated, his head shown flying and

68. On the iconography of Poina here, see Paton 1908, 411; and Aellen 1994, 39, 65, and 203
no. 9, pls. 13–14. Further bibiliography in Morelli 2001, 95n13.

FIGURE 3.3. Boston *Thersitoktonos* vase, detail: Menelaus restrains Diomedes.

whirling away from his body (figure 3.4).[69] The figure of Thersites is sur-
rounded by a variety of vessels that also appear to be flying chaotically in the

69. The name THERSITAS is inscribed immediately above his body. The head is turned so
as to face the body from which it was severed, allowing the artist to provide a frontal portrait, as
well as to give the impression that the head was rolling away. As Padgett et al. 1993, 99, note, "The
eyes of the liberated head are shut in death; the grizzled beard shows that Achilles has killed an
older man."

FIGURE 3.4. Boston *Thersitoktonos* vase, detail: Thersites' decapitated head flies from his body.

air, as if they had been violently knocked or deliberately thrown.[70] To the right, a slave (identified as *dmôs*)[71] appears to recoil in alarm, while on the left, Automedon observes the scene crouching, and perhaps taking refuge from the mayhem.

There can be little question that this vase represents some version of the *Thersitoktonos* ascribed to the *Aithiopis*, but it is impossible to tell how much of the detail found in the vase painting derived from the Cyclic poem. One wonders, for example, whether an avenging Poina made her appearance in the literary version; whether she was merely invoked in principle by Diomedes, aggrieved by the murder of his kinsman, or by Athena or Hermes, who also

70. Padgett et al. 1993, 103: "In the foreground and around Automedon...and the dead man are objects testifying to the violent action: a broken lustral basin, a tripod, a staff, a footbath, and a variety of metal vases, including two phialai, a kantharos, an oinochoe, and a volute-krater."

71. On the significance of the inscription *dmôs*, see Schmidt 2003, 171 and 2005, 202–3. Schmidt suggests that the generic identification of the slave might indicate that the painter was drawing from his engagement with a text (she suggests epic) rather than a performance. (I thank the late Professor Schmidt for sharing her ideas, and the references, on this topic with me *per litteras* before they were published.) See now also Morelli 2001, 100n33.

appear on the vase. In any case, the scene on the vase agrees with the summaries on all the major points: Achilles' slaying of Thersites angered Diomedes and caused a stir among the Greeks. Divine forces at some point entered the plot and vengeance was demanded of Achilles. The vase, however, offers some insight into a crucial aspect of the story that is lacking from the literary record, namely, the *occasion* on which Achilles killed Thersites. All we learn from the summaries is that Thersites ridiculed Achilles for falling in love with Penthesileia, and while it seems clear that Thersites must have abused Achilles to his face,[72] it is unclear what they were all were doing when this happened. In Quintus's account Thersites' rant seems to occur on the battlefield moments after Achilles' had killed Penthesileia, but no attempt at greater specificity is made, and Quintus seems to have had little interest in anything other than the abuse of Achilles and its consquences. In any case, the iconography of the Boston vase points in another direction, suggesting that the episode took place well after the battle in which Achilles had killed Penthesileia was over.[73]

Beneath Achilles' hut the artist was clearly trying to convey the details of a very specific scene as background to the pot's focal moment, when Achilles prepares to meet the challenge from Diomedes. The lower section, in other words, seems to represent an event in *past* narrative time that occasions the action in a *present* narrative time depicted in the central portions of the vase. Paton noted the peculiarity of the iconography in his early study of the vase, and in particular the fact that the scene seems far removed from the battlefield. He sensed too that the "presence and character of the scattered vases is surely of some significance,"[74] but he rejected prematurely, I think, a simple approach that may explain the context in which Thersites abused Achilles, and why his response was so controversial. The scattered vessels, in short, seem to indicate a banquet scene gone awry. Achilles' violent blow in this version sent Thersites' head and body rolling in different directions, and in their paths they overturned all the accoutrements of the room.[75] If Thersites mocked Achilles

72. In *Iliad* 2, Thersites rails against Agamemnon, but it not made clear exactly what Agamemnon was doing at the time. Presumably he was within earshot (Thersites addresses him in the second person, after all), but he never speaks; rather, Odysseus calls a swift halt to Thersites' abuse well before Agamemnon is allowed to react. One may wonder whether Odysseus functions here as a deliberate buffer, deflecting the possibility of a more extreme form of punishment from the person who was being directly abused, i.e., Agamemnon.

73. Morelli 2001, 60–62 and 153, suggests that Thersites' death (as depicted on the Boston vase and in Chaeremon's dramatic version of it) took place during an impromptu assembly at which the Greek leaders were arguing about the disposition of Penthesileia's armor.

74. Paton 1908, 415.

75. Paton 1908, 415, brought up the possibility of an "interrupted banquet," only to reject it on the grounds that "there is no sign of a table, most of the actors bear every mark of hasty arrival, and the attitude of Achilles is scarcely that of one who has been suddenly interrupted. . . ." Whether or not a table is necessary for indicating a banquet scene, Paton was misled by his assumption that the scene at the bottom of the vase must necessarily be taking place at the same time as the scene in

during some sort of convivial occasion, his abuse must be seen in a different light than if he confronted him in the flush of battle, when it would have been more difficult, not to mention inappropriate, for an audience to grasp markers of irony or other forms of poetic artifice.[76] A social setting such as a banquet, by contrast, would have provided Thersites with an ideal venue to engage in the type of comic performance that he was already known for among the Greeks at Troy (see *I.* 2.213–21). As we discussed earlier, his appearance and speech marked him as a comic type, a physically abject and therefore risible figure, whose role seemed always *épater le bourgeoisie* through his quarrelsomeness. When he engaged in this behavior in the unstaged moments of real life, such as in his altercation with Odysseus in *Iliad* 2, his behavior was more easily perceived as offensive insofar as there were no contextual cues to indicate that his mockery was anything other than what it claimed to be. The narrating Homer makes this clear enough in this scene by characterizing Thersites as a figure who is actually more worthy of blame than of dispensing it. In the *Thersitoktonos*, however, although we have very little detail of early versions, we can at least say that the punishment of Thersites was felt by some to be problematic, if not undeserved. The Boston vase may offer a clue as to why this was the case, for Thersites may have mocked Achilles on an occasion when, under normal circumstances, he ought to have had license to do so with impunity.

Invective discourse, after all, whether in the form of poetry, joking, or skolia, was frequently associated with sympotic contexts in early Greek culture, and the scene on the Boston vase, with its emphasis on the overturned vessels, may indicate that Thersites was killed during just such an occasion.[77] The importance of this possibility cannot be overstated, because it would mean that Thersites' mockery must be evaluated as a function of a social setting and performative context in which he was, paradoxically, as much a member of an in-group—a *philos*—as he was a pariah to his target. As Nagy has written, in explaining the dynamics of Archilochus's *psogos* against Lycambes, ". . . the

---

Achilles' hut. In fact, this seems absurd, given that Achilles was the one who had to have dealt the blow to Thersites in the first place, and he is here depicted as conferring with Phoinix in his hut in what appears to be a moment of contemplation, rather than one of violence and mayhem. Paton's own explanation of the scene is ingenious—"our artist had in mind a story in which Thersites met his death at the hands of Achilles while endeavoring to steal a treasure, which probably belonged to some god" (415)—but so speculative and tendentious as to be of little use. Paton was also troubled by the religious associations of some of the vessels in the scene, but at least half of them were appropriate to a banquet scene (note esp. the podanipter, the oinochoe, and the cantharus), and it would not have been inappropriate for the artist to intermingle lustral vessels with domestic ones.

76. On the banquet as a traditional locus in classical (and Near Eastern) literature and mythology of violence, see Paul 1991; and Bowie 2003.

77. On the association of *psogoi*, iambic poetry, joking, and other forms of comically transgressive modes, see Adrados 1975, 279; Pellizer 1983, 32; Nagy 1979, 244–45; Gentili 1988, 107–91; and Bartol 1992, p. 66–67.

iamboi composed against Lykambes qualify the poet as an *ekhthros* to his victim. Yet even an *ekhthros* may have to deliver his poetry in the context of a receptive audience—who would have to be, by contrast, *philoi* to him."[78] Adrados likewise described the symposium as possessing the "quality of a closed society with agonal and sporting elements."[79] A well-known passage from the *Homeric Hymn to Hermes* (55–58) confirms an early association between banquets, jocular sparring and formalized mockery,

> . . . Θεὸς δ' ὑπὸ καλὸν ἄειδεν
> ἐξ αὐτοσχεδίης πειρώμενος, ἠΰτε κοῦροι
> ἡβηταὶ θαλίῃσι παραιβόλα κερτομέουσιν,
> ἀμφὶ Δία Κρονίδην καὶ Μαιάδα καλλιπέδιλον,
> ὡς πάρος ὡρίζεσκον[80] ἑταιρείῃ φιλότητι,
> ἥν τ' αὐτοῦ γενεὴν ὀνομάκλυτον ἐξονομάζων·

> . . . and, testing it out, the god sang out improvised bits beautifully, as young men engage in scandalous mockery at festivals. He sang of Zeus the son of Cronos and finely-shod Maia, how they chattered in the spirit of companionable love, and recounting the tale of his own famous stock.

So too an elegiac poem, probably from the fourth century (*Adesp. eleg.* fr. 27W), mentions that jesting and comic mockery would routinely precede more serious performances at symposia:

> χαίρετε συμπόται ἄνδρες ὁμ[......· ἐ]ξ ἀγαθοῦ γὰρ
>   ἀρξάμενος τελέω τὸν λόγον [ε]ἰς ἀγα[θό]ν.
> χρὴ δ', ὅταν εἰς τοιοῦτο συνέλθωμεν φίλοι ἄνδρες
>   πρᾶγμα, γελᾶν παίζειν χρησαμένους ἀρετῇ,
> ἥδεσθαί τε συνόντας, ἐς ἀλλήλους τε φ[λ]υαρεῖν   5
>   καὶ σκώπτειν τοιαῦθ' οἷα γέλωτα φέρειν.
> ἡ δὲ σπουδὴ ἐπέσθω, ἀκούωμέν [τε λ]εγόντων
>   ἐν μέρει· ἥδ' ἀρετὴ συμποσίου πέλεται.

---

78. Nagy 1979, 243.

79. Adrados 1975, 279. Adrados also mentions a symposiastic association between "religious elements" and "obscenity and satire." A specific connection between obscenity and religious aspects of the symposium is difficult to gauge (see Bartol 1992, 66n2), but other ritual aspects of the Greek symposium are well attested. This answers Paton's denial that the Boston vase could represent a banquet scene on the grounds that there were religious vessels strewn around the area in addition to whatever vessels we might associate with dining.

80. On the reading ἠρίζεσκον (from *eris*) rather than ὡρίζεσκον, see Nagy 1979, 245 n.5. Nagy speculates that the young men ridiculing each other at a banquet were "reenacting" a "primal eris" that once took place between Zeus and Maia (Hermes's mother).

τοῦ δὲ ποταρχοῦντος πειθώμεθα· ταῦτα γάρ ἐστιν
ἔργ᾽ ἀνδρῶν ἀγαθῶν, εὐλογίαν τε φέρειν.   10

Greetings, fellow drinkers! [. . .] I begin with a good speech, and
will end up with a good speech. And whenever friends come together
for this sort of an affair, they should laugh and joke in accordance
with *aretê*, take pleasure as they convene, and insult and jeer in such
a way as to bring laughter. Let seriousness follow after, and let us
listen to people speaking in turn: This is the *aretê* of the symposium.
Let us obey the drinking-leader; for this is how good men behave,
and it brings good report.[81]

It is clear from both these passages, that within a sympotic setting, comic
mockery could be an integral part of the entertainment; line 4 of fr. 27W, in
fact, is explicit that this sort of activity could even be governed by a form of
aretê. These jocular encounters may have appeared unscripted and impromptu,
but they were entertaining to the company precisely because of the verbal skills
they elicited from the participants. In short, these contests were admired and
evaluated in accordance with a bona fide generic system.[82]

When we consider the iconography of the Boston krater in the light of this
literary background, it seems probable that, at least in the version that the
painter knew, Thersites had been mocking Achilles considerably after he had
killed Penthesileia, during some sort of occasion when the Greek troops had
gathered for a banquet. Indeed, it may be that Thersites' reputation as a persistent quarreler arose from his behavior at exactly this type of event. In *Iliad*
2, we remember, he was described as ἔχθιστος δ᾽ Ἀχιλῆϊ μάλιστ᾽ ἦν ἠδ᾽
Ὀδυσῆϊ, and the reason given is because he had a history of quarreling with
them (τὼ γὰρ νεικείεσκε). Although a symposiastic setting is not specified,
the iterative imperfect tense (νεικείεσκε) implies routine past behavior, and
the famous lines that introduce Thersites (212–15) suggest that he cultivated
a comic idiolect when wrangling with his targets:

Θερσίτης δ᾽ ἔτι μοῦνος ἀμετροεπὴς ἐκολῴα,
ὃς ἔπεα φρεσὶν ᾗσιν ἄκοσμά τε πολλά τε ᾔδη
μάψ, ἀτὰρ οὐ κατὰ κόσμον, ἐριζέμεναι βασιλεῦσιν,
ἀλλ᾽ ὅ τι οἱ εἴσαιτο γελοίϊον Ἀργείοισι

. . . Thersites of the endless speech, still scolded, who knew within
his head many words, but disorderly; vain, and without decency, to

---

81. See Ferrari 1988 for commentary on this poem.
82. On the question of whether the kind of jesting implied by this fragment included specifically iambic performances, see Bartol 1992, 66n9.

quarrel with the princes with any word he thought might be amusing
to the Argives. (trans. Lattimore)

From the standpoint of epic, Thersites' speech appeared indecorous and
chaotic, and could only be judged negatively, but he knew (εἴσαιτο) what
would draw a laugh and crafted his rhetoric accordingly. His habit of "quarreling with kings" was carried out with a distinct generic self-consciousness
that seems remarkably similar to the creative processes at work in the
symposiastic mockery that the infant Hermes sang about in his eponymous
hymn.

One might wonder how the deformed, buffoonish Thersites would have
found himself consorting with the likes of Odysseus and Achilles at banquets
on a military campaign, where presumably common soldiers did not much
consort with their social superiors. But what the *Iliad* passage does not reveal,
in its transparent effort to dehumanize Thersites, is that he quarrels with the
Greek leaders not as an insubordinate social inferior but as their social equal.[83]
As we noted above (p. 97), the *Thersitoktonos* shows that Thersites' kinship with
Diomedes makes him every bit as princely as those he routinely rails against,
and it is easy to imagine that he abused them as a *philos* among *philoi*.[84] As
the *Iliad* makes clear at 2.220, those for whom Thersites evidently reserved
his most intense abuse, Odysseus and Achilles, regarded him as ἔχθιστος,
but even their enmity would have evolved within the larger context of a community bound by ties of *philia*. As Nagy has said of Archilochus's mockery
of Lycambes and his daughters, although his "insults are against an *ekhthros*,
not a *philos* [, n]evertheless, they are in all likelihood framed for a general
audience of receptive *philoi*. . . ."[85] Likewise, every time Thersites would
contemplate what words would make his listeners laugh (ὅ τι οἱ εἴσαιτο
γελοίϊον Ἀργείοισιν), he was gauging the effects of his performance on an
audience of similarly "receptive *philoi*."[86] Certainly, the slaying of Thersites
would never have caused the problems it did if no one had felt some measure
of *philotês* toward him.

If, then, we are correct to infer from the Boston krater that Thersites ridiculed Achilles at an event where such behavior might have been expected,
possibly even welcomed, we begin to understand why his death created such a

83. See also above n. 21 on Thersites' social status.
84. There is also an Apulian calyx crater in Taranto in which Thersites oddly appears (his
identification assured by an inscription) in the company of such exalted figures as Helen, Leda,
Odysseus, and Menelaus (see Zimmermann 1997, 1207–9, catalogue no. 2). Schmidt (2003, 171)
suspects this scene might represent Helen's suitors—strange company for Thersites, to be sure,
but if so, it would corroborate the notion that he was the social equal of the other Greek princes.
85. Nagy 1979, 251.
86. As West 1974, 16, says of a set of particularly abusive elegiac couplets by Theognis (453–
56), "It is the perfection of its form, rather than the justice of the sentiment, that invites applause."

stir. From Achilles' point of view, Thersites had crossed a line in taunting him about Penthesileia. But from the audience's point of view, to kill a man for words spoken during a "performance" sanctioned by occasion and genre must have seemed an equal outrage, even if some of them might have found themselves sympathizing with Achilles' anger. This myth seems to illustrate, therefore, the perennial tension in satirical genres between the poeticized world of the satirist's production and the real world of his targets.

This tension was clearly felt and articulated on occasion in antiquity, as we can see, for example, from a passage in Plutarch (*Lycurgus* 12.6). In discussing the traditional mockery at Spartan *syssitia*, "common meals," he mentions some attempts at self-regulation when the mockery threatened to give real offense. Although mockery was customary on such occasions (αὐτοί τε παίζειν εἰθίζοντο καὶ σκώπτειν ἄνευ βωμολοχίας),[87] Plutarch notes, and normally targets did not mind being mocked (σκωπτόμενοι μὴ δυσχεραίνειν), if the mockery became unbearable, the target could ask for relief and the mocker would stop (μὴ φέροντα δὲ ἐξῆν παραιτεῖσθαι, καὶ ὁ σκώπτων ἐπέπαυτο). It would be good to know how common it was for someone to call a halt to formalized mockery of this sort; but even if it were merely an idealized notion Plutarch wanted to believe about Lycurgus's contribution to civilization, the anecdote points to an early awareness of the potential for performances of mockery or blame to be misconstrued by targets or audiences, no matter how many formal cues are provided by the mocker (for exampe, verbal or gestural) or the occasion itself. Achilles, as it seems from the Boston krater, was unprepared for the abuse he was to receive over Penthesileia, and no doubt uninterested at that point in the customs of after-dinner banter, and his intemperate response was lethal for Thersites.

Even though Thersites was a relatively minor figure in Greek myth, he was, in the end, chameleonic in revealing ways. As we have seen in this chapter, he was always a marginalized character with persistent comic associations, but assessments of his character varied according to the perspective of the narratives about him. In our comparison of the two epic narratives involving Thersites, we have found that the Iliadic episode treats him as purveying unjustified blame, and so he ends up in the eyes of the narrator (and of the audience within the narrative who witness the altercation) a *justifiable target* of Odysseus's anger. In the *Thersitoktonos* of the *Aithiopis*, by contrast, Thersites' "case" against Achilles' fleeting attachment to Penthesileia is likely to have been construed as legitimate, either because it was considered a genuine threat to

---

87. The phrase ἄνευ βωμολοχίας ("without buffoonery") implies perhaps a certain tameness or gentility to this form of jesting (see Nagy 1979, 245n3). But this probably refers to forms of diction (the mockery was perhaps less crude than it might have been), rather than a lessening of *ad hominem* bite. After all, as Plutarch says in the same passage, the Spartans felt it was important to know how to "endure mockery" (σκώμματος ἀνέχεσθαι).

military discipline, or because it was felt to constitute appropriate fodder for comic mockery. In both episodes, Thersites regards himself as a comic performer of sorts, but in the *Iliad* he becomes funny only when his own attempt at comedy fails and the Greek soldiers take malicious pleasure in the abject and humiliated state to which Odysseus reduces him. He is there, to be sure, an actor in a comedy, but the role of the self-righteous, controlling satirist with which he began is unexpectedly (for him) reversed, as his subversive attack on the political status quo is trumped by Odysseus's moral indignation. In the end, our epic narrator, Homer, treats Odysseus as the more appealing figure and the more successful mocker. In the *Thersitoktonos* tradition, however, Thersites is once again attacked for his blaming, this time fatally, but he seems here to emerge a veritable martyr for the comic cause, the satirist whose indignation was not only humorous, but was constructed so as to elicit the sympathy of an audience. He remains to the end, in short, a true satirist, even if it cost him his life.

These two episodes, therefore, are useful for clarifying the complex interrelationships we have been investigating throughout this study between the satirist and his target. In particular, they highlight what distinguishes the blamer from the blamed, the mocker from the mocked, in contexts where these roles are often blurred, if not interchangeable. We have seen how crucial a narrator's perspective is for cueing an audience to the distinction between these roles, especially when it comes to portraying the moral claims of two antagonists. A target can always mock back, and thus becomes the mocker. And vice versa, of course: The mocker can become the target when the original target counter-attacks more successfully. The terminology itself is labile and unstable, but a narrator has the power to clarify which antagonist at least *he* thinks *deserves*, within the parameters of the work, to be considered in which role. In so doing, he can make a more persuasive case—however disingenuous or comically absurd—for the justice of his mockery and blame. The figure of Thersites has proven to be an exemplary case of precisely this sort of narratological manipulation, for while he may be a blamer in both of the episodes we have examined, each narrative draws out different nuances of his blaming and shows how these nuances can only be assessed as a function of the *relationship* between two antagonists. In the end, only the narrator can sort out for the audience where their sympathies are "supposed" to lie when they witness a scene of reciprocal mockery and abuse.

4

Shifting Perspectives of Comic Abjection

Odysseus and Polyphemus as Figures of Satire

The preceding chapter has emphasized the importance of analyzing the contextual cues at work in ancient literary mockery, which allow us to understand how such poets could stake out their generic territory as satirists and construct for themselves an audience implicitly sympathetic to their putative goals. While the satirist has no actual control over how an audience will respond to his work, and will, in fact, routinely complain that people misunderstand him, he composes as if he imagines himself in the presence of an audience with whom he can collude against the rest of the world.[1] Satirical poetry, as we have repeatedly seen, depends upon precisely this sort of an oppositional stance: Whether the poet deploys invective, banter, parody, sarcasm or simple complaint in the service of his satire, his attitude is aggressive and confrontational, and as such demands, at least implicitly, that an audience take sides. Since the poet wants them to side with him, he will do whatever he can to represent himself as promoting the righteousness of his cause, providing all the requisite generic markers for distinguishing the difference between a true satirist and an unrighteous antagonist. The success of satire is thus dependent on an emotional and intellectual symbiosis between poet and audience in which each party both generates and fulfills the other's expectations.

We have seen in the case of Thersites just how delicate this relationship between poet and audience was, for although Thersites retained his role as the

---

1. See Goffmann 1974, 83–84, whose more general sociological analysis of interpersonal collusion in real life is equally applicable to satirical literature: "When two or more individuals cooperate in presenting a deception, covert communication among them is likely to be required, and even when not required, the grounds for indulging it are there. This is collusive communication; those in on it consititute a collusive net and those the net operates against, the excolluded." Put in literary terms, the relationship between a satirical poet and his audience forms a kind of Goffmanian "collusive net", within which both parties communicate by means of a "covert" sign-system based on generic coding. Those who fail to embrace the world fabricated by literary genre constitute Goffman's "excolluded" group, i.e., anyone who is not "in the know." Aristophanes, for example, conceptualizes members of his audience who are "in the know" as *sophoi* (as in, e.g., *Clouds* 426, *Frogs* 537).

quintessential figure of comic blame throughout antiquity, the slightest shift in emphasis in a given treatment of his story would be sufficient to transform him from a vulgar, socially malevolent buffoon (as in *Iliad* 2) to an outspoken figure of satire (as in the non-Iliadic traditions of the *Thersitoktonos*) with pretentions to social criticism. A transformation of this sort is a function of strictly literary maneuvers effected by an author: The details of Thersites' story may well remain consistent, but an author narrating them will know how to manipulate his audience's attitude toward them, such that one narrative will leave its audience sympathetic to Thersites, while another will leave them antipathetic to him. What we have suggested in the previous chapter, then, is that poets relied upon audiences to assess mockery and blame—by which I mean, they can determine where an audience's sympathies are "supposed" to lie within a poetic *psogos*—in terms of how much justice the antagonistic characters (or in first-person genres, the poet himself in his putative quarrels with others) are invested with in the narrative. We have moved beyond Nagy's monochromatic portrait of Thersites as a proto-iambographic poet to discover a more labile poetological figure, emblematic now of the self-righteous blame poet, now of that poet's reviled target. Both character-types engage in blaming, but when one is portrayed, for example, as a complete scoundrel, he will never succeed in convincing an audience that his own mockery has moral legitimacy. Homer himself, as we have seen, failed to portray Thersites as anything other than an unrighteous blamer of this sort, even though he hints that in other contexts Thersites might well be regarded as a more positive character, whose comic mockery might secure the moral high ground that it is never allowed to have in *Iliad* 2.[2] We can be quite sure, however, that if Thersites were writing his own account of the episode—that is, if he were no longer at the mercy of a third-person narrator, but could tell his own story in the first person, like a subjective satirist—he would have assumed an attitude of moral superiority, and done everything in his poetic power to construct for himself a sympathetic audience. Something like this might have occurred for a different part of

---

2. We might wonder whether the Thersites-scene in *Iliad* 2 represents an actual critique of blame poetry from within epic, something along the lines of what we see in Pindar *Pythian* 2.55–56, where Pindar suggests a critique of psogic poetry in contrast to *epinikion* (see above, pp. 70–71). But unlike Pindar, who evidently saw the *psogos* in stark opposition to his own praise poetry, and so repudiated the very notion of blaming, Homer is hardly uncomfortable with blaming in principle; see, for example, Martin 1989, 67–77, on the Homeric *neikos*, or, more generally construed, "flyting." In fact, as we discussed in the preceding chapter, Odysseus in *Iliad* 2 seems to take on the role of the self-righteous blamer, endorsed by the narrating poet. So there is no reason to suppose that *Thersites* somehow represents a kind of comic poetry repudiated by epic. What is at stake is the moral legitimacy of the mockery, not the mere fact of mockery itself. As we shall see in this chapter, Homer seems fully aware of the morphology of *psogoi*, and able to distinguish between "good" and "bad" mockery.

Thersites' story in the fourth-century *Thersitoktonos* comedies, which we discussed in the previous chapter.[3]

Homer has proven to be especially useful in our attempt to analyze the mechanisms of poetic abuse because of the way in which he embeds within his narrative various characters who appear to replicate the interaction of figures familiar to us from the literary *psogos*. Homer, however, does not situate any of these scenes of reciprocal abuse in an explicitly *poetic* context, and we should be clear, before we proceed to analyze another central Homeric scene of this sort, what it is that he can offer us. The intriguing fact about Thersites in Homer is that, even though his altercation with Odysseus occurs in a military setting, and thus outside of any context in which one might expect his abuse to be transformed into innocuous comedy, Homer's portrayal of Thersites has unmistakably comic features.[4] In the lost mythical accounts of Thersites, he probably never composed poetry as such, but he is still traditionally a highly poetic figure, insofar as his public speech was contrived in accordance with very specific performative conventions. In behaving as the quintessential *gelôtopoios*, the meaning of his *geloia* is strictly a function of the occasion for which he composes them. His desire to compose *geloia*, therefore, exists prior to their actual content: His mockery arises in the service of making people laugh, and the audience will be aware of this. It is in this sense that they will think of his behavior as poetic, effecting as it does the *poiêsis* of a *psogos* which takes on— like all literary mimesis—a separate and idiosyncratic reality informed by the generic and occasional contexts in which it occurs. What appears to be malevolent, aggressive abuse from a perspective outside these contexts turns out to be benign comedy, eagerly assimilated by an audience that understands the difference between *poiêsis* and lived reality unmediated by artistic form. It is true that the episode from Thersites' life-story found in the *Iliad* does not lead an audience to read his raillery as a *poetic psogos* against the Greek leaders; but it has nevertheless proved illuminating to see how a known figure of abuse and satire engages in verbal techniques that are socially acceptable as *poiêsis*, but dangerous when the hearer has no reason not to take the speech literally.

Although Thersites offers the most explicit example in Homer of a psogic discourse—a form of marked speech that owes its internal logic to the social practices from which it derives—other Homeric characters also adopt satirically abusive roles that seem equally imbued with poetological significance.[5]

3. Without more textual evidence, it is impossible to determine how Thersites was portrayed in these plays. It seems to me not unlikely that he was given ample space in these plays to plead his position, and to complain about the treatment he received at the hands of Homeric heroes (e.g. Lucian, *Ver. Hist.* 20; see also *Dial. Mort.* 30).

4. See discussion above, chapter 3.

5. I should emphasize here that am not concerned in this study with *every* instance of a quarrel between characters, or every time someone attacks someone else. I am, rather, interested in scenes in which confrontation and insult produce "comedy" of some sort, whether laughter in a work's

Chief among these is Thersites' main antagonist in *Iliad* 2, Odysseus, whose many guises elsewhere in the poems show him abusing other characters not only from a socially and politically superior vantage point, as he does with Thersites, but also while feigning abjection and weakness, as he does when taunted by the fellow beggar Irus (*Od.* 18.15–24).[6] Indeed, Odysseus finds himself in a variety of situations in which comedy arises from mocking speech, and his role in each is, characterisically, inconsistent. In our discussion of his behavior with Thersites in *Iliad* 2, for example, we found that Odysseus's role was analogous to that of the blame poet himself, in that his mockery affirmed a sense of righteousness that Homer took pains to highlight. Whatever mockery Thersites engages in against the Greek leaders, by contrast, remains unrighteous as it is presented by the narrating Homer. Thersites' verbal assaults were unquestionably *psogoi*, but they failed as satire[7] in that they are not allowed by the narrator to yield a sympathetic audience.[8] The same holds true for Odysseus's dealings with Irus: The two beggars inveigh against each other with mildly comical sarcasm and insult, but only Odysseus can be considered righteous within the narrative, and only he can be regarded as behaving analogously to a true satirist.[9]

---

putative audience, in the narrative's internal audience, or in both. Altercations within a given narrative that escalate to the point of reciprocal insult do not necessarily constitute an explicit form of comic discourse; whether such a scene is comic or not is strictly a function of how the poet manipulates the generic cues and crafts both his own, and his characters', points of view. For fuller discussion, see above chapter 1, pp. 24–27.

6. For a discussion of Odysseus's altercations with Irus, see Nagy 1979, 228–31. Odysseus also locks horns with Euryalus among the Phaeacians before his true identity is known; on which see Rosen 1990, where I argue that Hipponax was attracted to Odysseus's abject stances because of their comic potential. See also below p. 154.

7. While there is always some risk of anachronizing when we apply the term "satire" to literary forms found in periods where the term itself (or a close analogue or translation of it) did not exist, the lack of a term does not necessarily imply the absence of a concept which in other times was given that name. The word *satura*, for example, may have begun to appear only in late Republican Rome (see Coffey 1989, 11–23), but poets and audiences long before that were highly sensitive to the many nuances of comic mockery, including the criteria that allowed them to distinguish between what would later be known by the term *satura* and mere abuse. Among these criteria, the most critical (and this would have been recognized from the beginning, as we have seen in our analysis of *Iliad* 2) was that of the perceived righteousness or justice of mocker's cause. Martin's remarks on the term *neikos* (which he regards as a bona fide "genre") are instructive (1989, 68): ". . . an audience would not necessarily require dictional sign-posting for the occurrence of this genre at every turn . . . it might even be unmarked completely, when the poet allows the dramatic setting of the speeches itself to cue the audience to the genre involved."

8. In saying that Thersites is "not allowed by the narrator" to elicit sympathy from the audience, I do not, of course, mean that no member of any audience of *Iliad* 2 can ever feel sympathetic to Thersites. My point is only that Homer's narrative strategy makes it clear that from *his* point of view, no one is *supposed* to feel sympathy for him.

9. Contra Nagy (1979, 230–31), who views Irus as representative of a "blame poet," albeit an "unrighteous" one. As I have argued elsewhere (Rosen 1990, 29n1), the notion of an "unrighteous blame poet" is oxymoronic; one can be an "unrighteous blamer," but not an "unrighteous *blame*

In another Homeric scene, however, Odysseus emerges as a much more complex mocker, whose behavior generates comedy tinged with a moral ambiguity that seems at times even to risk alienating the audience. I refer to the well-known Cyclops episode in *Odyssey* 9, where Odysseus and the Cyclops Polyphemus end up in a full-blown confrontation which tempers its serious plotline with comic mockery from both principals. This scene has been profitably discussed from many angles, but never, to my knowledge, as a commentary on the dynamics of comic and satirical behavior. Yet, as I will argue in this chapter, this episode is in many ways fundamentally, if obliquely, concerned with such issues. To begin with, as we shall see below in greater detail, it calls attention to the idea of justice (*dikê*) as a criterion for evaluating a quarrel or physical confrontation, and problematizes the claims to self-righteousness that each antagonist offers in his own defense. Despite the fact that the story itself has roots in folktales of "good" (*qua* civilized culture) triumphing over "evil" (*qua* savage, uncultivated nature),[10] Homer constantly plays with the narrative perspective, never allowing Polyphemus or Odysseus to play a completely stable role. Rather, each of them is shown trying on different moral postures, different stances of abjection or superiority, and each attempts to play inconsistently with the sympathies of a putative audience at different points in the narrative. The episode, in short, seems at some level deeply concerned with the problem of mockery both as a lived phenomenon—the sarcasm, satire, and comedy that it entails, as well as its constant threat of physical violence—and as a poetic problem; that is, how the poet goes about representing

---

poet," for righteousness is a defining criterion for the blame poet/satirist. It is perfectly conceivable that a narrator would want to offer a critique of the satirist—to take him to task, for example, for engaging in satire, on the grounds (let us say) that such poetry is unedifying, indecorous, vel sim. Pindar does something like this when he complains that Archilochus is *psogeros* and that he "grows fat on hostilities" (*P.* 55–56; see above n. 2). This is different, however, from actually depicting a satirist in action, for if he did, it would be impossible for him to depict such a figure as unrighteous, since one cannot depict a satirist accurately without investing him with some measure of righteousness. A narrator could, of course, offer disapproving commentary on a satirist and his poetic activity within a narrative, but even this would not strip him of his claims to self-righteousness, which are part and parcel of what it means to be a satirist in the first place. *Pindar* may think that Archilochus is actually unrighteous in his *psogoi*, but as long as he acknowledges his status as a blame poet/iambographer (as he does in *Pythian* 2, for it is as a foil to praise poetry that he excoriates him), he concedes by definition Archilochus's generically motivated claims to self-righteousness. It remains possible for a satirist/blame poet to be portrayed as a failure, as someone who cannot sustain his claims to moral superiority—and this is essentially what happens with Thersites in *Iliad* 2—but if the narrator succeeds with this portrait, the character ceases to behave in this context as a satirist. In this sense, Thersites is a different case in Homer from Archilochus in Pindar. For Thersites is never allowed in the *Iliad* to behave as a *poet* of blame would, whereas in Pindar, Archilochus is never allowed to behave as anything else.

    10. On the question of the folkloric background of the Cyclops episode, see Hackman 1904; Page 1955, 1–20; Schein 1970; Glenn 1971; Mondi 1983; Heubeck and Hoekstra 1989; 19–20; and Cook 1995, 100n20.

two antagonists in narrative form and manipulating an audience's responses to each.

Such questions of the poetic representation of mockery will become even better delineated when we compare, later in this chapter, the Homeric Cyclops to his portrayal in Theocritus's sixth and eleventh *Idylls*. Theocritus's Cyclops has an obvious and explicit intertextual relationship with Homer *Odyssey* 9, although it is common for scholars to stress the stark contrast between the two portraits—Homer's Cyclops as unremittingly savage and "evil," Theocritus's Cyclops, now an absurd unrequited lover, as poignant, comical and bathetic. There can be little doubt that Theocritus, in keeping with the aesthetic of the Hellenistic idyll, was interested in teasing out from Homer, or assimilating from alternative traditions, more playful, melodramatic aspects of the Cyclops's story that would have had no comfortable place in epic. There are as many divergences, therefore, as points of contact between the two portraits of Cyclops, the most glaring being the fact that Odysseus does not figure directly in either of Theocritus's *Idylls*. One feature they share, however, is a central narrator (Odysseus in *Odyssey* 9; Polyphemus in Theocritus 11, and part of *Idyll* 6) who tells a comic story of abjection and beleaguerment, intended to enlist the sympathies of its audience. Theocritus's Cyclops, then, inextricably implicated as he is in his Homeric counterpart, takes on some of Odysseus's qualities, offering, as we shall see, his own form of self-righteousness and engaging in his own form of blaming. As the narrator, the Cyclops is no longer cast as a target of mockery, as in Homer, but presents himself as unworthily treated by others, and so deserving of his audience's sympathies. I shall be arguing, therefore, that Theocritus's desire to emphasize an alternate, non-Homeric portrait of Polyphemus resulted in a shift in perspective on both the dynamics of abuse that defined his relationship with Odysseus in *Odyssey* 9, and the poetic strategies involved in creating comedy out of it. Insofar as Odysseus in the *Odyssey* and Polyphemus in Theocritus 11 function explicitly within their respective narratives as poetological figures (that is, both are portrayed as performing their narrative in song),[11] we will want to pay close attention to the ways in which each poet manipulates narrative voice and genre in their treatment of these two characters. For we will find, in doing so, that Polyphemus and Odysseus, as singers of their own tales in each work, reveal a great deal about how their cre-

---

11. On Odysseus as an "epic" singer, see, e.g., Thalmann 1984, 171–84; Dougherty 2001, 52–59; and below [n. 16], although the identification is not straightforward for a number of reasons (e.g., within the context of the scene, Odysseus speaks in the first-person about his own experiences, whereas the epic singer would speak in the third-person about the experiences of others). As I discuss below, Odysseus is made to act *like* a poet (after all, he really *is* not a poet in *Odyssey* 9), but more like the poets we associate with subjective genres than with *epic* poets. In Theocritus 11, Polyphemus is said to have discovered that song is the best cure for his love-sickness (17–18), which he then proceeds to demonstrate with a performance in the first-person. On Polyphemus as a singer, see Manuwald 1990; also Köhnken 1996, 182–83, with n. 48.

ators, Homer and Theocritus, conceptualized the poetic structures that governed comic satire.

1. The Abject Odysseus

The Odysseus we encounter in *Odyssey* 9 is considerably different from the Odysseus who put the rebellious Thersites in his place in *Iliad* 2. Whereas there Odysseus behaved as a confident and uncompromising leader, in control, and projecting invincibility, his state of mind in *Odyssey* 9 is more vulnerable, in keeping with the precarious situation he finds himself in among the Phaeacians.[12] Having been thwarted at every turn in his attempts to return home from Troy, he is now delayed yet again in a country of questionable hospitality. At the end of Book 8, Demodocus's song about the fall of Troy causes Odysseus to weep (8.520–31), even though he was the one who requested it (8.487–98). As his host Alcinous sums up (8.539–41), all through dinner, ever since the singer took up his song of the Trojan war, his guest had not "ceased his pitiful lament" (ὀϊζυρὸς γόος). At the opening of Book 9, Odysseus acknowledges his sadness as he prepares to reveal his identity (9.12–13), and after identifying himself in lines 19–20, proceeds to catalogue the misfortunes of his νόστος πολυκηδής. Here, therefore, and indeed in so much of the *Odyssey*, we see a protagonist sunk in abjection and relentlessly confronted with new challenges. Odysseus, however, never succumbs to this abjection, and much of the poem's interest lies in the way he projects cockiness and arrogance even in the presence of a superficial sense of inferiority and disability.

I would like to argue in this chapter, in fact, that in this respect Odysseus adopts many of the characteristics associated with a satirist or blame poet, and that Homer, in pitting our perennially harrassed hero against a creature of grotesque fantasy such as the Cyclops, transforms his beleaguerement into a form of comedy. Homer achieves this subtly, yet forcefully, by making Odysseus the narrator of his own tale—a tale in which he allots himself the role of underdog against a seemingly insuperable, malevolent enemy. Two authorial perspectives, however, are at work here: Odysseus narrating a story that in its immediate context is presented as if it really happened, and Homer, who composes the framing narrative about Odysseus which his own audience (including ourselves)

12. See Cook 1999, who sees the *Cyclopeia* as a "microcosm of the interplay between active and passive heroism throughout the poem" (153). Odysseus's self-portrait in this episode as "abject," which I discuss in this section, is certainly one example of Cook's "passive heroics," although as I argue below, this is a form of heroics that in the end belongs generically more to comedy than epic. Austin (1983) also seems to be heading in this direction with his discussion of a "disequilibrium between the folkloric and the epic"and a "buffoonery in the story, the orgiastic revelry, the burlesque phallicism, [which] suggest a satyr play" (4).

will know to be fiction.[13] Odysseus, in other words, constructs his persona as if he were a subjective poet in performance (unlike the singer Demodocus, whose third-person narratives are more in keeping with traditional style of heroic epic), and the story he tells about himself in Book 9 is one of antagonism, mockery, and aggression. The fact that Homer, moreover, through an authorial voice distanced from that of Odysseus himself, casts Odysseus unambiguously as, if not exactly a poet (see above, n. 11), at least as a performer who stands in for one, ensures that his encounter with Polyphemus become not just a tale of aggression, but a representation of a bona fide poetic *psogos*, that is, of a fictionalized relationship in which a poet abuses a target from a standpoint of self-righteousness and indignation. Odysseus in effect takes over the narration from Homer, appropriates Homer's authorial standpoint as his own, and in so doing turns Homer's usual third-person omniscience into autobiography, into an account, in other words, of a *neikos* in which, as the first-person narration makes clear, he (that is, the speaker, now Odysseus) was *directly* involved.[14]

At the same time, Homer, as the ultimate creator of Odysseus's character,[15] can never completely let go of the narrative or allow Odysseus a life independent of his controlling hand, no matter how vivid Odysseus's self-presentation turns out to be. This complex narratological layering, as we shall see below, has several ramifications: First, it distances Homer's authorial voice from that of Odysseus in Book 9, and so encourages the audience to judge Odysseus's self-presentation independently from what they presume to be Homer's perspective. Second, in making Odysseus self-consciously play the role of a poet, we can catch a rare glimpse of how Homer conceptualized the specific *kind* of poetry that he has his character perform. As I shall argue below, there are even times in *Odyssey* 9 when Homer, through various metanarrative strategies, intersperses his own commentary on Odysseus's performance as a work of what we might want to call a form of "proto-satire."

At the opening of the book, as Odysseus prepares to identify himself to Alcinous, he notes in a famous passage the special charm that song has in its proper performance context:

13. In de Jong's (1987a, xiv) terminology, Odysseus here functions as the "focalizer," while Homer remains the narrator. Odysseus's story, moreover, would constitute "embedded focalization," and the larger whole a "complex narrator-text": "the external primary narrator-focalizer embeds in his narrator-text the focalization of one of the characters, who, thus, functions as an internal secondary focalizer."

14. This is not to say that Odysseus also becomes omniscient; "Jörgensen's law," which states (Jörgensen 1904) that "Homer" will always identify divine agents responsible for events, remains in effect. Odysseus will use generic terms such as *theos*, *daimôn*, or *Zeus*, unless the divinity has been identified to him. See Reinhardt 1948, 67–73 on Odysseus's first-person narration.

15. The "Narrator" in de Jong's (1987a) terminology.

οὐ γὰρ ἐγώ γέ τί φημι τέλος χαριέστερον εἶναι
ἢ ὅτ᾽ ἐϋφροσύνη μὲν ἔχῃ κατὰ δῆμον ἅπαντα,
δαιτυμόνες δ᾽ ἀνὰ δώματ᾽ ἀκουάζωνται ἀοιδοῦ
ἥμενοι ἐξείης. . . .

. . . for I think there is no occasion accomplished that is more
pleasant than when festivity holds sway among all the populace, and
the feasters up and down the houses are sitting in order and listening
to the singer. . . . (9.5–8;trans. Lattimore 1965)

With this description Odysseus has in mind the kind of poetry that Demodocus
has just been performing, namely heroic epic, and it is often supposed that, in
taking up the narration of Book 9, Odysseus assumes for himself the role of an
epic singer.[16] In fact, he seems rather to be at pains to differentiate the kind of
song he is about to perform from that which he had just described, and he locates the difference in the very nature of the authorial voice: Epic is typically
sung by a figure such as Demodocus in a third-person narrative about people
and events in which the singer is not personally implicated. Odysseus mentions, by contrast, that his performance will be narratologically different, and
implies that its effect will be different on its listeners. We may note the adver-
sative clause at the beginning of his speech (12–13): σοὶ δ᾽ ἐμὰ κήδεα θυμὸς
ἐπετράπετο στονόεντα ‖ εἴρεσθ᾽, ὄφρ᾽ ἔτι μᾶλλον ὀδυρόμενος στεναχίζω.
("But your heart has turned to ask about my sad pains, so that I weep and grieve
even more.") There may be nothing quite as fine as an epic performance at a
sumptuous banquet, he says, but Alcinous is asking Odysseus to tell of his
sorrows and explain why he broke down when he heard Demodocus singing
about the fall of Troy. Odysseus says that this will be a qualitatively different
enterprise, since it will make him, as narrator, even sadder (l. 13) than he had
been while listening to Demodocus's narration.[17] But this explanation also signals a genuine generic shift from the biographical mode of epic, with its tales

16. As Heubeck and Hoekstra 1989, 15 on 9.37–8, for example, put it: "Like his creator,
Odysseus is an epic poet: the grand saga of his *nostos* is comparable to the poem in which it is set."
But see above, n. 11.

17. Whether or not the audience would feel the same amount of pleasure in listening to
Odysseus's travails as they did in Demodocus's account of the Trojan War is uncertain, (see Heubeck
and Hoekstra 1989, ad loc. 12), although Odysseus does imply that the audience's experience of his
tale would be substantively different from their experience of Demodocus's. Although all forms of
song presumably would have their own *charis* and evoke some form of pleasure in an audience, the
immediacy of a first-person narration—especially one which the narrator claims, as Odysseus does,
will make him profoundly sad—is likely to make the relationship between poet and audience particularly fraught and unstable.

about heroic men and their deeds, to the autobiographical mode, where the singer's tale is identical with his own.[18]

There were several ancient poetic genres that can be considered "autobiographical" in the sense that their authorial voice emanates from the poet's professed subjectivity, his "ego,"[19] and virtually all of them were associated with lyric, elegiac or iambic forms. The status of Odysseus's narrative is, therefore, highly idiosyncratic, in that the tale he now tells, replicating Demodocus's role as an epic poet, is not what one would expect from epic narrators.[20] Rather, Odysseus narrates events of an "epic" that concern *himself*, and as such, his performance seems more at home in the personal genres associated with symposiastic performance. It has often been noted that the Odyssean books are woven together from various folktales of magic and fantasy, which at points seem somewhat misplaced within its larger epic frame;[21] and there is no question that such elements contribute to a shift in narrative strategy. But far more strik-

18. See above n. 11, on Odysseus as a poetological figure. Homer is explicit about making Odysseus act like a poet in Book 9. At the end of Book 8 (572–80), Alcinous had asked Odysseus to tell all about himself and explain his odd reaction to Demodocus's performance. Odysseus might very well have been made to do just that, and if he had in a straightforward manner, there would be little call to think of his narration as poetological in any special way; anything he uttered would be considered poetry only because Homer has to have him speaking in hexameter lines. But the opening of Book 9, where Odysseus explicitly contrasts what he is about to do with Demodocus's song, makes it clear that Homer wants to analogize Odysseus's performance with that of a bona fide poet.

19. This is not to say that such poetry must necessarily *be* autobiographical, only that its use of the subjective "I" *implies* that it is within its own performative moment. The exact nature and function of the subjective "I" in archaic Greek poetry, in particular whether it should be taken as genuine autobiography at one extreme, a complete fiction at the other, or something in between, has been a longstanding scholarly conundrum. Nagy (2004, 27) states the problem succinctly: "the main problem with the 'autobiographical I' is this: if indeed the self is expressed by way of a medium that controls the self-expression, to what extent can we think of that self as a genuine individual who is speaking about his or her genuine experiences? Or, to go to the other extreme, to what extent can we think of the self as fictional." See our discussion, above chapter 1, on the additional problems satire in particular poses for the question of the subjective "I." See also Rösler 1980, a foundational monograph that offers a what we might call a New Historical approach *avant la lettre* to the "I" of Greek lyric, and a follow-up in Rösler 1985. Further bibliography can be found in Gerber 1997, 6; and Nünlist 1998, 13–22.

20. Similar problems have arisen in the case of Hesiod's *Works and Days,* a work composed in epic hexameters yet narrated in the first person. Although this is not the place to enter into a protracted discussion of the work's generic identity, it is clear enough that *Works and Days* can hardly be considered *heroic* epos. (On the taxonomy of archaic epic poetry, see Ford 1992, 13–56, esp. 29–31.) In many ways, in fact, Hesiod shares with Odysseus's tale of the Cyclops a similar interest in establishing his own self-righteousness through the narration of a *neikos.* See Hunt 1981, who discusses the satirical elements of the poem. *Works and Days* has always been difficult to categorize, and one suspects that its generic elusiveness was deliberate. While the work contains satiric elements, therefore, it is difficult to conceptualize it as a bona fide work of satire, especially since in doing so one would expect considerably more evidence of comedy than we can find in it.

21. See, for example, Page 1973, in general on folktales in the *Od.*, and 4, 20, and 57, in particular, on the epic suppression of folktales in the *Od.* 9–12.

ing, it seems to me, is the abrupt deployment of the personal voice to serve as an epic narrator of the entire section.[22]

To return to Book 9 in particular, then, Homer signals at the opening that the poetic voice with which he will invest Odysseus begins to take on a distinctly nonheroic character, especially in its emphasis on Odysseus's sadness and abjection.[23] This sense of abjection—a sense, pervading the entire book, that he is cosmically oppressed in his attempt to return home, confronted by forces and people stronger than even his own normally superior physical abilities—pervades Odysseus's entire story, but its affiliation with satiric genres in Book 9 become apparent when Homer offsets Odysseus's complaints with contradictory gestures of self-aggrandizement. This strategy is typically adopted by satirical poets,[24] and is perhaps the fundamental way in which comedy is generated from an authorial stance that might otherwise come across as relentlessly petty. Lines 15–20 demonstrate this perfectly, beginning as they do with Odysseus noting his many god-sent woes, and ending with him asserting that his *kleos* extends to the gods:

κήδε᾽ ἐπεί μοι πολλὰ δόσαν θεοὶ οὐρανίωνες.
νῦν δ᾽ ὄνομα πρῶτον μυθήσομαι, ὄφρα καὶ ὑμεῖς
εἴδετ᾽, ἐγὼ δ᾽ ἂν ἔπειτα φυγὼν ὕπο νηλεὲς ἦμαρ
ὑμῖν ξεῖνος ἔω καὶ ἀπόπροθι δώματα ναίων.
εἴμ᾽ Ὀδυσεὺς Λαερτιάδης, ὃς πᾶσι δόλοισιν
ἀνθρώποισι μέλω, καί μευ κλέος οὐρανὸν ἵκει.

Many are the sorrows the gods of the sky have given me.
Now first I will tell you my name, so that all of you

22. I note that it is not the fact itself of a first-person narrative that is unusual (these are abundant in Homer), but rather the first-person narrative in which the narrator purports to function as an epic poet. On the narratology of Odysseus's performance—his *apologia*, as it is often called—before the Phaeacians in *Odyssey* 9, see de Jong 2001, 221–27: "[Odysseus's] *Apologue* is a first-person narrative, i.e., a narrative in which the narrator is internal, himself plays a role in the events (contrast the external primary narrator: 1.1–10 [i.e., Homer])."

23. This is not to say that Odysseus's authorial voice remains consistent throughout all the episodes he narrates. They are all consistently subjective, monological, and so (narratologically speaking) "non-epic," but their stances differ, as do the generic markers embedded within them. What distinguishes the Cyclops episode from the others is its flirtation with genuine comedy in the service of mockery, a quality that obviously resonated with later poets, such as Euripides in his *Cyclops* (on which see below, pp. 141–54), who were inspired by the Homeric treatment. Cook (1999), too, is sensitive to the comic resonance of Odysseus's behavior in the *Cyclopeia* when his trickster side is in evidence.

24. Examples abound from the iambographers to the Roman satirists. See, for example, Hipponax's abject stance in his rivalry with Bupalus (frr. 18–20 Dg.) and his brash threats against him elsewhere (frr. 121–22 Dg.), or the parabasis of Aristophanes' *Acharnians*, where the chorus complain on behalf of the poet that he was "wronged by his enemies" the year before (630), and proceeds to maintain at length that he is the "responsible for many good things among the Athenians" (631). See also below, chapter 6, on similar satiric strategies in Juvenal.

may know me, and I hereafter, escaping the day without pity,
be your friend and guest, though the home where I live is far away
 from you.
I am Odysseus son of Laertes, known before all men
for the study of crafty designs, and my fame goes up to the heavens.
 (9.15–20; trans. Lattimore)

Perhaps even more revealing is the claim here that the essence of his *kleos* is his wiliness. He might, after all, have singled out any number of qualities that he was famous for (*mêtis*, for example), but δόλοι here affiliate Odysseus, as has often been noted, with an entire history of folkloric trickster figures—figures who make their mark by outwitting people of superior physical and/or social power[25]—and this affiliation tendentiously prepares the audience for the imminent Cyclops episode. Performers who mock, satirize, or otherwise engage in comic blaming have long been associated cross-culturally with such trickster figures,[26] and Greco-Roman poetry offers no shortage of examples as well, from the archaic iambographer or Aristophanic *panourgos* or *ponêros* to the clever slave of Roman comedy or the often devious and disingenuous Roman satirist. Given the fact that Odysseus functions in this context as a surrogate poet, therefore, it is all the more revealing that he locates his *kleos* chiefly in his reputation as a trickster. For to do so in this particular poetological context all but explicitly identifies Odysseus as a *satirical* poet, and signals to the audience that in the tale they are about to hear they will find all the comic hyperbole, bravura, and moral self-righteousness that they would expect from a narrator of this sort.[27] At the same time, because Homer ultimately controls Odysseus's narration, it should not surprise us to find in his portrait of him here a high degree of self-consciousness about the poetics of satire, its morphology and dynamics.

It is entirely fitting, therefore, that Homer has Odysseus begin his tale with the Cicones, a story that emblematizes his interest throughout this book in the problem of assessing a first-person narrator's claims to self-righteousness and self-justification. The Cicones episode is very brief, lines 39–66, but its cen-

---

25. The foundational bibliography on the trickster-figure within folklore studies may be traced in Hynes and Doty 1993. On Archilochus and Hipponax as trickster-figures, see Philippson 1947; Miralles and Pòrtulas 1983, 11–50 (though not all of their arguments are convincing); and Miller 1994, 30–36, with discussion and further bibliography. On Odysseus as trickster, see now Cook 1999.

26. For a useful survey of the history and methodological approaches to trickster scholarship, see Hynes and Doty 1983, 13–32.

27. Technically speaking these lines introduce all of Books 9–12, not just Book 9; and certainly not all the episodes look like the production of a comic or satirical poet. But I assume, along with others, that Book 9 was conceptualized by the poet as a discrete unit, and derives from a well-attested tradition of *Cyclopeia*; see Cook 1995, 93n1 for extensive bibliography.

tral theme prepares us for the encounter with the Cyclops. Driven by the winds to the Cicones, Odysseus and his men sack and plunder the city in the expected heroic manner (41–43), and after dividing the spoils, Odysseus prudently orders them to depart. The men do not listen, however, but instead eat and drink along the shore, and so afford the Cicones ample time to muster a deadly attack against them. This scene is often justifiably paired with the one that immediately follows, the Greeks's encounter with the Lotus-eaters, in that both depict Odysseus's crew on the verge of abandoning their return in exchange for whatever pleasures of the moment lie at hand. In this respect, the crew is a kind of doublet for the Cyclops, who also responds primarily to his bodily desires for food and wine, at the expense of rational thinking and civility.[28]

By having Odysseus in this scene, then, adopt a morally superior stance in the face of the crew's weak-willed behavior, Homer leaves the audience with the impression that Odysseus's actions will be endorsed (by Homer *qua* external narrator) throughout the entire narrative. So if the crew's behavior here becomes linked to the Cyclops's behavior in the subsequent episode, when he finally appears, the listener will feel that Odysseus's opposition to him will be as justified as his complaint against the crew among the Ciconians. Odysseus, in short, assumes throughout this narrative a very explicit moral high ground, and his tale seems constructed to offer Alcinous not merely a description of his wanderings, but also a self-aggrandizing moral commentary on his behavior, especially as a kind of *apologia* for his dealings with the Cyclops.[29] Odysseus's antagonistic posturing, whether in his stance against his crew as they threaten to sink into lassitude among the Ciconians or Lotus-eaters, or against the Cyclops in his cave, is—from his narratological vantage point at least—morally right. It arises, moreover, as a *response* to an imagined or anticipated sense of indignation, and never allows the listener to think of him as the *initiator* of any dispute. Someone else is always at fault, and Odysseus feels called upon to set things straight and chastise where appropriate, even if it entails, as it does with the Cyclops, wiliness and deceit. By this point in our study it should be clear that these are defining characteristics of the satirist, whose attacks are almost always in some sense reactionary in the face of a perceived affront to his moral sensibilities.

This attitude goes far to explain why the Cyclops episode is permeated with questions of proper social behavior, and why Odysseus seems to be obsessed with explaining his actions in moral terms. Odysseus, after all, runs the risk of being accused of behavior not much different from that of his crew

28. So Cook 1995, 56: "the crew succumb to the temptations of Paradise, and in so doing regress to a precivilized condition."

29. See Olson 1995, 47: "There is no sign in the text that Odysseus sees this attack as in any way reprehensible, or as a mistake *per se*; the Ciconians were Trojan allies . . . and this is therefore simply heroic business as usual."

among the Ciconians, for when, at line 224–25, the crew beg Odysseus to leave the Cyclops's cave after they have raided his stores of food (ἔνθ' ἐμὲ μὲν πρώτισθ' ἕταροι λίσσοντ' ἐπέεσσι ‖ τυρῶν αἰνυμένους ἰέναι πάλιν . . .), he refuses because, as he said, he wanted to see whether the Cyclops would give him a guest-gift (ἀλλ' ἐγὼ οὐ πιθόμην, ἦ τ' ἂν πολὺ κέρδιον ἦεν, ‖ ὄφρ' αὐτόν τε ἴδοιμι, καὶ εἴ μοι ξείνια δοίη, 228–29). He repeats this assertion later at 267 when he first addresses the Cyclops, making sure to point out that this would be the "proper" behavior in such a situation:

ἱκόμεθ', εἴ τι πόροις ξεινήϊον ἠὲ καὶ ἄλλως
δοίης δωτίνην, ἥ τε ξείνων θέμις ἐστίν.
ἀλλ' αἰδεῖο, φέριστε, θεούς· ἱκέται δέ τοί εἰμεν.

. . . but now in turn we come to you and are suppliants
at your knees, if you might give us a guest present or otherwise
some gift of grace, for such is the right of strangers. Therefore
respect the gods, O best of men. . . . (9.267–69; trans. Lattimore)

De Jong (2001, 226) has pointed out how often Odysseus relies on the hindsight of experience in his tale to Alcinous, which allows him to evaluate situations and characters for his listeners even when, narratologically speaking, he would not yet have had access to this sort of information. His attitude toward the Cyclops is a case in point, since from the very beginning he characterizes him with the kind of detail he could only know if he had actually lived through the experience he is recounting. Odysseus's emphasis on the moral character of the Cyclops is all the more striking, therefore, since it reads as if he is attempting to offer a *post facto* defense of behavior that might otherwise appear to be rather compromised. Was it really necessary, after all, for Odysseus to disturb the Cyclops? Why did he refuse to listen to his crew's pleas to return to the ship while they had a chance, especially since they had just survived two incidents that demonstrated the lethal consequences of delaying a departure?[30] These questions may not be articulated in the text, but Odysseus goes out of his way to answer them by infusing his narrative with moral indignation—explicit and implicit—against the Cyclops. Odysseus's first-person voice here is crucial, for it is the perceived *subjectivity* of the narrator that transforms into indignation what would be mere description in a third-person narrative.[31] Odysseus, in other words, is recounting events that

30. These are famous questions to ask of the story, if only because the text itself encourages us to do so: At 9.228 Odysseus notes with hindsight that he would have been better off if he had heeded the crew's warnings. On the question of Odysseus's behavior throughout this passage, and more specifically the question of whether he can be construed as guilty of hybris, see Reinhardt 1948, 78–85; Newton 1983; Friedrich 1987 and 1991 (with further bibliography).

31. Such indignation can only be expressed in a narrative when there is at least the pretense of a personalized voice, one that belongs to a character who has some sort of personal interest in the

he lived through, so any evaluative description of a character that he offers will come across as a subjective response, not a factual statement (although he obviously wants the listener to believe it as fact) of the sort an omniscient narrator might attempt to provide. The care Odysseus takes, therefore, to construct a negative impression of the Cyclops, and to defend his own actions along the way, is a rhetorical strategy by which he can emphasize his own rectitude, and ensure that the listener's sympathies will always remain with him.

Indeed, the tone of Odysseus's initial instructions to the crew at 172–76 shows just how narcissistic and self-righteous his role in the episode will become. This is the crucial moment in which Odysseus must justify an action that is, if not simply gratuitous, then certainly dramatically unmotivated.[32] And yet his solution is to make it seem as if his encounter with the Cyclops was just the opposite. He does this by convincing the listener that the moral turpitude of the Cyclops was serious enough to warrant his own intervention. More accurately, Odysseus only *suspects* at this point that the Cyclops would be unjust, but it is clear that the epithets he applies to him here are projected back from hindsight:

ἄλλοι μὲν νῦν μίμνετ᾽, ἐμοὶ ἐρίηρες ἑταῖροι·
αὐτὰρ ἐγὼ σὺν νηΐ τ᾽ ἐμῇ καὶ ἐμοῖσ᾽ ἑτάροισιν
ἐλθὼν τῶνδ᾽ ἀνδρῶν <u>πειρήσομαι</u>, οἵ τινές εἰσιν,
ἤ ῥ᾽ οἵ γ᾽ <u>ὑβρισταί τε καὶ ἄγριοι οὐδὲ δίκαιοι,</u>
<u>ἦε φιλόξεινοι, καί σφιν νόος ἐστὶ θεουδής.</u>

"The rest of you who are my eager companions, wait here,
while I, with my own ship and companions that are in it,
go and find out about these people, and learn what they are,
whether they are savage and violent, and without justice,
or hospitable to strangers and with minds that are godly."
(9.172–76; trans. Lattimore)

---

events that he recounts. If *Homer* states that Polyphemus is lawless and savage, he need not be expressing indignation at this "fact." If he were to make it clear, however, that he disapproved of such qualities in Polyphemus, as an aside to the audience, or by some other such rhetorical device, a personal relationship with the listener is thereby momentarily established, and an implicit "I" emerges for as long the aside lasts. In this respect, the indignation of Odysseus that I see at work here resembles the *indignatio* of the Roman satirist (which we will take up below in chapter 6), although Homer himself offers a rich vocabulary of anger, most of which involve an individual's perception of an affront to his personal *timê*. See Cairns 2003, for an excellent survey of the terminology for anger (and "indignation," although he does not himself focus on this concept) in Homer.

32. See Austin 1983, 14–16, on the question of Odysseus's motivations in the *Cyclopeia*: "Beware the Trickster's ribald laugh. The Trickster's laugh reveals all the necessities of the story as a flimsy sham. No necessity, not a single real, external necessity motivates the plot of this adventure."

Many have often wondered why, in any event, Odysseus is portrayed as feeling compelled to distract himself and his crew from their efforts to return home by taking on an unnecessary and dangerous venture. His explicit motivation is that he wants to "make trial" of the inhabitants of the island (πειρήσομαι), certainly to find out who they are, but really (as 175–76 make clear) to assess their moral stature. Is he merely stirring up unnecessary trouble? Why should he care, after all, whether these people whom he has never met, and has no real need to meet now, are immoral or not?[33] The answer is intimately tied, I would suggest, to the way in which Homer has Odysseus fashion himself throughout this episode as a satirist-like figure, for Odysseus must convince his listeners that people who behave like the Cyclops simply *must* be "corrected" in some way. If the world around him is awry, the satirist channels his *indignatio* at this state of affairs into blame, and acts as if he has no choice but to castigate and correct. As such, he regards himself not as the initiator of antagonism, but as the innocent respondent to a preexistent undesirable situation, and so confirms his status as a self-righteous underdog, always "fighting the good fight."[34] Behind lines 172–76, therefore, lies a train of thought something like this: "I wanted to find out if these people were unjust and savage, because if they were, then naturally it would be my responsibility to do something about that. The equilibrium of the world, after all, cannot sustain such behavior, and I'm the only one capable of standing up to it."

From the absurdity of these claims the essential comic underlay of satire is generated. Odysseus's explanation in these lines of why he got involved with the Cyclops to begin with exudes disingenuousness, since it reads more as a distraction from his main goal of *nostos* (especially given the ironic object lesson of the recent distractions of the Ciconians and Lotus-eaters), than as the necessary exercise of moral reconnaissance that he says it is. The disingenu-

33. Some scholars have tried to put something of a positive spin on Odysseus's motivations by seeing his visit to the Cyclops as a function of Odysseus's search for knowledge. As Cook (1995, 100), for example, says of lines 174–76: "Odysseus defines his mission as a test: 'I shall go to see if they are civilized.' If the Cyclopes had been, then Odysseus and his men could have been assured of their escape from the enchanted world." This may have been true enough, but Odysseus himself never adds that explanatory coda to his thinking, and if we imagine that it was implied, one wonders why he would have chosen this particular moment to distract himself and his men from the business of returning home. But Cook, and others, are right to lay emphasis on Odysseus's professed obsession with the question of how much justice and piety the Cyclopes have. As a motivation for visiting the Cyclopes, this too may not seem compelling, but it helps explain why Odysseus seems to embark on this adventure almost willfully assuming in advance that he will end up feeling indignant at what he will find there. Olson (1995, 50–52) also takes a sympathetic view of Odysseus's motivations, although he does recognize, at least, that Odysseus, in the course of his narrative, tries deliberately to shift the blame for what happens in the encounter with the Cyclops away from himself.

34. This is a common enough sentiment across ancient satirical genres, as, for example, in a passage from the parabasis of Aristophanes, *Wasps*, 1029–37, where the chorus praises the poet for standing up to political "monsters" at great personal risk.

ousness of the passage is further increased by the fact that even the putative internal listeners of Odysseus's tale (that is, the court of Alcinous) will realize that his evaluative epithets of the Cyclops are retrojected onto an earlier part of the narrative sequence, however much they might agree with them.[35] Can the Cyclopes, in other words, really be considered savage and unjust before, or in the absence of, an encounter with Odysseus and his men?[36]

The long description of the Maron's wine at 9.193–215, moreover, offers a glimpse of the comic touches that will pervade the entire episode, and serves to undermine, in typical satirical fashion, the smug self-righteousness of 172–76. After describing the hedonistic delights of this wine, Odysseus offers an explanation of why he decided to bring it with him:

. . . αὐτίκα γάρ μοι ὀΐσατο θυμὸς ἀγήνωρ
ἄνδρ᾽ ἐπελεύσεσθαι μεγάλην ἐπιειμένον ἀλκήν,
ἄγριον, οὔτε δίκας εὖ εἰδότα οὔτε θέμιστας.

. . . for my proud heart had an idea that presently
I would encounter a man who was endowed with great
    strength,
and wild with no true knowledge of laws or any good customs.
    (9.213–15; trans. Lattimore)

As it turns out, Odysseus admits that he was expecting to find an adventure, and he brought the wine in preparation for it, implying that he had already worked out the entire trick in advance. Once again, Odysseus adopts a tone of self-righteousness—he figured that the people he would meet would be "savage" and "ignorant of justice and laws"—but the ruse he anticipates, namely, getting his antagonist drunk with irresistible wine, belongs more to a lowdown, amoral, comic world than to that of the high-minded ethicist.[37] In keeping with

35. The Phaeacians had their own unhappy history with the Cyclopes, as the opening of Book 6 makes clear. Lines 2–6 mention that the Phaeacians were once neighbors of the Cyclopes, but were forced to relocate to Scheria because the arrogant, stronger Cyclopes kept plundering them.

36. As Austin says (1983, 34, n. 9), "The trickster-hero violates every code of civilized behavior, as nowhere else in the *Odyssey*, and does so before the Cyclops demonstrates any deviant behavior." This statement must be modified in light of the fact that Homer has already let his audience know (see previous note) that, at least from the Phaeacian perspective, the Cyclopes were unjust and savage. But Odysseus would have had no way of knowing this himself, and if anything, might be seen as taking a risk with his story. For the one time that Alcinous had mentioned the Cyclopes to Odysseus (7.205–6, where he notes that the Phaeacians were related to the "Cyclopes and the savage race of Giants"), his attitude was ambiguous, and potentially even vaguely sinister (see Rose 1969, 393).

37. The wine trick of *Odyssey* 9 seems to be a Homeric innovation (cf., Röhrich 1962, 62), which suggests that the poet was actively interested in adding comic touches. Wine may well have associations with culture, civilization, agriculture, etc. (Cook 1995, 96), but its intoxicating effects

figures we later associate with satire, Odysseus embodies contradictory impulses, adopting at one moment an indignant ethical pose, and at another jettisoning that in favor of the role of a rakish *ponêros*. Homer has, in short, combined in this passage the trickster-Odysseus with the moralizing sensiblities of the satirist.

The connections between trickster figures and comic satirists have often been noted, especially in recent discussions of the iambographers,[38] and it is easy to see that Odysseus is made to cast himself in such a role in *Odyssey* 9. His role as poetic narrator makes it all but explicit that he is here engaged in the refashioning of his own character before multiple audiences (the Phaeacians, as well as ourselves), and his story is designed to highlight the qualities that satirists traditionally claim for themselves. Perhaps the best illustration of this can be seen in the famous "No-One" (*outis/mêtis*) ruse: Earlier in the episode Polyphemus, in a feigned attempt to honor traditional protocols of *xenia*, had asked Odysseus (355) to announce his name, and Odysseus, with characteristic foresight, identified himself as "No-One." After he and his men had blinded Polyphemus, Odysseus is able to rely on this false name to escapes trouble from the neighboring Cyclopes, who had come to investigate Polyphemus's distress.[39] Using a trick name (usually "Myself") against an adversary has numerous parallels in folktale,[40] and the Greek language offers the extra bonus of the pun on *mê-tis*, that is, a word that means both "No-one" in certain grammatical constructions (cf., for example e.g., lines 403–6),[41] and, with a different pitch accent, "crafty intelligence" (*mêtis*, cf., for example, line 422, as well as Odysseus's epithet *polymêtis*). Nothing could sum up the paradoxical qualities of the satirist better than this pun, which juxtaposes a note of personal inconsequentiality ("I'm a nobody") with self-assurance and bravado ("I'm crafty and clever"). Indeed, no matter how much a satirist can revel in his own abjection, in the end he must assert some measure of power and affirm his superiority over his antagonist. This self-aggrandizing impulse would explain the final scene in Book 9, in which Odysseus feels moved, over the strenuous objections of his crew, to tell the Cyclops his real name (491–505).

---

can undo all such regulating forces and lead to licentiousness, irrationality, and general disorder— to a world, in other words, that readily engenders comedy. This point did not escape Euripides a few centuries later, as we shall see below (pp. 141–54), whose satyr play *Cyclops* continually plays up on the comic, bawdy effects of too much unmixed wine.

38. See above, nn. 25 and 26.

39. That is, when Polyphemus complains to the other Cyclopes that "No-one" was responsible, they leave him alone and urge him to look to his father Poseidon for protection (409–11).

40. For discussion and further bibliography, see Heubeck and Hoekstra 1989, 33. As Hackman's study (1904) makes clear, the use of "Nobody" for "Myself" in folk-tale versions of these stories is extremely rare. This striking fact led O'Sullivan (1987, 7–8) to suggest that the Odyssean tale served as a model for subsequent versions recorded by folklorists.

41. Discussion in Podlecki 1961, 130–31; also Heubeck-Hoekstra 1989, ad loc. 35.

This scene can be analyzed in several ways, though most would agree that Odysseus's final interaction with the Cyclops replicates traditional elements of a heroic *aristeia*, such as the battle vaunt and claims to personal *kleos*.[42] Obviously, if Odysseus had departed from the Cyclops and left him thinking that "No-One" had injured him, Odysseus would not be able to claim the credit for the deed. But what does he get from this *kleos*? In fact, more abjection; for, as is often noted, by revealing his true name, he allows the Cyclops to call down on him the curse that will delay his homecoming, increase his suffering and destroy his crew along the way. The Odyssean *mêtis* that inspired the "*Outis*" trick may have allowed him to escape the Cyclops initially, but Odysseus's overpowering desire to reap *kleos* from it comes with a heavy price. This is a type of *kleos* with epic roots[43] but it has much in common with the *kleos* implicit in what Hellenistic scholars dubbed *kômôidein onomasti* that is, the mockery of individuals *by name*.[44] The phrase itself referred to the naming of targets by comic poets (specifically, they had in mind poets of Athenian Old Comedy), but mockery *onomasti* implies a highly personalized relationship between poet and target, in which the identity of each party is equally important; anonymous mockery is virtually unthinkable, and the mocker who believes himself to be in the right (that is, the satirist) will have particular difficulty restraining himself from claiming credit for his attacks. Such egocentric thinking certainly lies behind the vaunts of the heroic battlefield, but the twist of abjection that follows Odysseus's revelation in this scene aligns him distinctively with the comic satirist, whose triumph over his enemies is so often compromised by self-irony.

In fact, the final joke of the "*Outis*" trick consists in just this sort of ironic self-abasement, especially when we keep in mind that *Odysseus* is the narrator of the episode, and thus *he* is the one we are supposed to think is responsible for composing even negative remarks about himself. After Odysseus finally identifies himself to Polyphemus at 502–5, Polyphemus (as Odysseus recounts it) recalls that he had once received a prophecy from the seer Telemus that he would one day be blinded by Odysseus (507–12). He implies that, since then, he was on the watch for the arrival of Odysseus, but that he was thrown off track because he always expected Odysseus to be a "great and fine person."

---

42. On the *aristeia* as the basic building block of the *Odyssey*, cf. Schröter 1950, esp. 121–84, on the *Mnêstêrophonia*; on the *Cyclopeia* as *aristeia*, Heubeck and Hoekstra 1989, 38–39; Peradotto 1990, 46–47, 148–56; and Cook 1995, 94–96.

43. See Segal 1994, 85–109, who finds considerable ambivalence and irony in Homer's presentation of *kleos*, especially in the *Odyssey*.

44. See Steinhausen 1910 and Halliwell 1984 on the Hellenistic interest in cataloguing the targets of comic poets, largely according to the nature of a *komoidoumenos*'s moral deficiency or actual crime. For the dynamics of *kômôidein onomasti* in Aristophanes, especially the tensions it creates between "serious" and "comic" interpretations for an audience, see Mastromarco 2002 and Ercolani 2002.

Instead—he now discovers—Odysseus turns out to be "small, inconsequential and weak:"[45]

ἀλλ' αἰεί τινα φῶτα μέγαν καὶ καλὸν ἐδέγμην
ἐνθάδ' ἐλεύσεσθαι, μεγάλην ἐπιειμένον ἀλκήν·
νῦν δέ μ' ἐὼν ὀλίγος τε καὶ οὐτιδανὸς καὶ ἄκικυς
ὀφθαλμοῦ ἀλάωσεν, ἐπεί μ' ἐδαμάσσατο οἴνῳ.

But always I was on the lookout for a man handsome
and tall, with great endowment of strength on him, to come here;
but now the end of it is that a little man, niddering, feeble,
has taken away the sight of my eye, first making me helpless
with wine. (9.513–16; trans. Lattimore)

With the term οὐτιδανός Odysseus has the Cyclops make his own pun, recapitulating the "*Outis*" ruse. One has the impression, in fact, that the Cyclops is shown rationalizing how he could have been duped by Odysseus's name-trick in the first place: The man who called himself "*Outis*" actually *looked* the part (οὐτιδανός), so why would it not be natural for him to assume that this was Odysseus's real name? The effect of these lines, then, is to denigrate Odysseus's physical appearance. But because Odysseus's victory over the Cyclops has proven that appearances can hardly be trusted, and that an "*Outis*" who relies on *mētis* can in the end overpower brute force, his stance of abjection is transformed into an ironized emblem of its opposite, and out of this emerges comedy. Odysseus gives the lie to the Cyclops's low opinion of him, and ends up himself with the last laugh.

Odysseus's ironic self-presentation in this passage is consistent with the way in which Homer portrays him elsewhere in the *Odyssey*. Perhaps the most striking parallel with the Cyclops episode, however, is Odysseus's quarrel with Irus in Book 18, another scene that emphasizes a contrast between Odysseus's unimpressive physical appearance and the reality of his actual strength.[46] Nagy persuasively linked Irus to the quarrels (*neikea*) associated with blame poetry, although, as I argued in the case of Odysseus and Thersites in the preceding chapter, I think he has reversed the roles of poet and target in this scene. Clearly

45. One wonders what difference it would have made to Polyphemus if he had known from the start that he was dealing with Odysseus. He seems to imply with these lines that he might have treated him differently out of fear of the prophecy, although this would perhaps be inconsistent with his earlier profession that the Cyclopes have no care for the gods (see lines 272–80), and so would not care for any of their pronouncements about future events.

46. Homer's emphasis on Odysseus's middling physical appearance was evidently picked up by Hipponax in his own self-presentation, and used for similar purposes, namely to cultivate a stance of abjection, but then to surprise his target (and audience) with unexpected superiority, both moral and physical. See Rosen 1990, and further, below p. 154.

it is Odysseus here who has righteousness on his side, and as such, from the perspective of the narrative, himself plays a role analogous to that of a blame poet against an unrighteous target, Irus, who is presented as richly deserving of Odysseus's mockery.[47] The comedy of their altercation arises in large part from Odysseus's portrayal as seemingly physically inferior to his antagonist, and socially inferior to those witnessing the quarrel. At lines 26–31, Irus likens Odysseus's speech to that of an old servant-woman (". . . how garrulously the pig[48] talks, just like an old servant-woman . . ." . . . ὡς ὁ μολοβρὸς ἐπιτροχάδην ἀγορεύει, ‖ γρηῒ καμινοῖ ἴσος) and again taunts him with his old age ("for how could you fight with a younger man?" πῶς δ᾿ ἂν σὺ νεωτέρῳ ἀνδρὶ μάχοιο; 31). This sets the stage (almost literally!) for a comic performance, with the suitors as an appreciative audience, as lines 33–41 make clear:

ὣς οἱ μὲν προπάροιθε θυράων ὑψηλάων
οὐδοῦ ἔπι ξεστοῦ πανθυμαδὸν ὀκριόωντο.
τοῖϊν δὲ ξυνέηχ᾿ ἱερὸν μένος Ἀντινόοιο.
ἡδὺ δ᾿ ἄρ᾿ ἐκγελάσας μετεφώνει μνηστήρεσσιν·
"ὦ φίλοι, οὐ μέν πώ τι πάρος τοιοῦτον ἐτύχθη,
οἵην τερπωλὴν θεὸς ἤγαγεν ἐς τόδε δῶμα·
ὁ ξεῖνός τε καὶ Ἶρος ἐρίζετον ἀλλήλοιϊν
χερσὶ μαχέσσασθαι· ἀλλὰ ξυνελάσσομεν ὦκα."
ὣς ἔφαθ᾿, οἱ δ᾿ ἄρα πάντες ἀνήϊξαν γελόωντες,
ἀμφὶ δ᾿ ἄρα πτωχοὺς κακοείμονας ἠγερέθοντο.

So, in front of the towering doors, and upon the threshold
polished smooth, these two hurled jagged words at each other
and Antinoos, the sacred prince, stirred them on to battle,
and laughing sweetly he spoke aloud to the rest of the suitors:
"Friends, in the past nothing has ever happened to match
this entertainment that the god has now brought to the palace;
for the stranger and Irus are now making ready for battle
with their fists. Come, let the rest of us speed the encounter."
So he spoke, and the rest of them all sprang up, laughing,
and gathered all in a group around the two ragged beggars.
    (18.33–41; trans. Lattimore)

47. Nagy points out (1979, 228–31) that Irus is characterized as envious and gluttonous, and argues that "the story of Irus in effect ridicules the stereotype of an unrighteous blame poet. Like the unrighteous blamers, who are righteously blamed by praise poetry, Irus has *eris* 'strife' with a good man [Odysseus] . . . and makes *neikos* 'quarreling' against him." As I have argued in the preceding chapter, the notion of an "*unrighteous* blame poet" strikes me as an oxymoron, at least when he is quarreling with an antagonist who can be considered, as Odysseus is here, "righteous." See above, pp. 75 and 120n9.

48. On the meaning of the obscure word, *molobros*, see Russo, Fernandez, and Galiano-Heubeck 1992, 28 (ad *Od.* 17.219).

The imminent fight between Odysseus and Irus is real enough, and will certainly yield blood and pain, but it is regarded as pure comic spectacle—an occasion for laughter (*gelôs*) and delight (*terpôlê*)—by the suitors. Odysseus, for his part, knowing full well that he will have no trouble beating Irus, nevertheless encourages the suitors's lust for a good show by playing up his old age and general state of abjection:

ὦ φίλοι, οὔ πως ἔστι νεωτέρῳ ἀνδρὶ μάχεσθαι
ἄνδρα γέροντα δύῃ ἀρημένον· ἀλλά με γαστὴρ
ὀτρύνει κακοεργός, ἵνα πληγῇσι δαμείω.

Friends, it is not possible for a man who is older
and worn with sorrow to fight with a younger man, but my villainous
belly drives me to do it, and fall to his fists. (18.52–54 trans. Lattimore)

What the suitors expect is little more than a skirmish between two base buffoons, the one an old, feeble and hungry loser, the other a gluttonous, arrogant poseur.[49] It seems like a ridiculous mismatch to them, and it is not surprising that they find it laughable. Their delight is further enhanced by Odysseus's unexpected victory over Irus: As soon as Odysseus knocks him down with a blow to the neck, the suitors can barely contain themselves:

δὴ τότ᾽ ἀνασχομένω ὁ μὲν ἤλασε δεξιὸν ὦμον
Ἶρος, ὁ δ᾽ αὐχέν᾽ ἔλασσεν ὑπ᾽ οὔατος, ὀστέα δ᾽ εἴσω
ἔθλασεν· αὐτίκα δ᾽ ἦλθεν ἀνὰ στόμα φοίνιον αἷμα,
κὰδ δ᾽ ἔπεσ᾽ ἐν κονίῃσι μακών, σὺν δ᾽ ἤλασ᾽ ὀδόντας
λακτίζων ποσὶ γαῖαν· ἀτὰρ μνηστῆρες ἀγαυοὶ
χεῖρας ἀνασχόμενοι γέλῳ ἔκθανον.

They put up their hands, and Irus hit him on the right shoulder,
but Odysseus struck the neck underneath the ear, and shattered
the bones within, and the red blood came in his mouth, filling it.
He dropped, bleating, in the dust, with teeth set in a grimace,
and kicking at the ground with his feet, and the haughty suitors
held up their hands and died with laughing. (18.95–100; trans.
  Lattimore)

---

49. Cf. lines 3–4, which describe Irus as famous for his insatiable eating and drinking, and his gluttonous stomach. Though he looked big, Homer notes that he had no "strength" or "power." The bystanders of this scene are in for a further surprise, when, at 66–72, Odysseus girds himself for the fight by tying up his rags, and so reveals an impressive physique after all (which Athena proceeds to enhance, 70).

After Odysseus props up the defeated Irus outside as a scarecrow, the suitors are described as "laughing sweetly" (ἡδὺ γελώοντες, 111) as they bestow upon him the promised prize of food. Odysseus is here rewarded for a successful comic performance much as an actor or dramatist might be in the Greek theater several centuries later.

It should be clear, then, that the Irus episode in *Odyssey* 18 bears a striking resemblance to the Cyclops episode in its presentation of Odysseus: In both we find an Odysseus who feigns weakness and abjection, and who confronts an antagonist ruled exclusively by his passions and obsessed with food. In both cases Odysseus overcomes his adversary through a combination of ingenuity and strength[50] and generates laughter from his victory and subsequent mockery of his enemy.[51] Indeed, it is this comic element, combined with the self-righteousness assumed by Odysseus in each episode, that allows us to construe him as a figure whose behavior replicates the performance of a literary satirist.

On the matter of self-righteousness, however, the episodes subtly diverge, for whereas in the Irus episode there is never any doubt that Odysseus's behavior is intended to be perceived as morally justified, in the Cyclops episode his moralizing stance is never fully convincing and in the end seems highly contrived. The central action of the episode, after all—Odysseus's blinding of the Cyclops—may seem justified enough as a response to the Cyclops's feasting on his men, but only until one realizes that the Cyclops's savage behavior is itself a response to *Odysseus's* gratuitous intrusion into the Cyclopean world. Whereas Odysseus wants his audience to believe that *he* is reacting to the Cyclops's attacks on his men, the narrating Homer seems eager not to let it go unnoticed that it is the *Cyclops* who is reacting to Odysseus's unexpected and

---

50. It is easily overlooked that Odysseus's victory over Irus required some forethought, since there was always the potential danger that the suitors would gang up on him even if he were to overpower Irus. This is why he makes the suitors swear at lines 55–57 that they will not interfere at all in the fight. Line 51 makes it clear that Homer regards this gesture as a function of Odysseus's *mêtis*: τοῖς δὲ δολοφρονέων μετέφη πολύμητις Ὀδυσσεύς.

51. Despite the fact that Odysseus is responsible for the disaster that befalls his crew in the Cyclops's cave, he remains amused at his own cleverness, especially when his *Outis*-ruse succeeds in neutralizing the threat from the other Cyclopes, 9.413–14: ὣς ἄρ᾽ ἔφαν ἀπιόντες, ἐμὸν δ᾽ ἐγέλασσε φίλον κῆρ, ‖ ὡς ὄνομ᾽ ἐξαπάτησεν ἐμὸν καὶ μῆτις ἀμύμων. This laughter is not identical to the laughter of an *audience*, but it does seem to model Odysseus's κῆρ as a kind of audience for his μῆτις. Moreover, Odysseus's laughter is a direct response to an unintentionally comic scene he has just witnessed himself, namely the confused exchange between the Cyclopes and Polyphemus. Only Odysseus (and his men, although they are not mentioned) can appreciate the full malicious comedy of the scene. Perhaps Odysseus's own laughter as he contemplates the effect of his trick functions as a cue to the audience (Homer's and Odysseus's alike) to join in with their own laughter.

unwelcome taunts.[52] So much is clear from the lines in which Odysseus formally introduces himself to the Cyclops (9.266–71), where he repeats the explanation of his visit which he had used earlier in his narrative (. . . ἡμεῖς δ' αὖτε κιχανόμενοι τὰ σὰ γοῦνα ‖ ἱκόμεθ', εἴ τι πόροις ξεινήϊον ἠὲ καὶ ἄλλως ‖ δοίης δωτίνην, ἥ τε ξείνων θέμις ἐστίν, 228–29) and demands in the name of Zeus, protector of suppliants, that the Cyclops treat them with appropriate respect:

> ἀλλ' αἰδεῖο, φέριστε, θεούς· ἱκέται δέ τοί εἰμεν.
> Ζεὺς δ' ἐπιτιμήτωρ ἱκετάων τε ξείνων τε,
> ξείνιος, ὃς ξείνοισιν ἅμ' αἰδοίοισιν ὀπηδεῖ.

> Therefore
> respect the gods, O best of men. We are your suppliants,
> and Zeus the guest god, who stands behind all strangers with honors
> due them, avenges any wrong toward strangers and suppliants.
>   (9.269–71; trans. Lattimore)

There can be little doubt that, from Homer's perspective as the omniscient narrator, Odysseus is the aggressor in this episode, even though Homer has him work hard within his own embedded narrative to make it seem as if the Cyclops is the aggressor. In this respect, in fact, there are parallels between Odysseus's behavior in Book 9 and Thersites' in *Iliad* 2, for both initiate their quarrels and use mockery to express their indignation against their enemies, and both are portrayed as underdogs pitted against a more powerful antagonist. Both, likewise, revel in their verbal wit, which relies on sarcasm, threat and insult. But while Iliadic epic, as we saw in the preceding chapter, is incapable of showing Thersites' indignation as legitimate, the Odyssean narrator makes it less straightforward how we are supposed to judge the aggressive Odysseus. The hero's aggression and mockery are really only fully legitimized in his *own* account, and the startling retrospective regrets about his encounter with the Cyclops that Homer puts into his mouth suggests, I would argue, a genuine ambivalence— from the perspective of the framing narrator, at least—about how we ought to judge Odysseus's behavior in this episode.

---

52. Do we anachronistically impute our own moral sensibilities to Homeric culture when we criticize Odysseus's foray to the Cyclopes' island? Perhaps, one might argue, any self-respecting Greek audience would have applauded Odysseus's proactive incursion to the Cyclopes in order to discover their moral status, and punish them if he found them deficient. The text makes clear, however, as we noted earlier (above, n. 30), that Odysseus regrets what he put his men through, and Homer does not leave us with the impression that any amount of knowledge Odysseus may have obtained about the Cyclopes could have justified the many deaths his crew suffered as a result.

The central interpretive problem of this ambivalence, then, is this: Is it accurate to claim that Odysseus's behavior in the Cyclops episode is an example of comic, satirical mockery, in which the underdog Odysseus, fueled by righteous indignation, has the last laugh on his putatively invincible antagonist, Polyphemus? Or is Odysseus's taunting of Polyphemus fraught with moral paradox and founded upon *un*righteous indignation and a kind of comedy that exposes the blamer as blameworthy himself, much as we saw the Paphlagonian portrayed in Aristophanes' *Knights*? While the Cyclops incident was hardly composed as a systematic disquisition on poetic satire, the fact that these tensions and ambivalences are never resolved in the episode does suggest an awareness that the comedy inherent in mockery is rarely a stable poetic category. In the case of the Cyclops, it is as if Homer cannot quite decide who is more blameworthy, Odysseus or the Cyclops, and so, likewise, he cannot quite decide where to locate the comic aspects of the altercation between them. Does the narrative that Homer has Odysseus "sing" to the Phaeacians constitute what we might call a "*psogos* against the Cyclops," that is, a work of poetic mockery intended to generate comedy *at the expense* of the Cyclops? Certainly, the character Odysseus could make that claim for himself; but would Homer leave it at that? As I have argued, Homer seems to exhibit some anxiety about where the blame really lies in this skirmish, and he at least seems interested in questioning Odysseus's mockery of the Cyclops, without necessarily condemning it. Fundamentally, Odysseus recounts his tale as a self-righteous satirist might, adopting the expected postures (righteous indignation, abjection, wiliness, for example) and deploying the appropriate literary tropes (verbal mockery, vaunting, personal insult, laughter). But by the end of the episode, from the perspective of *Homer's* audience (as opposed to Odysseus's internal audience of Phaeacians), he becomes, rather, something of a satirist *manqué*, deficient in the one area which, as I have argued, defines the true satirist, namely his ability to convince his audience (however disingenuously or ironically) that his blaming—and their laughter in response—is morally justified.[53]

2. The Post-Homeric *Cyclopeia*: The Rehabilitated Odysseus in Euripides and Philoxenus

There is, to be sure, a good deal of comedy in Homer's *Cyclopeia*, and much of the entertainment lies in watching the antagonists spar with each other in a battle

---

53. I should note here that this does not make Odysseus here "an unrighteous blame poet," a phrase Nagy has used to describe Irus in *Od.* 18 (see above, n. 47). We might conclude that Homer is subtly suggesting that Odysseus is an unrighteous or unjustified *blamer*, which we could say describes the *targets* of blame poets, but blame poets themselves need to be conceptualized as justified if they are to be characterized as poets to begin with.

of wits and physical strength. The heroic narrative demands that Odysseus be victorious and the last laugh he has on the Cyclops is the malicious laughter implied in any form of battle-vaunting, which reduces the adversary to a state of deserved (from the victor's point of view) abjection and makes him look ridiculous. On the battlefield, however, warriors faced each other believing that they had equivalent moral standing (both normally enter the fray willingly and believing their cause to be right), and the joyous laughter of victory that belittles the defeated party reflects in the victor his *aristeia* rather than *ponêria*. Homer, as we have seen, cannot quite seem to decide which of these ethical terms would describe Odysseus's victory over Polyphemus: Odysseus's confrontation with the grotesque monster is recounted clearly, if superficially, from the perspective of an anthropocentric comic world, in which the civilized man will triumph over the uncivilized beast, but any laughter the passage elicits always seems tempered by Homer's reluctance to grant either Odysseus or Polyphemus the complete moral high ground.

Such a portrait of Odysseus is not inconsistent with other scenes in the *Odyssey* where Homer places him in similarly compromising or unflattering situations, and later Greek authors enjoyed exploiting Odysseus's reputation for *ponêria* as much as they did his *polytropeia*.[54] The story of Odysseus's encounter with the Cyclops, however, seems to have had a curiously monolithic afterlife in Greek comic literature after Homer: Most of the subtle moral questioning of Odysseus's character that runs through *Odyssey* 9 is abandoned and the episode retold in more simplistic, clear-cut terms, as a classic tale of right and wrong, man and monster. After Homer, we have no versions of the episode until the later fifth century, but our evidence for this period, and the following century, suggests that Odysseus was usually cast as the unambiguously wronged party, and the Cyclops as the unjust aggressor.[55] What seems to have captured the imagination of post-Homeric authors was not any moral anxiety they might have detected in Homer's version of the episode, but rather the simple tale of a hero, reduced to abjection by a troubled *nostos* and his captivity at the hands of a powerful, carnivorous monster. As far as we can tell, these authors either omitted or downplayed the fact that in Homer Odysseus's attack on the Cyclops was ultimately unprovoked (i.e., Odysseus was himself

54. See Stanford's survey (1963, 102–17) of the many unflattering portrayals of Odysseus in Greek tragedy.

55. With the exception of Euripides' *Cyclops*, to which we turn below, nothing substantial remains from the fifth-century treatments of the Cyclops episode. Cratinus's *Odysseis*, insecurely dated to the early 430's (see Kassel-Austin, 4.192) would be an excellent play to consider, since it seems to have been a sustained parody of *Odyssey* 9, but no more than 25 lines survive, and only two of the fragments consist of more than two consecutive verses. See Cratinus frr. 143–57 K-A; Holland 1884, 158–65; Nesselrath 1990, 237–39; and Rosen 1995, 129–32. Comic versions of the epic episode also seem to have been popular in Sicilian comedy and satyr play even prior to Euripides. See Holland 1884 149–58 on Epicharmus, and 165–67 on Aristias.

responsible for initiating the encounter with the Cyclops), and this allowed them to grant Odysseus the moral high ground throughout the episode. This, in turn, offered a straightforward recipe for comedy—it was certainly always clear at whom the audience should laugh—and one by-product of the plot's new-found moral clarity was an Odysseus whose behavior replicated what we have come to expect of a satirist. In these versions, that is, Odysseus is cast in the role of an indignant and self-righteous underdog, whose success depends on verbal dexterity rather than physical superiority. In this section, we will examine two important versions of the episode from the fifth century, which suggest that authors could self-consciously situate Odysseus within a tradition of satiric poetry, ever sensitive to the ways in which the smallest nuance in the depiction of a given character could make a difference to an audience's understanding of genre and poetics.

In the extant literature, the tradition of an explicitly comic Cyclops begins with Euripides' satyr play of that name, produced probably in the last decade of the fifth century.[56] This play has borne a heavy burden over the centuries as the only extant example of a complete Greek satyr play, and now it must also serve as our only complete example of a play from the classical period dramatizing the Cyclops episode. While it could never be mistaken for its Homeric model, it is a strikingly conservative treatment of the story, as is often noted, hewing closely to the basic plot of *Odyssey* 9. If anything, as we shall discuss in greater detail below, Euripides glossed over much of the moral ambiguity in the Homeric version by making Odysseus come to the Cyclops's island for a legitimate purpose (he and his men needed food) rather than simply to make mischief under the pretense of establishing *xenia*, and so stripped down the Homeric plot to its most essential elements: Odysseus arrives at the Cyclops's island, is trapped in his cave, tricks him with the "No-man" ruse, and ends up blinding him with a fiery stake. The more specific correspondences and discontinuities between the two have been well studied by others,[57] so we need not dilate upon them here except to note that, insofar as the play is a parody of *Odyssey* 9,[58] it reflects a particularly heightened degree of literary gamesmanship on Euripides' part. Not every deviation from Homer will prove to be a profound literary gesture—some were probably motivated simply by

56. Seaford 1982 argues for 408 BCE as the most likely date of production. See also Seaford 1984, 48.

57. See, e.g., Holland 1884, 167–75; Wetzel 1965; Ussher 1978 111–21 (and *passim*); and Seaford (1984) 51–59. Konstan 1981 urges a reading of Euripides' *Cyclops* less necessarily implicated in the Homeric version.

58. I use parody here in its least negative sense: As a variation on a target text, it is necessarily "parasitic" (i.e., it could not exist in its current form without a specific antecedent), but this need not imply repudiation or censure of the original text. Silk's (1993) acute remarks about Aristophanes' parody of tragedy are also applicable to Euripides' parody of Homer. See also Arnott 1972, who discusses the paratragic elements in Euripides' *Cyclops*.

generic differences or dramaturgical demands[59]—but we can at least assume that Euripides (and his audience) would have understood them all as some form of commentary on the Homeric target text.

For our purposes, the most significant change from Homer's version lies in the portrait of Odysseus as an essentially blameless victim. This change is hardly subtle and has often been noted,[60] but it needs to be re-examined as part of our analysis of the relationship between Odysseus and the Cyclops in its capacity as a marker of literary genre. What we will find is an Odysseus constructed to interact with the Cyclops in much the same way as satirical poets such as Hipponax or Aristophanes interacted with their targets. This is not to say that Euripides regarded Odysseus and Cyclops as poetological figures, or to suggest that the primary function of *Cyclops* was to offer a commentary about satire; but Euripides certainly had to make some conscious decisions about how he might transform an epic Odysseus into a comic one. And the decisions he made—granting Odysseus the moral high ground, playing up his physical weakness and self-doubt in contrast to the Cyclops—suggest that *his* Odysseus would become comic by tapping into specific poetic traditions of satire in a way that epic would never fully endorse. How self-consciously Euripides made such literary decisions (by which I mean, whether he invented his new version himself, or inherited it from other, now lost, antecedents) will never be known, but our discussion below should make it clear that the Odysseus of his *Cyclops* behaves according to a poetics readily available to Euripides and his contemporary audience.

From the very opening of the play, it is clear that Odysseus is edgy and vulnerable in a way alien to the Homeric portrait. In his opening lines to Silenus at 96–98, Odysseus mentions his and his men's thirst and hunger:

ξένοι, φράσαιτ᾽ ἂν νᾶμα ποτάμιον πόθεν
δίψης ἄκος λάβοιμεν εἴ τέ τις θέλει
βορὰν ὀδῆσαι ναυτίλοις κεχρημένοις;

---

59. Since Euripides' *Cyclops* was a satyr play, for example, the addition of satyrs to the *dramatis personae* would be natural, if not expected, as would the chatter about wine, Dionysus, and inebriation. As for dramaturgy—to take one example—to conform with tragic staging conventions, the blinding of Polyphemus takes place off-stage and is not even described on-stage after the fact, whereas in Homer it is recounted in a detailed narrative. Further discussion in Wetzel 1965, esp. 1–40; and Seaford 1984, 51–52.

60. Most recently Kovacs 1994, 55: "In Homer Odysseus's motives for seeking out the Cyclopes is curiosity and a desire for guest-gifts, and no one reading the epic can help feeling that there was something culpably rash in the whole adventure. In Euripides, Odysseus and his men approach the cave of Polyphemus because they are in need of food and water . . . and then are unfairly accused of stealing what they have offered to pay for. Sympathy for Odysseus is therefore strengthened and there is no admixture of blame."

Strangers, could you tell me where we might find a stream of water to slake our thirst, and whether anyone is willing to sell provisions to needy sailors? (96–98; trans. Kovacs 1994)

and again at line 133, he reiterates that they are seeking food: (ὅδησον ἡμῖν σῖτον, οὗ σπανίζομεν, "sell us some bread, which we lack"). When he identifies himself to Silenus at 103, Silenus makes as if to banter with him, lightly mocking him with the epithet κρόταλον δριμύ:

Σι. χαῖρ᾽, ὦ ξέν᾽· ὅστις δ᾽ εἶ φράσον πάτραν τε σήν.
Οδ. Ἰθακος Ὀδυσσεύς, γῆς Κεφαλλήνων ἄναξ.
Σι. οἶδ᾽ ἄνδρα, κρόταλον δριμύ, Σισύφου γένος.

(Sil.): Greeting, stranger! But tell me your name and country. (Od.) Odysseus, of Ithaca, lord of Cephallene. (Sil.) I know of the man, the wheedling chatterer, Sisyphus's son. (102–104; trans. Kovacs)

But Odysseus responds without engaging the insult, as if enervated by his predicament: "yes, that's me; but don't wrangle with me . . ." (ἐκεῖνος αὐτός εἰμι· λοιδόρει δὲ μή). At least in the first half of the play, Odysseus seems to prefer the high road: no unnecessary quarreling, no interest in deception or playing games. His behavior is vividly contrasted to that of the satyrs, who characteristically give themselves over to their bodily appetites as much as they can.

ὡς ὅς γε πίνων μὴ γέγηθε μαίνεται·
ἵν᾽ ἔστι τουτί τ᾽ ὀρθὸν ἐξανιστάναι
μαστοῦ τε δραγμὸς καὶ παρεσκευασμένον
ψαῦσαι χεροῖν λειμῶνος ὀρχηστύς θ᾽ ἅμα
κακῶν τε λῆστις. εἶτ᾽ ἐγὼ ⟨οὐ⟩ κυνήσομαι
τοιόνδε πῶμα, τὴν Κύκλωπος ἀμαθίαν
κλαίειν κελεύων καὶ τὸν ὀφθαλμὸν μέσον;

The man who does not enjoy drinking is mad: in drink one can raise *this* to a stand, catch a handful of breast and look forward to stroking her "meadow" with his hands, there's dancing and forgetfulness of cares. Shall I not kiss such a drink and tell the bonehead Cyclops— and the eye in the middle of his head, too—to go hang? (168–74; trans. Kovacs, modified)

With their interest in the unbridled enjoyment of food, drink, and sex we are clearly in a comic world, although Odysseus maintains a serious demeanor, in much the same way as Dicaeopolis remains earnest in Aristophanes' *Acharnians*, at least until he has accomplished what he set out to do (namely, to secure a private peace with Sparta). Like Dicaeopolis (and any number of other Aristophanic protagonists on a mission, such as the Sausage Seller in *Knights*, or Bdelycleon in *Wasps*), Odysseus's sang-froid serves as an implicit repudiation of the satyrs's behavior, even if that repudiation is not meant to be taken seriously. The exchange between them at 175–87 is revealing on this point:

Χο. ἄκου᾽, Ὀδυσσεῦ· διαλαλήσωμέν τί σοι.
Οδ. καὶ μὴν φίλοι γε προσφέρεσθε πρὸς φίλον.
Χο. ἐλάβετε Τροίαν τὴν Ἑλένην τε χειρίαν;
Οδ. καὶ πάντα γ᾽ οἶκον Πριαμιδῶν ἐπέρσαμεν.
Χο. οὔκουν, ἐπειδὴ τὴν νεᾶνιν εἵλετε,
    ἅπαντες αὐτὴν διεκροτήσατ᾽ ἐν μέρει,
    ἐπεί γε πολλοῖς ἥδεται γαμουμένη,
    τὴν προδότιν, ἣ τοὺς θυλάκους τοὺς ποικίλους
    περὶ τοῖν σκελοῖν ἰδοῦσα καὶ τὸν χρύσεον
    κλῳὸν φοροῦντα περὶ μέσον τὸν αὐχένα
    ἐξεπτοήθη, Μενέλεων ἀνθρώπιον
    λῷστον λιποῦσα. μηδαμοῦ γένος ποτὲ
    φῦναι γυναικῶν ὤφελ᾽, εἰ μὴ ᾽μοὶ μόνῳ.

(Chorus leader): Listen, Odysseus. We would like a little chat with you.
(Od): Of course, since you are my friends and I am yours.
(Ch. leader): Did you capture Troy and take Helen prisoner?
(Od): Yes, and we sacked the whole house of the sons of Priam.
(Ch. leader): Once you had caught the girl, didn't you all then take turns banging her, since she takes pleasure in having more than one mate? The traitor! She saw the parti-colored breeches on the man's legs and the gold necklace around his neck, and went all a-flutter after them, leaving behind that fine little man Menelaus. O would that the female sex were nowhere to be found—but in my lap. (175–87; Kovacs)

Although the satyrs begin as if they want to have a meaningful chat about his experiences at Troy, it soon becomes clear that they are more interested in launching a *psogos* against Helen for what they regard as her wanton, not to mention treacherous, behavior. It is hardly surprising, however, that their moral indignation is a mere façade, and the scene ends with a silly sexual joke. Throughout, Odysseus plays the straight man to their buffoonery, never responding to their coarse humor.

There is much comedy in these contrasts, and in the decidedly unheroic portrait of Odysseus that Euripides seems at pains to reinforce in the early scenes of the play. Whereas the Homeric Odysseus is generally poised to confront the next challenge,[61] the Euripidean Odysseus seems, initially at least, simply beleaguered. Indeed, when the Cyclops's arrival is first announced (193), Odysseus's initial response is only fear and an inclination to flee:

Σι. . . . . οἴμοι· Κύκλωψ ὅδ᾽ ἔρχεται· τί δράσομεν:
Οδ. ἀπολώλαμέν τἄρ᾽, ὦ γέρον· ποῖ χρὴ φυγεῖν;
Σι. ἔσω πέτρας τῆσδ᾽, οὗπερ ἂν λάθοιτέ γε.
Οδ. δεινὸν τόδ᾽ εἶπας, ἀρκύων μολεῖν ἔσω.

(Sil.): Oh no! Here comes the Cyclops. What are we to do?
(Od.): Then we are done for, old man. Where should we flee to?
(Sil.): Inside this cave, where you could avoid being seen.
(Od.): A dangerous suggestion, this, going into the net. (193–96; trans. Kovacs)

He needs to remind himself, in fact, of his own heroic stature:

Σι. οὐ δεινόν· εἰσὶ καταφυγαὶ πολλαὶ πέτρας.
Οδ. οὐ δῆτ᾽· ἐπεὶ τἂν μεγάλα γ᾽ ἡ Τροία στένοι,
εἰ φευξόμεσθ᾽ ἕν᾽ ἄνδρα, μυρίον δ᾽ ὄχλον
Φρυγῶν ὑπέστην πολλάκις σὺν ἀσπίδι.
ἀλλ᾽, εἰ θανεῖν δεῖ, κατθανούμεθ᾽ εὐγενῶς
ἢ ζῶντες αἶνον τὸν πάρος συσσώσομεν.

(Sil.): No danger: There are many hiding places in the cave.
(Od.): I shall not do it. Troy would groan loudly if I were to run from a single man when I stood my ground so often, shield in hand, against a throng of Trojans without number. Rather, if I must die, I will die nobly—or live on and also retain my old reputation. (197–202; trans. Kovacs)

It is shame, in other words, that keeps him from fleeing—fear that cowardly behavior *now* would diminish his reputation for heroism.[62] He wills himself into a heroic posture, that is, but only as an after-thought. We may expect this

61. Though certainly not always: see, e.g., *Od.* 10.50–52, where Odysseus contemplates suicide after his men loose the winds from Aeolus's bag, or 10.496–98, where he sinks into a brief depression, and again contemplates suicide, after Circe tells him that he must visit Teiresias in Hades. Still, these moments are fleeting, and insofar as they form part of Odysseus's own narrative to the Phaeacians, they serve his own dramatic, self-aggrandizing, purposes as well, for the more dire he can portray his predicament, the more heroic is his resolve to endure it.

62. Seaford (1984, 141) remarks that *Cyclops* 198–200 "brings out the contradiction in *Od.* 9.263–67, where Od. combines mention of the glory of the Trojan War with supplication." Perhaps, but the passage in *Cyclops* seems to highlight, if anything, the disingenuousness of Odysseus's supplication in the *Odyssey* passage, where the hero states undiplomatically, not to mention menacingly, that they have come as suppliants to see if they might receive guest-gifts (Homer *Od.* 9.266–68). Euripides' Odysseus does eventually bring this up (*Cyclops* 299–301) but only after all his other, more rational arguments have failed to elicit mercy from Polyphemus.

kind of behavior from a diffident, dithering comic character, but hardly from a self-assured Homeric hero.

Odysseus is further assailed in a highly ironic departure from the Homeric version of the episode. Just when it seems as if he has found an insider friend and ally in Silenus, now serving as Polyphemus's slave, Silenus turns on him as soon as he has the chance. At 228–40, when Polyphemus has returned and spots Odysseus and his men, Silenus tries to cover up his drunken state by claiming that Odysseus had attacked him and threatened to steal Polyphemus's food, and then to attack Polyphemus himself.

> τούς τ᾽ ἄρνας ἐξεφοροῦντο· δήσαντες δὲ σὲ
> κλῳῷ τριπήχει, κατὰ τὸν ὀφθαλμὸν μέσον
> τὰ σπλάγχν᾽ ἔφασκον ἐξαμήσεσθαι βίᾳ,
> μάστιγί τ᾽ εὖ τὸ νῶτον ἀπολέψειν σέθεν,
> κἄπειτα συνδήσαντες ἐς θάδώλια
> τῆς ναὸς ἐμβαλόντες ἀποδώσειν τινὶ
> πέτρους μοχλεύειν, ἢ 'ς μυλῶνα καταβαλεῖν.

And they said that they would collar you like a dangerous dog and right under your very eye violently pull out your guts, flay your back nicely with a whip, then bind your hand and foot and throw you onto the rowing benches of their ship and sell you to someone who needs to move heavy rocks or throw you into a mill. (234–40; trans. Kovacs)

Silenus's speech here is worthy of the finest invective passages in Aristophanes, as the following repartee between the Sausage-seller, the Paphlagonian, and a slave from *Knights* vividly illustrates:

> ΑΛ. ἐγὼ δὲ βυνήσω γέ σου τὸν πρωκτὸν ἀντὶ φύσκης.
> ΠΑ. ἐγὼ δέ γ᾽ ἐξέλξω σε τῆς πυγῆς θύραζε κύβδα.
> ΟΙ. Α´ νὴ τὸν Ποσειδῶ κἀμὲ τἄρ᾽, ἤνπερ γε τοῦτον ἕλκῃς.
> ΠΑ.   οἷόν σε δήσω ‹ν› τῷ ξύλῳ.
> ΑΛ.   διώξομαί σε δειλίας.
> ΠΑ.   ἡ βύρσα σου θρανεύσεται.
> ΑΛ.   δερῶ σε θύλακον κλοπῆς.   370
> ΠΑ.   διαπατταλευθήσει χαμαί.
> ΑΛ.   περικόμματ᾽ ἔκ σου σκευάσω.
> ΠΑ.   τὰς βλεφαρίδας σου παρατιλῶ.
> ΑΛ.   τὸν πρηγορεῶνά σου 'κτεμῶ.
> ΟΙ. Α´ καὶ νὴ Δί᾽ ἐμβαλόντες αὐ-   375
>   τῷ πάτταλον μαγειρικῶς
>   εἰς τὸ στόμ᾽ εἶτα δ᾽ ἔνδοθεν
>   τὴν γλῶτταν ἐξείραντες αὐ-

τοῦ σκεψόμεσθ᾽ εὖ κἀνδρικῶς
κεχηνότος   380
τὸν πρωκτόν, εἰ χαλαζᾷ.

(Sausage seller): And I'll stuff your arse like a sausage skin.
(Paphlagonian): And I'll drag you out of doors by the buttocks, head
    downwards.
(Slave A): By Poseidon, if you drag him, you'll have to drag me too!
(Pa): How I'll clap you in the stocks!
(SS): I'll indict you for cowardice.
(Pa): Your hide will be stretched on the tanning bench.
(SS): I'll flay you into a thief's hold-all.
(Pa): You'll be spread out and pegged to the ground.
(SS): I'll make mincemeat out of you.
(Pa): I'll pluck out your eyelashes.
(SS): I'll cut out your crop.
(Slave A): And, by Zeus, we'll shove a peg in his mouth as the
butchers do, then pull out his tongue and take a good and proper
look at him, there with his gaping . . . arse, to see if he's measly.
(*Knights* 364–81 trans. Sommerstein 1981)

There is a formalized, almost formulaic, quality to such passages that serves to
emphasize their fundamental comic absurdity[63] while apportioning the proper
levels of abjection among the principal players. In the case of the *Cyclops* passage, our sense of Odysseus's abjection grows even stronger when Silenus falsely
imputes to him a laundry list of vituperative threats against Polyphemus.

Since Polyphemus chooses to believe Silenus rather than the chorus—who
take Odysseus's side and maintain his innocence—Euripides effectively has
Polyphemus replicate the moral calculus found in Homer, where Odysseus
could be accused of the sort of *ponêria* that Silenus now charges him with, and
where we *could* understand why Polyphemus might be indignant enough to
eat Odysseus and his men. This creates a complex, ironized narratology: Just
when Odysseus is portrayed as unproblematically moral (he went out of his
way, after all, to follow normal social protocols in trying to secure food from
the satyrs at the beginning of the play), he is frivolously charged with unjust
behavior and thrown into deeper abjection. Abject and oppressed characters
in comic genres, when confronted with powerful and unjust adversaries, respond with indignation, as Euripides has Odysseus do at 285–308:[64]

    63. See Rosen 1988, 68–70. On dictional continuities between satyr play and Old Comedy,
see Voelke 2003; and López Eire 2003.
    64. There seems to be little cause for emending the λέγομεν of 287 to ψέγομεν, as Kovacs
does (1994, ad loc.), though if his reading were right, it would be fitting for Euripides to have
Odysseus conceptualize his speech here as a ψόγος.

Οδ. θεοῦ τὸ πρᾶγμα· μηδέν' αἰτιῶ βροτῶν.   285
    ἡμεῖς δέ σ', ὦ θεοῦ ποντίου γενναῖε παῖ,
    ἱκετεύομέν τε καὶ λέγομεν ἐλευθέρως·
    μὴ τλῇς πρὸς ἄντρα σοὺς ἀφιγμένους φίλους
    κτανεῖν βοράν τε δυσσεβῆ θέσθαι γνάθοις·
    οἳ τὸν σόν, ὦναξ, πατέρ' ἔχειν ναῶν ἕδρας   290
    ἐρρυσάμεσθα γῆς ἐν Ἑλλάδος μυχοῖς·
    ἱερᾶς τ' ἄθραυστος Ταινάρου μένει λιμὴν
    Μαλέας τ' ἄκρας κευθμῶνες ἥ τε Σουνίου
    δίας Ἀθάνας σῶς ὑπάργυρος πέτρα
    Γεραίστιοί τε καταφυγαί· τά θ' Ἑλλάδος   295
    †δύσφρον' ὀνείδη† Φρυξὶν οὐκ ἐδώκαμεν.
    ὧν καὶ σὺ κοινοῖ· γῆς γὰρ Ἑλλάδος μυχοὺς
    οἰκεῖς ὑπ' Αἴτνῃ, τῇ πυριστάκτῳ πέτρᾳ.
    νόμος δὲ θνητοῖς, εἰ λόγους ἀποστρέφῃ,
    ἱκέτας δέχεσθαι ποντίους ἐφθαρμένους   300
    ξένιά τε δοῦναι καὶ πέπλους ἐπαρκέσαι,
    οὐκ ἀμφὶ βουπόροισι πηχθέντας μέλη
    ὀβελοῖσι νηδὺν καὶ γνάθον πλῆσαι σέθεν.
    ἄλις δὲ Πριάμου γαῖ' ἐχήρωσ' Ἑλλάδα
    πολλῶν νεκρῶν πιοῦσα δοριπετῆ φόνον   305
    ἀλόχους τ' ἀνάνδρους γραῦς τ' ἄπαιδας ὤλεσεν
    πολιούς τε πατέρας. εἰ δὲ τοὺς λελειμμένους
    σὺ συμπυρώσας δαῖτ' ἀναλώσεις πικράν,
    ποῖ τρέψεταί τις;

It was the doing of a god: blame no mortal for it. But, O noble son of
the seagod, we at once entreat you and give you our frank censure:
do not have the hardness to kill benefactors who have come to your
house and to make of them a godless meal for your jaws. It was we
who kept your father safe in the possession of his temple seats in
every corner of Greece: the harbor of sacred Taenarum and the
recesses of Cape Malea remain inviolate, safe is the rock of Sunium
rich in silver, sacred to the goddess Athena, safe are Geraestus's
refuges. We did not suffer the great disgrace of surrendering Greek
possessions to the Trojans. In these events you also have a share,
dwelling as you do in the far reaches of Hellas, under Aetna, the rock
that drips with fire. But if you are deaf to these considerations, there is
a law among mortals that one must receive shipwrecked suppliants,
give them the gifts hospitality requires, and provide them with
clothing. <It is this treatment we ought to receive from you,> rather
than to have our limbs pierced with spits for roasting beef and to fill
your maw and belly. Priam's land has wrought enough bereavement

on Greece, drinking down the spear-shed blood of many corpses. She has widowed wives and brought old women and greybeards childless to the grave. If you mean to cook and consume those left, making a grim feast, where shall anyone turn for refuge? (trans. Kovacs)

In this speech, Odysseus implores the Cyclops to spare him and his men, and to show them a modicum of charity as shipwrecked and destitute men deserve. (He mentioned guest-gifts and clothes, 301, though it is clear from the opening of the play that he and his men were primarily driven to the island by their need for food). He ends with a plea typical of any moralizing satirist, namely that Polyphemus should give up his life of gluttony and, well, "be good"!:

> ἀλλ᾽ ἐμοὶ πιθοῦ, Κύκλωψ·
> πάρες τὸ μάργον σῆς γνάθου, τὸ δ᾽ εὐσεβὲς
> τῆς δυσσεβείας ἀνθελοῦ· πολλοῖσι γὰρ
> κέρδη πονηρὰ ζημίαν ἠμείψατο.

> Listen to me, Cyclops: Give up this gluttony and choose to be godly instead of impious: For many have found that base gain brings punishment in its train. (309–12; trans. Kovacs)

No character within a comic work such as this, however, and certainly no satirist worth his salt, can get away for long with this kind of sanctimoniousness, and Euripides impishly undermines Odysseus's pieties with Silenus's advice to the Cyclops that he should eat them anyway: "and if you bite down on the tongue, Cyclops, you'll become a terribly shrewd chatterbox!" (. . . ἢν δὲ τὴν γλῶσσαν δάκῃς, ‖ κομψὸς γενήσῃ καὶ λαλίστατος, Κύκλωψ).[65]

After Polyphemus utterly rejects Odysseus's pleas for mercy (316–45), Odysseus calls upon Athena and Zeus for their help, in an outburst epitomizing his abjection, and warns them against neglecting his prayer:

> Οδ. αἰαῖ, πόνους μὲν Τρωϊκοὺς ὑπεξέδυν
> θαλασσίους τε, νῦν δ᾽ ἐς ἀνδρὸς ἀνοσίου
> ὠμὴν κατέσχον ἀλίμενόν τε καρδίαν.
> ὦ Παλλάς, ὦ δέσποινα Διογενὲς θεά,
> νῦν νῦν ἄρηξον· κρείσσονας γὰρ Ἰλίου
> πόνους ἀφῖγμαι κἀπὶ κινδύνου βάθρα.

---

65. See Seaford's remarks about Odysseus (1984, 56): "Odysseus is of course no heroic representative of *nomos*, humanity, and Athenian democratic values. He is in Euripidean tragedy so associated with crafty self-interest that the audience of *Cyc.* must have regarded his rhetorical plea as an example of the πολλῶν λόγων εὑρήματα ὥστε με θανεῖν ['all those many words I discovered to keep myself from being killed,' *Hec.* 250] with which he once saved his life when recognized in Troy by Hecuba, only to treat her without thanks or pity after the Greek victory."

σύ τ', ὦ φαεννὰς ἀστέρων οἰκῶν ἕδρας
Ζεῦ ξένι', ὅρα τάδ'· εἰ γὰρ αὐτὰ μὴ βλέπεις,
ἄλλως νομίζηι Ζεὺς τὸ μηδὲν ὢν θεός.

Oh, alas, I have escaped hardships at Troy and on the sea only to put
in now at the fierce and harborless heart of this godless man! O
Pallas Athena, Zeus's divine daughter, now, now is the time to help
me! For I have come into trouble greater than at Troy and to the
very uttermost of danger. And you, Zeus, Protector of Guests, who
dwell in the bright realm of the stars, look on these things! For if you
take no note of them, men mistakenly worship you as a god when
you are in fact Zeus the worthless. (347–55; trans. Kovacs)

Dale pointed out that this form of "challenging-nouthetetic" prayer is common in late Euripides,[66] but when deployed for comic effect, as it is here, we
can trace its roots to parodic forms found in the Greek iambus. Hipponax, as
we saw in chapter 1, offers several passages of comic complaint to various
gods for their neglect of his needs and his consequent suffering.[67] Like those
iambographic speakers (likely Hipponax himself), Odysseus too fashions himself as the oppressed underdog, who, in his desperation, must put himself at
the mercy of the gods. This is a pedestrian, lowly sort of protagonist whose
risibility lies in an implicit contrast with his far more powerful and elevated
antagonists. In the case of *Cyclops*, Euripides transforms his Odysseus into a
compromised figure, who belongs more in the benighted all-too-human present
than in any mythical past when humans were routinely imagined as larger than
life. As if to leave no doubt about such a comic devaluation, Euripides has
Odysseus explicitly distance himself from the mythical discourse with which
his own story would have been known to the audience. For at 375–76, after
the Cyclops has finished devouring his men, he exclaims:

Οδ. ὦ Ζεῦ, τί λέξω, δείν' ἰδὼν ἄντρων ἔσω
κοὺ πιστά, μύθοις εἰκότ' οὐδ' ἔργοις βροτῶν;

O Zeus, what am I to say when I have seen in the cave terrible
things, incredible things such as one meets only in stories, not in the
deeds of mortals?
(375–76; trans. Kovacs)

66. Dale 1963; Seaford (1984, 172 ad loc.) augments her list of parallels. See also Kleinknecht
1937, 73 on parodies of hymnic invocations.
67. See also Hipponax frr. 47 and 48 Dg., which broach similar themes. On the latter, see
Rosen 1987.

Odysseus, in other words, numbers himself among mere mortals, who normally only hear about the horrible events he has just witnessed from *mythoi*. In describing the Cyclops as a figure drawn from *mythoi*, and his deeds as beyond human belief, Odysseus thereby distances himself even further from any heroic stature the audience might have expected him to have from their knowledge of Homer. Euripides' Cyclops certainly presents a challenge of Homeric proportions to Odysseus, but this Odysseus is not particularly eager to meet it.

In the end Odysseus has the last laugh, since he overcomes the Cyclops in the same manner as his Homeric forebear—getting him drunk and blinding him. The effect of the outcome, however, is different in each version. Whereas Homer's Cyclops is portrayed as morally suspect simply by virtue of his primitive, non-human status, and so Odysseus has no compunction about assailing him with little initial provocation, Euripides' Cyclops is given a chance to demonstrate his moral failings first, and suffers only as a direct consequence of them. Both versions of the episode, as we have noted, aim for the comedy that arises when characters mock or satirize each other. But the precise nature of this comedy—Who laughs at whom? Why? And how does the text direct the responses of its putative audience?—differs according as each poet conceptualizes the relationship between his antagonists. Euripides is able to clarify the moral and generic ambiguity we find in Homer's version of the story by constructing his own version that draws more straightforwardly on a well-established poetics of satire. Indeed, the final lines of the *Cyclops* typify the major components of such a poetics:

Κυ. οἴμοι γελῶμαι· κερτομεῖτέ μ᾽ ἐν κακοῖς.
Χο. ἀλλ᾽ οὐκέτ᾽, ἀλλὰ πρόσθεν οὗτός ἐστι σοῦ.
Κυ. ὦ παγκάκιστε, ποῦ ποτ᾽ εἶ; Οδ. τηλοῦ σέθεν
    φυλακαῖσι φρουρῶ σῶμ᾽ Ὀδυσσέως τόδε.
Κυ. πῶς εἶπας; ὄνομα μεταβαλὼν καινὸν λέγεις.
Οδ. ὅπερ μ᾽ ὁ φύσας ὠνόμαζ᾽ Ὀδυσσέα.
    δώσειν δ᾽ ἔμελλες ἀνοσίου δαιτὸς δίκας·
    κακῶς γὰρ ἂν Τροίαν γε διεπυρώσαμεν
    εἰ μή σ᾽ ἑταίρων φόνον ἐτιμωρησάμην.

(Cyc.): Oh, you are mocking me, deceiving me in my troubles!
(Od.): I shall no more. He's right in front of you.
(Cyc.): O you complete scoundrel, where in the world are you?
(Od.): At some distance, where I can keep the person of Odysseus
    here safe from harm.
(Cyc.): What? This is a new name you use.
(Od.): The very one my father gave me, Odysseus, and you were
    destined to pay the price for your unholy feast. For it would have
    been a sad affair, if we had burned down Troy but then I failed to

punish you for the murder of my companions. (687–95; trans.
Kovacs, modified)

Here we find an indignant, formerly abject mocker, Odysseus (known up to
this point by the abject tag "*Outis*," that is, "nobody"), who finally gets the
better of his target, Cyclops (note the vocabulary of comic abuse here: γελῶμαι,
κερτομεῖτε, ὦ παγκάκιστε), and has justice unambiguously on his side ("you
were destined to pay the price for your unholy feast . . . It would have been a
sad affair if we had burned down Troy, but then I failed to punish you for the
murder of my companions.")

It is impossible to know for sure whether Euripides consciously depicted
his Odysseus and Cyclops as players in a literary game of *psogos* and satire that
went beyond the parameters of satyr play, but there is no doubt that others
throughout antiquity did so. If our evidence were better, in fact, it is not unlikely that we would find Odysseus and Polyphemus first deployed as paradigms of satirist and target, respectively, by none other than Hipponax. I have
discussed elsewhere the likelihood that Hipponax assimilated the motif of
"Odysseus as underdog" into his poetic quarrels with his own targets, and
identified himself (as his speaking persona) with the Odysseus whom Homer
portrays in a less than flattering light. We need not rehearse the argument
here,[68] except to say that such an assimilation to the Homeric Odysseus would
have been a particularly effective conceit in his ongoing *contretemps* with Bupalus,
since it would have allowed Hipponax to maintain a simultaneously abject and
mock-heroic stance in his dealings with his adversary. For like Odysseus,
Hipponax too seems to have portrayed himself as someone whose unremark-
able, even deficient, appearance belied an unexpected physical strength,[69] and
this would presumably lead him in the end to a comic "victory" over Bupalus.[70]

---

68. See Rosen 1990, esp. 17–19, for full discussion. Here I argued that Hipponax found in
Homer an Odysseus who was often superficially diffident and abject, but in the end, superior and
self-righteous (one thinks of his altercations with Euryalus [8.133–85] or Irus [18.1–107], or
Antenor's description of him as he observes him from the walls of Troy in the Iliadic *teikhoskopia*,
Il. 3.217–24). At some point in his work, it seems, Hipponax modeled himself, *qua* satirist, on just
such a Homeric Odysseus. See also Miralles and Pòrtulas 1988, 37–44 on the possibility that
Hipponax parodied the Homeric *Doloneia* (*Iliad* 10). On the possibility that Archilochus, too, might
have drawn on the Homeric Odysseus for aspects of his own self-presentation in his iamboi, see
Seidensticker 1978.

69. See Hipponax test. 19, 19a, 19b Degani. To judge from these testimonia, Hipponax seems
to have gone out of his way to portray himself as small, weak, and thin, not to mention ugly, when
in fact he was extremely strong, and could (for example) hurl an empty vase incredibly far. See
discussion in Rosen 1990.

70. The evidence for Hipponax' deployment of Odysseus is more or less confined to frr. 74–
78 Dg., fragments from an Oxyrhynchus papyrus (P.Oxy. 2174) first edited by Lobel. Although it
is difficult to piece together anything coherent from this papyrus, there are enough suggestive phrases
to make the connection reasonably secure (a title ΟΔΥ[ΣΣΕ, is the first hint; as Lobel puts it: "it is
allowable to recognize . . . the title and some of the details of a 'Return of Odysseus'—seaweed

Hipponax is, of course, well known as an early parodist of Homer,[71] and it would be consonant with his poetic program to work out a comic version of *Odyssey* 9 at some point in his literary skirmishing with targets. It must be admitted, however, that there is slim evidence among the scattered fragments of Hipponax for a Cyclops scene, in which the poet assumed the role of Odysseus in a *psogos* directed against a target construed as a Cyclops character, however tantalizingly suggestive it may be. So we must look to a somewhat later period to find more secure evidence for an Odysseus capable of being conceptualized as an *explicitly* satirical figure in his dealings with the Cyclops. We turn here, therefore, to the dithyrambist Philoxenus of Cythera, who composed a poem in the generation after Euripides entitled *Cyclops or Galateia*. In this work (written before 388, when it was parodied in Aristophanes' *Wealth* 290–301), Philoxenus evidently added a new twist to the Odysseus-Cyclops story as it had been inherited from Homer, namely Polyphemus's amatory interest in the nymph Galatea.[72] The comic potential of pairing a grotesque monster with a beautiful sea-nymph is obvious, and in the next section we will see how Theocritus developed the story for his own purposes in the third century. Most relevant at this point is an ancient tradition that Philoxenus composed his *Cyclops* as a political allegory directed against the tyrant Dionysius I of Syracuse, in which poet and tyrant supposedly lay behind the figures of Odysseus and Cyclops, respectively. As is typical of biographical claims of this sort, the evidence is late and indirect, and we have no way of judging its authenticity, but, as we shall see below, it is persistent across a variety of sources and reveals much about the explicitly satirical potential of the Cyclops story.

Athenaeus (1.6e-7a) derives his version of the anecdote about Philoxenus and Dionysius from the historian Phaenias (late fourth-century BCE), and offers a charming, if garbled, account. Philoxenus and Dionysius were evidently good friends for a time, at least until Philoxenus was caught with Dionysius's mistress, whose name, as the story goes, happened to be Galatea:

---

after a snack, questions about family, Phaeacians, the lotus, perhaps a dreadful giant, an auger, embers, not to mention more problematical indications," 67). See also Masson 1962, 144, who suggested that "il pouvait s'agir d'Ulysse ou d'un personnage assimilé au héros."

71. Athenaeus (698b-c) records the famous statement attributed to Polemon (second-century BCE) that Hipponax was the "inventor" (*heuretês*) of parody, citing the obvious Homeric burlesque in fr. 126 Dg: Μοῦσά μοι Εὐρυμεδοντιάδεω τὴν ποντοχάρυβδιν . . . Hipponax's engagement with Homeric texts, however, could be considerably more subtle: cf., for example, Hipponax fr. 37 Dg., where the collocation of φαρμάσσων and ἐμβάπτων in a context of food preparation seems to allude to a similar collocation at Homer *Od.* 9.391–93, a simile used to describe the blinding of the Cyclops.

72. See Holland 1884, 184–209; Arnott 1996, 139–41; Sommerstein 2001, 156–58; also, Kugelmeier 1996, 255–62 (on Aristophanes' parody of Philoxenus in *Wealth*); and now Hordern 1999.

συνεμέθυε δὲ τῷ Φιλοξένῳ ἡδέως ὁ Διονύσιος. ἐπεὶ δὲ τὴν ἐρωμένην
Γαλάτειαν ἐφωράθη διαφθείρων, εἰς τὰς λατομίας ἐνεβλήθη· ἐν
αἷς ποιῶν τὸν Κύκλωπα συνέθηκε τὸν μῦθον εἰς τὸ περὶ αὐτὸν
γενόμενον πάθος, τὸν μὲν Διονύσιον Κύκλωπα ὑποστησάμενος, τὴν
δ᾽ αὐλητρίδα Γαλάτειαν, ἑαυτὸν δ᾽ Ὀδυσσέα

Dionysius used to enjoy getting drunk with Philoxenus. But when
Philoxenus was caught *in flagrante delicto* with his mistress Galatea,
he was sent to the stone quarries. There he composed his *Cyclops*,
in which he told the story of what happened to him, representing
Dionysius as the Cyclops, the flute-girl [that is, Dionysius's mistress]
as Galatea, and himself as Odysseus.

As Hordern (1999, 446) has pointed out, this anecdote does not actually say
that Philoxenus's *Cyclops* was intended as a satire against Dionysius, although
the scholia to Aristophanes' *Wealth* 290 confirm that tradition. Even if this
tradition has some basis in truth, it seems too conveniently coincidental that
Dionysius' mistress would have the same name as a sea-nymph known from
myth, and it is no surprise that alternate explanations of Philoxenus's sentence
in the quarries arose in antiquity.[73] But even if we can never get to the bottom
of Philoxenus's biography,[74] the stories that circulated about him in antiquity
suggest that from a relatively early period the Odysseus-Cyclops episode, as it
was inherited from Homer, was felt to be easily adaptable to the kinds of poetic structures and conventions that we have come to identify in this book with
comic satire. I suggested in the previous section that Euripides' *Cyclops* can
be analyzed along these lines, but what makes the case of Philoxenus's *Cyclops*
even more compelling is the self-consciousness with which it associates the
Cyclops story with the dynamics of poeticized personal satire. It seems to have
taken no great effort of the imagination to map the characters of a putatively
real-life interpersonal drama of abjection and injustice (Philoxenus thrown into
prison by a tyrant) on to the characters in the Homeric episode (Odysseus
imprisoned by the Cyclops), and so to turn the proto-comedy of *Odyssey* 9 into
explicit satire. The episode's narrative strategy is simplified, as it is now told
from the subjective perspective of an indignant speaker with a straightforward

73. See Arnott 1996, 140; and Hordern 1999, 447–48 for alternative explanations of Philoxenus's
punishment.

74. See Webster 1970, 21 on the possibility that the alleged connection between Philoxenus
and Dionysius I arose from parodies of Philoxenus's dithyramb among contemporary comic poets
(though he does not completely discount the idea that it could be genuine). Webster also discusses
(20–22) the evidence for Middle Comic versions of the Cyclops story; see also Sommerstein 2001,
156. For other comic traditions about the tyrant Dionysius, see Hunter 1983, 116–22 (on the fragments of Eubulus's *Dionysios*); Webster 1970, 28; and Sommerstein 2001, 174–76, on line 550 (lam-
pooning Dionysius) of Aristophanes' *Wealth*.

agenda of complaint, and its new allegorical mode allows him to direct the outcome of the story to his own advantage: What seems in real life to be an insurmountable challenge (imprisonment in a quarry) can in a poetic version be transformed into a vehicle by which an abject hero vindicates himself and overcomes a powerful, but unjust, adversary.

It is fascinating, in fact, to watch this very process played out in Athenaeus's account of Philoxenus and his relations with Dionysius, in the section that leads into the part quoted above. This passage (1.6 e-f) offers a humorously bizarre anecdote in which Philoxenus essentially replicates key components of the Odysseus-Cyclops episode:

Φαινίας δέ φησιν ὅτι Φιλόξενος ὁ Κυθήριος ποιητής, περιπαθὴς ὢν τοῖς ὄψοις, δειπνῶν ποτε παρὰ Διονυσίῳ ὡς εἶδεν ἐκείνῳ μὲν μεγάλην τρίγλαν παρατεθεῖσαν, ἑαυτῷ δὲ μικράν, ἀναλαβὼν αὐτὴν εἰς τὰς χεῖρας πρὸς τὸ οὖς προσήνεγκε. πυθομένου δὲ τοῦ Διονυσίου τίνος ἕνεκεν τοῦτο ποιεῖ, εἶπεν ὁ Φιλόξενος ὅτι γράφων τὴν Γαλάτειαν βούλοιτό τινα παρ' ἐκείνης τῶν κατὰ Νηρέα πυθέσθαι· τὴν δὲ ἠρωτημένην ἀποκεκρίσθαι διότι νεωτέρα ἁλοίη· διὸ μὴ παρακολουθεῖν· τὴν δὲ τῷ Διονυσίῳ παρατεθεῖσαν πρεσβυτέραν οὖσαν εἰδέναι πάντα σαφῶς ἃ βούλεται μαθεῖν. τὸν οὖν Διονύσιον γελάσαντα ἀποστεῖλαι αὐτῷ τὴν τρίγλαν τὴν παρακειμένην αὐτῷ.

Phaenias says that the poet Philoxenus of Cythera, who was quite the gourmand, was dining once with Dionysius, when he saw that a huge mullet had been put in front of that man, but a small one was placed in front of himself. Taking it up in his hands, he put it up to his ear. When Dionysius asked him why he was doing this, Philoxenus said that he was composing his "Galatea" and wanted to learn a few things from the fish about Nereus's daughters. And [he said] the fish, when asked, answered that it was caught too young, and so had not followed him; but it said that the fish which had been served to Dionysius, because it was older, knew all the things Philoxenus wanted to know. And so Dionysus laughed and sent the fish lying in front of him over to Philoxenus.

This part of Athenaeus's story represents Philoxenus and Dionysius in a relationship characterized by bantering goodwill. But we may notice that Philoxenus here is actually portrayed as a subordinate, unhappy with his inferiority to his host, but determined to get the better of him by guile and cleverness. To Athenaeus (or more precisely to Phaenias, his source), it is clear that Philoxenus concocts the absurd story of the mullet because he is indignant at the size of his portion: "when he saw that Dionysius had a large mullet in front of him, and that his was small. . . ." Like the Homeric Odysseus confronting the Cyclops, when he finds himself in an inferior position he resorts to deception in order to get his way. It does not much matter whether Dionysius is actually taken in by Philoxenus's ruse—Athenaeus says he laughed, and then gave Philoxenus his larger fish—or whether he saw through it from the start and was rewarding Philoxenus for his imaginative and amusing story.[75] Nor (again) does it matter whether the story is true. The point is, rather, that in antiquity people evidently could not resist assimilating Philoxenus himself to the Odysseus he constructed in his *Cyclops*, and that what interested them most about this character was his role as self-righteous, self-aggrandizing, and deceptive satirist. And as if to emphasize a specific correlation between Philoxenus and the Odysseus of the Cyclops episode, Athenaeus mentions that Dionysius would routinely get drunk with Philoxenus.[76] It is hardly a stretch to suppose that this detail was intended to allude to, at least in its original source (perhaps in a comedy; see below, n. 77), Dionysius's identification with the Cyclops in Philoxenus's allegorical version of the episode, portrayed as overcome by Odysseus's potent wine.[77]

---

75. Erwin Cook has suggested to me that this scene may be modeled on the passage at the end of *Od.* 14, where Odysseus tells Eumaeus a story in order to get a cloak from him. Eumaeus is pleased with himself for getting the point of Odysseus's yarn (14.508–12), and Odysseus ends up with a cloak to sleep in at the end (14.520).

76. See previous note; in the Eumaeus episode of *Od.* 14, Odysseus prefaces his tale by blaming the wine for what he is about to say (463–65).

77. A late testimonium (c. 410 CE; see Hordern 2004, 286 for dating and further bibliography) about Philoxenus's *Cyclops*, Synesius's *Epistles* 121 (*Patr. Gr.* 66.1500 B–D Migne = Philoxenus fr. 5, 818 *PMG*), is worth mentioning here. Synesius's letter offers rich detail of a version of the story usually assumed to derive from Philoxenus (Holland 1884, 192–97; Sommerstein 2001, 156; and Hordern 2004, 285–86), although he may also have been drawing on versions from Middle Comedy (for evidence, Sommerstein 2001, 156). This passage reveals a tradition that easily conceptualized Odysseus and Polyphemus as characters engaged in a psogic agon of sorts, where the tone is sarcastic and satirical, but always highly moralistic. Synesius ends his account of the story by making an allegorical connection between himself and his target; Synesius recounts how Odysseus tried to persuade Polyphemus to move the stone blocking the opening to the cave by promising him magic spells that would help him win over Galatea. In reply, Synesius says,

πρὸς οὖν ταῦτα ὁ Πολύφημος ἐξεκάγχασέ τε ὅσον ἐδύνατο μέγιστον καὶ τὼ χεῖρε ἐκρότησε. καὶ ὁ μὲν Ὀδυσσεὺς ᾤετο αὐτὸν ὑπὸ χαρμονῆς οὐκ ἔχειν ὅ τι ἑαυτῷ χρήσαιτο, κατελπίσαντα τῶν παιδικῶν περιέσεσθαι· ὁ δὲ ὑπογενειάσας αὐτὸν, "ὦ Οὖτις," ἔφη, "δριμύτατον μὲν ἀνθρώπιον ἔοικας εἶναι καὶ ἐγκατατετριμμένον ἐν πράγμασιν. ἄλλο μέντοι τι ποίκιλλε· ἐνθένδε γὰρ οὐκ ἀποδράσεις." ὁ μὲν οὖν Ὀδυσσεύς (ἠδικεῖτο γὰρ ὄντως) ἔμελλεν ἄρα τῆς πανουργίας ὀνήσεσθαι, σὲ δὲ Κύκλωπα μὲν ὄντα τῇ τόλμῃ Σίσυφον δὲ τοῖς ἐγχειρήμασι δίκη μετῆλθε καὶ νόμος καθεῖρξεν, ὧν μή ποτε σύγε καταγελάσειας.

"Polyphemus laughed out his loudest and clapped his hands with delight. Odysseus thought that he couldn't contain himself with joy, excited by his hope of possessing his beloved, but the giant only chucked him under the chin. 'Noman,' said he, 'you have all the airs of a very shrewd little fellow and one experienced in affairs; but try some other scheme, for you will not escape from here.' Odysseus, unjustly treated, then prepared to profit by his cunning, but as to you, a Cyclops in audacity and a Sisyphus in your actions, it is justice which has pursued you, and law which has closed in upon you. May you never be able to mock at these!"

Like Euripides'*Cyclops*, Philoxenus's version seemed to have focused on an unproblematically just Odysseus and unjust Polyphemus. As such, when Philoxenus came to allegorize them in his *Cyclops* in the service of a satirical agon between "real" people, it was easy to see which character he would map himself on to (Odysseus), and which would stand in for his adversary (Polyphemus).[78] But the detail of Galatea, a character who added a comic love interest to an otherwise heroic encounter, seems to have been something new with Philoxenus, and offered a potential complication to the easy assumption that Polyphemus was always an incorrigibly "bad" character.[79] Indeed, the notion of a lovesick Polyphemus opened up the door not only to high comedy, but also to a potential reevaluation of his character as it had evolved in Greek literature after Homer's treatment in *Odyssey* 9. The appearance of Galatea in the story of Polyphemus, I suggest, allowed authors of the late classical and Hellenistic periods to reconsider nuances of his character once found in Homer but gradually lost as the story became simplified in the service of pure comedy. A "love-story" of Polyphemus and Galatea is, to be sure, still comedy; but it is a comedy that invests the erstwhile ogre with a human subjectivity that Homer came close to conveying, but stopped short of fully exploring.

3. Cyclops Rehabilitated: Lovesongs of Polyphemus in Theocritus

Homer's occasional touches of sympathy for the Cyclops in *Odyssey* 9 are often noted and certainly add to the impression that his character may be less monolithic than one might at first suppose. Indeed, Homer seems continually on the verge of allowing the Cyclops to offer his own "*psogos* against Odysseus," a narrative that, if it were to exist, might begin by questioning Odysseus's intrusion into his secluded, and heretofore innocent, life. The narrative strategy of Book 9 could never allow this, since Odysseus himself is made to tell the

---

78. In fact, the allegory seems clumsy: If Polyphemus is supposed to represent the tyrant Dionysius, and Dionysius already has the real Galatea as his mistress, why would he be portrayed as lovesick over the sea-nymph Galatea, who would be unattainable by him in his guise as Polyphemus? And if Odysseus was supposed to be a cipher for Philoxenus, where does the real-life Galatea—with whom Philoxenus supposedly had had an affair—fit in? According to the version given in Synesius (see above n. 77), Odysseus tried to get himself out of the cave by offering Polyphemus love spells and charms with which he could win over Galatea—hardly the kind of assistance we would expect the real-life Philoxenus to offer his adversary Dionysius!

79. The closest we get to a sympathetic portrait of Polyphemus in *Odyssey* 9 is probably the famous address to his favorite ram at 446–61, although this, as told by Odysseus himself, is surely intended, from his perspective at least, as mockery. Is it possible that Polyphemus's relationship with Galatea evolved out of this relationship to his ram (as suggested to me by Erwin Cook; see above, n. 75)?

tale, but if it could (and Homer himself, as we have seen, offers some encouragement for us to entertain the fantasy), we might find the Cyclops adopting the same satirical postures and tropes as Odysseus in his own narrative. From such a perspective, the Cyclops, not Odysseus, would have "right" on his side, and his abjection, insofar as it would in such a hypothetical case be a *reaction* to an unprovoked wrong committed against him, would align him comfortably with the figure of the satirist as we have come to understand him throughout this study.

Homer, as we have seen, offers only a small glimpse at an alternative, righteously indignant Cyclops in *Odyssey* 9, a hint that the moral standing of the antagonists in that book might be more nuanced than the character Odysseus would want us to believe, and that the Cyclops might plausibly have a different story to tell if given the chance. Although the notion of a sympathetic Cyclops remained undeveloped in Homer, however, it resonated with later authors who took the Homeric tale on a famous erotic tangent, and altered the narrative perspective in such a way as to give voice to the Cyclops's abjection, rather than that of Odysseus. This is a Cyclops in many respects highly dependent on Homer's portrait in *Odyssey* 9, but his transference from the epic to the amatory world affords him a new subjectivity unavailable in Homer, and with that, in turn, the opportunity to construct a new relationship with the putative audience of his own song. Even though the story of Polyphemus and Galatea does not figure in the Homeric episode, no ancient audience who heard it could fail to recognize Polyphemus's Homeric provenance. And as I shall argue below, the story of the comically erotic Polyphemus arose, at least in part, as a response to, or even commentary on the nuances of Homer's *Cyclopeia* discussed above, namely, the occasional touches of pathos shown toward the Cyclops, Odysseus's morally questionable behavior, and, especially, the unstable roles of blamer and target within the narrative.

Theocritus *Idyll* 6 and *Idyll* 11 both concern the love of the Cyclops for Galatea, though they focus on different periods of the relationship. We begin with *Idyll* 11, however, because it deals with events chronologically prior to those in *Idyll* 6, even though we cannot tell which was composed first.[80] The first indication that we have come a long way since *Odyssey* 9, and will encounter a Cyclops who has shed most, if not all, of the monstrous qualities so obvious there, comes in the opening lines of the poem, where both the speaker, Theocritus, and his addressee, Nicias, are linked with the lovesick Polyphemus:

οὐδὲν ποττὸν ἔρωτα πεφύκει φάρμακον ἄλλο,
Νικία, οὔτ᾽ ἔγχριστον, ἐμὶν δοκεῖ, οὔτ᾽ ἐπίπαστον,

80. See Köhnken 1996; and Hunter 1999, 244–45. It is not unreasonable to suppose that *Idyll* 6 was composed later than 11, but whether we should consider the two as "companion pieces" (as Segal 1977, 48) remains an open question.

ἢ ταὶ Πιερίδες· κοῦφον δέ τι τοῦτο καὶ ἁδύ
γίνετ᾽ ἐπ᾽ ἀνθρώποις, εὑρεῖν δ᾽ οὐ ῥᾴδιόν ἐστι.
γινώσκειν δ᾽ οἶμαί τυ καλῶς ἰατρὸν ἐόντα
καὶ ταῖς ἐννέα δὴ πεφιλημένον ἔξοχα Μοίσαις.
οὕτω γοῦν ῥάιστα διᾶγ᾽ ὁ Κύκλωψ ὁ παρ᾽ ἁμῖν,
ὡρχαῖος Πολύφαμος, ὅκ᾽ ἤρατο τᾶς Γαλατείας.

There's no other remedy for love, Nicias, neither oil nor lotion, it
seems to me, except for the Muses; and this is gentle and sweet for
humankind, but it's not easy to find, as I think you know since
you're a physician, and deeply loved by all the nine Muses. So at
least my compatriot the Cyclops fared most easily—the legendary
Polyphemus, when he fell in love with Galatea. . . . (11.1–8)

Nicias seems to be in love, and, though a doctor himself, is looking for a remedy for the pain of eros. Theocritus offers the example of the Cyclops—a figure he refers to as ὁ παρ᾽ ἁμῖν, "one of our compatriots"—who found the best
pharmakon against lovesickness to be song. Theocritus's recommendation, then,
which comes with the authority of native affiliation (the Cyclops, too, he says,
was a "Sicilian"), is that Nicias act like the mythical Cyclops. This is a simple
enough point, but it remains one of great significance, for it establishes immediately that the poem is not itself going to be a mockery directed *against* the
Cyclops (as one might easily expect from any post-Homeric treatment of Cyclops) but will rather deploy the Cyclops as a sympathetic, positive paradigm.
To accomplish this, the gruesome aspects of the Homeric Cyclops must be
considerably downplayed, and the poem's focalizing voices assimilated to one
another. That is, the "I" that opens the poem, Theocritus, essentially "becomes" the "I" of Polyphemus's embedded song (beginning at line 19), since
Theocritus has himself "endorsed" the song as a useful means of overcoming
lovesickness. It would make little sense, after all, for Theocritus to identify himself with Homer's sociopathic Cyclops—at least if he did so without irony—
who was, first of all, a fundamental enemy of humans, and second, uninterested
in anything remotely amorous.

Narratologically, then, *Idyll* 11 is a departure from *Odyssey* 9, for whereas
the Homeric Cyclops was denied direct representation in his own voice (he is
only quoted by Odysseus as part of his own narrative), *Idyll* 11 essentially *is*
the Cyclops's voice, framed only by Theocritus's introductory opening (1–19)
and two simple verses in conclusion (80–81). Indeed, as if to redress the Cyclops's inability to speak for himself in the Odyssean narrative, Theocritus has
him replicate the narrative context of Book 9, where Odysseus serves as his
own "singer" before the Phaeacians. For Theocritus, at least, there was little
question that Odysseus was a poetological figure in *Odyssey* 9, and in adapting
Odysseus's role as a "singer" to the Cyclops in *Idyll* 11, he signals, even more

explicitly, in fact, that Polyphemus's song is as much about poetry and poetic genre, as it is about love.[81] If Odysseus, then, as I have argued above, can be held to assume the role of the satirist in *Odyssey* 9, setting himself up as a self-righteous, abject blame poet against a threatening antagonist, how do we view the Cyclops in *Idyll* 11 when he breaks into song in a gesture intended to mimic the song of the Homeric Odysseus?[82]

At first sight, Polyphemus's song seems to be completely different from Odysseus's: Odysseus's song, for one, is embedded in epic, Polyphemus's in bucolic, and each one sings a song appropriate their respective contexts. Odysseus recounts a past heroic adventure (with himself cast as the hero), and Polyphemus sings a tale of his own unrequited love. These obvious differences in content, however, tend to obscure a remarkable resemblance between the two *as psogoi*. All the qualities that mark Odysseus in *Odyssey* 9 as a satirist-figure—his stance of physical and emotional abjection and oppression, the indignation against an antagonist that inspires comic mockery—likewise characterize the Theocritean Cyclops. We find Polyphemus, for example, poignantly, if comically (to the audience, anyway), adducing his physique as the reason Galatea flees his advances:

γινώσκω, χαρίεσσα κόρα, τίνος οὔνεκα φεύγεις·
οὔνεκά μοι λασία μὲν ὀφρὺς ἐπὶ παντὶ μετώπῳ
ἐξ ὠτὸς τέταται ποτὶ θὥτερον ὣς μία μακρά,
εἷς δ᾽ ὀφθαλμὸς ὕπεστι, πλατεῖα δὲ ῥὶς ἐπὶ χείλει.

I know, beautiful girl, why you flee. It's because a hairy brow
stretches across my entire forehead, in one long length from one ear
to the other; beneath it there is one eye, and over the lip a flat nose.
(11.30–33)

Like Thersites in *Iliad* 2, like Odysseus quarreling with Irus or pitting himself against the Cyclops in the *Odyssey*, Polyphemus's physical abnormality denies him the respect he seeks and rouses his indignation.[83] In his erotic de-

---

81. As Hunter (1999, 219) remarks: "More generally . . . the Cyclops is trapped in the language, not just of Homer, but of Odysseus. T[heocritus]'s creation is forced to express himself with words and phrases which prove already loaded against him, even where they do not refer specifically to *Odyssey* 9 . . . he is a pathetic victim of poetic tradition, who functions as a (comic) paradigm for the position of a dactylic poet in a post-Homeric world."

82. Note the pun on "Outis" in line 38, which links Polyphemus to Homer's Odysseus with unmistakable irony: συρίσδεν δ᾽ ὡς οὔτις ἐπίσταμαι ὧδε Κυκλώπων, ‖ τίν, τὸ φίλον γλυκύμαλον, ἁμᾷ κἠμαυτὸν ἀείδων ‖ πολλάκι νυκτὸς ἀωρί. ["And I know how to pipe like no-one else of the Cyclopes here, very often singing well into the night of you, my dear sweet apple, and of myself.]"

83. In the case of Thersites and Odysseus, they themselves do not claim that their physical appearance is responsible for their quarrels, as Polyphemus blames his own physique for his erotic frustration, but even so, Homer takes pains to portray Thersites' and Odysseus's abjection as at

lirium, he lashes out against his own mother, whom he blames for not interceding forcefully enough on his behalf. Indeed, his mother is implicated in his trouble throughout the poem, for it was through her that he first met Galatea:

ἠράσθην μὲν ἔγωγε τεοῦς, κόρα, ἁνίκα πρᾶτον
ἦνθες ἐμᾷ σὺν ματρὶ θέλοισ᾽ ὑακίνθινα φύλλα
ἐξ ὄρεος δρέψασθαι, ἐγὼ δ᾽ ὁδὸν ἁγεμόνευον.

I fell in love with you, girl, when you first came with my mother to pick hyacinths from the hill, and I led the way. (11.25–27)

At first he gently takes his mother to task for being unable to endow him with gills, with which he would be able to pursue his love beneath the sea:

ὤμοι, ὅτ᾽ οὐκ ἔτεκέν μ᾽ ἁ μάτηρ βράγχι᾽ ἔχοντα,
ὡς κατέδυν ποτὶ τὶν καὶ τὰν χέρα τεῦς ἐφίλησα

Alas that my mother bore me without gills, with which I might have dived down to you and kissed your hand. . . . (11.54–55)

But at line 67, his indignation becomes explicit and leads to open blame:

ἁ μάτηρ <u>ἀδικεῖ με</u> μόνα, καὶ <u>μέμφομαι αὐτᾷ</u>·
οὐδὲν πήποχ᾽ ὅλως ποτὶ τὶν φίλον εἶπεν ὑπέρ μευ,
καὶ ταῦτ᾽ ἆμαρ ἐπ᾽ ἆμαρ ὁρεῦσά με λεπτύνοντα.
φασῶ τὰν κεφαλὰν καὶ τὼς πόδας ἀμφοτέρως μευ   70
σφύσδειν, <u>ὡς ἀνιαθῇ</u>, ἐπεὶ κἠγὼν ἀνιῶμαι.

My mother alone wrongs me, and I blame her; for never once has she said nice things about me to you, and yet she sees me wasting away day by day. I will say that my head and both my feet ache, so that she may be in pain since I too am in pain.

The path he proposes here—to tell his mother how much he suffers, and blame her for it so that she will suffer as much as he does—promises relentless misery for himself, as he pines for an unobtainable object of desire. In the famous lines that immediately follow, he briefly checks himself, realizes that his *mania* has gotten the better of him, and asks himself whether he might be better off if he returned to his usual routine, undistracted by love.

---

least partially defined by their physical deformity. The same can be said for Hipponax in his quarrels with Bupalus; see Rosen 1990; and above n. 69.

ὦ Κύκλωψ Κύκλωψ, πᾷ τὰς φρένας ἐκπεπότασαι·
αἴ κ᾽ ἐνθὼν ταλάρως τε πλέκοις καὶ θαλλὸν ἀμάσας
ταῖς ἄρνεσσι φέροις, τάχα κα πολὺ μᾶλλον ἔχοις νῶν.
τὰν παρεοῖσαν ἄμελγε· τί τὸν φεύγοντα διώκεις;

O Cyclops, Cyclops, where have your wits wandered? You would
show far more sense if you would go weave cheese-baskets, and
collect shoots for your lambs. Milk the one that's near; why pursue
him who runs away? (11.72–75)

These lines imply that it is unreasonable to suppose that someone with
such a deep passion will be able to transcend it, and we are left with a sense of
inevitability about Polyphemus's abjection. Hunter has noted that the clause
θαλλὸν ἀμάσας ‖ ταῖς ἄρνεσσι φέροις may recall a passage in *Odyssey* 17
(224), where the goatherd Melanthios insults the disguised Odysseus, an echo
which, as Hunter puts it (1999, 241), "reveals the hopelessness of his wish to
'show more sense': he [Polyphemus] can no more do this than escape his own
future." I would argue, in addition, that this passage recalls specific aspects of
Odyssey 9 that highlight this hopelessness even more forcefully. It seems, in
any case, that Polyphemus here plays out in his own mind the dispute between
Odysseus and his crew at key moments in the narrative of *Odyssey* 9. The first
occurs at lines 224–30, when the men beg him not to wait around for the
Cyclops to return, but rather to take their fill of his food-supplies, and leave
while they were safe:

ἔνθ᾽ ἐμὲ μὲν πρώτισθ᾽ ἕταροι λίσσοντ᾽ ἐπέεσσι
τυρῶν αἰνυμένους ἰέναι πάλιν, αὐτὰρ ἔπειτα   225
καρπαλίμως ἐπὶ νῆα θοὴν ἐρίφους τε καὶ ἄρνας
σηκῶν ἐξελάσαντας ἐπιπλεῖν ἁλμυρὸν ὕδωρ·
ἀλλ᾽ ἐγὼ οὐ πιθόμην, ἦ τ᾽ ἂν πολὺ κέρδιον ἦεν,
ὄφρ᾽ αὐτόν τε ἴδοιμι, καὶ εἴ μοι ξείνια δοίη.
οὐδ᾽ ἄρ᾽ ἔμελλ᾽ ἑτάροισι φανεὶς ἐρατεινὸς ἔσεσθαι.   230
ἔνθα δὲ πῦρ κήαντες ἐθύσαμεν ἠδὲ καὶ αὐτοὶ
τυρῶν αἰνύμενοι φάγομεν, μένομέν τέ μιν ἔνδον
ἥμενοι, ἧος ἐπῆλθε νέμων. φέρε δ᾽ ὄβριμον ἄχθος
ὕλης ἀζαλέης, ἵνα οἱ ποτιδόρπιον εἴη.
ἔντοσθεν δ᾽ ἄντροιο βαλὼν ὀρυμαγδὸν ἔθηκεν·   235
ἡμεῖς δὲ δείσαντες ἀπεσσύμεθ᾽ ἐς μυχὸν ἄντρου.
αὐτὰρ ὅ γ᾽ εἰς εὐρὺ σπέος ἤλασε πίονα μῆλα,
πάντα μάλ᾽, ὅσσ᾽ ἤμελγε, τὰ δ᾽ ἄρσενα λεῖπε θύρηφιν,
ἀρνειούς τε τράγους τε, βαθείης ἔντοθεν αὐλῆς.
αὐτὰρ ἔπειτ᾽ ἐπέθηκε θυρεὸν μέγαν ὑψόσ᾽ ἀείρας,   240

From the start my companions spoke to me and begged me to take
some of the cheeses, come back again, and the next time to drive
the lambs and kids from their pens, and get back quickly to the
ship again, and go sailing off across the salt water; but I would not
listen to them, it would have been better their way, not until I
could see him, see if he would give me presents. My friends were
to find the sight of him in no way lovely. There we built a fire and
made sacrifice, and helping ourselves to the cheeses we ate and sat
waiting for him inside, until he came home from his herding. He
carried a heavy load of dried-out wood, to make a fire for his
dinner, and threw it down inside the cave, making a terrible crash,
so in fear we scuttled away into the cave's corners. Next he drove
into the wide cavern all from the fat flocks that he would milk, but
he left all the male animals, billygoats and rams, outside in his
yard with the deep fences. Next thing, he heaved up and set into
position the huge door stop, a massive thing. . . . (trans.
Lattimore)

Later, at lines 494, when Odysseus and the remaining crew have begun their
escape from the Cyclops, his men again entreat him not to turn back and taunt
his antagonist.

"σχέτλιε, τίπτ᾽ ἐθέλεις ἐρεθιζέμεν ἄγριον ἄνδρα:
ὃς καὶ νῦν πόντονδε βαλὼν βέλος ἤγαγε νῆα
αὖτις ἐς ἤπειρον, καὶ δὴ φάμεν αὐτόθ᾽ ὀλέσθαι.
εἰ δὲ φθεγξαμένου τευ ἢ αὐδήσαντος ἄκουσε,
σύν κεν ἄραξ᾽ ἡμέων κεφαλὰς καὶ νήϊα δοῦρα
μαρμάρῳ ὀκριόεντι βαλών· τόσσον γὰρ ἵησιν."

"Hard one, why are you trying once more to stir up this savage man
who just now threw his missile in the sea, forcing our ship to the
land again, and we thought once more we were finished; and if he
had heard a voice or any one of us speaking, he would have broken
all our heads and our ship's timbers with a cast of a great jagged
stone, so strong is his throwing." (9.494–99; trans. Lattimore)

In both cases, Odysseus fails to listen: In the first case, he states openly that it
would have been better if he had; in the second, as we have previously discussed, his refusal to listen results in the Polyphemus's curse, which called
down relentless suffering upon Odysseus's return. Theocritus's Polyphemus
internalizes this very debate between passion and rationality at line 72, where
his momentarily rational mind enjoins his irrational, manic side to overcome

his passion for Galatea, just as Odysseus's crew vainly pleaded with their master to restrain his irrational impulses to meddle with the Cyclops.

Within the confines of *Idyll* 11, therefore, Polyphemus's abjection remains inescapable, even if the very act of singing his song is supposed to alleviate his lovesickness.[84] The self-pity and psogic blaming that arises from this abjection combine to create a character who self-consciously seeks the sympathies and approval of his audience, as well as collusion with them against all the things that oppress him. In short, this is the type of figure we have been associating throughout this study with the poet of satire and mockery. But this is only half of the picture, for alongside the satirist's sense of beleaguerement and oppression, we typically find an almost contradictory stance of superiority and self-importance. Indeed, it is the apparent paradox of such a portrait—the whining underdog who simultaneously sings his own praises—that accounts for a good deal of the comedy that satire has to offer. Theocritus's Polyphemus in *Idyll* 11 follows this pattern in almost textbook fashion, as for example, in the continuation of the passage just quoted above, he boasts that, in fact, he could take a lover even more desirable than Galatea if he chose to:

εὑρησεῖς Γαλάτειαν ἴσως καὶ καλλίον᾽ ἄλλαν.
πολλαὶ συμπαίσδεν με κόραι τὰν νύκτα κέλονται,
κιχλίζοντι δὲ πᾶσαι, ἐπεί κ᾽ αὐταῖς ὑπακούσω.
δῆλον ὅτ᾽ ἐν τᾷ γᾷ κἠγών τις φαίνομαι ἦμεν.

Perhaps you will find another, more beautiful, Galatea. Many girls urge me to spend the night in play with them, and they all giggle when I pay attention to them. Clearly even on land I seem to be a somebody. (11.76–79)

Polyphemus ends his song with these lines, leaving his listener with the impression of a highly sexualized, attractive man, as if to offset the self-pity that suffuses the rest of his narrative. Polyphemus's sexual braggadoccio is a gesture that aligns him with figures from iambographic poetry and Old Comedy, who, like Polyphemus, will often fixate on their sexuality in their efforts to compensate for an otherwise abject self-portrait.[85]

84. See Hunter 1999, 221–22, for a discussion of the *autarkeia* for which Cyclopes were famous in antiquity (and Cook 1995, 97–102 for the ethical implicaton of *autarkeia* within the *Cyclopeia*). The Polyphemus of *Idyll* 11, however, as Hunter implies, is incapable of realizing such *autarkeia*, since eros has caused him to desire a creature who is fundamentally unattainable (see line 75). Polyphemus, in short, is here doomed to abjection.

85. A few examples from both genres: the end of Archilochus fr. 196aW (the "Cologne Archilochus"), the lurid sequence of fragments in Hipponax, frr. 17–35 Dg., Dicaeopolis's interaction with the Megarian at Aristophanes' *Acharnians* 719–835, Cinesias's behavior with Myrrhine in *Lysistrata* 848–951.

Theocritus further explored Polyphemus's attempts at self-aggrandizement in *Idyll* 6, to which we shall now briefly turn. This poem recounts a later stage in the relationship between Polyphemus and Galatea, when Polyphemus's manic passion for her had subsided, and it is *she* who now seems to be in pursuit of him. This short *Idyll* is structured as a singing contest between two *boukoloi*, Damoetas and Daphnis: Daphnis sings (6–19) of how Galatea pursues Polyphemus, who shows no interest in her; Damoetas (21–40) sings in the voice of Polyphemus, who claims to be on to her tricks and uninterested in playing up to her teasing. On the surface, the poem suggests that Polyphemus has by now regained his senses, and that the self-pity of *Idyll* 11 has given way to a sense of self-possession and dignity. As recent discussion has shown, however, the poem is, for all its apparent simplicity, strikingly enigmatic, especially when it comes to any assessment of the Polyphemus's character. This is not the place for us to confront all the interpretive challenges of this poem, but several points are relevant to our concerns in this chapter. First, despite the fact that Polyphemus *appears* to have overcome his earlier abjection, when he was head-over-heels in love with Galatea, the poem never allows his abjection to disappear entirely; in fact, as we shall see in a moment, it simmers continually beneath the surface. Second, it is worth noting in relation to the first point, that the contest between the two cowherds is structured as a kind of *psogos*. More precisely, the unusual form of the song partially describes in the third-person Galatea's role in the *psogos* (Daphnis telling the story of Galatea's bantering abuse of Polyphemus), and partially represents that *psogos* in the first person from Polyphemus'point of view (Damoetas's impersonation of Polyphemus, who recounts his disdain for Galatea).[86]

Once again, Polyphemus finds himself pitted against an antagonist, and though he tries to remain in control of his feelings and behavior, he never fully succeeds. Daphnis describes how Galatea "attacks" Polyphemus, pelting his flocks and dog with apples, and verbally taunting him with abusive epithets:

βάλλει τοι, Πολύφαμε, τὸ ποίμνιον ἁ Γαλάτεια
μάλοισιν, δυσέρωτα καὶ αἰπόλον ἄνδρα καλεῦσα·
καὶ τύ νιν οὐ ποθόρησθα, τάλαν τάλαν, ἀλλὰ κάθησαι
ἀδέα συρίσδων. πάλιν ἅδ', ἴδε, τὰν κύνα βάλλει,
ἅ τοι τᾶν οἴων ἕπεται σκοπός·
. . . .
ἁ δὲ καὶ αὐτόθε τοι διαθρύπτεται· ὡς ἀπ' ἀκάνθας
ταὶ καπυραὶ χαῖται, τὸ καλὸν θέρος ἁνίκα φρύγει,
καὶ φεύγει φιλέοντα καὶ οὐ φιλέοντα διώκει,

<hr/>

86. On the form of the poem, see E. Bowie 1996, 96–97; and Hunter's remarks 1999, 243–44.

καὶ τὸν ἀπὸ γραμμᾶς κινεῖ λίθον· ἦ γὰρ ἔρωτι
πολλάκις, ὦ Πολύφαμε, τὰ μὴ καλὰ καλὰ πέφανται.

Polyphemus, Galatea throws apples at your flock, calling you
'unlucky in love' and a 'goatherd.' And you don't look her way, you
miserable wretch, but sit there playing your pipe sweetly. Look,
she's hitting the dog again, who follows you as a guard over your
sheep. (6.6–10)

. . . .

And from there too she flirts with you, and like the dry hairs on a
thistle when the fine summer parches it, she flees the one who loves
her, and pursues the one who doesn't, leaving no stone unturned.
For often, Polyphemus, things that are not beautiful appear beautiful
to love. (6.15–19)

Galatea's intentions are ultimately inscrutable, but her teasing is sexual
(διαθρύπτεται) and probably mildly malicious (καὶ φεύγει φιλέοντα καὶ οὐ
φιλέοντα διώκει). In any case, it succeeds in irritating Polyphemus, who responds by claiming, at least, to see through her games:

εἶδον, ναὶ τὸν Πᾶνα, τὸ ποίμνιον ἀνίκ' ἔβαλλε,
κοὔ μ' ἔλαθ', οὐ τὸν ἐμὸν τὸν ἕνα γλυκύν, ᾧ ποθορῶμι
ἐς τέλος (αὐτὰρ ὁ μάντις ὁ Τήλεμος ἔχθρ' ἀγορεύων
ἐχθρὰ φέροι ποτὶ οἶκον, ὅπως τεκέεσσι φυλάσσοι)·
ἀλλὰ καὶ αὐτὸς ἐγὼ κνίζων πάλιν οὐ ποθόρημι,
ἀλλ' ἄλλαν τινὰ φαμὶ γυναῖκ' ἔχεν·

I saw her, by Pan, when she was pelting the flock, and she never
escaped my notice, no, by my sweet single eye, by which I can see to
the end, (and may the seer Telemus, with his hateful prophesies,
carry those hateful things to his home, and save them for his children); But I for my part, teasing her in return, do not give her a
glance, but I tell her I have another as a wife. (6.21–26)

Scholars have pointed out how these opening lines are fixated on eyes and vi-
sion, and the allusion to Telemus in line 23 all but assures that the blinding
scene of *Odyssey* 9 lies behind them. It was Telemus, after all, who had proph-
esied to the Cyclops that he would one day be blinded by Odysseus (see above
p. 135).[87] Hunter writes: "The Theocritean Cyclops's scorn for the prophet

87. Note also line 17–18, which may also conjure up Odyssean associations: καὶ φεύγει
φιλέοντα καὶ οὐ φιλέοντα διώκει ‖ καὶ τὸν ἀπὸ γραμμᾶς κινεῖ λίθον· The phrase "she moves
the stone from the line" was a proverbial metaphor from the language of board games that used a

reminds us of how, all too late, he was to acknowledge his skill; nevertheless, the fact that Polyphemus, unlike his Homeric model, is fully conscious of the prophecy is part of the presentation of a Cyclops who believes himself 'in control.'"[88] Polyphemus's control, in other words, is merely delusional, and the allusions to *Odyssey* 9 serve to reinforce a sense of poignancy about his vain attempts to transcend fully his earlier *mania* for Galatea. The reader's sympathies are thereby directed toward Polyphemus and (in contrast to the narratological perspective of *Odyssey* 9) against Odysseus and all he represents. Despite his bravado and claims to superiority over Galatea, he remains, in short, as doomed in *Idyll* 6 as he was in *Idyll* 11, and ultimately as doomed as he was in *Odyssey* 9.[89]

Conclusions: The Comedy of Abjection

It is worth remembering that the context for all this doom is comic: we are witness in this poem to the coy sparring of two ill-matched lovers who will never be able to connect, and the "beauty-and-the-beast" motif assures a certain lightness of touch. There is poignancy, to be sure, in the continual evocation of the Homeric background in *Idyll* 6, but by the end of the poem Theocritus has focused our attention rather on Polyphemus's humorous stance of self-delusion. Certainly the final lines of Polyphemus's song, sung in his voice by Damoetas, are unmistakably comic:

ἦ γὰρ πρᾶν ἐς πόντον ἐσέβλεπον, ἦς δὲ γαλάνα,
καὶ καλὰ μὲν τὰ γένεια, καλὰ δέ μοι ἁ μία κώρα,
ὡς παρ᾽ ἐμὶν κέκριται, κατεφαίνετο, τῶν δέ τ᾽ ὀδόντων
λευκοτέραν αὐγὰν Παρίας ὑπέφαινε λίθοιο.

For I recently looked into the sea, and it was calm, and my beard appeared beautiful, and so did my one eye, as far as I judge, and it showed off the gleam of my teeth whiter than Parian marble.
(6.35–38)

---

stone as a playing piece. Moving a stone from the line was, then, a desperate act by a player admitting defeat; see Hunter 1999, 252. Possibly λίθον refers to the huge stone in front of the opening of Polyphemus's cave in *Odyssey* 9: Galatea, that is, as she harrasses Polyphemus with her on-again-off-again behavior manages to distract him, much as Odysseus had done in *Odyssey* 9, where the result was to have the stone removed from the door so that he and his men could escape.

88. Hunter 1999, ad loc. 254.

89. Gow 1950, ad loc. 124, notes that Polyphemus's aside to Telemus here recalls Eurymachus's retort to the prophet Halitherses at *Od.* 2.178. Since Eurymachus was later killed by Odysseus (22.79–88) the allusion, as Hunter puts it (1999, 254), "bodes ill for Polyphemus . . . but it distances him from the Homeric Cyclops."

On the surface we have come a long way from the utter despair that Polyphemus felt in *Idyll* 11 over his physical appearance, and his new-found self-esteem (as we might call it) seems almost noble. But the ultimate absurdity of his vanity is inescapable, and we laugh, in the end, at the inconcinnity between the actual grotesqueness of his appearance and his professed belief that he is attractive.[90]

The Polyphemus that we are left with by the end of the poem, therefore, has much in common with the various poets of comic mockery and satire we have encountered in this book: He sings a tale suffused with self-righteousness and indignation, his abjection is profound and pervasive yet tempered by an ironically inflated sense of self, and, although the audience will find him a laughable figure in the end, he retains their sympathies throughout the narrative. While it is impossible to say how self-consciously Theocritus went about creating such a satirical Polyphemus—did he actually conceive of his Polyphemus, for example, as an Archilochus or Hipponax *redivivus*?—it seems likely that he was responding at least in part to the generic ambiguities evident in Homer's version of the story in *Odyssey* 9. As we have discussed in this chapter, Odysseus and Polyphemus in that book are set against each other in a relationship of antagonism and mockery, but without consistent cues as to who ends up with the most persuasive claims to self-righteousness. Despite the horrifying details of the Homeric episode, comic elements do abound in it, whether in Odysseus's cocky verbal jousting of the Cyclops or in the grotesque portrayal of the Cyclops's physical appearance. For Homer, though, the comedy was largely at the expense of the Cyclops: The audience laughs along with Odysseus *at* the Cyclops, and the larger narrative of the *Odyssey* more or less demands that they ultimately sympathize with Odysseus.

Homer's version of the story may contain comedy, but, as should be clear by now, this comedy is not formally satirical. Odysseus mocks Polyphemus mercilessly, and the audience can laugh at his bravado, but the relationship that Homer constructs between the mocker and the mocked has more in common with epic traditions of battle vaunting or "flyting" than satire.[91] In the former, the vaunter's mockery derives from a stance of self-possession and superiority; he may be self-righteous and morally indignant at his target, but it is less important for the narrative that the target actually deserves such indignation. The narrative is not really about questions of justice or morality, but more about the comedy that arises when the strong humiliate the weak. There is often an element of gratuitous cruelty to this kind of laughter, as we have seen in the Greek army's reaction to Odysseus's treatment of Thersites, or Odysseus's laughter at the blinded Cyclops. In satire proper, by contrast, mockery will typically assume a moral cast endorsed by the narrator, with the

---

90. See Hunter's discussion, 1999, ad loc. 258–59.
91. See above n. 2.

mocker positioned as a weaker party contending with a stronger—usually with palpable irony, since the satirist's abjection will presume a moral superiority worth far more than whatever power his target may possess. As we have seen, Homer complicates the moral positions of the two antagonists just enough to make it unclear exactly where the blame lies, and who should legitimately have the proverbial last laugh.

In the Cyclops episode of *Odyssey* 9, Homer seems most interested in portraying Odysseus as the quintessential heroic vaunter, whose exploits serve to aggrandize his stature within the broader narrative. It would be a mistake, I think, to make too much of the weak rationale for Odysseus's attack on Polyphemus, since this episode was presumably not composed as an object lesson in heroic ethics. But, as we have seen in this chapter, there are narratological cracks throughout this episode—the morally compromised Odysseus, hints of a more poignant, pitiable Cyclops, etc.—and whether or not the Homeric poet himself had any intention of foregrounding them, they were widened and explored by subsequent authors, especially those interested in developing the episode's comic potential.

5

Satiric Authenticity
in Callimachus's *Iambi*

It has by now become something of a commonplace to conceptualize the Hellenistic period as a time when Greek poets maintained a highly self-conscious relationship with the literary traditions of the past, and although it is an easy position to overstate, these poets did seem to have been peculiarly concerned to situate themselves explicitly in relation to their literary forebears. Theocritus is certainly one case in point, as we saw in the previous chapter, and his particular interaction with Homer in *Idylls* 6 and 11 offers considerable insight into the generic dynamics and narratology of satirical poetry. We turn in this chapter to Theocritus's contemporary, Callimachus, whose collection of *Iambi*, as the title suggests, addressed similar concerns even more explicitly. Indeed, this work is quintessentially Hellenistic in its obsession with its literary provenance: As we shall see, it is suffused from beginning to end with the spirit of Hipponax, now transformed by Callimachus into a veritable patriarch of the archaic iambus and everything that genre stood for.

We might expect this work, then, to become a treasure trove of ancient commentary on poetic satire, and an essential tool in our attempt to understand how at least some ancient poets (and their audiences) understood this type of poetry. Such expectations can be reasonably well fulfilled, but only if we proceed with considerable caution. To begin with, like much of Callimachus, the *Iambi* are imperfectly preserved in papyrus fragments: These fragments, which include some exegetical material from subsequent commentators, probably give us a fairly accurate idea of what the collection was like—the structural principles of the work, and the basic subject or theme of each *Iambus*. But, like so much Hellenistic poetry, the *Iambi* are extremely dense, allusive, and playfully enigmatic; even when we have a run of complete lines, interpretation can be difficult, and the many intermittent lacunae and large swathes of missing verses obviously compound the difficulty. We have an obligation to do what we can with whatever evidence exists, and this includes a certain amount of speculation about what Callimachus might have written in the parts we no longer have. The *Iambi* certainly have received their fair share of analysis and explication since the discovery of the various papyri that provide us with what text and scholiastic commentary we have, and two very fine recent studies of the collection, appearing within three years of each other, show just how much these poems continue to intrigue.[1] As often happens with fragmentary texts, however, a number of orthodoxies about the *Iambi* have gradually emerged, which, upon fresh scrutiny, sometimes seem to have arisen more from wishful thinking than judicious inference. In this chapter, therefore, I would like to reconsider several of these orthodoxies that have direct bearing on our study of ancient mockery and satire. Our focus will be quite specific, but at the same time its ramifications will be broadly applicable to the entire collection, since I will be concerned primarily with the fundamental question of how exactly Callimachus conceptualized the iambus—specifically, how he conceptualized the vituperative and comic aspects of the archaic iambus of Hipponax in relation to his own iambi.

The central question about Callimachus's *Iambi*, in fact, is a function of how we believe we should understand his relationship with Hipponax. Callimachus begins and ends the work with clear allusions to the early iambographer, and as scholars have amply documented, the other poems are peppered with Hipponactean allusions. To put the question simply: What is Hipponax's role in the work? As we shall see, there is little question that he is brought on as some sort of figure of poetic authority, but is the point that he should serve as a mentor, who will guide Callimachus in the composition of his own iambi? Or is Callimachus more interested in somehow transforming the archaic iambus into something "new" or "better" than its original form? In either case, can Callimachus's *Iambi* tell us anything about what he regarded as an appropriate form and function of the genre?

Let me anticipate in brief the argument of this chapter: Prevailing scholarly consensus holds that Callimachus's purpose in composing the *Iambi* was to "reform" a genre that was in its archaic form unnecessarily and indecorously vituperative. To quote just a few of the most recent versions of this notion: "The opening poem is not just an *étude* in the style of an old master—it makes explicit the considered re-creation and adaptation of choliambic poetry . . . The studied crudity of the old Iambus appears ennobled, the hatred has mellowed" (Kerkhecker 1999, 2). Again Kerkhecker (293): "the [iambic] tradition is a foil for innovation and experimentation. Callimachus moves from an aggressive form of poetry to one in which the author himself is no longer immune from criticism." And most recently: ". . . [the opening of *Iambus* 1 provides] a reference to the kind of invective for which Hipponax became celebrated, and at the same time a rejection of that invective" (Acosta-Hughes 2002, 39). There

---

1. Kerkhecker 1999 and Acosta-Hughes 2002. Both offer convenient descriptions, with bibliography, of the physical remains of the text (Kerkhecker, xvii–xxiv, and 116–22 on *Iambi* 5–7; Acosta-Hughes, 3–5), though Pfeiffer's conspectus (1953, ix–l) is still fundamental. See Lehnus 1989 for an exhaustive bibliography on the *Iambi* through 1988. The next ten years are well covered in Kerkhecker 301–30.

is certainly something comforting in these conclusions, since they are in accord with the tendency in recent decades to think of virtually every Hellenistic poet as continually striving to "re-fashion" or "re-make" his poetic antecedents, or to create "hybrid" forms. And in the case of the *Iambi* there is at least some truth to the idea that Callimachus was trying to compose a form of iambus that bore his own stamp and could serve as a representative of the genre appropriate to his own era.

It is, however, far less clear than is generally assumed that Callimachus's "new" iambus necessarily implied a repudiation of the Hipponactean iambus, specifically of its "invective" style of mockery and abuse, its *aischrologia*, and stances of intense anger and indignation. As I hope to show in what follows, Callimachus's relationship with Hipponax was not predicated on a platform of rejection and reform, but rather of recovery and authenticity. By this I mean that Callimachus wanted to distill from Hipponax a putatively "true" version of the iambus, and so to demonstrate through his own *Iambi* that he understood—perhaps, he might say, better than most of his contemporaries—the idiosyncrasies of the genre, and its efficacy, when properly composed, as a mode of satire and comedy. It is not that Callimachus merely wanted to replicate Hipponax as some sort of historical novelty, but rather that he found Hipponax's work to be the paradigmatic instantiation of the very poetics he was striving for in his own attempts at composing iambi. What this means, as we shall see in detail below, is that the primary movement in Callimachus's *Iambi* was not in fact, as most scholars seem to hold, one of "distancing" from Hipponax, nor is it quite one of "nostalgia" either; rather, I would argue, it is a movement of appropriation and amalgamation in the service of composing a form of iambus which, in the end, no matter how different in detail from Hipponax, will remain true to Hipponactean poetics.[2]

This reading of Callimachus's *Iambi* will have significance for the broader questions we are asking in this book about the ways in which poetic mockery and satire were conceptualized in classical antiquity. For we will find a Callimachus who has a very clear, almost analytical, conception of satirical poetics and a sense that its history remains essentially stable and articulable. Iambus turns out for Callimachus to be, on the one hand, a variegated literary form, but on the other, one that displays certain continuous characteristics which we have construed throughout this study as "satirical." Callimachus, I shall argue, well understood that "iambus" and "iambic" were not necessarily synonymous terms; an iambus only became iambic when it became a form of satire, when it featured some configuration of the elements we have isolated as satirical—mockery, *aiskhrologia*, didactic posturing, a self-righteous stance.

---

2. Barchiesi's notion (2001) of Horace's relationship to Archilochus in the *Epodes* bears some similarity to the relationship between Callimachus and Hipponax I argue for here (Barchiesi also comments briefly, 158, on Callimachean iambus). See further, below, n. 27.

One might well imagine that an iambus could display different *degrees* of satire and mockery, that the genre could evolve from one of vituperation to one of mild, jovial banter—certainly this is the picture of Callimachean iambus that scholars now largely endorse. The point I would like to make in this chapter, however, is that Callimachus did not, in fact, see things this way; instead, he saw the essence of the iambus as "fixed" by poets such as Hipponax, and any significant loss of its essential "iambic" elements would eventually obliterate its identity as a form of iambus. A "gentle, mild" iambus is, on this view, an oxymoron. The Callimachus of the *Iambi*, I suspect, would more likely want to ask how there can be a "real" iambus without iambic content and style. As I shall argue, most scholars have been largely misguided in thinking that Hipponax is brought on as a patriarchal literary figure urging Callimachus to reconceptualize the iambus as something no longer "aggressive." Callimachus wanted to situate himself within a venerable tradition of iambus as he conceived of it, and wanted to do it right: His iambi would be appropriate enough to his own age and a showcase for his literary talents, but at the same time true to its heritage as a genre that never shied away from satirical invective and mockery.

1. The Problem of Hipponax: *Iambus* 1

Not until Horace's *Sermones* do we find a Classical poet who writes satire with quite as much generic self-consciousness as Callimachus in the *Iambi*. The collection is framed by two poems (1 and 13), which are explicitly programmatic, and show that Callimachus was interested as much in second-order questions about the nature and history of the iambus as he was in simply composing them. Moreover, the other poems in the collection, despite their highly lacunose state, strongly suggest that Callimachus was experimenting with various forms that he associated with the archaic iambus of Hipponax and Archilochus, such as animal fable (*Iam.* 2), self-righteous didacticism (*Iam.* 1, 2, 3, and 5 especially), unadorned invective (4), parody (*Iam.* 8 and 11), or *aischrologia* (*Iam.* 9).[3] Recent scholarship on the *Iambi* has addressed these poems and

---

3. Scholars traditionally regard the first four *Iambi* as "Hipponactean," and, except for the thirteenth (which was probably the last poem in the collection, although see Acosta-Hughes 2002, 9–13 for the most recent discussion, with bibliography, of that controversy), the other poems as either marginally Hipponactean or utterly non-Hipponactean. It should be emphasized, however, that so much of Hipponax is lost that it is difficult to speak meaningfully about what is really "Hipponactean," beyond using the term as a synonym for "vituperative" or "satirical." These adjectives may characterize accurately enough the fragments of Hipponax that that we have, but they hardly do justice to what was a rich and varied poetic oeuvre. For further discussion, see below p. 191. For an overview of the Callimachean *Iambi*, with attention to their connections with the archaic iambus, see Clayman 1980, 55–65. For a more detailed account, Puelma Piwonka 1949, 206–309 is still excellent.

the many literary issues that arise in them fruitfully, and it is not my purpose here to enter into anything like a comprehensive discussion of them. My focus in this chapter, rather, will be the "program" itself, that is, what was Callimachus striving to create, or re-create, by means of his forays into this archaic genre? We shall concentrate, therefore, on the two explicitly programmatic *Iambi*, 1 and 13, in which the poet engages with Hipponax as a figure of literary authority, and Iambus 4, which is almost certainly an allegory about poetics.

Iambus 1 opens with considerable *éclat*: Hipponax appears from the underworld and demands the attention of his listeners. He announces that he has come with an iambus in hand, which is not of the kind he himself once composed against Bupalus (φέρων ἴαμβον . . . βοͿυπ̣ιάλͺειͺον), although he offers no further explanation of what it was.[4] The bulk of the legible parts of the poem tells the parable of Bathycles' cup, left at his death to his sons to bestow on the wisest of the Seven Sages. Each of the wise men refuses to keep it himself and passes it on to another, until it is finally dedicated to Apollo. Presumably the moral of the story is that even great men should remain humble and self-effacing. The Florentine diegesis claims that Hipponax tells this story to a gathering of literary scholars (*philologoi*) whom he apparently chastises for treating each other with *phthonos*,[5] and people have inferred from this that the parable was intended as an object lesson in collegiality.[6] The standard interpretation of the poem seems at first glance logical enough: Hipponax arrives not to promote the harsh iambus he was best known for, but something new and different; something intended to foster harmony among his audience of *philologoi*. Modern scholars routinely assume, then, that this *Iambus* sets the program for the rest of the collection—that Callimachus is attempting to compose a new, in some sense "less Hipponactean" form of iambus.

This is reading of the poem, however, which I shall argue is far less secure than might at first appear, and a fresh examination, free of as many in-

---

4. The legible text breaks off from lines 5 to 8, but enough survives for us to conclude that Hipponax did not pursue the matter. A scholium to Hephaestion (116.10–16 Consbruch) quotes lines 3–4 (φέρων . . . βοͿυπ̣ιαλͺειͺον), but as Kerkhecker (1999, 33, n. 144) notes, "the vagueness of the scholium…and the fact that the quotation stops where it does, suggest that there was no positive statement." (See also next note on this scholium).

5. ὑποτίθεται φθιτὸν Ἱππώνακτα συγκαλοῦντα τοὺς φιλολόγους εἰς τὸ Παρμενίωνος καλούμενον Σαραπίδειον· ἤκουσι δ᾽ αὐτοῖς κατ᾽ εἴλας ἀπαγορεύει φθονεῖν ἀλλήλοις (2–6).

The scholium cited in the previous note suggests that Callimachus's purpose in this scenario was enigmatic: It seems "novel" to him but he cannot quite be sure, as his use of the word δοκεῖ indicates: [referring to the varying character of iambic meter] παρὰ Καλλιμάχῳ δὲ καινὸν εἶναι δοκεῖ ὡς "φέρων ἴαμβον οὐ μάχην ἀείδοντα τὴν βουπάλειον."

6. "Callimachus denounces envy, jealousy, and carping philistinism." Kerkhecker 1999, 42. See also Schmidt 1990, 126–27.

herited preconceptions as possible, may lead us to a clearer understanding of Callimachus's iambic program. The root of the confusion arose first in the interpretation of lines 3–4, "[I have come]...bearing an iambus that does not sing [of] the Bupalean battle" (φέρων ἴαμβον οὐ μάχην ⌊ἀείδ⌋οντα ‖ τὴν βο⌊υπ⌊άλ⌋ειον). Scholars were intrigued and puzzled by these lines even in antiquity,[7] but a basic consensus has long prevailed that when Hipponax announces a "battle" which is "not Bupalean," this must be synonymous with "not aggressive," and so "gentle." As Acosta-Hughes (2002, 39) has most recently put it: "It is precisely this type of invective, poetry in iambic meter that serves to do battle against Bupalus, that the speaker of these lines declares not to be his."

This assumption is, it seems to me, open to objection on many grounds. To begin with, it is difficult to imagine what Callimachus might mean by a "battle" that was supposed to be nonaggressive. Presumably, the iambus he bears still offers *makhê*, only not one that involves Bupalus.[8] Callimachus does seem to play with his readers by leading them momentarily to suspect that his iambus will have no *makhê* whatsoever (as if to say "the iambus I bear does not sing of battles . . ."), but the adjective *Boupaleion*, which has been delayed until the following line, immediately clarifies the situation,[9] that is, it simply will not be a Bupalean battle. Further, there is something paradoxical, if not simply absurd, in having Hipponax offer a putatively "enlightened," nonaggressive form of poetry, but then directly launch into the very kind of abuse he has supposedly just eschewed. Lines 6 and 7 are fragmentary, but there is enough there to conclude that he is insulting his audience:

ὦ]νδρες οἳ νῦν[‖]κέπφ[
κα]τηύλησθ' οἱ με[‖ Διω]νύσου

O men of today! . . . bird-brained [
You have been bewitched by the music of Dionysus. . . .

There is, moreover, plenty of other typically Hipponactean invective at other points in the poem. Lines 26–30 certainly do not hold anything back—

---

7. See above, n. 3, for example.
8. Hunter 1997, 49, senses this as well, although he is not focused there on its ramifications: "The phrasing and enjambment [of vv. 3–4] . . . is a clear provocation: the *iambos* is carried like a spear, but Callimachus/Hipponax is not 'looking for a fight', or rather not a fight with Boupalos, thus leaving him free to fight with anyone else."
9. A point well made by Acosta-Hughes 2002, 39.

ὤπολλον, ᾦνδρες, ὡς | παρ᾽ αἰπόλῳ μυῖαι
ἢ σφῆκες | ἐκ γῆς ἢ ἀπͅὸ θύματος Δελφͅοί.
εἰ̣ληδὸ̣ν [ἐσ]|μεύουσιν |· ὦ Ἑκάτη πλήθευς.
ὁ ψιλοκόρσͅης τὴν πνͅοͅὴν ἀναλώσει
φυσέων ͺὄκͺͅͅ|ως μὴ τὸͅν τρίβωνα γυμνώσῃ.

O Apollo! The men swarm in throngs like flies around a goatherd or
wasps from the ground, or Delphians at a sacrifice. Hecate—what a
crowd! The bald one will waste his breath blowing so as not to be
stripped of his cloak.

—and the end of the poem, though desperately lacunose, seems full of vituperation.[10] Scholars recognize these traditionally invective touches, but do not
seem troubled by their inconcinnity with the notion that the person speaking
them has claimed to be bringing a "non-invective" iambus. The special pleading necessary to explain why a Hipponax who is supposed to be enjoining a
"new iambus" behaves exactly like an "old iambicist" is puzzling. As a recent
example, we may consider Kerkhecker on lines 78–98:

> "High-minded exhortation gives way to sarcasm and caricature. Com-
> pared with the Seven Sages, the scholars are a sorry lot. With ample
> scope for taunts, mockery and ridicule, Hipponax is himself again. It is
> part of the game that Callimachus can let Hipponax have it his way,
> without compromising his own superior refinement; that he can indulge
> in Hipponactean waspishness, without demeaning his own fastidious
> detachment; that he can have his cake and eat it."

One wonders what has become by this point of Kerkhecker's notion that
Callimachus's Hipponax was brought on to repudiate the very "waspishness"
that he now seems to revel in. Kerkhecker would explain this paradox by speaking of a "game" that Callimachus was playing in the poem, but he never clarifies
what the nature and purpose of such a "game" might be (unless it would be simply to confuse the reader: what does he stand to gain by allowing himself to "have
his cake and eat it" in this regard?) Nor is there any substantial textual warrant
for us to claim that Callimachus thought his poetry displayed "superior refine-
ment" or "detached fastidiousness" in comparison to Hipponactean poetry.
These are appealing notions that are certainly in keeping with prevalent ideas of
the Hellenistic "aesthetic," but in the end they are largely scholarly fictions. The
fact of the matter remains that, whatever Hipponax might have said about the
purpose of his *anabasis* in the sad tatters of lines 4–8, he proceeds throughout

---

10. See lines 78–98, with discussion in Acosta-Hughes 2002, 2002, 54–59: "Much of these
lines consists of invective, even mutual insult, so characteristic of the iambic genre" (54).

the rest of the poem to replicate the kind of poetry he was admired for—by turns mocking, satirical, parodic, and always full of comedy and riposte. That much is doubtless uncontroversial enough; but to this I will add that there is virtually no internal evidence to support the now firmly entrenched notion that Hipponax is deployed as a "model in contradistinction to whom Callimachus composes his own choliambic verses" (Acosta-Hughes 2002, 32).

It is easy to see, however, that scholars have been led in this direction by the testimony of the *Diegesis*, which states that Hipponax urged the *philologoi*, gathered at the temple of Sarapis, "to renounce *phthonos* against one another" (*apagoreuei phthonein allêlois*). We must turn, therefore, to three interrelated questions that emerge from this text: First, what is the point of Hipponax's injunction to the *philologoi* to avoid *phthonos*? Do we infer from this, as scholars have generally supposed, that Hipponax is repudiating a distinctly "psogic" iambus in favor of a "milder" form? Second what does Hipponax mean by recounting the fable of Bathycles, evidently as some sort of object lesson for the *philologoi*? Does it illustrate the dangers of *phthonos*, perhaps? Is it intended, again, to herald a new form of iambus? Third, can we use the *Diegesis* to explain what Hipponax means when he states in the opening lines of *Iambus* 1 that the iambus he bears "does not sing of a Bupalean battle." That is, should we assume that Hipponax's protreptic against *phthonos* means that a *makhê* that is "not *Boupaleios*" is one that repudiates vituperative satire? And if it does not, what might Hipponax mean by the expression?

In order to discuss these questions adequately, we must bring to bear all the lessons we have learned throughout the course of this study about the ways in which ancient satire actually worked—its tropes, thematic conceits, performative dynamics, and so forth. In particular, we will want to keep in mind such things as the satirist's elusive, unstable subjectivity, his stance of moral self-righteousness and indignation, and his comically inflated claims of moral superiority. We must keep in mind as well another common feature of satire that is often obscured by the satirist's flashier histrionics and frequent flirtations with scandal, namely his ultimate desire (however disingenuous and/or tacit) for tranquility, harmony and peace. It may seem paradoxical to impute such desires to a figure who makes a career out of poeticizing aggression and mockery, but as we have seen earlier (see, e.g., on Thersites, p. 96), such modes imply a dissatisfaction with some status quo, and a return to some imagined time when life was "different" and "better." As self-proclaimed figures of moral righteousness, satirists generally do not present *themselves* as *gratuitously* rancorous or prone to excessive anger.[11] While it may at first glance seem

---

11. See the final chapter on Critias's judgment of Archilochus. He takes him to task for portraying himself in a negative light; among his charges is that he represents himself as attacking his friends and enemies. Does this mean that he portrayed himself as *unnecessarily* angry? I doubt it: Almost certainly he would have been proud of his attacks, and would have regarded them as completely justified.

counterintuitive to imagine an iambographer such as the Callimachean Hipponax recommending a path of tranquility and harmony rather than one of continual strife and confrontation, such a stance is fully consonant with an iambographer's aims qua *satirist*. Simply because the iambus is an appropriate genre for invective and *psogos*, does not mean that poet has to represent himself as "liking" such tropes or recommending them to others. Behind every satirical attack, in fact, lurks the implicit notion of a "perfect world," in which one does not have to endure whatever or whomever the poet is ranting about at any given moment; satire tends to imply a yearning for precisely the sort of tranquility and peace that Hipponax is made to endorse in *Iambus* 1. The comic irony of satire arises when it becomes clear that the satirist is by and large constitutionally incapable of ever knowing how to enjoy such a harmonious state, even if it were to stare him in the face (and certainly Hipponax's incongruously vituperative tone throughout *Iambus* 1 bears this out—despite his calls for "peace," he cannot himself let go of his famously splenetic temperament). The satirist represents himself as essentially doomed to be constantly on the attack, martyring himself, as it were, to the pursuit of some putative "better world" in order to benefit all those who deserve it (that is to say, the members of his audience—real or imagined—who are sympathetic with him).[12] *Psogos* is, in short, a mode that the satirist claims to be *forced* to deploy in the face of an unjust world, with the implicit goal (unattainable, of course, and, from the poet's point of view, ironically undesirable) that what we all really want is a world in which *psogos* is not necessary in the first place.

Most of the time in ancient satire (and indeed throughout the entire history of the genre), this assumed desire for a peaceful, non-psogic world remains latent and implicit. But it surfaces in explicit ways often enough for us to feel secure that when Callimachus's Hipponax exhorts the *philologoi* to such a life in *Iambus* 1, we need not assume he is turning his back on vituperative satire. One noteworthy example from Aristophanes will be useful here. In the famous parabasis of Aristophanes' *Frogs* (718–37), the chorus leader comes forth to chastise the Athenian demos for favoring the wrong sort of people in the aftermath of the oligarchic attempt of 411 and the more recent defeat of the fleet at Arginusae. The speaker's advice to the Athenians bears an uncanny resemblance to Hipponax's injunctions to the *philologoi* in *Iambus* 1, for in each case a poet (or, as in Aristophanes' case, a putative stand-in for the poet) urges a group to set its priorities straight by relinquishing their scorn against people whom they should welcome (back) and respect:

τῶν πολιτῶν θ᾽ οὓς μὲν ἴσμεν εὐγενεῖς καὶ σώφρονας
ἄνδρας ὄντας καὶ δικαίους καὶ καλούς τε κἀγαθοὺς

---

12. See Rosen and Baines 2002, 107–13 on Juvenal's claims that he is "forced" to engage in satire by the corrupt world around him.

καὶ τραφέντας ἐν παλαίστραις καὶ χοροῖς καὶ μουσικῇ,
<u>προυσελοῦμεν</u>, τοῖς δὲ χαλκοῖς καὶ ξένοις καὶ πυρρίαις   730
καὶ <u>πονηροῖς κἀκ πονηρῶν εἰς ἅπαντα χρώμεθα</u>
ὑστάτοις ἀφιγμένοισιν, οἷσιν ἡ πόλις πρὸ τοῦ
οὐδὲ φαρμακοῖσιν εἰκῇ ῥᾳδίως ἐχρήσατ' ἄν.
Ἀλλὰ καὶ νῦν, <u>ὦνόητοι, μεταβαλόντες τοὺς τρόπους</u>
χρῆσθε τοῖς χρηστοῖσιν αὖθις· καὶ κατορθώσασι γὰρ   735
εὔλογον, κἄν τι σφαλῆτ', ἐξ ἀξίου γοῦν τοῦ ξύλου,
ἤν τι καὶ πάσχητε, πάσχειν τοῖς σοφοῖς δοκήσετε.

Similarly with regard to our citizens: those whom we know to be well-
born virtuous honest, fine, upstanding men, reared in wrestling-schools
and choruses and culture, we spurn with contempt, and in all our affairs
we make use of those men of base metal, aliens, redheads, low fellows of
low ancestry, Johnnies-come-very-lately, whom formerly the city
wouldn't have used lightly in a hurry even as scapegoats. But even at
this late time, you foolish folk, change your ways and honour the honest
again. That will be creditable for you if you are successful, and if you
trip up at all, well, even if something does happen to you, at least
discerning people will think it's happening "on a respectable tree"!
(*Frogs* 727–37 trans. Sommerstein 1996, modified)

Because the Athenians disrespect (προυσελοῦμεν) the wrong people, the
coryphaeus urges them to "change their ways" (μεταβαλόντες τοὺς τρόπους)
and make everything right again. Aristophanes addresses his audience here with
the mildly insulting ὦνόητοι, just as Hipponax calls the *philologoi* κέπφ[οι
("bird-brained") in line 6 of *Iambus* 1; both passages, in other words, engage
in blame from a perspective of moral indignation, but both have as their ultimate goal the restoration of a state of social harmony.[13] Despite the Aristophanic
speaker's explicit desire for the audience to "be nice" to one another, and identify properly who is a *philos* and who an *ekhthros*, no one has ever been led to
take this passage as an Aristophanic repudiation of his more aggressive satiric
strategies.

We have still not answered, however, the question of what Hipponax
means when he tells the *philologoi* not to engage in *phthonos* against each other.
Does this not imply that they have been attacking each other in some fashion,
and that Hipponax regards this as a bad thing that ought to stop? And if so,

13. Indeed, in broad terms the same can be said of most of Aristophanes' plots, which likewise aim at harmony and peace, even if it takes a play's worth of mockery and abuse to achieve it.
One thinks of *Peace*, *Birds*, *Lysistrata*, and *Ecclesiazusae*, in particular, though all of his plots (with
the possible exception of *Clouds*, which has a potentially darker, more ambiguous ending than most)
imply some sort of utopian goal. For the utopian themes in Greek comedy, see now Farioli 2001.

does this mean he now finds fault with all blame and mockery, as most scholars seem to assume? Is this, in fact, the point of the fable of Bathycles' cup, which he proceeds to recount? As we address these questions, we should keep in mind that a satirical *psogos* is normally directed by the poet against a target conceptualized as an enemy, an *ekhthros*. In keeping with a satirist's stance of indignation at the state of the world around him (or at individuals within his ambit), he will want to make clear distinctions between "us" (all right-thinking people, including his audiences) and "them" (his *ekhthros/i* and all those imagined to be blatantly against him or unsympathetic to his idiosyncratic calculus of right and wrong). In *Iambus* 1, the *philologoi* are apparently conceived of as a community of scholars; toward each other, in other words, they are an "us" rather than a "them." Why, then, have they been showing *phthonos* toward each other? This is decidedly not the kind of behavior even an iambographer would endorse among a group of people who conceive of themselves as a community of *philoi*. The moral of the fable seems to be that truly wise men understand that complete knowledge is ultimately unattainable and that anyone who would accept a prize for being wise cannot possibly *be* wise. When applied to the *philologoi*, the fable suggests that they have been competing with each other in self-serving and arrogant ways over their intellectual skills, and may have been reduced to engaging in *psogoi* against each other.

What, then, is Hipponax's role in this little scene of internecine strife? I would suggest, in view of our discussion above, that he is brought on by Callimachus for the primary purpose of castigating the *philologoi* for misunderstanding what a *poetic psogos* really is, and misusing it against each other as an instrument of *phthonos* rather than of comedy. Hipponax's speech to the assembled crowd functions as itself an *epideixis* of a "proper" *psogos*,[14] replete with invective, *aiskhrologia*, fable, didacticism and *indignatio*, with the implication that whatever the *philologoi* have been doing to each other either should be recast as poeticized, comic mockery among *philoi*, or redirected outward against those considered to be genuine enemies, against an imagined "them" instead of "ourselves." There is no reason, it seems, to assume that Hipponax's injunction to the *philologoi* against *phthonos* amounts to an injunction as well against a *psogos*.[15] Hipponax has nothing to say against *psogoi* directed at true

14. Certainly, as recent scholars have duly noted, Hipponax levels plenty of mockery against the *philologoi*, and the Diegesis does say that his purpose was to take them to task for their behavior. See, for example, lines 25–30, with discussion in A-H 50–53 and K 33–34. Kerkhecker 1999 (following Falivene 1993, 925) infers from the fact that individual *philologoi* are not mentioned by Callimachus that Callimachus "includes himself among the victims of this poem." From this he concludes that "iambic criticism has (here) turned conciliatory. The Iambicist corrects himself as well as others" (34). It should be said, however, that the text itself can hardly sustain on its own this series of inferences.

15. I suspect that much of this would have been made clear in lines 12–25, which are, unfortunately, too fragmentary to be of much use. Still, it is worth noting a number of tantalizing phrases which indicate that Hipponax had poetics on his mind in this section: *Mousa*, 17, *i]ambon hosti[s*, 21, *penta]metra*, 23.

(or constructed) enemies, that is, targets who are thought to deserve abuse, only against those which are aimed at undeserving targets, such as fellow members of a community of *philologoi*.

If anything, Callimachus seems at pains in this opening, programmatic poem to distinguish between iambic-psogic discourse and other forms of abusive interaction among people, and to articulate a distinctly poeticized abuse that exists as a species of comic speech marked off from the everyday. Why would Callimachus bring on a *poet* to castigate a group of *philologoi*,[16] who, presumably, were spending their days squabbling with each other in prosaic and banal, but very real, unpoeticized discourse?[17] It seems almost inconceivable that an iambographic *poet* would be introduced to offer advice to a group of people, who are not themselves iambographers, about how to compose iamboi. Unless these *philologoi* were abusing each other in choliambic verse, which seems highly unlikely, it is difficult to imagine why Hipponax would be offering them advice on how to compose poetic *psogoi*! It seems much more likely, rather, that Hipponax's own *psogos* against the *philologoi* in *Iambus* 1 functions no differently from any of his other *psogoi*, that is, as a satirical attack against some target, suffused with hints of didacticism and self-righteousness. As such, Hipponax would be railing against the *philologoi* for behaving in a manner that ill suits men of such status, on a didactic theme which might be called "Against *phthonos*." The universal scholarly assumption that Hipponax's complaint against the *philologoi* is somehow a pronouncement about the poetics of iambus and that this pronouncement, therefore, forms the basis of Callimachus's program for a "new iambus," seems untenable. Hipponax's confrontation with the *philologoi*, in short, *is a psogos*,[18] and it is only *about* the *psogos* insofar as it may suggest to them that a true *psogos* should be directed at putative enemies, not at members of one's own community, and that a truly *poetic psogos*—constructed, fictionalized mockery mediated by poetic form—should, moreover, always result in comedy, not *phthonos*.

Although the end of the poem (78–98) is desperately fragmentary, there are sufficient remnants to support this notion that Callimachus's program in *Iambus* 1 was to promote and defend his own *iamboi* as deeply Hipponactean,

---

16. Even if such a group also included poets, the *phthonos* they evidently exhibit toward one another presumably has to do with their interactions with each other in real life, not with how they compose poetry. See Kerkhecker 1999, 26.

17. The *philologoi* may well have included poet-scholars such as Callimachus, but there is no indication in the text that Callimachus is thinking of these scholars here as specifically poets.

18. Acosta-Hughes's formulation is appealing (2002, 146), but not strong enough in that it treats Hipponax's *psogos* as mere "advice": "Here in *Iambus* 1 'Hipponax' is revealed to be a source of advice to the Alexandrian literati on their aberrant behavior, a figure of wisdom from a far place . . . a sage in a choliambic setting." I would also add that "sage" is far too dignified a term for the figure of Hipponax either in Callimachus or in his own poetry. "Pretending sage" would be closer to the truth: The didacticism of the iambographer is rarely, if ever, stable and ideally undercut at some point by irony and other forms of humor.

rather than to distance himself from that archaic form. Much would be clarified, no doubt, by the lacuna immediately following the end of the fable of Bathycles (77), where one assumes that Hipponax related the fable to the *philologoi*.[19] But even without such a transition, it is clear that the rest of the poem constitutes a defense of vituperative satire. Lines 78–80 amount to a satirist's *apologia* for his *psogoi* against critics, who claim that he is irrational or even mad:

ἀλλ' ἢν ὁρῆ τις, "οὗτος Ἀλκμέων" φήσει
καὶ "φεῦγε· βάλλει· φεῦγ'" ἐρεῖ "τὸν ἄνθρωπον."
ἕκαστ[ο]ς αὐτὸν.[..]α. αρθα κηρύσσει

But if someone should see [him], he will say "That's Alcmeon!" and "Flee! He hits!" he'll say, "Flee that man!" Each one him . . . will announce. . . .

It has been long noted that this conceit became a favorite of the Roman satirists,[20] who reveled in presenting themselves as (comically) abject and misunderstood by those who were afraid of their mocking censure. In his *Epodes* (6.11–14), Horace at one point even appropriates for himself the image of a mad, charging bull in claiming to follow in the footsteps of Archilochus and Hipponax:

cave cave, namque in malos asperrimus
    parata tollo cornua,
qualis Lycambae spretus infido gener
    aut acer hostis Bupalo.

Beware, beware! For I raise my horns most savagely, aimed at bad people, just as that son-in-law spurned by the treacherous Lycambes, or Bupalus's bitter enemy!

Kerkhecker (1999, 45) laconically remarks, "If we can use [Horace] as a guide, 78f report insults hurled against the Iambicist." Horace (and the other Roman poets who used this trope) may indeed be a useful guide to what Callimachus's Hipponax is up to at the end of *Iambus* 1, but no one seems to follow through on the implications for an interpretation of the entire poem.[21] It is worth re-

19. Kerkhecker 1999, 44: "The lacuna preceding 78 leaves room for comments on the scholars' reactions."
20. Further bibliography in Kerkhecker 1999, 45nn211, 212. See esp. Puelma Piwonka 1949 214–15; and Clayman 1980, 60–61.
21. See, e.g., Acosta-Hughes 2002, 55: "the fact that [this passage is] cited apparently from one or more of the speakers' critics is important both as an example of Callimachus's scene-painting

membering that all the Roman examples serve to explain and defend "psogic" satire, and they display all the hallmarks of irony we would expect of the satirist: He feels beleaguered by a segment of humanity who are offended by his work, but maintains simultaneously that only he is able to take the high road, to retain his moral integrity in the face of a compromised world.

No one knows quite what to do with the fragmentary lines that follow, but it is clear that they form Hipponax's valediction to the *philologoi* before he must return to the underworld:[22]

ε τα[..]́.. [   ]. αι. ηξει. [85
    τὰ τρά͵χηλα γυμνάζει
        ]...... ουσκορ. μος
    μαν]θάνοντες οὐδ' ἄλφα
        ]... κονδύλῳ καπηλεῦσ[αι
]....... νι[.]ασυλλο.   90
    ]ουσερ. ρ.. ροσῳ [πέ]πλον
    ]ηρ μοῦνος εἶλε τὰς [Μο]ύσας
    ] οι χλωρὰ σῦκα τρωγούσα[ς
    ]λου καὶ γέλωτος [
    μὴ] πίθησθε· καὶ γὰρ η. [95
    ]... ι τοῦ Χάρωνος ιγ.... γ[
        ]ώλυε κἀποπλεῖν ὥρη
        ]ήσας ε[   ]τω κυσω

[exercises the throat . . . knowing not even alpha . . . to trade in
blows . . . cloak . . . alone took the Muses . . . eating green figs . . .
and of laughter . . . do not] be persuaded; for indeed . . . of Charon
. . . and the hour to sail away . . . to the ass] (trans. Acosta–Hughes
2002).

Before Hipponax takes his leave, however, it is also reasonably clear that he is in some capacity concerned with the workings of satire. Lines 88–94 are mere scraps, but it is still remarkable how much of what remains can be related to the satirical tropes that have by now become familiar to us:[23] people's ignorance (μαν]θάνοντες οὐδ' ἄλφα),[24] physical violence (κονδύλῳ καπηλεῦσ[αι),

---

in the *Iambi*, and as an illustration of the socially marginalized status of the iambic poet." This is unobjectionable enough, but it does not do much to explain what Hipponax's point is in citing his critics.

22. Suggested by Pfeiffer 1949, 171 ad loc. "Charon" (the ferryman in Hades) is mentioned at 96, and the next line mentions a "time to sail away . . ." (κἀποπλεῖν ὥρη).

23. See Acosta-Hughes 2002, 57–59, for a useful commentary on these lines.

24. For bibliography, see Kerkhecker 46n217. Acosta-Hughes 2002, 57, although I think he may make too much of the "literariness" of the image: "In a series of images taken from the stock

isolation and abjection as a poet (?)[25] (μοῦνος εἷλε τὰς [Μο]ύσας), a type of unelevated poetry (χλωρὰ σῦκα τρωγούσα[ς),[26] and of course the mention of laughter (καὶ γέλωτος). If [πέ]πλον is the correct supplement line 91, the mention of a cloak may well recall Hipponax's fragments which complain about his poverty and cold, and his desire for a new cloak (for example, frr. 42, 43 Dg.) and I suspect this line has some connection with "trading in blows" of line 89 (κονδύλῳ ϗαπηλεῦϩ[αι): a fist fight, for example, may result in the loss of, or damage to, the poet's cloak. Rounding it all off is Hipponax's role as poet-advisor (μὴ] πίθησθε· καὶ γὰρ η[), another typically satirical stance.

But what does all this talk about iambic poetry have to do with the rest of the poem? How does it relate to the fable Hipponax has only just finished telling, and what point does he want to leave his audience of *philologoi* with? Above all, since the poem is a program piece introducing the rest of the collection, what is the point about the *Iambi* as a whole that *Callimachus* wants to communicate to his readers? While certainty will always be impossible, given the fragmentary state of the ending, it seems extremely likely that Callimachus has Hipponax offer a strong defense of the traditional iambus just before he returns to the Underworld, and that this defense is explicitly motivated by the reaction he gets to his fable from the *philologoi*. The *philologoi* have been constructed throughout the poem as the target of an iambic *psogos*, that is, a group in need of the satirist's moral censure. The target of a *psogos* is never happy being attacked, and will be expected to fight back in one way or another, for without this predictable reaction there will be no comedy, and the satire will fail. After Hipponax tells his fable as an object lesson for the *philologoi*, we might reasonably expect them to take umbrage at his presumption to lecture them about their behavior. This was presumably noted in the missing line 78, where they may well have said that Hipponax was "crazy" or "mad." The defense of iambus that Hipponax proceeds to offer is really a continuation of his *psogos*: Satirists are routinely classified as "madmen" because the people who are afraid

---

of archaic iambic verse, this one stands out for the novelty of its presence in this choliambic setting—for its quality of *not* belonging." This presupposes that writing and "literariness" were in some sense alien to the archaic iambus, which is hardly well established. Insulting someone by saying that he is so stupid that he "doesn't even know the first letter of the alphabet" would surely have packed an insulting punch in the sixth century BCE as well as in the third. Line 86 (τὰ τράχηλα γυμνάζει = "exercising the throat") seems likely to be part of this insult, i.e., referring to stupid people, who presume to have something to say.

25. Kerkhecker 1999, 47: "Line 92 . . . may refer to someone who is alone in practicing a certain kind of poetry (perhaps the Iambicist)?" See also Schmidt 1990, 127, who suggested that it referred to one of the *philologoi*, who claimed Apollo's *sophia* for himself.

26. Bibliography in Kerkhecker 1999, 47n220; "Munching green olives" is an emblem for poverty. See also Tarditi 1978; Cozzoli 1996, 131–40; and Acosta-Hughes 2002, 58–59, esp. n. 84.

of them—like these *philologoi*—are too blind to their own moral failings and cannot distinguish between a satirist's useful advice and the rantings of a lunatic. As ever, though, the satirist cannot have it any other way, or he would fail to be funny: His targets must be doomed never to take a satirist's advice, and the satirist himself remains doomed always to be misunderstood, and so humorously paranoid and angry.

Callimachus, therefore, has brought on Hipponax to serve as an authoritative model because he realized that iambus is a genre that needs more contextualizing than probably any other. Callimachus could well have written his opening *Iambus* in his own voice, as a *psogos* against his fellow literati. But the decision to use Hipponax as his voice here serves to call attention to the highly literary nature of the iambus, doubtless as a means of counteracting the genre's pretenses to representing "reality." *Iambus* 1 concludes by having the master of the vituperative iambus himself sanction the practice for Callimachus's own time. Hipponax functions in the poem as Callimachus's cicerone, showing him how a *psogos* is done, what sort of reaction to expect from one's targets, and how to stick firmly to one's poetic principles. His return to the underworld allows Callimachus from that point on in the collection to work in this genre independently of his predecessors, but always implicated in the tradition that they had established. Callimachus may indeed feel that his iambus will be a newer, more contemporary form than its Hipponactean ancestor, but it hardly seems the case that he located this novelty in a repudiation of satiric vituperation and a conscious move toward a milder form of satire. Callimachus himself must surely have realized that a "gentle iambus" would have been something of a contradiction in terms.

A critical question, however, remains: If Hipponax was not advocating some form of "gentler" iambus, what would he have meant when he said that he brought with him an iambus that "did not sing of a Bupalean battle"? (φέρων ἴαμβον οὐ μάχην ⌊ἀείδ⌋οντα ‖ τὴν Βο⌊υπ⌋άλ⌊ε⌋ιον). If, as I argued earlier pp. 177–78, nothing in the text compels us to assume that the phrase implies a repudiation of vituperative satire, to what, then, could it possibly refer? Several simple answers suggest themselves: First, in keeping with Callimachus's intention to write a programmatic poem for his own time—that is, not a mere pedantic, museum piece—it would make perfect sense for Callimachus to resurrect an archaic Hipponax, who could distance himself from the iambus which was appropriate to his own lifetime when he feuded with Bupalus in his poetry, but no longer appropriate to Callimachus's. When the redivivus Hipponax now says that he bears an iambus that does not sing about his battles with Bupalus, he means this literally: The iambus he now bears is directed against Callimachus's targets, the *philologoi*, not Bupalus, and this is why Hipponax's now characterizes his "battle" as "not Bupalean." The battle is now Callimachean, and Bupalus has become irrelevant to the cast of characters Callimachus will assemble in his *Iambi*. While its *poetic form* will remain "Hipponactean" (as the rest of *Iambus* I demonstrates), its content can now be called "Callimachean."[27]

2. *Iambus* 13: Hipponax without Ephesus and the Question of *Polyeideia*

The idea that Callimachus was trying in his *Iambi* to work out his own poetic relationship with Hipponax and the archaic iambus has been well recognized and discussed, especially in the recent scholarship.[28] The question of how exactly Callimachus conceived of his own attempts at iambus, however, seems less well understood. My argument in the previous section, that Callimachus did not intend his "modernized" version of the iambus to look or feel radically different from an archaic iambus when it came to that genre's most distinctive literary hallmarks gains additional support, I think, when we turn to *Iambus* 13, a poem that probably rounded out the collection of *Iambi* and served as a kind of programmatic coda to the whole work.[29] In many ways, as has often been pointed out, *Iambus* 13 serves as a kind of companion piece, or counterpoint, to *Iambus* I, taking up as it does Callimachus's debt to Hipponax once again. Just as *Iambus* I announced the iambic program of the poems that would follow, *Iambus* 13 offers a retrospective apologia for the entire collection.

The first general point to make is that this poem bears all the marks of a traditional iambus. The Diegesis tells us that the poem is a response to critics (καταμεμφομένους, Dieg. IX.33 Pf.), which will lead us to expect an indig-

---

27. I suspect that something similar is at work in Horace's famous remark in *Epistles* 1.19.23–25, where, in referring to his *Epodes*, he says that he followed the "meters and spirit of Archilochus" (*numeros animosque ‖ Archilochi*), but not the "content and the words that assailed Lycambes" (*non res et agentia verba Lycamben*). While some have taken this to mean that Horace intended his *Epodes* to be less vituperative than Archilochus's iambi (e.g., Kerkhecker 1999, 275–76, "Horace's way of appropriating Archilochus without Lycambes owes much to Callimachus's Hipponax without Bupalus"; see also Fraenkel 1957, 35–36 [on *Epode* 10]; Mayer 1994, 263–64; and Watson 2003, 12), it would not surprise me if Horace had conceived of his *Epodes* as a work every bit as "Archilochean" as the original Archilochean iambus, but more appropriate for the contemporary Roman audience. Much depends on what Horace meant when he said that he followed the *animos* of Archilochus in *Epist.* 1.19.24 (quoted above). See Mankin 1995, 6–9; and more broadly on the iambic cast of the *Epodes*, Cucchiarelli 2001, 130–43. See also Barchiesi 2001, with whose subtle assessment of Horace's relationship to Archilochus I am in sympathy; e.g. his conclusion, 156, that ". . . there is no reason to differentiate a conventional iambic voice from a contemporary, 'engaged' voice, and to imagine the second voice as more independent from Archilochean influence."

28. See, e.g., Hunter 1997; Konstan 1998; *passim* in Kerkhecker 1999, specifically, 293–94, which summarizes his conclusions; and Acosta-Hughes 2002, *passim*, especially 32–47.

29. The problem of frr. 204–207 Pf., which follow *Iambus* 13 (fr. 203 Pf.) in some of the papyri and have sometimes been thought to constitute the real ending of the collection, has been well examined by Kerkhecker 1999, 271–95. He concludes that 13 was in all likelihood the last poem in the work; Acosta-Hughes 2002, 9–13, operates on the same assumption. Although the question is less critical for our purposes here, their arguments seem reasonable to me.

nant poet, harassed by what he will portray as unjust criticism. In the course of his presentation, he will present himself as belittled and misunderstood by his detractors, and will offer mockery and abuse of his own in defending himself. The poem is structured as a dialogue, a common device in ancient satirical genres that allows the poet to dramatize his struggles with the world with particular vividness. In keeping with so many of the examples we have already discussed in this study, the poet ends up portraying himself as simultaneously abject and indignant, whiny and supercilious, but in the end morally superior to all his critics. The tone—when properly understood by a knowing audience—will be light and jovial, even if the putative "message" is supposed to be serious. Again, this is a satirical stance we have encountered many times, that is, a poet's insistence on the moral gravitas of his work, even as he undermines it, or at least problematizes it, with his arsenal of comic tropes. While this poem concerns a world of poetic rivalries and professional *phthonos* idiosyncratic to Callimachus, if one changes the names and historical circumstances it is easy to imagine in their place a Hipponax feuding with Bupalus, Archilochus with Lycambes, or Aristophanes with Cratinus, Eupolis or Cleon. Clayman's general remarks (1980, 61) about the poetic affiliation between Hipponax and Callimachus, are well applied to *Iambus* 13: "Both Callimachus and Hipponax . . . share a cluster of attitudes which are interdependent. They perceive their own virtues as unrewarded, indeed they are misunderstood and attacked. The poets take it badly; decry the injustice of it all; pity themselves and in their outrage attack the attackers. . . ."

Iambus 13, however, concerns the nature of Callimachus's relationship with Hipponax, and specifically Callimachus's answer to charges that his *Iambi* have somehow debased an authentic Hipponactean poetics, through what the Diegesis calls *polyeideia* ("variety of poetic form").[30] The legible part of the papyrus begins with a critic apparently faulting him for not "mingling with Ionians, nor going to Ephesus, where those who want to produce choliambs draw their inspiration not without learning:"

ἐκ γὰρ ...... [. οὔτ'] Ἴωσι συμμείξας
οὔτ' Ἔφεσον ἐλθών, ἥτις ἐστι αμ.[
Ἔφεσον, ὅθεν περ οἱ τὰ μέτρα μέλλοντες
τὰ χωλὰ τίκτειν μὴ ἀμαθῶς ἐναύονται·

for from . . . [neither] having associated with the Ionians
nor having gone to Ephesus, which is . . .
Ephesus, from which place those who intend to compose in the
"limping meter' [choliambic poetry] take their inspiration not
      unlearnedly (11–14)

---

30. On the term as referring to Callimachus's entire poetry collection, see Acosta-Hughes 2002, 9 and 68.

Several lines later, the critic specifies further that he objects to Callimachus's interweaving of Ionic and Doric elements, and to the "chattering" style that seems to result. Finally, the critic charges Callimachus with being a bit mad:

ἀλλ᾽ εἴ τι θυμὸν ἢ ᾽πὶ γαστέρα πγεϙϭ.[
εἶτ᾽ οὖν ἐϖ . . . ἀρχαῖον εἴτ᾽ ἀπαι. ‖[..].[
τοῦτ᾽ ἐμπ[έ]πλεκται καὶ λαλευσ‖[..]..[
Ἰαστὶ καὶ Δωριστὶ καὶ τὸ σύμμικ|τον[.
τ[ε]ῦ μέχρι τολμᾷς; οἱ φίλοι σε δήσ|ουσ[ι,
κ[ἢ]ν νοῦν ἔχωσιν, ἐγχέουσι τὴν[κρᾶσιν   20
ὡς ὑγιείης οὐδὲ τῷγυχι ψαύεις
ην δητϙϭωϭυπιπε[...]... αι Μοῦσαι."

"But if in some regard [inspires?] heart or stomach . . . whether then . . . ancient or . . . this is interwoven and chatter[ing?] . . . In the Ionic and Doric and the intermingled fashion . . . Until what point will you venture? Your friends will tie you down, if they have sense, and will pour the [blending?] as you do not touch sanity with your fingertip [it truly so much?]. . . . Muses." (16–22; trans. Acosta-Hughes)

This famous passage has been amply discussed by other scholars and we need not revisit familiar territory here,[31] but one question we must ask is this: If, as I have been arguing, Callimachus was interested in maintaining a distinctly Hipponactean tone in his *Iambi*, and was not so much focused on creating a "new" form of iambus as an authentic one, what function does the critic's attack on Callimachus in *Iambus* 13 actually serve? His charge is, after all, that Callimachus deviated far too much from his Hipponactean original. When Callimachus responds as he does at the very end of the poem by defiantly agreeing that he has indeed "never visited Ephesus or associated with Ionians" (63–66), does this mean that he regards his *Iambi*, in fact, as a significant departure from Hipponax? This is more or less the current scholarly consensus about what Callimachus is after in the *Iambi*. Kerkhecker's remarks are indicative of the way most people read the collection; he speaks of the iambic tradition as "a foil for innovation and experimentation" (294), and finds Callimachus's "I" to be different from that of the archaic iambicist: "Callimachus says 'I' to account for himself. His is private poetry; self-effacing, not self-enhancing; self-analytical, and wryly self-critical; an individual sensibility much opposed to Archilochean indignation." What I would like to propose instead, however, is that such contrasts which scholars imagine to exist between an archaic and

31. Full, complementary treatments can now be found at Kerkhecker 1999, 255–65; and Acosta-Hughes 2002, 74–78; although Clayman 1980, 44–47 remains foundational. Further bibliography can be found in these studies.

Callimachean iambus are vastly overstated, and that in fact the main task of *Iambus* 13 is to argue against them.

As I see it, scholars take a wrong turn when they assume that the critic's charge of *polyeideia* is meant to identify *in reality* something innovatively Callimachean about his *Iambi*. Just because the critic believes that *polyeideia* is one of the reasons Callimachus's iambi seem less Hipponactean than they should be, does not mean that the charge is correct or justified. Indeed, Callimachus himself (if we can trust the Diegesis) is evidently at pains justify his *polyeideia* by citing the authority of the fifth-century poet Ion of Chios. Lines 30–33, at any rate, seem to refer to the idea that no writer should be held to one genre alone:[32]

τίς εἶπεν αυτ̣[...]λε..ρ.[....].
σὺ πεντάμετρα συντίθει, σὺ δ᾽ ἡ[ρῷο]ν,
σὺ δὲ τραγῳδε[ῖν] ἐκ θεῶν ἐκληρώσῳ;
δοκέω μὲν οὐδείς, ἀλλὰ καὶ το. δ..κεψαι

who said...
you compose pentameters, you in the [heroic] meter,
and is it your god-given lot to write tragedy?
No one, I think . . . but also. . . .

The fact is that *polyeideia* can apply equally to the archaic iambus itself: It was as much a farrago as Roman satire was later said to be. Hipponax himself may have been best known for writing in the Ionian dialect and choliambic meter, but he nevertheless dabbled in any number of other forms, genres, and rhetorical modes. And Archilochus was even more catholic than Hipponax in his engagement with different meters and generic registers. Partly this can be attributed to a propensity for parody and generic "parasitism" which seems intrinsic to so many satirical genres, but there seems little doubt that Archilochus and Hipponax had themselves a particular fondness for *polyeideia*.[33] In other words, as Callimachus seems to say to his critic, not only is it unjust to object to *polyeideia* (because it is a poetic approach with considerable ancient authority), but the charge of *polyeideia* is particularly misplaced here as an example of how the poet has deviated from some putatively original Hipponactean iambus (since Hipponax was polyeidetic himself). *Polyeideia*, in short, does *not* seem to be

32. See Scodel 1987, 208; and Acosta-Hughes 2002, 82–89. Also Clayman 1980, 48 for a summary of the "polyeidetic" features of Callimachus's *Iambi*. On the possibility that Callimachus is here humorously conflating three distinct Ions (the eponym of the Ionians, the poet Ion of Chios, and the Ion of Plato's dialogue of the same name), see Hunter 1997, 46–47.

33. In the ten line lacuna after line 33, it would not surprise me to find that, after citing Ion as an antecedent in *polyeideia*, Callimachus then adduced Hipponax himself (or perhaps Hipponax and Archilochus together) as paradigms of *polyeideia*. For a catalogue of the many possible components that went into an iambus, see Bowie 2002, 36–37; and Watson 2003, 11.

an emblem of Callimachean innovation in the *Iambi*, but rather the opposite, a lost generic quality he has *recovered* in an attempt to be "authentically" Hipponactean without actually "being" Hipponax.[34]

The end of *Iambus* 13 (52–66), in fact, bears out this reading:

.].ναἱοιδος ἐς κέρας τεθύμωται
κοτέω]ν ἀοιδῷ κἠμὲ δει..ταπραχ...[
  ]δ[ύ]γηται τὴν γενὴν ἀνακρίνει
κα[ὶ] δοῦλον εἶναί φησι καὶ παλίμπρητον   55
καὶ τοῦ πρ......ου τὸν βραχίονα στίζει,
ὥστ' οὐκ αικε[.....]ῳσιν α λ..υϛαι
φαύλοις ὁμι[λ]εῖ[ν....].ν παρέπτησαν
καὐταὶ τρομεῦσαι μὴ κακῶς ἀκούσωσι·
τοῦδ' οὕνεκ' οὐδὲν πῖον, ἀ[λλὰ] λιμηρά   60
ἕκαστος ἄκροις δακτύλοις ἀϙκνίζει,
ὡς τῆς ἐλαίης, ἣ ἀνέπαυσε τὴν Λητώ.
μηθ. [..]............y ᾀείδω
οὔτ' ἰΈφεσοϳν ἐλθὼϳν οὔτ' ἰἸωϳσι συμμείξας,
Ἔφεσον, ὅθεν περ οἱ τὰ μέτρα μέλλοντες   65
τὰ χωλὰ τίκτειν μὴ ἀμαθῶς ἐναύονται

. . . rage rising in his horns angry with the singer and me . . . and says that I am a slave and one bought and sold repeatedly and . . . brands my arm, that not . . . to associate with men of little worth . . . have flown by and themselves tremble lest they be badly spoken of. For which reason nothing fat, but famine-causing bits each one scrapes off with his fingertips as though from the olive tree, which gave rest to Leto. not . . . I sing neither going to Ephesus nor associating with the Ionians, to Ephesus, whence they intending to produce the limping metra, are not unlearnedly inspired. (trans. Acosta-Hughes)

In a reprise of the image of the crazed, angry satirist of *Iambus* 1 (78–81), Callimachus again assumes a posture of comic abjection. Earlier in *Iambus* 13,

34. Hunter 1997, 43 has put it well: "Callimachus has placed into the mouth of his 'critics' features of his poetry which he wishes to advertise." I also essentially agree with Hunter that for Callimachus "the recreation of archaic poetic forms should not be, as his 'critics' are made to suggest, the search for a 'historical authenticity' in which the resulting poems, written in conditions as near as possible to those of the original (i.e., by going to Ephesus to 'give birth to lame verses'), would be fit for nothing other than a museum." But as I have argued, the critics misunderstand what an authentic Hipponactean iambus was in the first place. *Polyeideia*, in short, turns out to be a *mark* of authenticity, which Hipponax actually does seek; the battle between Callimachus and his critics is a battle over what constitutes an authentic Hipponactean iambus, not an antagonism between a turgid authentic one and a contemporary "inauthentic" one. See further below.

as we saw, the satirist's madness was part of his critic's indictment against him (20–22), but here the poet revels in it as a defining feature of who he is. People may be angry at him (53), accuse him of being low-born or slavish (54–55), and so question the very poetic enterprise he has embarked upon (58–59), but Callimachus remains defiant: This is what satire has always been about, from Hipponax to his own time. Satirists are, as always, doomed to be misunderstood, because if they are not, there can be no satire, no *psogos*, no antagonism with a hostile audience, hence no comedy. Callimachus's critic thinks he understands what iambus is, and has some notion of a "pure," unadulterated Hipponactean form. Callimachus, however, has a far more sophisticated understanding not only of the actual history of satire, but of its actual *dynamics*. The critic evidently wants Callimachus to replicate Hipponax, whatever exactly that would entail—he seems to regard a "proper" iambus as pure invective written in choliambs. But Callimachus makes it clear that this is generically, as well as historically, inaccurate, since the poetry of Hipponax was demonstrably (even by us today) about far more than simple *psogos*. It is Callimachus, then, not the critic, who is the real "purist." His self-construction as an abject comic figure, a misunderstood madman, from whom the Muses want to keep their distance,[35] is an inheritance from the archaic iambus; if the critic was complaining about Callimachus's compromised self-presentation in his *Iambi*[36] (as we might infer from Callimachus's defensiveness about it in 54–56), he has failed to understand how satire really operates, synchronically as well as diachronically. Ultimately, Callimachus seems to be commenting on how to make the genre his own, while remaining authentic to its origins. His critics charge him with "innovation," but he responds by pointing out that what they take to be innovation is actually authenticity.

The famous final lines of the Iambus (quoted above, 64–66) now make sense: The critic wanted him to "visit Ionia and Ephesus"—metaphorically, that is, to become as much like Hipponax as possible—and faulted him for his failure to do this. Callimachus's response is essentially to point out that his

---

35. Lines 57–62 seem to refer to the Muses, possibly picking up the critic's earlier mention of them at line 22, and now suggesting that they want to distance themselves from vituperative poetry. But whose? The lacunae make it impossible to tell for sure, although scholars have come to assume that Callimachus is directing these lines against his critic; i.e., the Muses recoil from the kind of *psogos* that his argumentative opponents engage in (e.g., Kerkhecker 1999, 266; Acosta-Hughes 2002, 99: "the Muses show the same revulsion before the poet's critic that the poet feels himself.") In fact, there is no real textual warrant to take it this way, and if anything, the ὥστε clause of line 57 seems to suggest that it refers to the poet himself: In other words, it offers the "result" of the preceding lines, which seem to highlight the satirist's hallmark stances of abjection. ὥστε, that is, continues the thought from κα[ὶ] δοῦλον εἶναί φησι . . . (55): someone calls the poet a "slave", etc., *with the result that* [the Muses] . . ." end up distancing themselves from this sort of poetry.

36. See below, chapter 7, on Archilochus and the "problem" of a satirist's negative self-presentation.

poetry *is* in fact very Hipponactean, but that he did not need to become him in any sort of antiquarian way to achieve this. One needs to know and understand Hipponax, but not to imitate him in a rote, unreflective way, as his critic seems to want. The final lines, then, help also to explain our earlier problem with the *Boupaleios makhê*, for that phrase has a similar import. Bupalus himself, a character with great resonance for Hipponax's audience, is irrelevant for Callimachus', and so he can be abandoned; but what Bupalus stands for—the satirist's comic bête-noire—is what Callimachus wants to preserve for his own time. Callimachus realized, in other words, that the dynamics of satire transcend time and place; he does not need a real "battle with Bupalus," nor any other kind of "visit to Ephesus" to compose effective iambi. Callimachus, I would suggest, wanted to compose traditional Hipponactean satire, but realized that the only way to do this without creating a mere historical novelty was to distill from Hipponax the elements of iambus that are transferable to any historical context.[37]

Clayman (1980, 51) articulated what must have been a very real dilemma for Callimachus when she wrote that his *Iambi*

> . . . could only exist after the old Ionic forms and the other genres he exploits had lost their vitality. By the third century, the poetic genres of the archaic and classical ages had long since peaked. What Alexandrian could write an Homeric epic or an Aeschylean tragedy or an Hipponactean iamb and expect to be taken seriously? Any Hellenistic poet worthy of the name *had to invent new forms or radically alter the old ones to make themselves some working space.* The doctrine of genre purity, which is the position of Callimachus's critics in *Iamb* 13, led only to sterile imitation. (my emphasis)

Clayman is certainly correct, I think, to say that Callimachus would have regarded what the critic wants from him as a "sterile imitation." But the alternative, as I have argued, does not have to be a "new" or "radical" *form.* The "old Ionic forms" had indeed lost so much of their vitality by Callimachus's time that most people—the critic included—had only the most superficial understanding of what the original forms were like. In the case of the iambus, most people would have conceptualized it as a genre of mere *psogos,* and would not have stopped to think of it as the polyeidetic form that it actually was. The "learning" about the iambus which, the critic implies, one could acquire by (metaphorically) "visiting" Ionia (Ἔφεσον, ὅθεν περ οἱ τὰ μέτρα μέλλοντες

---

37. Hunter 1997, 43 concludes that Callimachus is looking to the Hipponactean iambus for "a flexible frame in which the various resources of the literary heritage could be used to produce a living poetry." I am sure this it true, although, as I have also argued here, the poetry he is ultimately after would look—as far as we can judge from a comparison of two very fragmentary poets— very Hipponactean.

‖ τὰ χωλὰ τίκτειν μὴ ἀμαθῶς ἐναύ̣ονται) turns out to be a sham, as Callimachus recognizes at the end of the poem. Callimachus, then, did not so much have to "invent new forms" as to recover the true original, and make it work for his own time.[38] It was a form of imitation completely in keeping with both his scholarly cast of mind and his fertile poetic imagination.

Whether or not Callimachus's critic was real or fictional,[39] he highlights the fact that *Iambus* 13 is constructed as a formal *psogos*. All the traditional structures of a traditional *psogos* are in place: The critic attacks the poet for what he perceives as some transgression, here a literary one; the poet presents himself as harassed and indignant; there is the obligatory note of comic abjection (the poet's self-portrait as mad, and abandoned by the Muses); and then the defense and counterattack, launched from a stance of "knowledge" and self-righteousness (the poet knows that the critic's attacks are unfair and misguided, and he will set him straight). As we have come to expect, the poet allows himself to be portrayed negatively at the outset by his putative enemy and revels in his own beleaguerment , but ends up with the moral high ground. By the end of the poem, the critic has become the poet's target, and serves as a foil to the poet's ultimate project of self-aggrandizement.

3. *Iambus* 4: An Allegory of Satire

I have been arguing so far that Callimachus, in the two explicitly programmatic *Iambi* that frame the collection (1 and 13), displayed a sophisticated understanding of the dynamics of poetic satire, and was concerned to situate his own attempts at this kind of poetry authentically and authoritatively within a literary history that stretched back to the Ionian iambus. To be sure, Callimachus recognized that the iambus was an appropriate genre for vituperative satire, but he also understood it to be far more than that, as the varied forms and subjects of his *Iambi* amply attest. Like his mentor Hipponax, he strove for a robust style of comic mockery, but one highly mediated by all the poetic tropes and posturing that we have come to associate with satirical poetry. The prevalent idea that Callimachus somehow wanted to transform the frank, aggressive

---

38. See Kerkhecker 1999, 267–68: "The critic's notion of true *Hipponax nachfolge* is seen to fall short of the poet's moral concerns and his allegiance to the Hipponax of *Iambus* 1: he is aggressive only in the service of gentleness." We should remember, however, that whatever the "moral" high ground Callimachus would want to claim for himself here over against his critic would have been indicated by the generic protocols of the iambus itself—it was hardly an innovation on Callimachus's part intended to distinguish himself from the original Hipponax. Hipponax was as morally self-righteous as any poet of satire worth his salt. As for the paradoxical notion that Callimachus sought to be "aggressive only in the service of gentleness," we should, again, remember that the *Iambi* themselves never put the matter this way, and that scholars have drawn this conclusion by spinning out an entire programmatic narrative from the Diegesis of *Iambus* 1.

39. See Acosta-Hughes 2002, 76n14, who also cites apposite remarks in Clayman 1980, 47.

satire of Hipponax into something milder and more peaceful, we have seen, is based on an incomplete understanding of Hipponactean iambus, and a misunderstanding of how Callimachus conceptualized his relationship with the archaic iambographer.

Perhaps the chief misunderstanding has been to assume that the scenes of quarreling and mockery in the *Iambi* must in some sense reflect actual aspects of Callimachus's autobiography, and that he "uses" Hipponax to defend himself against very real antagonists, who existed outside his poetry. As we have seen throughout this study, it is in the nature of satirical poetry to claim that the poet's enemies do in fact exist, but a knowing audience will understand that such claims usually come laden with comic irony and can hardly be taken at face value. This is not to say that Callimachus's antagonists—any more than Archilochus's or Aristophanes'—did not exist in the real world, only that we need not assume any *necessary* connection between how he represented them poetically, and what his relationship might have been with them in the real world. As we shall see in a moment, Callimachus was well aware that, however much (if at all) he drew on his own personal experiences for his subject matter, poetics would have trumped autobiography every time: What mattered most was what the poet did with his subject matter within the parameters of the iambic genre. Callimachus realized that the iambus was properly accessible really only to an audience who had been initiated into the poetics of the *psogos* and the particular form of comedy that it engenders. Without this knowledge, they tend to find only vituperation and rancor without the comedy, and mistake the *mimesis* of a *neikos* for the real thing. And an audience that does not properly understand the satirical *psogos* as both poeticized and comic is likely to find it a violation of the civility and decorum that normally hold for the real world.

If such notions lay implicit in our readings of *Iambi* 1 and 13 above, they seem all but explicit in *Iambus* 4, to which we may now turn. As I shall argue, this poem is essentially concerned with the question of "initiation" into a world of poetic satire—who is "allowed" access to it, who is capable of understanding it. In the process of sorting out the answers to these questions, the poem offers a paradigmatic example of the type of iambus that Callimachus endorses in the programmatic 1 and 13, that is to say, an iambus that poeticizes mockery with as much vituperative wit, stylistic *polyeideia*, and edgy humor that we might expect from an Ionian iambographer. It is, as we shall see, an iambus "in action," a full-blown psogic agon in the form of an Aesopic fable, which can readily be allegorized as a contest between the poet and his adversaries. In the end, the poem offers commentary not only on how to "do" the iambus, but also on how to "be" an audience for iambic satire, and how to recognize the mediating effects that poetic genre has on the representation of material that purports to derive from the poet's own life.

The Diegesis is an instructive place to begin, since its distillation of the diffuse plot makes it clear that the poem was a psogic *neikos*:

Διεφέρετο ὁ ποιητὴς πρός τινα τῶν ἐφαμίλλων· Σῖμος δέ τις παρατυχὼν παρυπέκρουεν ἄμφω παρενδεικνύμενος ἴσος εἶναι

The poet was arguing with one of his rivals when a certain Simus, who happened to be nearby, interrupted the two of them, pointing out that he was equal [to them].

As this summary makes clear, there are really two quarrels in progress here: The first is the dispute the poet is having with "one of his rivals." The second—which is essentially what motivates the iambus—is the *psogos* into which the poet enters with the interloper, Simus. The focal point of the poet's *psogos* against Simus is yet another agon, the fable of the laurel and olive, who quarrel with each other about which tree is superior. The fable is told to Simus because it features a character who behaves like Simus, that is, a bramble bush, which tried to intercede in the dispute between the two trees and urge them to calm their hostilities. Thus, as the bramble bush's role in the dispute between the trees replicates Simus's role in the dispute between the poet and his rival, the allegory of the fable is assured, and it becomes clear that the real point of the *Iambus* is how one should respond to a *neikos* between rival poets.

There has been much excellent scholarly commentary on this poem, especially in recent years, and little disagreement that the fable is intended as an allegory about poets and poetics.[40] Scholars have dutifully noted the "narrative frame" around the fable—the poet's confrontation with Simus—but it is surprising how little interest is shown in its function within the poem.[41] They

---

40. Opinions have varied as to how each tree in the fable maps on to a poet or poetic style, though most scholars now tend to identify the olive with the Callimachus of the *Iambi*, and the laurel as one of his adversaries or rivals. See Acosta-Hughes 2002, 191n62 for earlier bibliography on the question. He himself sees the agon as one of "contrasting aesthetics, one grand [laurel], one subtle [olive]," although he resists specific identification of each, and prefers to see the laurel and olive as "emblematic of the larger program of *Iambi* as a collection" (192). While I think it is certainly true that each tree incorporates various poetic elements that can found elsewhere in Callimachus's *Iambi*, it seems tendentious to conclude from this that both trees "are instances of the reinvention of a genre, a reinvention that, while conscious of the earlier form and deliberately alluding to an ancient tale, or Hipponax of old, then transcends any boundary that the evocation of the earlier form might invite in the minds of the poem's audience." Acosta-Hughes 2002, is led to this conclusion by conceptualizing the archaic iambus as not much more than a "medium of personal invective" (192), when in fact, there is little about the form of *Iambus* 4 that might not have been found in an archaic iambus.

41. See, e.g., Kerkhecker 1999, 112–13: "Prima facie, the fable is told to put down the intruder. This is the point of 103 echoing the opening line. However, that becomes clear only late in the poem. Before we get there, the speaker dwells on the trees' quarrel in so much detail and with so much glee that we suspect the *fabula docet* is little more than a pretext." Kerkhecker goes further

tend to concentrate, instead, on the nature of the allegory itself: which tree represents which poet? or if not a poet, what sort of poetic style? Which tree "wins" the agon, and can claim superiority? These are important questions, to be sure, but, as I shall argue, their real importance lies ultimately in the ways in which they serve the larger framework of the poem. In the end it is the Simus/bramble connection we are left with, reminding us that the point of the poem is not so much an attempt to persuade an audience of the superiority of one kind of poetry over another, but rather a plea for two quarreling parties to be left in peace by outsiders precisely so that they can *continue* their wrangling—*not* so that they can attempt to reconcile their differences.

That the entire *Iambus* is composed for the "instruction" of the interloper Simus—which is to say, as a *psogos* "against" him—is clear from the opening line 6, where the speaker announces that he will tell Simus a fable, directed at him: ἄκουε͵ δὴ τὸν αἶνον· ἔν κοτε Τμώλῳ ‖ δάφνην ἐλαίῃ νεῖκος οἱ πάλαι Λυδοί ‖ λέγουσι θέσθαι . . . As we saw in chapter 3, the Aesopic fable and the archaic iambus, both genres of censure and didactic posturing, were closely associated with each other, and Callimachus exploited their affinities throughout his *Iambi.*[42] Here, the fable is addressed explicitly to the person thought to be in need of its message, the "son of Charitades" of line 1, παῖ Χαριτά͵δεω. This is the figure identified by the Diegesis as "Simus," a name often regarded as "iambic" because of its comic potential ("snub-nose,"[43]) and presumably mentioned somewhere in the lost sections of the poem. Archilochus had opened one of his epodes similarly, with a vocative patronymic and the promise of a censorious fable (fr. 185W):

ἐρέω τιν' ὕμιν αἶνον, ὦ Κηρυκίδη,
    ἀχνυμένη σκυτάλῃ,
πίθηκος ἤει θηρίων ἀποκριθεὶς
    μοῦνος ἀν' ἐσχατιήν. . . .

---

than most in acknowledging the structural frame of Simus—bramble. Earlier scholars, as he notes (q.v., with bibliography) have been largely preoccupied with the allegory of the trees. Lelli 1996 does invest the bramble with some significance, but his argument that the bramble represents a rough, archaizing poet, unworthy of the more refined poetics that the laurel and olive stand for, does not really account for the bramble's failed attempt to get the two trees to stop quarreling.

42. See Acosta-Hughes 2002, 170–74; also Kerkhecker 1999, 86.

43. Pfeiffer 1949, 177 ad loc. See Kerkhecker 1999, 83n1. Acosta-Hughes 2002, 194: "The adjective *simus* [snub-nosed] is something of a topos in Hellenistic poetry and in later satiric literature for characterizing people in an ironical or comic light; it is particularly frequent in bucolic poetry . . ." (see 194 for further examples). It is worth remembering that the name never occurs in the Iambus itself. Is it even a proper name here, or might the Diegesis be using it loosely as a term of opprobrium?

> I shall tell you a fable, O Kerykides [= "son of Herald], with a
> painful message stick: A monkey went out alone in remote parts,
> apart from the other animals. . . .

Whatever happens in Callimachus's fable, therefore, we cannot lose sight of
the fact that it is directed at a target, and must ultimately remain applicable to
his situation. But what exactly *is* his situation?

The Diegesis says that Simus "interrupted the poet while he was arguing
with one of his rivals," which the poet found highly presumptuous.[44] The poet
may indeed have been engaged in a literary debate, as most scholars tend to
think, but there is little indication that Simus was trying to horn in on this
topic. It was evidently the rancor and aggression that concerned him, as both
the Diegesis (12–14) and the text itself make clear (98–100), and the fable serves
to illustrate just how misplaced and unwelcome Simus's concern for calming
the antagonists was. The opening line itself implies that this will be the theme
of the poem, for when the speaker exclaims, "One of us?—surely not!—son of
Charitades . . ." he himself wants to fence off whatever *neikos* he is having with
his antagonist as a defense against an outsider like Simus. That is, the speaker
actively desires his *neikos*; whatever occurs in such a context is a private affair
that will be inaccessible to the vast majority of the "uninitiated." Simus stumbles
upon a *psogos* between two *poets*, but he cannot distinguish this mimetic *neikos*
from a real one. The joke is that the speaker then turns the *psogos* on Simus
himself, calling him (according to the Diegesis, since these particular lines have
been lost) a "Thracian" and a "boy-thief."[45] The fable, then, follows in an
iambographic vein, with the sole purpose of illustrating to him why Simus had
no business intruding on what has become the "marked" territory of the speaker's
quarrel. The speaker essentially is saying to Simus with this fable:

> "once upon a time there were two trees, and they had a quarrel about
> their respective merits. They mocked and taunted each other, claimed
> to be superior to the other, and competed with each other for clever-
> ness and wit in the process. An outside shrub came along and mistook
> this for the actual quarreling of everyday life; but he was incapable of
> understanding that the context of the quarrel was highly contrived, and
> representational in what amounts to *literary* terms. You are like the
> bramble, Simus, and like him you don't realize that the quarrel you

44. Here I follow Kerkhecker's enlightening explanation of the diction of the Diegesis, 84:
"Simus does not claim to be their equal, he only implies it...through his attempt at peacemaking.
The poet resents, not the interruption itself, but the assuming intimacy of a man of no consequence."
As he explains in n. 6: "*parhypekroue parendeiknumenos* = 'he interrupted, thus implying,' 'his in-
terruption implied'."

45. See Lelli 1996, who takes the charge of pederasty against him seriously.

witness between me and my adversary is likewise contrived and literary. If you could understand the poetic *psogos*, the literary iambus, you, Simus, would see that the iambic poet, like the trees of the fable, thrives on the *neikos*, indeed, *requires* an adversary for him to compose such poetry."

The fable of the laurel and olive trees, therefore, functions as an *epideixis* for Simus of a proper literary *psogos*. It is likely enough, as scholars have long held, that the laurel and olive represent the positions taken, respectively, by the poet and his rival in the argument alluded to by the Diegesis. If this is so, we are meant to envision the poet's agon as one suffused with comic invective and mockery, since such elements also characterize the trees' speeches. Whatever the exact nature of the agon that mapped on to the fable of the trees, it seems reasonable to infer that, like the two trees in the fable, Simus had come upon two poets trying to prove that each is superior to the other. Since Callimachus barely mentions such an agon in this poem (if he did, it would have had to be in the lost opening lines, 2–4; we learn about it, in fact, only from the Diegesis) it is fruitless to speculate much further about what he might have had in mind. But to judge from the ways in which each tree argues her case, it is likely that the point of any poetic agon on which the fable was based would not have led to an *objectively* clear winner. For even though it is easy enough to see that the olive tree is made to "defeat" the laurel, the victory is largely rhetorical, that is, the olive's speech is contrived to manipulate the audience's sympathies against the laurel with obvious (and humorous) tendentiousness, and it becomes clear that a "victory" for either is almost meaningless. In the arboreal realm both trees play indisputably important functions in human endeavors, as each makes abundantly clear; and what do we conclude when we take the trees as metaphors for poetic activity? Are two genres being pitted against each other here? If so, which tree represents which genre? The issue cannot be settled because Callimachus is deliberately enigmatic, but this seems to be precisely the point: What matters is not whether he can convince an audience that one type of poetry is "better" than the other, but rather that he can construct an agon so that his side *appears* to win. It is simply an exercise in futility to try to decide whether (for example) iambus is "better" than some other genre, since pitting any bona fide poetic genre—each with its own demonstrable merits, charms, or even utility—against another is a wholly artificial confrontation to begin with.[46]

46. Comparing poets who compose in the same genre (two iambic poets, let us say), might make for a more genuine contest; but the fable of the trees does not seem to allow for such a metaphorical interpretation of the agon. Pitting laurel against laurel, or olive against olive (as ciphers for poets working within the same tradition) is very different from pitting a laurel against an olive, two distinct species of trees.

Clayman, I think, sensed something very much along these lines when she argued that the agon of the trees was ultimately a contest of rhetorical styles. As she puts it (1980, 29): "In *Iamb* 4 Callimachus exaggerates the rhetorical nature of the fable by presenting it in the form of a debate elaborately constructed in the fashion of professional rhetoricians. . . . While illuminating the nature of the genre, the arboreal rhetoricians also parody human rhetoricians and the verbal tricks of their trade." For "professional rhetorician" I would substitute "professional poets," who marshal their own rhetorical forces to persuade their audiences in ways appropriate to their chosen genres. This is why, I suggest, it makes far better sense to locate the point of the fable in its form and structures—that is, as a successful satirical *psogos*—rather than in its actual content.

Let us take a closer look. The fable represents a confrontation between two figures, each of whom feels enough *indignatio* to be moved to attack the other. But the relationship between the two is carefully orchestrated: Only one can be portrayed as initiating the quarrel (the laurel: δάφνην ἐλαίη νεῖ[κος οἱ πάλαι Λυδοί ‖ λέγουσι θέσθαι, 7–8) and only one will end up victorious (the olive, τὰ τρί᾿ ἡ δάφνη κεῖται, 80). Both antagonists are invested with a stance of self-righteousness, but only one can ultimately be endorsed by the narrative as having right on her side. Each has the potential to operate as a satirist, but one of them has to end up the target. It is not especially difficult in this case to see where things are heading, when we recall that true satirists are not normally portrayed as attacking unless they feel provoked, and unless they are given the moral high ground. Here, the olive behaves like a reactionary satirist, responding to the laurel's apparently gratuitous insults.[47] The laurel's speech is pure, classic invective: she repeats three times in her speech the insulting vocative, "Brainless olive . . ." (ἄφρων ἐλαίη, 18, 28, and 40), and alternates mockery (making fun of the olive's bi-colored leaves, 23–24, and her association with death rituals, 40–43) with shameless self-aggrandizement (ἱρὴ γάρ εἰμι· πῆμα δ᾿ οὐχὶ γινώσκω, 37, "for I am holy, and I don't recognize suffering"; ἀ[γν]ὴ γάρ εἰμι, κοὺ πατεῦσί μ᾿ ἄνθρωποι, "for I am pure, and men don't trample on me," 39).

The olive has no choice but to respond, and her strategy will surely remind us of another classic *neikos*, that between Stronger and Weaker Logos in Aristophanes' *Clouds*, where Weaker Logos confounds Stronger Logos's barbs by immediately turning them into compliments:

---

47. If Pfeiffer's placement of line 13 is correct, †ἐγὼ φαύλη πάντων τῶν δένδρων εἰμί† ("of all the trees I am worthless"), the olive displays exactly the same sort of feigned abjection we expect of a satirist. The line originally was cited by the rhetorical author [Trypho], in a work *On Tropes* (Spengel, *Rhet. Gr.* III, p. 206, 15), as an example of ironic self-deprecation, which he called *asteïsmos* (the example he offers is the rich man who claims to be the poorest of all people).

Κρ. καταπύγων εἶ κἀναίσχυντος.
Ητ. ῥόδα μ᾽ εἴρηκας.
Κρ. καὶ βωμολόχος.
Ητ. κρίνεσι στεφανοῖς.
Κρ. καὶ πατραλοίας.
Ητ. χρυσῷ πάττων μ᾽ οὐ γιγνώσκεις.
Κρ. οὐ δῆτα πρὸ τοῦ γ᾽, ἀλλὰ μολύβδῳ.
Ητ. νῦν δέ γε κόσμος τοῦτ᾽ ἐστὶν ἐμοί.

(Stronger Argument): You're a shameless faggot.
(Weaker Argument): Your words are like roses!
(Stronger Argument): And an impudent trickster.
(Weaker Argument): You're crowning me with lilies!
(Stronger Argument): And a father-beater.
(Weaker Argument): You don't realize it, but you're spangling me with gold.
(Stronger Argument): Those names weren't gold in the old days, they were lead.
(Weaker Argument): But now I regard them as an honour.
(Aristophanes, *Clouds* 909–14 trans. Sommerstein 1982)

In like manner, the olive remains cool and collected (τὴν δ᾽ ἀπήλ.[λαξε ‖ μάλ᾽ ἀτρεμαίως ἡ τεκοῦσα τὸ χρῖμ[α, 44–45) and picks up on the laurel's final (and for her, presumably the most devastating) taunt, that the olive is associated with corpses, burial and mourning.[48] The olive claims, however, that these are in fact her finest attributes (. . . τῶν ἐμῶν τὸ κ[άλλιστον ‖ . . . ἤεισας· οὕτω μὴ κάμοιμ[ι ποιεῦσα, 46–48) and she regards it as an especially great honor to escort great men who have died in war (49). So far, the olive appears to be taking a higher road than the laurel; she opens her speech without counterinsult, indeed with open flattery, however disingenuous (ὦ πάντα καλή), and her remarks about an olive's role in death rituals seems almost reverent. But it soon becomes clear that the olive is no pushover, that she is up for confrontation herself, and that she can pack an even more forceful verbal punch than her adversary. Her boast that she takes more pleasure in accompanying corpses to burial than the laurel does in being brought by Dorians from Tempe to the festival of Apollo at Delphi (55–56: γηθέω δὲ πλεῖον ἢ σὺ τοῖς ἁγινεῦσιν ‖ ἐκ τῶν σε Τεμπέων, [alluding to the laurel's remarks at 34–35]) is a gratuitous and fabricated *ad hominem* claim (how could she *possibly* know this?), and

---

48. Dawson 1950, 52–53 cites other parallels from Aristophanic agones.

indicates that her initial calm demeanor was repressing a groundswell of indignation.

The olive is a savvy satirist, however, and has far better control of her rhetoric than the laurel; just as she realizes that she is on the verge of engaging the laurel in her own vituperative terms, she checks herself (59–61): . . . ἀλλ' ἄριστον ἡ σωπή.‖ ἐγὼ μὲν οὔτε χρηστὸν οὔτε σε γρύζω ‖ ἀπηνὲς οὐδέν· ("But silence is best. I grumble nothing good nor hurtful against you.") Claiming that she has no interest in saying herself anything "hurtful" (*apênes*), she abruptly begins a fable of her own—two chattering birds who themselves debate which of the two trees is superior—through which she can carry out obliquely her final blow to the laurel. As Dawson has said (1950, 52), "The olive's attitude is not so much one of modesty as a clever display of *eirôneia*, enabling the tree to enumerate its virtues and at the same time avoid the charge of arrogance by attributing the details of its defense to the chattering birds." The fable-within-a-fable is a clever enough device, but it has the additional effect of portraying the olive as the "true" satirist in this agon, the one who has mastered his ironic postures and deploys poetic tropes that had become associated explicitly with satirical genres. Poets of the iambus, in particular, often mocked their targets by indirect methods, whether through impersonating other characters or employing devices such as fables, through which they could humorously off-load their *psogoi* onto animal ciphers.[49] The olive, therefore, despite her pretenses to humility and abjection, ends up on top, as she uses the birds of her fable, like a savvy iambographer, to build up the case that is presented as defeating the laurel (64–91).[50]

An analysis of the agon along these lines, furthermore, helps to explain why the laurel is the one who ends up chastising the uppity bramble bush, who tries to calm the two antagonists down. One might expect it to be the olive who would take on this role, since she would be in the superior position at the end of the scene, and would more neatly be analogous to the speaker at the opening of the *Iambus*, who recounts the fable as an object lesson to Simus against intruding on the disputes of his superiors. In the end, however, the laurel is presented as the satirist's target who "loses" (or is in the process of losing) the quarrel, so it is natural for this party to remain angry: She has not had an opportunity to respond, now that the two trees are in the thick of it, and, seething, she is gearing up for a second round (93–95):

ὡς εἶπε· τῇ δ' ὁ θυμὸς ἀμφὶ τῇ ῥήσει
ἤλγησε, μέζων δ' ἢ τὸ πρόσθεν ἠγέ[ρ]θη
τ]ὰ δεύτερ' ἐς τὸ νεῖκος . . .

49. On indirect abuse Archilochus, see West 1974, 32; and Bossi 1990, 47. On iambus and animal fable, see Rosen 1984 and 1988, 29–33; Gerber 1997, 59–65.
50. If she is meant to stand for a poetic genre, as some have supposed, her victory is a victory for the iambus over whatever genre the laurel is supposed to represent.

So she spoke. But the heart of the other was grieved at this speech,
and she was aroused more than before for a second quarrel, until. . . .
(trans. Acosta-Hughes)

The olive, by contrast, has scored her points, as the birds of her fable make clear, and has no reason to be particularly angry, especially if the quarrel were to end right there. Now, this does not mean that she approves, any more than the laurel does, of the bramble's rude intrusion on their argument. But within the context of the story, it is the laurel who feels most immediately interrupted, since she was just on the verge of responding to the olive's stinging attacks, and so she is the one we would expect to react first to the possibility that she would not be able to have her say. There is nothing in the text, in any case, to indicate that the olive would have been sympathetic to the bramble's plea for mildness and harmony. The fact that the speaker at the beginning of the poem (identified by the Diegesis as "the poet") chastises Simus for interrupting the quarrel shows him to be in complete sympathy with the laurel's response to the bramble, and if we are right to identify the speaker with the superior olive at the end, then there is no question that both of these characters endorse the laurel's attitude toward the bramble's attempt to stop the trees from quarreling.

It is difficult, in fact, to imagine how either tree could find anything to like about the bramble's plea:

"οὐκ ὦ τάλαιναι παυσόμεσθα, μὴ χαρταὶ
γενώμεθ' ἐχθροῖς, μηδ' ἐροῦμεν ἀλλήλας
ἄνολβ' ἀναιδέως, ἀλλὰ ταῦτά γ' β. μ:"   100
τὴν δ' ἄρ' ὑποδρὰξ οἷα ταῦρος ἡ δάφνη
ἔβλεψε καὶ τάδ' εἶπεν· "ὦ κακὴ λώβη,
ὡς δὴ μί' ἡμέων καὶ σύ. . . ." (98–103)

"Miserable ones, will we not cease, lest we become
objects of fun to our enemies, nor let us say unhappy things
shamelessly of one another, but these. . ."
The laurel looked at her from under her brow like a bull
and said the following. "O evil source of disgrace,
So even you are one of us . . . ?" (trans. Acosta-Hughes)

The bramble warns that the trees should stop abusing each other, so they not end up being ridiculed by their enemies. But asking two parties not to say nasty things about each another, or to worry about what other people will think of them, especially people regarded as their enemies, essentially amounts to a plea for "non-iambic" behavior—what bona fide iambus could do without "shameful" satire, and the attempt to demean its targets by making them appear ridiculous? What the bramble fails to realize is that the quarrel he is witnessing is a *poetic* quarrel, that each antagonist attacks the other within a formalized literary setting, and that the goal of the *psogos* is ultimately a form of comedy. This is why Simus is construed by the speaker, and the bramble by the laurel, as an outsider who has no business entering into the "closed" world of the poetic *neikos*, which will only make sense to those who have come to understand the poetics of satire. Without such an understanding, poetic satire once again appears to be simply an unpleasant, indecorous, even scandalous form of "real-life." The bramble succumbs to just such a confusion: He cannot understand that the *neikos* he witnesses is a constructed, literary representation of reality, and so he self-righteously tries to put a stop to it.[51]

Iambus 4 is certainly a programmatic poem, but as I have argued in this chapter, Callimachus is not interested in faulting the aggressive, psogic side of the iambus; rather he revels in the genre and seeks to promote as authentic a version of it as he can.[52] Unlike many of his modern critics, Callimachus seems to have realized that the moralizing substratum of satirical poetry is as much a trope as its invective, and that the two can coexist in the same work without interfering with the work's comic goals. As we have repeatedly seen throughout this book, vituperative poetic satire is particularly and deliberately elusive: Audiences can never be entirely sure whose voice they are hearing when the "I" of the poem attacks an adversary or laments the state of the world. But the poets who worked in these genres, understood that it takes two parties to make an agon and that only one of them can be portrayed as "justified." The three programmatic *Iambi* that we have examined in this chapter all show Callimachus exploring these dynamics—that is, the relationship between the mocker and the mocked, the taxonomy of abuse (for example, When is abuse considered justified within an iambus? When is it merely offensive? How does it become comic?), and the engagement with one's generic forebears. The Callimachus that emerges is a poet who wanted to revive an old, moribund form of comic poetry, not as if to dust off a museum piece and put it on display, but in order to show that the form still had plenty of life in it, that there was a qualitative, aesthetic difference between the pedestrian insults and mockery of everyday life and their representation as fictional poetry. What he found in the archaic iambus, in fact—and in Hipponax in particular—was a poetic form which was at root comic and satirical, but which was also so much more. The

51. See Kerkhecker's remarks (1999, 114–15): "*Iambus* IV is a game of Chinese boxes. The speaker introduces the tale of laurel and olive, and the olive introduces the device of the birds. Opponent and subject of the quarrel remain obscure; what matters is, how it is conducted. The poem is not about a quarrel, but about quarrelling; not about poetics, but about manners." Kerkhecker is absolutely right, I think, that the real point of the *Iambus* is the question of how a *neikos* is conducted, but if anything, it seems to emphasize the idea that "manners" exist in a very different sphere from poetics, and that a figure who behaves like the bramble needs to be chastised within the context of Callimachus's *Iambi* precisely for confusing the two.

52. Acosta-Hughes 2002, on all the Hipponactean allusions in the poem.

archaic iambus achieved its comedy not only by attacking people, or engaging in gratuitous *aiskhrologia*, but just as often by assimilating other literary devices or traditions that could exist in other contexts quite independently of the iambus and its psogic associations. One thinks of such things as the Aesopic fable tradition, various forms of literary parody, and the ubiquitous pretense of moralizing and protreptic.

The entire collection of Callimachus's *Iambi* bears out his sensitivity to the fact that the authentic iambus of an Archilochus or Hipponax, was a multifarious, often scrappy, genre, with its unpredictable combination of the elevated and low, and its comically parasitic relationship with other discrete literary traditions, all masterminded by a poet whose motives remain either inscrutable or unstable. Even the *Iambi* that are traditionally felt to signal a distinctly Callimachean departure from the archaic iambus, most notably *Iambi* 6–12, are probably less innovative than has often been thought. For even though we are greatly hindered here by their highly lacunose state, enough remains to suggest that the topics, themes, and diction would not be out of place as well among the archaic iambographers.[53] Callimachus certainly would have known that he could not really compose iambi that could in any meaningful sense "be" the iambus of a by-gone era, and Depew has done well to remind us that this is particularly the case when ancient genres are conceptualized, as they routinely were in the Hellenistic period, as "occasion-based." For no poet could ever hope to recreate the exact historical and cultural conditions under which an early exemplar of the genre was composed and performed.[54] It seems true enough that Callimachus's *Iambi* could not, as Depew (329) puts it, "*do* what traditional examples of the genre do," insofar as he could not replicate some hypothetically original performative occasion. But at the same time, as I hope this chapter has shown, he remained interested in exploring precisely those elements of the iambic genre that seemed to transcend localization in time and place, and would be recognizable as "iambic" in any poetic context.

53. Depew 1992, 328: ". . . only 1–4 are relatively unproblematic instances of the genre. The later *Iambi* deviate more and more from what we or the Alexandrians might consider to be straightforward instances of the genre. Eight, for example, is an epinician composed in a stichic meter, 9–13, experiment even more freely with metrical and thematic possibilities. . . ."

This assumes that we have anything like an accurate sense of what a "straightforward instance" of the iambus was in antiquity. It is well known that the term "iambus" need not always imply a meter (see discussion in West 1974, 22–25, Rosen 1988, 3–7 and Brown 1997. 13–16); certainly Archilochus in particular, and even Hipponax (cf., e.g., 126 Dg.), did not limit their satirical repertoire to iambic or choliambic meters.

54. This is a particularly acute problem for the reception of satirical poetry once it takes on a life of its own after the death of the poet and is disseminated far beyond the local culture in which it was originally performed. For discussion of this problem in the case of the ancient reception of Archilochus, see chapter 7.

6

Mockery, Self-Mockery, and the Didactic Ruse

Juvenal, Satires 9 and 5

1. From Greece to Rome

Up to this point in our study we have been concerned largely with Greek conceptions of poetic mockery and satire, partly because the Greek material is so rich and varied in itself, but more importantly because when we first begin to encounter satirical genres in Roman literature, these poets had already become highly sensitive to the diachronic evolution of the genres they were working in, and whatever a prehistory of comic satire might have looked like in ancient Rome, the fact remains that all the Roman satirical poets who have come down to us, beginning with Ennius and Lucilius, position themselves in at least some relationship with Greek antecedents. At the same time, however, as I have been arguing throughout, while ancient poets of satire could be explicit about their participation in a literary tradition, they also recognized that the various types of poetry associated with that tradition could be analyzed in terms of distinct typological elements, abstracted from any associations they might have had with specific works that might be conceptualized as part of an orderly, linear history. In short, ancient poets of comic satire tended to be as conscious of the synchronic aspects of their poetics as they were of the diachronic.

The literary-critical vocabulary never seems quite adequate to account for such typologies, but we have been using terms such as "conceits" or "tropes" to describe phenomena that recur among all satirists (for example, poets who may claim to be indignant, angry or impoverished), "dynamics" to describe the larger contexts in which such poetry is composed (for example, the ways in which the relationship between poet, target and audience is configured), and we have isolated dictional features (for example, *aiskhrologia*, invective, unelevated language), metrical preferences, and performative contexts which also serve to distinguish this kind of poetry. Across time, language and genre, we have continually seen poets mix and match these various elements, whether in accordance with their own aesthetic proclivities, the cultural demands of the time, or some inscrutable combination of the two. However diverse the various examples of poetic mockery and satire turn out to be in the grand sweep from the archaic Greek iambus through Roman satire, all such poetry was fundamentally energized by the assumption (either explicit or implicit) that there is comedy to be found in the poetry of personal attack, and certain strategies for achieving it. Poets of mockery and satire work with these basic literary ingredients as a skilled cook works with a recipe: Each produces in the end a confection at once idiosyncratic and unique, yet instantly recognizable as an example of a broader tradition unified at a fundamental level by a set of shared goals.[1]

All the poets we have considered up to this point themselves would, to varying degrees, be aware of these goals, and would have realized that success in this type of poetry depended to a great extent on an effective orchestration of the various players, who give such poetry its generic identity, including the poet's own constructed role as a self-righteous mocker and his relationship with targets and audiences, and of the narratological ambiguity that arises from their often dissonant interplay. In the preceding chapter, we found in Callimachus a poet who for the first time began to address such issues self-consciously, and as we proceed in time across the Greco-Roman literary tradition, we find further corroboration that satirical poets were sensitive to a poetics that transcended the particular morphologies of their chosen genre, and evidence for increasingly sophisticated literary gamesmanship in the service of comic mockery.

For the Roman tradition, we had an early glance at such gamesmanship in chapter I in our discussion of Horace *Sermones* 1.4, where we confronted a famous paradox: Roman satire was a genre composed in Latin dactylic hexameters, intensely wedded to Roman culture, and famously conceptualized, at least by Quintilian in the first-century CE, as an almost autochthonous, idiosyncratically Roman invention.[2] In its form, at least, it was not, in other words, like any of its

---

1. It should be said here that the "goals" of a literary *tradition* are not necessarily identical to those of a *genre*. Aristophanes' goals as a poet of Athenian Old Comedy (construed as a localized, historically-bound genre), for example, will at least in some respects differ from his goals as a poet of satire, though they will certainly intersect at times. Put another way, the things Aristophanes needs to do in order for his plays to work on the Athenian stage will include satire, but much more as well. Similarly, Aristophanes may have occasionally found his desire to write a successful comedy (i.e., one that won him the prize in the contest) in conflict with some of the things satirists routinely did. My point is only that when a poet such as Aristophanes mocked individuals in his plays, he was drawing on a literary tradition that might include elements that existed independently of Old Comedy. The same can be said for other traditions as well, such as traditions of "religious" or "technical" discourse; these too existed independently of the genre in which they are deployed (i.e., Old Comedy). See, e.g., Willi 2003.

2. Probably the most frequently quoted ancient remark on Roman satire, Quintilian *IO* 10.1.93:

Satura quidem tota nostra est, in qua primus insignem laudem adeptus Lucilius quosdam ita deditos sibi adhuc habet amatores ut eum non eiusdem modo operis auctoribus sed omnibus poetis praeferre non dubitent. ["Satire is completely our own, in which the first practitioner, Lucilius, ac-

Greek antecedents—it was not composed in iambics or choliambics, was not a form of drama, and certainly not Greek in its themes and characters (except when Greeks were held up to ridicule)—and yet Horace was perfectly comfortable, in the opening lines of *Serm.* 1.4, affiliating his satires with the poets, and poetics, of Old Comedy. As we noted earlier, scholars have often pointed out that, in making such a claim, Horace was either disingenuous or misguided, since there were demonstrably many other literary influences on the *Satires* besides Old Comedy.[3] To be sure, the passage comes off as charmingly naïve and comically self-aggrandizing, but it also shows an astute, reflective Horace, inching his way toward conceptualizing satire primarily in terms of poetic tropes and dynamics, and only secondarily in terms of its particular instantiations. It mattered little to him whether the specific literary components of Old Comedy could map on to anything in either Lucilius or his own *Satires*, as long as he could recognize in all of them a common project of creating comedy from mockery and from the many strategies that the poet of mockery must deploy in order to be effective.

Our focus in this chapter will not, however, be Horace's satires, but rather his successor in the genre, Juvenal—more precisely, one exemplary poem of his, Satire 9. Juvenal was active in the first to second centuries CE, and some may find the large leap from Callimachus, across nearly four centuries, somewhat jarring. There is surely plenty one could say, after all, about the rest of Horace's satirical poetry, not only his *Sermones*, but also his *Epodes*, a collection of poems modeled explicitly, as we saw in the preceding chapter, on Archilochus, and scholars have already told us much about Horace's manipulation of a variety of loosely affiliated "sources"—archaic iambus, Old Comedy, New Comedy, Hellenistic iambus, didactic philosophical traditions, Lucilian satire, for example—in writing this kind of poetry.[4] Paradoxically for our interests here, however, Horace sometimes seems to tell us too much: His own evident delight in speaking ironically and disingenuously about his satirical poetry can often obfuscate by leading us in two directions. Sometimes he will leave us with the impression that his poetic material (the targets he chooses, for example, or the behavior he wants to satirize, etc.), is driving the specific ways in which he deploys his "sources"—in other words, that he *first* chooses his subject matter and then works his literary antecedents into his particular treatment of the material. But at other times, he leaves the impression (as with the opening of *Serm.* 1.4) that his material comes into being *as a function of* an a priori poetic

---

quired great esteem, and has fans even to this day who are so devoted to him that they not only categorically prefer him to other satirical authors, but to all poets of any sort."]

See Coffey 1989, 2–3; and Freudenburg 1993, 179.

3. See discussion and bibliography in chapter 1, above, pp. 5–8.

4. I have treated Horace and the broader satirical tradition from a comparative point of view, elsewhere, in Rosen and Marks 1999; and Rosen and Baines, 2002.

"system" that he has abstracted, whether intuitively or self-consciously, from the various antecedents available to him.

Juvenal's *Satire* 9, by contrast, will offer us a test case equally as programmatic as anything we find in Horace, but far less obscured by the superabundance of explicit programmatic discourse that we find in Horace. Juvenal's satirical poetics in this poem, as we shall find, is remarkably consistent with the poetics of all the earlier satirical poets we have considered in this book, yet it mentions none of them explicitly. Instead, as I shall argue, it offers commentary about what satire *is* and *should be* without worrying about what it was in the hands of *others*, and as such it becomes an impressively comprehensive paradigm of the kind of abstracted poetics of satire for which I have been arguing in this study.

2. Juvenal's Ninth *Satire*

Scire uelim quare totiens mihi, Naeuole, tristis
occurras fronte obducta ceu Marsya uictus.
quid tibi cum uultu, qualem deprensus habebat
Rauola dum Rhodopes uda terit inguina barba?
[nos colaphum incutimus lambenti crustula seruo.]   5
non erit hac facie miserabilior Crepereius
Pollio, qui triplicem usuram praestare paratus
circumit et fatuos non inuenit. unde repente
tot rugae? certe modico contentus agebas
uernam equitem, conuiua ioco mordente facetus   10
et salibus uehemens intra pomeria natis.
omnia nunc contra, uultus grauis, horrida siccae
silua comae, nullus tota nitor in cute, qualem
Bruttia praestabat calidi tibi fascia uisci,
sed fruticante pilo neglecta et squalida crura.   15
quid macies aegri ueteris, quem tempore longo
torret quarta dies olimque domestica febris?
deprendas animi tormenta latentis in aegro
corpore, deprendas et gaudia; sumit utrumque
inde habitum facies. igitur flexisse uideris   20
propositum et uitae contrarius ire priori.
nuper enim, ut repeto, fanum Isidis et Ganymedem
Pacis et aduectae secreta Palatia matris
et Cererem (nam quo non prostat femina templo?)
notior Aufidio moechus celebrare solebas,   25
quodque taces, ipsos etiam inclinare maritos.
"utile et hoc multis uitae genus, at mihi nullum

inde operae pretium. pingues aliquando lacernas,
[munimenta togae, duri crassique coloris]
et male percussas textoris pectine Galli   30
accipimus, tenue argentum uenaeque secundae.
fata regunt homines, fatum est et partibus illis
quas sinus abscondit. nam si tibi sidera cessant,
nil faciet longi mensura incognita nerui,
quamuis te nudum spumanti Virro labello   35
uiderit et blandae adsidue densaeque tabellae
sollicitent, αὐτὸς γὰρ ἐφέλκεται ἄνδρα κίναιδος.
quod tamen ulterius monstrum quam mollis auarus?
'haec tribui, deinde illa dedi, mox plura tulisti.'
computat et ceuet. ponatur calculus, adsint   40
cum tabula pueri; numera sestertia quinque
omnibus in rebus, numerentur deinde labores.
an facile et pronum est agere intra uiscera penem
legitimum atque illic hesternae occurrere cenae?
seruus erit minus ille miser qui foderit agrum   45
quam dominum." sed tu sane tenerum et puerum te
et pulchrum et dignum cyatho caeloque putabas.
"uos humili adseculae, uos indulgebitis umquam
cultori? iam nec morbo donare paratis?
en cui tu uiridem umbellam, cui sucina mittas   50
grandia, natalis quotiens redit aut madidum uer
incipit et strata positus longaque cathedra
munera femineis tractat secreta kalendis.
dic, passer, cui tot montis, tot praedia seruas
Apula, tot miluos intra tua pascua lassas?   55
te Trifolinus ager fecundis uitibus implet
suspectumque iugum Cumis et Gaurus inanis,
nam quis plura linit uicturo dolia musto?
quantum erat exhausti lumbos donare clientis
iugeribus paucis! melius, dic, rusticus infans   60
cum matre et casulis et conlusore catello
cymbala pulsantis legatum fiet amici?
'improbus es cum poscis' ait. sed pensio clamat
'posce,' sed appellat puer unicus ut Polyphemi
lata acies per quam sollers euasit Vlixes.   65
alter emendus erit, namque hic non sufficit, ambo
pascendi. quid agam bruma spirante? quid, oro,
quid dicam scapulis puerorum aquilone Decembri
et pedibus? 'durate atque expectate cicadas'?
uerum, ut dissimules, ut mittas cetera, quanto   70

metiris pretio quod, ni tibi deditus essem
deuotusque cliens, uxor tua uirgo maneret?
scis certe quibus ista modis, quam nempe rogaris
et quae pollicitus. fugientem saepe puellam
amplexu rapui; tabulas quoque ruperat et iam   75
signabat; tota uix hoc ego nocte redemi
te plorante foris. testis mihi lectulus et tu,
ad quem peruenit lecti sonus et dominae uox.
instabile ac dirimi coeptum et iam paene solutum
coniugium in multis domibus seruauit adulter.   80
quo te circumagas? quae prima aut ultima ponas?
nullum ergo meritum est, ingrate ac perfide, nullum
quod tibi filiolus uel filia nascitur ex me?
tollis enim et libris actorum spargere gaudes
argumenta uiri. foribus suspende coronas: 85
iam pater es, dedimus quod famae opponere possis.
iura parentis habes, propter me scriberis heres,
legatum omne capis nec non et dulce caducum.
commoda praeterea iungentur multa caducis,
si numerum, si tres impleuero." iusta doloris,   90
Naeuole, causa tui; contra tamen ille quid adfert?
"neglegit atque alium bipedem sibi quaerit asellum.
haec soli commissa tibi celare memento
et tacitus nostras intra te fige querelas;
nam res mortifera est inimicus pumice leuis.   95
qui modo secretum commiserat, ardet et odit,
tamquam prodiderim quidquid scio. sumere ferrum,
fuste aperire caput, candelam adponere ualuis
non dubitat. [nec contemnas aut despicias quod
his opibus] numquam cara est annona ueneni.   100
ergo occulta teges ut curia Martis Athenis."
O Corydon, Corydon, secretum diuitis ullum
esse putas? serui ut taceant, iumenta loquentur
et canis et postes et marmora. claude fenestras,
uela tegant rimas, iunge ostia, tolle lucernam,   105
e medio fac eant omnes, prope nemo recumbat;
quod tamen ad cantum galli facit ille secundi
proximus ante diem caupo sciet, audiet et quae
finxerunt pariter libarius, archimagiri,
carptores. quod enim dubitant componere crimen   110
in dominos, quotiens rumoribus ulciscuntur
baltea? nec derit qui te per compita quaerat
nolentem et miseram uinosus inebriet aurem.

illos ergo roges quidquid paulo ante petebas
a nobis, taceant illi. sed prodere malunt   115
arcanum quam subrepti potare Falerni
pro populo faciens quantum Saufeia bibebat.
uiuendum recte est, cum propter plurima, tum ex his
[idcirco ut possis linguam contemnere serui.]
praecipue causis, ut linguas mancipiorum   120
contemnas; nam lingua mali pars pessima serui.
[deterior tamen hic qui liber non erit illis
quorum animas et farre suo custodit et aere.]
"utile consilium modo, sed commune, dedisti.
nunc mihi quid suades post damnum temporis et spes   125
deceptas? festinat enim decurrere uelox
flosculus angustae miseraeque breuissima uitae
portio; dum bibimus, dum serta, unguenta, puellas
poscimus, obrepit non intellecta senectus."
ne trepida, numquam pathicus tibi derit amicus   130
stantibus et saluis his collibus; undique ad illos
conueniunt et carpentis et nauibus omnes
qui digito scalpunt uno caput. altera maior
spes superest, [tu tantum erucis inprime dentem]
* * * *
gratus eris: tu tantum erucis inprime dentem.   134a
"haec exempla para felicibus; at mea Clotho   135
et Lachesis gaudent, si pascitur inguine uenter.
o parui nostrique Lares, quos ture minuto
aut farre et tenui soleo exorare corona,
quando ego figam aliquid quo sit mihi tuta senectus
a tegete et baculo? uiginti milia fenus   140
pigneribus positis, argenti uascula puri,
sed quae Fabricius censor notet, et duo fortes
de grege Moesorum, qui me ceruice locata
securum iubeant clamoso insistere circo;
sit mihi praeterea curuus caelator, et alter   145
qui multas facies pingit cito; sufficiunt haec.
quando ego pauper ero? uotum miserabile, nec spes
his saltem; nam cum pro me Fortuna uocatur,
adfixit ceras illa de naue petitas
quae Siculos cantus effugit remige surdo."   150

    Naevolus, I'd like to know why I so often run into you looking
gloomy with an overcast scowl like the beaten Marsyas. What are
you doing with a face like Ravola's when he was caught rubbing

Rhodope's crotch with his wet beard? [We give a beating to the slave who licks the pastries.] I can't imagine a more miserable face on Crepereius Pollio, who goes around offering triple the interest rate and cannot find anyone foolish enough to take him up. Where have all those wrinkles suddenly come from? It's a fact that you used to be happy with nothing much, playing the homebred knight, an elegant dinner guest with biting humor and forceful witticisms bred within the city limits. Now everything's the reverse. Your face is grim, your unoiled hair a bristling forest, your skin has completely lost that glossiness which you used to get from strips soaked with hot Bruttian pitch—instead, your legs are neglected and dirty with sprouting hair. Why this emaciation, like a chronic invalid's, tormented for ages by a fever that comes every third day and that long ago became a member of the household? We can detect the tortures of the soul as it lies deep in the sick body, and we can detect its delights, too. From there the face derives both moods. So you've apparently changed your life plan and you're going the way opposite to your past. After all, its not so long ago, as I recall, that you were often to be found at the shrine of Isis and at the Ganymede in the temple of Peace and at the secret Palace of the imported Mother and at Ceres (is there, then, any temple where women don't prostitute themselves?), a lover more notorious than Aufidius, and (something you keep quiet about) laying their husbands too.

"Many people find even this way of life profitable, but I get no reward for my efforts. From time to time I get a coarse overcloak loosely made by a Gallic weaver's comb, or some thin silver plate of inferior quality. Its fate that rules humans—even the parts hidden under our clothes have their fate. You see, if the stars abandon you, nothing will be achieved by the unprecedented length of your long cock, though Virro with drooling lips has seen you in the nude and his many coaxing love letters assail you nonstop. 'For the man can't help being attracted by the—pathic.' Yet what monstrosity is worse than a stingy pervert? 'I paid you this, then I gave you that, and later you got still more.' He computes it while wiggling his arse. All right, let's get out the calculator and the slave boys with their records: count five thousand paid in total and then let's count up my exertions. Or is it easy and straightforward to drive a penis worthy of the name into your guts and there meet yesterday's dinner? The slave who ploughs the soil will have an easier life than the one who ploughs his master."

But I thought you used to consider yourself a soft, pretty boy, good enough for the heavenly cup?

"Will you rich men ever gratify your lowly hanger-on or I your follower? Are you unwilling to spend money even on your sickness now? There's your recipient of a green parasol and large amber balls when his birthday comes round or rainy spring begins and, lounging on his soft chaise lounge, he fondles his secret Ladies' Day presents. Tell me, you little love bird, for whom are you keeping all those hills and farms in Apulia that tire out all those kites within your pastureland? The productive vines from your Trifoline land, or the ridge which overlooks Cuma, or hollow Gaurus keep you well supplied—after all, is there anyone who seals more vats of vintages that will keep for years? Would it be a big deal to make a gift of a few acres to your exhausted client s loins? Tell me, is it better that your rustic child, along with his mother and toy houses and puppy playmate, becomes a bequest to your friend who clashes the cymbals? 'It's impertinent of you to beg, he says. But my rent shouts, 'Beg!' and my slave boy makes his demands, as single as the broad eye of Polyphemus—clever Ulysses' means of escape. I'll have to buy another, since this one isn't enough, and both will have to be fed. What'll I do when winter starts blowing? What'll I say, please, to the boys' shoulder blades and feet in December's northerly gales? 'Hang on and wait for the cicadas'?

"But though you ignore and disregard my other services, how do you value the fact that if I had not been your devoted and obedient client, your wife would still be a virgin? You know very well indeed how often you asked for that favor—the different ways you wheedled and the promises you made. Your bride was actually walking out on you when I grabbed her and embraced her. She'd even destroyed the contract and was already in the process of making a new arrangement. I spent the whole night on it and only just managed to retrieve the situation, with you sobbing outside the door. My witness is the couch—and you—you could surely hear the sound of the bed and its mistress' voice. There are many households where a lover has saved a marriage that's shaky and starting to fall apart and already more or less dissolved. Which way can you turn? What are your priorities? Is it no service, no service at all, you ungrateful cheat, that your little son or your daughter is my child? After all, you acknowledge them as your own and you're delighted to splash all over the newspapers the proofs of your virility. Hang the garlands over your doors: now you're a daddy—and it's me who's given you something to contradict the gossip. Because of me you possess the privileges of a parent, and you can be mentioned in people's wills, you can receive bequests intact, and some nice unexpected gifts too. What's more, many benefits will come along with those gifts if I make up the number to a full three.

You have a perfectly justifiable case for feeling resentment, Naevolus. But what does he say in reply?

"He takes no notice. He's looking out for another two-legged donkey.—Make sure you keep these confidences of mine absolutely to yourself. Keep quiet, and lock my complaints away inside you. An enemy kept smooth by pumice is deadly. The man who's just shared his secret with me is blazing with hatred, as if I'd betrayed everything I know. He'll have no hesitation in using a knife or breaking my head open with a cosh or lighting a candle at my door. And [you shouldn't disregard or belittle the fact that, for wealth like his] the cost of poison is never high. So please keep my secrets hidden, like the Council of Mars at Athens."

O Corydon, Corydon! Do you think a rich man can ever have a secret? Even if his slaves keep quiet, his horses will talk and so will his dog and his doorposts and his marble floors. Close the shutters, put curtains across the chinks, fasten the doors, turn out the light, make everyone leave, don't let anyone sleep close by—all the same, what the master does at the second cock-crow will be known to the nearest shopkeeper before dawn, along with all the fictions of the pastry cook, the head chefs, and the carvers. After all, is there any allegation they refrain from concocting against their masters? Rumors are their revenge for getting belted. And there'll always be someone who'll seek you out at the crossroads, even if you don't want to hear, who'll drench your poor ear with his drunken story. So it's them you need to ask what you were wanting of me a little while ago, to keep quiet. But they actually like betraying secrets better than drinking stolen Falemian wine in the quantities that Saufeia used to down when she was carrying out a public sacrifice. There are lots of reasons for living a proper life, but especially this, that you get to ignore the tongues of your slaves. The tongue, in fact, is the very worst part of a bad slave.

"The advice you've just given me is sound, but too general. What do you suggest I do right now, after all my wasted time and cheated hopes? The fleeting blossom, you know, the briefest part of our limited and unhappy life, is speeding to an end. While we drink and call for garlands and perfumes and girls, old age is creeping up, undetected."

Don't worry, you'll never be without a pathic patron as long as these hills stay standing. From all over the world they come here in their carriages and ships, everyone who scratches his head with one finger. There's one other prospect which is even better: [...words missing]You'll be most welcome. Just keep on chewing that love salad.

"Keep those examples of yours for the lucky ones. My Clotho and Lachesis are pleased if my cock can feed my belly. Ah, my own tiny Hearth Gods (I always make my requests with a few grains of incense or meal and a simple garland), when will I ever make a catch that will save my old age from the beggar's mat and stick? All I want is an income of twenty thousand from secure investments, some silver cups, plain, but the sort that would be banned by the censor Fabricius, and two hefty bodyguards from the Moesian gang to enable me to take my place safely in my hired litter at the noisy racecourse. In addition, I'd like an engraver, stooped by his work, and an artist who can do multiple portraits in moments. That's enough. But when will I even be poor? It's a feeble prayer, with little hope of success. The trouble is that when Fortune is summoned on my behalf, she has already plugged her ears with wax fetched from the ship which escaped from the songs of Sicily thanks to its deaf crew." (text and trans. Braund 2004)

What makes Satire 9 especially illuminating is that it deploys virtually every trope we have come to associate with poetic satire and mockery from Homer to Horace, and makes a vivid case for satire as a discrete form of marked fictional discourse, inscrutable to notional "outsiders," and operating in an elusive, perennially unstable moral universe. This is a *comic* instability, of course, and the audience's inability to locate a fixed moral center to the poet's mockery, despite its implicit didactic pretense, pales in importance when compared to the laughter it occasions. All the paradoxes and contradictions of satire that we have explored in other authors are gradually brought into focus in Satire 9, as Juvenal toys with the very notion of "mocker" and "target", and ultimately endorses the very stance of comic abjection that he simultaneously complains of and hopes to transcend. As we shall see, Juvenal accomplished all this by embedding within the poem a kind of alter-ego, an interlocutor character named Naevolus, who behaves like a satirist even though he is not one. At the same time, Juvenal plays the expected role of the satirist *in propria persona*, interacting with a bitter, complaining, satirical Naevolus, and interviewing him, in fact, as if he were interviewing himself. In the end, it becomes almost impossible to decide who is the actual target of blame; is it Naevolus, the obscene, squalid gigolo, or his venal, selfish, sexually dysfunctional patron, Virro? And with whom are the audience's sympathies directed by the poem to reside? Naevolus's complaints about Virro are vivid and persuasive, but are we supposed to "feel sorry" for a man who prostitutes himself and offers no apologies for a lifestyle that is portrayed as, at the very least, indecorous, if not morally reprehensible? Only Virro emerges from the poem as a clear target of satire, and yet it is Naevolus whose unseemly behavior is narratologically foregrounded throughout.

It is, indeed, this very question of the poem's moral perspective that makes it so perfectly emblematic of the hermeneutic conundra especially idiosyncratic to satirical genres. As we have repeatedly seen, whatever one calls it in any given context—satire, *psogoi*, *iamboi*—the poetry of mockery insists on its own moral, didactic agendum. Any attack on a target, as we have seen at length in chapter 3, will imply the poet's indignation at some aspect of the person or things he attacks, and a desire to "teach" his putative audience some lesson about it. In Juvenal 9, this didacticism is adopted by the two principal characters: (1) The speaking poet, who makes fun of Naevolus and, indirectly, Virro; and (2) Naevolus, who mocks Virro and everything he stands for. Do these two didactic voices end up clashing or merging? This is the essential crux, as I would argue, of all satirical poetics, namely how an audience can reconcile a poem's didactic pretense with all the transgressive impulses, whether dictional or thematic, that inevitably arise in its relentless drive toward comedy. Juvenal 9, as we shall see, articulates this crux brilliantly by creating in Naevolus a character whose ability to function simultaneously as both satirist and target confounds any attempt to locate in the poem any real moral stability. Instead, not unlike the point we take away from the Laurel's censure of the Bramble in Callimachus *Iambus* 4, the poetry of mockery is a "closed" fictional world that is rarely, if ever, what it purports to be. One moment it makes claims about its didactic purposes that seem serious enough; the next, it undermines them with its own stances of *ponêria*.

Such ambiguities have two parallel, but antithetical, consequences: First, they make it virtually impossible to decide where the "meaning" of satirical poetry actually resides. Second, they encourage audiences to *believe* that the meaning of satire is in fact straightforward and *un*ambiguous. Indeed, the more a satirist can achieve the two simultaneously, the more successful he has been, for in deceiving the second group (those who take a satirist's claims at face value), he has secured for himself a kind of *carte blanche* to proceed with his "true" project of satiric *ponêria*—that is, his forays into scandalous diction, compromised self-representation, and other similarly comedic gestures. For now he can gratify an audience of "insiders," those who, like Callimachus's Laurel and Olive trees, understand satire as a closed, fictive space, and who revel in, rather than problematize, its comic ironies. At the same time, however, he can mitigate the potentially "damaging" effects of his poetic *ponêria* in the eyes of those inclined to take satire at face value by cultivating a façade of high moral purpose.

Certainly the reactions of scholars in recent centuries to Juvenal 9 bear out such an analysis, where we consistently find attempts to "explain away" the Satire's luridness by emphasizing its moral message. One nineteenth-century French editor (Dusaulx 1826, 105–6), in a reaction typical of the period, was tormented by the problem and wished that Juvenal had restrained himself in the satire, though he consoled himself by concluding that Juvenal's purpose was ultimately didactic: Nothing about "humor" or "comedy" ever enters into his discussion.[5] Some scholars, however, were capable of a more balanced view, and could admit publicly, even in the nineteenth century, that much of the success of the satire is a function of its humor. Ludwig Friedländer in 1895 showed only passing interest in the moral aspects of the poem and in fact judged it one of Juvenal's best:[6]

> If one can distance oneself from the repugnant subject matter, one can count this satire as one of Juvenal's best. The characterization of Naevolus, who regards the looseness of his trade as natural and who complains that his wages do not correspond to his performance, is executed with jesting and humor that reminds us of Petronius.

Friedländer was one of Juvenal's "inside" readers: He saw immediately that the passage is driven by humor and irony (for example, the simple fact that Naevolus takes it for granted that his profession as a gigolo is "acceptable"), that the jokes align the work with other ancient poets working in related comedic traditions, such as Petronius, and that (as he proceeds to note) the poem is particularly admirable for its liveliness and formal coherence.[7]

For his own day Friedländer was something of an outlier in his response to Satire 9, and even in our own relatively tolerant era there persists a tendency to assume that, however much we laugh along with Juvenal's portrait of Naevolus, the point of the poem is fundamentally a serious attack on his character and behavior. Certainly since the early 1960's scholars of Juvenal have—at least in principle, if not in practice—recognized the dangers of taking Juvenal too literally, and they have often invoked the poet's use of "masks" and "personae"

---

5. From an English commentary on Juvenal from 1835, we find a similarly awkward, equally humorless, attempt to "salvage" the Satire:

> "This satire relates to that most execrable practice in which the ancients, to their eternal shame, so universally indulged. Juvenal's purpose was to impress the minds of others with the same loathing which he himself felt for this disgusting vice ... This piece has many beautiful and many moral passages, exclusive of the grand and important lesson which it is our duty to gather from it; that a life of sin is a life of slavery. . . ." (Stocker 1835, 227)

6. "Wenn man im Stande ist von dem widerlichen Gegenstande abzusehn, wird man diese Satire zu den besten Juvenals zählen. Die Charakteristik des Nävolus, der die Zulässigkeit seines Gewerbes als selbstverständlich betrachtet und darüber klagt, dass der Lohn nicht den Leistungen entspricht, ist mit einem an Petron erinnernden Witz und Humor durchgeführt." (Friedländer 1895, 433).

7. Anderson 1982 [1964], 305 comments on the nineteenth-century discomfort with Juvenal's sensationalism in Satires 2, 6, and 9: "At best, the typical editor deplores Juvenal's lack of good taste in dealing with sex; at worst, he may attempt any number of autobiographical interpretations to explain these three on the whole skillfully composed poems."

to ironize and undermine any apparent seriousness of tone.[8] W. S. Anderson's work on Roman Satire in the 1950s and 1960s was foundational in showing the complexity and subtlety of Juvenal's satirical masks, with all their contradictions, hypocrisies, rhetorical posturing, and so on. He was acutely sensitive, moreover, to the near impossibility of ascribing a stable moral position to either the historical satirist or even the satiric "persona" he adopts in a poem,[9] and continually urged us to resist the temptation to take at face value any autobiographical claims made by the satirist within the work:

> In my opinion, the reader today should start as the Roman audience did nineteen hundred years ago, with a clear realization that the poet is a rhetorical artist and that what he allows to be said in his poems, whether in the first or the third person, does not correspond exactly to his own psychological state: the poet dons a mask or creates an objective character. (Anderson 1982 [= 1964], 313)

But while "*persona* theory" has been highly successful in reminding readers that we need not *necessarily* hear a poet's autobiography every time he speaks with his own voice in a poem, it actually does not fully *solve* the problem of how to interpret the satirist's voice; it merely defers it and makes it more complicated. We may put the matter this way: *Persona* is a metaphor appropriated from the terminology of the theater. The satirist puts on a mask—a *persona*— in his poem, just as a dramatist writes for actors, who will put on a mask on the stage in order to represent a given character. The analogy breaks down, however, at one crucial point; for in satire the putative actor behind the mask always *is*, in fact, the poet himself, the author of the work. We are not watching real actors on a stage when we read or listen to one of Juvenal's satires, so when the poet speaks in the first person, there are no physical cues (in the form of a

---

8. The "rehabilitation" of Juvenal in the twentieth century from straightforward moralist (as best represented at the time by Highet 1954) to more elusive ironist took its cue from Kernan's study of satire English Renaissance satire (1959), began in earnest with Anderson 1957 and Mason 1962, continued with Anderson 1964, and became more or less orthodox by the time of Martyn 1979. See Martyn 1979, 219–20n1 for a brief history and further bibliography; and Freudenburg 1993, 3–17. See also Braund 1982, who, in a review of Bellandi 1980, offers a succinct account of the tensions between the literary and biographical/psychological approaches to Juvenal. More recently, see Iddeng 2000, 107–108, and passim, for a critique of persona theory. Iddeng (109n6) notes some early challenges to persona theory, and attempts to offer some of his own. His arguments to repudiate persona theory are compromised by an incorrect assumption that "the line between fiction and factual prose was never drawn." As he continues: "We have no record of a substantially different approach by the readers or the audience to different types of writing." See in particular below, chapter 7, for discussion of a variety of evidence that contradicts this statement.

9. See, for example, Anderson (1982, 311): "I suggest, then, that Juvenal has carefully delineated the character of his satirist first by placing him in situations where his extreme anger and his limited perspective tend to render his motives suspect, and then by attributing to him assertions which at times border on the pathological, and at other times seem remarkably close to self-irony."

costumed actor, for example) to indicate that we are supposed to conceptualize the poet's "I" as such. The audience will realize that, even if we do not believe what the authorial "I" of the satire is saying, no one but the poet himself could be playing the part. If, by contrast, we imagine an actual drama in which some actor wears a mask that purports to identify him with the poet, we have physical proof in front of us that this actor is a mimesis of the poet, not the poet himself; we have no reason to assume (and would in most cases, probably be wrong if we did)[10] that the *actor* is the poet himself. In the case of a real poet, we can actually *see* the distinction, physically, between the poet (who wrote the lines) and the *persona* of the poet (the mask worn by the actor, who plays out the part of the poet in front of us) in a way that nondramatic satire does not allow. It is far more difficult in the case of nondramatic satire, therefore, to avoid an association between the actual poet and a character that claims to be speaking for that poet within the poem itself. When Anderson speaks of the poet who "dons a mask or creates an objective character," it is important to realize that any attempt at objectivity is, by necessity, largely disingenuous on the part of the poet, part of the game to keep the audience slightly confused about what to think, but ultimately always aware that a real author is somewhere pulling the strings.

There is a second reason why the *persona* metaphor does not ultimately solve the problem of what to make of a satirist's self-representation. To spin out the analogy with dramatic poets who write for actors in masks: A playwright may create an objective character purporting to be the playwright himself and played by an actor on the stage, who may well say things that the playwright himself would never utter in real life; but the fact remains that that character is that playwright's creation, and as such, nothing will ever stop the audience from wondering "why" the *author* had this actor do and say what he does as he plays his part. Likewise in the case of satire, "*persona* theory" may give a character who claims to be the author a certain amount of license and autonomy within the drama of the satire, and a listener may even be savvy enough to

---

10. One probable exception, from the Greek theater, was Cratinus's *Pytine*, the fifth-century Old Comedy in which Cratinus himself is said to have played the lead. The play's title refers to a "Wine-bottle" and the plot seems to have taken a comic look at Cratinus's alleged drinking problem. I have suggested elsewhere that this play ended up portraying Cratinus as reveling in a state of comic abjection. For discussion and bibliography, see Rosen 2000; also Biles 2002 and Ruffell 2002. If Cratinus actually did play himself in the production of 423 BCE, one wonders whether this would have made him more or less "credible" as a witness for his "real" self in the eyes of the Athenian audience. See also chapter 7 in relation to Archilochus's famously "compromised" self-presentation in his own poetry. Certainly the notion of the "real" poet putting on an actual *persona* (or *prosôpon*, to use the Greek term for "mask") in order to represent himself on the stage would bring us a little closer to "*persona* theory" as it is applied to Roman satire, where a reader cannot ever quite escape the idea that it is actually the *poet himself* who is wearing the mask; and that simply begs the question once again of what that author can mean by donning a particular mask.

divorce completely the poet's *persona* from the poet himself, but in the end, that same listener may legitimately ask why the poet decided to put on the mask that he did in his poem.[11] In short, then, "*persona* theory" does little to resolve the perennial problem of satire, namely, its fundamental didactic and moral claims. Even a decision simply to downplay such claims, and privilege the comedic aspects of satire (as Friedländer, and others, might do)[12] can only sweep the conundrum temporarily under the rug: For eventually an audience will want to know what the *point* of all the joking is. And if one responds that the point is simply to raise a laugh, an attentive listener might still want to know why the jokes were configured as they were; why, in fact, are some people and things singled out for mockery and blame, and others not?[13]

It should come as no surprise that such interpretative problems become more or less urgent in proportion to the level of "scandal" one find in a work. In the case of Satire 9, the poem's depiction of unconventional sexuality, its obscenity, its rhetorically exaggerated culture of depravity, are just the kinds of thing that have pushed moral buttons since antiquity, and constantly call attention to their own "transgressiveness." But audiences will seek an explanation of such sensationalism, and although they might conclude that Juvenal is himself depraved (as some have occasionally done throughout history), this would certainly not be in keeping with the poet's professed project of *indignatio* and self-righteous posturing. So if they play along with Juvenal's didactic pretense, they will find it almost impossible not to assume, however well versed they are in *persona* theory and cognizant of the perils of the "intentional fal-

11. In this regard, we may consider this remark by Anderson (1982 [=1964], 305): "That Juvenal's satirist abhors vice hardly needs to be argued. After all by definition *indignatio* means righteous fury over something *indignum*; and the indignant speaker characteristically describes himself or is described as afire, impatient, erupting, quite unable to endure the crimes which he denounces." Anderson proceeds to make the point that Juvenal routinely ironizes this *indignatio* (e.g., in his refusal to leave Rome in Satire 3, despite his relentless complaining about the city). He concludes: "Juvenal has from the beginning revealed the complex nature of his satirist's abhorrence and so made the *persona* dramatically more interesting: the satirist hates and loves the city, abhors and yet is fascinated by its vices, a lonely prophet in the corrupt city." In other words, thinking of Juvenal's "I" as a *persona* makes the poem "more interesting," but can do little to persuade an audience that they must necessarily separate the *indignatio* of the *persona* from that of the poet. In the end, Rome is still a "corrupt city," as Anderson notes, and it was Juvenal himself who had to decide to make his *persona* complain about it in Satire 3. An audience may well want to know whether Juvenal is trying to persuade them that Rome is in fact "corrupt," even if Juvenal's "*persona*" makes sure that they can never know for sure.

12. This is essentially Martyn's (1979) approach as well.

13. For a judicious, if somewhat different, critique of the metaphor of the mask in persona theory, see Rudd 1976, 175–81. While not denying that Roman satirists sometimes used "masks" for strategic purposes, he finds the metaphor somewhat unfortunate in that masks imply a certain "rigidity" (see his quotations from Lucretius *DRN* 3.58, and Seneca *Epist.* 24.13; "They are talking as if the face were a single static entity. But a face can change expression as a voice changes tone; whereas a mask is rigid," 178–79). See also Volk 2002, 10–13, on the problem of the relationship between persona/mask and the author in (non-satirical) Latin didactic poetry.

lacy," that Satire 9 represents an essentially straightforward attack on characters such as Naevolus and Virro. Read this way, the satire ends up feeling like the moral tract it purports to be within its genre, even if the satirist makes us laugh at himself as well as his targets along the way. But things do not end here, for a poem like Satire 9, by virtue of its pervasive scandalous comic material, can offer only the veneer of didacticism, for the very act of laughing at such material amounts to complicity in the poet's very act of transgression. If, for example, we laugh at an obscenity, even one directed against a target for allegedly didactic purposes, we have essentially uttered the same obscenity as the poet; we may not literally say the actual words, but we hear them, or read them, and so must in some sense articulate them in order to know that they are funny. This kind of satire, then, gives the lie to its own didactic claims at the very moments when it seems to be urging its audience to be taking them seriously.

As we shall see in what follows, the common critical obsession with locating *actual* moralizing in the poem—instead of understanding the rhetoric of moralizing that suffuses it—has interfered with a full appreciation of its poetic strategies. The satirical poet himself, as I have argued throughout this study, no doubt takes a wry pleasure in leaving some of his audience convinced of his didactic seriousness, some humored but still confused in their quest to pin down his "real" sentiments, and others simply scandalized by his *ponêria*. Our task here will be to show that Juvenal's Ninth Satire is very much concerned not only with sorting through precisely these responses to satire and mockery, but also with articulating a fundamental insight that comedy and didacticism are, in the end, if not antithetical to one another, then certainly in constant tension.

3. Naevolus the Satirist—Naevolus as "Juvenal"

Satire 9 addresses two of Juvenal's favorite themes: the inequities of the client-patron relationship, and the kind of amoral, self-serving behavior that we find in the poet's interlocutor, Naevolus, a gigolo now spurned by his rich, effeminate patron. As we have seen, its lurid subject has often disturbed commentators, even as it has also frequently been praised as one of Juvenal's most successful efforts, particularly because of the way in which it effects its satire so economically through the character of Naevolus. Susanna Braund (1988) has offered a rich and detailed analysis of the poem in her study of Juvenal's third book, *Beyond Anger*, and has demonstrated meticulously the care with which Juvenal constructed his portrait of Naevolus. For Braund, Naevolus is one of Juvenal's most disreputable characters: he embodies qualities that often appear in other Juvenalian characters, but here he takes them to even greater extremes. Thus, while many characters (including of course, the poet's *persona* as well) might display anger, *ira*, Naevolus is *really* angry ("an excessive and intemperate over-reaction of anger").[14] Other qualities that Braund sees as extreme in Naevolus, are his "pessimism," his "greed," his "scorn for effemi-nacy," a pervasive "brashness," and a lack of "aesthetic sensibility"—"traits which are for the most part indisputably unpleasant." Insofar as Naevolus's personality is such an extreme version of many character types familiar from other poems of Juvenal, Braund argues, he is a somewhat parodic figure, and his dyspeptic complaint about his patron, "a parody of the usual complaint of the neglected client" (139). "These features," she concludes, "all make it hard for us to sympathise with Naevolus, and distance us from him." Braund con-trasts the portrait of the speaker, Naevolus's interlocutor, which is predominantly "ironic." That is, he displays a feigned sympathy with Naevolus's complaints, and offers incongruous, and so humorous, philosophical advice, all in an effort to assert his own moral superiority over Naevolus.

As an analysis of the satirical character types that Juvenal develops in the poem, Braund's discussion is invaluably illuminating, but I am certain that there is more to be discovered when we explore further the way in which Juvenal configures the relationship between Naevolus and the speaker. One problem arises when Braund makes this intriguing suggestion (1988, 170):

> [i]ndirectly and obliquely, perhaps, Satire 9 can be seen as an allegory
> of the procedure of satire . . . Naevolus's position is very similar to that
> of the archetypal satirist. He has an invective to deliver, but because
> he is fearful of the consequences, he delivers it not directly to the
> victim (= the patron) but to a (supposedly) disinterested audience
> (= the speaker), whom he then attempts to bind to secrecy.

Braund realizes that most of Naevolus's personal qualities derive essen-tially from his *ira* and *indignatio*, and that his tirade against his patron shares certain qualities with the kinds of ranting we find elsewhere in Juvenal's own satirical voice. But if Naevolus is as distasteful to "us" as Braund has argued, if we are supposed to be "distanced" from him, and "unsympathetic," why exactly, we might ask, would Juvenal want to make such a disreputable figure into an "allegory" of his own poetic enterprise? If our response to Naevolus is supposed to be as Braund has argued, that is, if is it "indisputable" that we must take seriously Naevolus's moral shortcomings, do we assume that Juvenal's point in doing this was to show that all satirists are really moral reprobates like Naevolus? This certainly is the obvious conclusion to draw, but it is not one that makes much sense if Juvenal's mockery of Naevolus is, in fact, meant to be taken seriously. Braund's intense focus on Naevolus as a *serious* negative moral exemplum has, it seems, kept her from taking the next natural step in the argument, namely,

---

14. Braund 1988, 137; ". . . Naevolus's long outburst shows him to be a gloomy, jealous, scorn-ful, brash, angry man."

to identify Naevolus the satirist with the Juvenalian satirist himself, and to have Juvenal thereby *embrace* the character of Naevolus wholesale as a kind of ironized poetic alter-ego.[15] This reading recovers a comic element in the poem that arises when the ostensibly moral satirist paints *himself* into the portrait of the character he is supposed to be attacking. In fact, as I shall argue, the specifically literary cast that Juvenal gives to this relationship between two interlocutors of the poem (Naevolus and Juvenal) is crucial to our understanding of the relationship between the poet and his target throughout all of his satires.

I would like to argue, then, that (a) Naevolus is invested with the role of the satirist in Satire 9 precisely because he serves as a type not only of the satiric narrator in general (Braund's fundamental insight), but of the Juvenalian satiric *persona* in particular, and (b) this literary conceit is part of the poem's larger program, which addresses the nature of the posturing and pretenses that the poet must affect in order to be a successful satirist. Such poses, in short, are depicted as character traits of a disreputable, degraded gigolo such as Naevolus. The unsavory portrait of Naevolus, in other words, functions programmatically by suggesting, with great comic irony, that the Juvenalian satirist (the sort or satirist described at length in the programmatic first Satire)[16] must at some level *become* what he attacks, and that this form of satire demands that he invariably play the role of an abject, disempowered underdog. In the remainder of this section, therefore, we will be amplifying and corroborating Braund's suggestion that Naevolus behaves like a satirist, but then arguing that the poem's central focus is poetics rather than, in any significant sense, morality.

A number of curious verbal and thematic elements in Satire 9, in fact, strongly suggest that the poem is more concerned with the activity of satire and the nature of the satirist than with criticizing the behavior of any of its characters. Indeed, the beginning and end of the poem offer a programmatic frame that leads easily, I think, to such a conclusion. The very opening lines of the poem seem to be urging the audience to construe Naevolus as a cipher for Juvenal the satirist:

> scire velim quare totiens mihi, Naevole, tristis
> occurras fronte obducta ceu Marsya victus.

---

15. Braund has recently revisited Satire 9 briefly in Braund 2004, 424–26, and has reformulated her earlier position on Naevolus as a case of "metasatire—satire using satire to talk about the processes of satire." She has read an earlier version of the argument I am putting forward here for Naevolus as Juvenal's alter-ego, and finds it compatible with her own treatment of Satire 9 in Braund 1988. (see also Braund 2004, 424n24). See now also Plaza 2006, 166, who (though apparently unaware of Braund's two treatments of Naevolus) flirts with the notion of Naevolus as a satirist-figure: "Naevolus is almost the impersonation of that adynaton, *saturam scribens cinaedus.*" ["the pathic homosexual writing satire," alluding to *Sat.* 4.106]. Ultimately, however, Plaza rejects the idea, ("[t]he witty male prostitute may be dismissed in the end"), though she does concede that briefly, at least, Juvenal had encountered in Naevolus his "underground self."

16. See, e.g., analysis in Braund 1996, 110–21.

> Naevolus, I'd like to know why I so often run into you looking
> gloomy with an overcast scowl like the beaten Marsyas. (trans.
> Braund)

Braund (1988, 158) has argued that the comparison of Naevolus to the mythological figure Marsyas highlights a certain "rustic" quality in him, in contrast to the *urbanitas* of the speaker (who is attacking this rusticity).[17] Marsyas was a satyr, after all, and satyrs were "rustic" to the Romans. But the heart of the Marsyas myth concerns a musician-performer, inventor of a form of aulos, who hybristically challenged Apollo himself to a musical contest.[18] They agreed that the winner could do whatever he chose to the loser, and when Apollo, predictably, won, he had poor Marsyas flayed alive. The comparison of the pained Naevolus to Marsyas (*ceu Marsya victus*), in other words, surely evokes the entire story of Marsyas as a defeated *performer*, a figure who construes himself as a superior musician, but has been plunged into abjection by an opponent, who had an unfair advantage (that is, the agon was between a human and divine—a lopsided, doomed pairing).

Another problem with Braund's characterization of Naevolus as *rusticus* is that a few lines later, 9–11, he is described as once having been quite the opposite, that is, practically *urbanus*. Braund is well aware of this passage[19] but remains focused on Naevolus's current "rustic" or non-urbane appearance and behavior. It strikes me as highly significant, however, that Naevolus is said to have *not always* been as disheveled as he now appears to be: In fact, it almost seems as if Juvenal is imputing to Naevolus an essential character of wit and *urbanitas* that he has perhaps only temporarily lost because of his current situation. Indeed, if we focus more on the image of Naevolus-cum-Marsyas as "harried poet" in the opening lines, then lines 9–10 offer striking literary commentary. The Naevolus of an earlier, more carefree, time, was a happy-go-lucky socialite:

> . . . certe *modico* contentus agebas
> vernam equitem, conviva *ioco mordente* facetus
> et *salibus* vehemens intra pomeria natis.

---

17. This seems somewhat at odds with a point Braund makes earlier in her treatment (1988, 146), namely that Juvenal's mention of Marsyas may also be part of a multifaceted allusion to Alcibiades's speech in Plato's *Symposium*. There, as Braund notes, Socrates is likened to Marsysas on several occasions from 215a5–222b7. But of course, the point of Alcibiades's mention of Marsyas is not to portray Socrates as a *rusticus*, but rather to equate the satyr's sublime musicianship with the profundity of Socrates' soul. For Socrates as a paradigmatic "ironist" among the Roman satirists (especially Horace), see Braund 1988, 143–57.

18. See Courtney 1980, ad loc, 427. For early accounts of the contest, see Hdt. 7.26 and Xen. *Anab.* 1.2.8.

19. "Naevolus commences his reply [at line 27] by trying to live up to the speakers' picture of his former sophistication" (1988, 150).

MOCKERY, SELF-MOCKERY, AND THE DIDACTIC RUSE

It's a fact that you used to be happy with nothing much, playing the homebred knight, an elegant dinner guest with biting humor and forceful witticisms bred within the city limits. (trans. Braund)

Naevolus is certainly far more than a "witty . . . jester or buffoon," as Braund describes him here. Rather, the mention of public activity that included a moderate outlook on life, and a biting and risqué wit, tempered by charm, is reminiscent of the ways in which Horace describes his own satiric project in the *Sermones*, especially as he works through it in *Sermones* 2.1, where he settles for a somewhat genteel Lucilian approach.[20] In happier times, it seems, Naevolus would have been perceived as a witty Horatian dinner guest; now, as a "flayed Marsyas," a ruined artist, he has sunk to an even lower level of poetic degradation, and his *indignatio* reaches a pitch that Juvenal had claimed for himself in the first Satire.[21]

These programmatic opening lines of the satire are balanced by the final lines (147–150), which seem to offer yet more literary commentary, specifically on the relationship between Juvenal's satire and his audience. Here Naevolus complains that Fortuna refuses to hear his prayers:

> . . . votum miserabile. nec spes
> his saltem; nam cum pro me Fortuna vocatur,

20. Braund insists that Naevolus is a kind of *rusticus*, while Juvenal is *urbanus*, for why would Juvenal want someone he is portraying as a boorish *rusticus* be emblematic of the kind of poetry he was supposed to be writing as an urbane sophisticate? (See Braund's remarks, 1988, 157: "We have established the nature of the speaker's [= Juvenal's] ironic character. We have also seen that he considers himself superior to Naevolus. There is enough evidence in the poem to justify calling this superiority *urbanitas*. . . . Thus the speaker's sustained use of irony helps characterise him as *urbanus*. Moreover, it seems that he regards Naevolus as *rusticus* (although he does not use this word), an unsophisticated Philistine.") The problem is resolved, however, by the argument I am proposing here, which would have Juvenal appropriating for himself Naevolus's abjection as an emblem of the perennially beleaguered satirist. It is, in other words, an ironized abjection, which may appear as *rusticitas* to others, but is in fact supposed really to be an "underappreciated" *urbanitas*. See now Plaza 2006, 165, who also calls attention to Naevolus' native wit, and the curious associations this conjures up with Horace in his *Sermones*.

21. Possibly Juvenal wants to contrast here two strands of Roman satire, an urbane Horatian-style *sermo* and his own deliberately less decorous form of *satura* (a notion that runs somewhat parallel to Freudenburg's argument [see1993, 107] that Horace was concerned to combine the Aristotelian "liberal jest" with rougher, iambographic strands). On the idea that Juvenal conceptualized his particular form of *indignatio* as distinctly non-Horatian, see Bellandi 1973. For Juvenal, however, I would not want to overemphasize the contrast. Horace may project a more outwardly genial speaking voice than Juvenal, and he may be less openly "angry," but his model still remains the famously vituperative Lucilius, and, if he were alive in Juvenal's time, he would doubtless claim, at least, to be sympathetic to Juvenal's fiery, comical tirades. Indeed, as Horace implies, he would be as fiery as Juvenal if he only thought he could have gotten away with it himself. It is true, however, as Jensen 1981–82, 159, points out, that Horatian targets (Jensen's example is the "vicious" *avarus*) are often portrayed as genuinely tormented, in contrast to many Juvenalian reprobates, who seem to enjoy their vices with impunity.

227

adfixit ceras illa de nave petitas
quae Siculos cantus effugit remige surdo.

It's a feeble prayer, with little hope of success. The trouble is that
when Fortune is summoned on my behalf, she has already plugged
her ears with wax fetched from the ship which escaped from the
songs of Sicily thanks to its deaf crew. (trans. Braund)

The allusion to Odysseus and the Sirens is extremely oblique, but when
it is mapped out, its implications are illuminating: Naevolus calls upon Fortuna
here in the same way as the Sirens called upon Odysseus in the Homeric passage to which these lines allude (Hom. *Od.* 12.165–200). Just as, in Homer,
Odysseus puts wax in his ears to avoid the songs of the Sirens, here Fortuna
plugs her ears with wax (indeed, wax derived from Odysseus's ship!, 149) in
order not to hear Naevolus. Naevolus, in other words, plays the role of the
dangerous Homeric Sirens whose song (*Siculos cantus*) can only bring trouble
to anyone who hears them. In equating Naevolus with the Sirens in these lines,
then, Juvenal equates Naevolus's *miserabile votum* with a *poetic* form (the Sirens'
"*votum*" for Odysseus to stay with them forever, articulated to him in seduc-
tive song)[22] that is generally perceived to be pernicious to its intended audience.
As we have seen repeatedly in our previous discussions, satirical poetry was often imagined to be pernicious, and more often than not, it was the poets themselves who were the first to say so as a topos of ironic self-aggrandizement.[23] We
may recall Horace's complaint at *Serm.* 1.4.81–91 that the satirist is wrongly
perceived by the public as injurious, the warning of Persius's friend in his first
Satire (1.107–10), or Juvenal's own programmatic remarks about Lucilius at
1.165–68, where the earlier satirist comes at his audience as if with a drawn sword,
and makes them sweat with guilt. In the closing lines of Satire 9, therefore,
Naevolus, now cast as a dangerous Siren-like singer, plays the role of a similarly
subversive, dangerous satirist, continually frustrated by a public that shuts out
his poetry as something harmful, just as Odysseus shuts out the Sirens.[24]

If I am right to suggest that Juvenal has deployed Naevolus in Satire 9 as
an alter-ego who in some sense reflects the prototypically beleaguered, abject
life of the satirist, one might at first wonder why he would have created quite

22. Courtney (1980, 445) notes that the point of the comparison with the Sirens is that
Naevolus "would try to tempt Fortune by offering her a share of his prosperity in a *votum* (147),"
but says nothing about whether it is significant that the Sirens are "singers."

23. See discussion, with bibliography, in chapter 5 (above, pp. 184–86).

24. The analogy is interestingly reminiscent of Thersites' difficulties with Odysseus in *Iliad*
2, as discussed at length in chapter 2 above. Odysseus there famously squelches Thersites' dissent
and punishes him for his mockery of the Greek leaders. In the Odyssean episode of the Sirens,
likewise, Odysseus is victorious, successfully withstanding the Sirens' attempt to overpower him
with their song.

as unseemly and disreputable a character to serve in this capacity. Time and again in our study, however, we have seen satirical poets perfectly capable of assuming disreputable roles if they seem contextually appropriate (Archilochus and Hipponax as sexual rakes, for example, or Aristophanes' use of the *ponêros* Sausage-seller in *Knights* to carry out his attacks on Cleon)—and Satire 9 would certainly not be the first time when Juvenal adopted behavior that was intended to make him look indecorous, if not simply vulgar. Certainly, Juvenal was not elsewhere above adopting a stance of self-righteous moralism only to have it "degenerate" into comic narcissism and ironic self-parody.[25] So the "brashness" of Naevolus, "his complete lack of awareness of cultured conduct, his lack of aesthetic sensibility" (141), which Braund thinks makes him qualitatively different from all the other beleaguered complainers of Juvenal's earlier satires, in fact aligns him all the more closely with the unstable and morally ambiguous stance of the Juvenalian satirist himself.

Many passages within the satire might serve to illustrate this point, but several are particularly striking and worth close scrutiny. At line 63, after Naevolus has been complaining about how stingy his wealthy patron, in particular, his refusal to repay his sexual services with land, he quotes the patron's rebuff: *improbus es cum poscis* (lit.: "You're *improbus* to ask for this . . ."). *Improbus*, as Braund has shown, generally implies "breaking the rules of proper social conduct," and for her, this term again illustrates Naevolus's lack of *urbanitas*.[26] But Naevolus's tirade, we have already seen, has many affinities with a satirist's complaint. When Juvenal complains about someone and mocks him, as Naevolus does here with Virro, we are not normally privy to the target's response. But this is exactly what Juvenal has Naevolus record for us here in line 63: "It's impertinent of you to beg," replies Virro. Since Naevolus's complaint against Virro is essentially a satirical *psogos* analogous to any of Juvenal's own rants elsewhere in his work,[27] Virro's epithet for Naevolus, *improbus*, then, is equally applicable to Juvenal when he is like-

25. *Contra* Braund (1988,157): "Unlike Plato's Socrates or 'Horace' in *Serm.* 1.9, 2.3 and 7, [Juvenal] does not direct the irony against himself. Rather, it is entirely at the expense of his interlocutor (cf. Hor. *Serm.* 2.4), whom he humours and manipulates in order to mock him." A surprising claim, it seems, given the fact that at the end of Satire 9 (130–33), the speaker Juvenal consoles Naevolus with the thought that Rome will never have a shortage of *pathici* to satisfy him. It is difficult not to read this as irony directed by Juvenal at himself, for what has happened to his authorial stance of censure? Does he now suddenly "really" approve of Naevolus's lifestyle?

26. See Braund 1988, 137, where she wonders whether the patron's charge of *improbitas* against Naevolus might actually be "right," in view of Naevolus's subsequent long, over-the-top, tirade.

27. Or at least in his first three books. Scholars have long noted what appears to be a shift in the character of Juvenal satires after the third book (7–8), from openly vituperative to somewhat more tempered and philosophical (or "Democritean"). In the nineteenth century Ribbeck 1865 saw this as a "problem," and suggested that the later books were forged. Few have taken this seriously, but many find the difference in tone between the earlier and later books noteworthy. See e.g., Highet 1954, on Book 3: "The beginning of a failure in Juvenal's powers . . ." (104); on Book 4, ". . . the

wise in his vituperative mode.[28] Of course, from the point of view of the satirist, who quotes such unfavorable judgments against himself, the charges are entirely unfounded and unjust; but they intensify the satirist's typical stance of abjection in the eyes of his audience, and thereby give more (comic) justification to their attacks.[29]

In terms of the dynamics of satire, then, it is not difficult to see a fusion between the indignant Naevolus and the indignant Juvenal. But there are other ways in which the equation is corroborated within Juvenal. In one of the rare explicit references in Juvenal to the term *satura*, Satire 4.106, a connection with Satire 9 seems inescapable. Here, one of Domitian's councillors, Rubrius, rushing into the court to advise the emperor on what to do about the monstrous fish which had recently been brought before him, is described as "more *improbus* than a *cinaedus* writing satire" (*et tamen improbior saturam scribente cinaedo*). This is a humorously gratuitous, self-referential image,[30] especially since its import is not entirely transparent on first reading. Is Rubrius, for example, "more *improbus* than a *cinaedus* writing satire" (with emphasis on the word *cinaedus*), implying that it is a "shameful" thing even to imagine a *cinaedus* writing satire? Or does the phrase imply, comically, that everyone associates *cinaedi* with satire-writing anyway, that is, that *improbitas* is somehow inherent in the very

---

work of an aging man . . . a strange blend of sombre melancholy with tenderness and even gaiety" (123). See also Bellandi 1980, for a further attempt to account for the "two Juvenals," and Braund 1988, 197: ". . . we see a marked development of Juvenal's satiric *persona* throughout his poetic career. The simple, indignant persona of the first two Books is replaced in Book III by a more complex, ironic *persona*." This is a vast topic in itself, which we cannot address here, although I do think that such a movement has often been overstated. There are quasi-philosophical moments in the earlier books, and sufficient *indignatio* in the later ones to make it questionable whether, as has often been felt, Juvenal somehow "abandoned" the direction he charted for himself in the first satire by the time he wrote the later books.

28. Horace engages in the same conceit in *Serm.* 4, where he too imagines what the satirist's target will think of the satirist and "quotes" what he might say against him. See e.g., *Serm.* 4.26–31, 78. For further discussion of this passage, see Rosen and Marks 1999, 907–909.

29. Naevolus's own *improbitas* serves also as an excellent emblem of the entire satiric enterprise. His *improbitas* emerges, that is, precisely as a function of the aggressive priapic stance of the Roman satirist that Amy Richlin has so well discussed (1992 [1983] 202): "The satirist in effect rapes Rome with Naevolus as his agent—an agent at whom he jovially sneers." This agent, I would add, is also "Juvenal" the satirist himself. All the more comically pathetic and almost programmatic, then, becomes Naevolus's famously obscene rhetorical question at 43–44 (*an facile et pronum est agere intra viscera penem || legitimum atque illic hesternae occurrere cenae?*) The satirist, like Naevolus, is by definition always disenfranchised, and when he reacts, he does so with phallus erect, so to speak—one that is *legitimus* at that, unlike (he would way) those of his targets. Yet despite this show of power and virility, the satirist's desire for some sort of cosmic justice is, as usual, destined to remain unfulfilled. See also Miller 1998, 260–61.

30. In her commentary on Juvenal Book 1, Braund (1996, 258) writes of this line: "the fleeting self-referentiality . . . affirms the robust masculinity of the speaker, who evidently regards 'a sodomite writing satire' as far removed from his self-image."

profession? The placement of *cinaedus* at verse-end functions as a *paraprosdokian*, and piles on even more comic abjection to the image that the reader initially encounters: "If you remember that all satirists are naturally *improbi*, well then imagine that Rubrius is even *improbrior* than that; then, imagine not only an *improbus* satirist, but a *cinaedus* writing satire!" This surprise double-dose of authorial self-flagellation is humorous because the audience is taking in the work of "someone writing satire." Is its author a *cinaedus*? Is he *improbus* too, like Rubrius? An answer, of course, is irrelevant: The point is that the satirist has winked at the audience with the suggestion that the didactic underpinnings of the genre might be less solemn and more playful than one might be led to believe.

Perhaps even more arresting is the fact that we encounter our *cinaedus* again in Satire 9, this time as part of a Greek quotation from Homer, deployed by Naevolus in another moment of ironic self-denigration:

> nam si tibi sidera cessant,
> nil faciet longi mensura incognita nerui,
> quamuis te nudum spumanti Virro labello
> uiderit et blandae adsidue densaeque tabellae
> sollicitent, αὐτὸς γὰρ ἐφέλκεται ἄνδρα κίναιδος.

> You see, if the stars abandon you, nothing will be achieved by the unprecedented length of your long cock, though Virro with drooling lips has seen you in the nude and his many coaxing love letters assail you nonstop. 'For the man can't help being attracted by the—pathic.' (9.33–37; trans. Braund)

The Greek quotation parodies a famous line from Homer (*Od.* 16.294, 19.13), but substitutes κίναιδος ("pathic") for σίδηρος ("iron," "sword"). The word for *cinaedus* once again occurs at verse-end as a *paraprosdokian*, a surprise that instantaneously lowers the epic tone of the phrase. The associations begin to accrue: From Satire 4 we learn that satirists can be *improbi*, and can be humorously associated with *cinaedi*; in Satire 9, Naevolus is called *improbus* by the target of his own complaint, and earlier refers to himself as a *cinaedus*. Through it all, we have seen a Naevolus whose self-righteous *indignatio* mimics that of the satirist himself. The case for Naevolus as Juvenal's alter-ego, therefore, seems increasingly assured.

The context in which Naevolus imagines Virro calling him *improbus* highlights another theme that links him with a prototypical satirist: Poverty. Indeed the bulk of Naevolus's tirade concerns allegations that he cannot support himself adequately on the beneficence of his patron. To illustrate this briefly we may compare a section of Naevolus's complaint with complaints delivered elsewhere in the voice of the poet. In lines 27–40 of Satire 9, for example,

Naevolus complains about the cheap coats and dishes he gets from his patron, as well as the patron's stinginess.

> utile et hoc multis uitae genus, at mihi nullum
> inde operae pretium. pingues aliquando lacernas,
> [munimenta togae, duri crassique coloris]
> et male percussas textoris pectine Galli
> accipimus, tenue argentum uenaeque secundae.

> Many people find even this way of life profitable, but I get no reward
> for my efforts. From time to time I get a coarse overcloak loosely
> made by a Gallic weaver's comb, or some thin silver plate of inferior
> quality. (trans. Braund)

Complaints about poverty are part of the stock in trade of satirical abjection and *indignatio*, and by now, Naevolus's own complaint of his poverty will remind us of similar gestures in other satirists, such as Hipponax and Callimachus, who likewise portray themselves on occasion as destitute "have-nots" deserving the sympathy of their audience.[31] Juvenal's programmatic first Satire has much to say about the oppressed, impoverished client, as well, but lines 132–38 sum up the attitude well:

> uestibulis abeunt ueteres lassique clientes
> uotaque deponunt, quamquam longissima cenae
> spes homini; caulis miseris atque ignis emendus.
> optima siluarum interea pelagique uorabit
> rex horum uacuisque toris tantum ipse iacebit.
> nam de tot pulchris et latis orbibus et tam
> antiquis una comedunt patrimonia mensa.

> The old and weary clients leave the porches, abandoning their
> wishes—although the hope of dinner is the one that lasts longest.
> The poor souls have got to buy their cabbage and firewood. Mean-
> while their lord will be devouring the choicest produce of woodland
> and sea, reclining alone among the empty couches. The fact is, they
> consume entire fortunes at a single table chosen from all those
> splendid, large round tables of such antiquity. (trans. Braund)

31. On Hipponax, see chapter 1 pp. 11–12, Callimachus, see chapter 5 (above, pp. 192–93, with bibliography). The theme of poverty also occurs prominently in Hesiod's *Works and Days*, and although this is obviously not, generically or formally speaking, a work of "satire," its didactic stance and authorial stance against a target, Perses, give much of it a satiric cast, as Hunt 1981, 197, has well argued. See also our discussion about Odysseus in his role as a disguised beggar in Hom. *Odyssey* (above, chapter 4, 120).

Once again, we find complaints about insufficient material support, and a contrast with the rich patron's own extravagant lifestyle. In Book 3 (that is, poems 7–9) Juvenal's complaints about boorish rich patrons are perhaps somewhat more restrained than in the earlier books,[32] but they nevertheless make the same point about the satirist's perennial indigence. In Satire 7, for example, Juvenal focuses on how a *poet* suffers from inadequate patronage; predictably, modern critics have responded to this passage with more sympathy than when similar complaints elsewhere in Juvenal (including Naevolus's) come across more as irate outbursts. The examples Juvenal offers in Satire 7, however, of poets who were well supported (unlike poets of his own age) are superficially exalted enough, but these poets too are merely looking for the same banal things in life that the Juvenalian *cliens* elsewhere also lacks: Horace, he says, had plenty of food and wine, and so could compose the *Odes*; Vergil had enough to buy a blanket, had a slave and a place to live, and so could compose the *Aeneid*. So why should the contemporary poet not have the bare necessities of life provided for him as well?

> sed uatem egregium, cui non sit publica uena,
> qui nihil expositum soleat deducere, nec qui
> communi feriat carmen triuiale moneta,
> hunc, qualem nequeo monstrare et sentio tantum,
> anxietate carens animus facit, omnis acerbi
> inpatiens, cupidus siluarum aptusque bibendis
> fontibus Aonidum. neque enim cantare sub antro
> Pierio thyrsumque potest contingerc maesta
> paupertas atque aeris inops, quo nocte dieque
> corpus eget: satur est cum dicit Horatius 'euhoe.'

But the outstanding bard—the one with no common vein of talent, the one who generally spins nothing trite, the one who coins no ordinary song from the public mint, the likes of whom I cannot point out, but can only imagine—he is the product of a mind free from worry and without bitterness, a mind that longs for the woods and is fit to drink the springs of the Muses. Unhappy poverty, you see, cannot sing inside the Pierian cavern or grasp the thyrsus: it lacks the cash which the body needs, night and day. Horace was full when he spoke the Bacchic cry "Evoe!" (7.53–62; trans. Braund)
....

32. See Braund 1988, 135–43 on Naevolus's relationship with his patron in Satire 9; also Bellandi 1974.

magnae mentis opus nec de lodice paranda
attonitae currus et equos faciesque deorum
aspicere et qualis Rutulum confundat Erinys.
nam si Vergilio puer et tolerabile desset
hospitium, caderent omnes a crinibus hydri,
surda nihil gemeret graue bucina. . . .

A great soul, not one perplexed about buying a blanket, is needed for
visions of chariots and horses and the gods' faces and the kind of
Fury that drove the Rutulian crazy. After all, if Vergil hadn't had a
slave boy and decent lodgings, all the snakes would have fallen from
the Fury's hair and no terrifying blast would have sounded from her
silent war trumpet. (7.66–71; trans. Braund)

Naevolus's own version of this at the end of Satire 9 is humorously hy-
perbolic, as if Juvenal himself were parodying the trope:

O parui nostrique Lares, quos ture minuto
aut farre et tenui soleo exorare corona,
quando ego figam aliquid quo sit mihi tuta senectus
a tegete et baculo? uiginti milia fenus   140
pigneribus positis, argenti uascula puri,
sed quae Fabricius censor notet, et duo fortes
de grege Moesorum, qui me ceruice locata
securum iubeant clamoso insistere circo;
sit mihi praeterea curuus caelator, et alter   145
qui multas facies pingit cito; sufficiunt haec.
quando ego pauper ero?

Ah, my own tiny Hearth Gods (I always make my requests with a
few grains of incense or meal and a simple garland), when will I ever
make a catch that will save my old age from the beggar's mat and
stick? All I want is an income of twenty thousand from secure
investments, some silver cups, plain, but the sort that would be
banned by the censor Fabricius, and two hefty bodyguards from the
Moesian gang to enable me to take my place safely in my hired litter
at the noisy racecourse. In addition, I'd like an engraver, stooped by
his work, and an artist who can do multiple portraits in moments.
That's enough. But when will I even be poor? It's a feeble prayer,
with little hope of success. (9.137–47; trans. Braund)

In the last line, Naevolus claims that he is only looking for a time when he
can call himself basically "poor," as opposed to his current position of utter

destitution.[33] But all the material things he prays for are obviously far too extravagant for someone looking only to bring himself to a comfortable level of "poverty," and the pièce de resistance—an engraver (*caelator*) and painter (*alter qui multas facies pingit*) to accompany him as his Moesian slaves carry him above the crowds—makes it clear that even Naevolus, and by extension his creator Juvenal, is not taking himself terribly seriously here.[34] Once again, we can see that Juvenal has acribed to Naevolus precisely the kind of literary posturing that he elsewhere assumes for himself when representing himself as a poet of satire.

33. Courtney 1980, ad loc. 444: "*paupertas* does not indicate penury, but a modest sufficiency…of course the irony of the passage consists in the fact that his wishes are not all that modest (cf. *modico contentus*)."

34. The addition of an engraver and a painter to Naevolus's retinue seems oddly gratuitous here. For Braund (1988, 156), it simply reveals Naevolus's true character: "[H]ow can Naevolus consider an engraver and an artist as essential? Once again, Naevolus condemns himself. In musing on his 'basic' requirements for life, he has revealed his greed." But this seems a decidedly humorless reading of a lighthearted and ironic passage. I wonder in fact whether we are somehow meant to transfer their role as visual artists to the realm of poetry, especially if I am right to suggest (see above pp. 227–28) that the final lines of the poem end up analogizing Naevolus to a satirical poet of sorts. Does not the satirist "engrave" vivid images of his characters, or paint the portraits of *multas facies*? Perhaps the famous programmatic lines of Satire 1 lie not far in the background of this passage: *quidquid agunt homines, votum, timor, ira, voluptas, || gaudia discursus, nostri farrago libelli est*. This may help to explain another curiosity in Satire 9 (lines 63–65, quoted above) that constitute Naevolus's response to the charge against himself of *improbitas* that he puts into the mouth of Virro. Naevolus objects that he is driven to ask for more money from his patron simply in order to pay the rent (*pensio*); and his slave chimes in with a similar plea (64). In order to emphasize that he only has a single slave, Naevolus uses the odd simile of Polyphemus's single eye: "as single as Polyphemus's broad eye, because of which crafty Ulysses escaped." A nexus of associations comes into play: Naevolus complains that one slave is insufficient for his needs, in keeping with his subsequent cries of poverty, which are, in themselves, as we have discussed, typical fare for the satirist. The allusion to Polyphemus is obviously literary and elevated (insofar as it alludes to an epic passage), although the scene itself is one that features an agon between "high" and "low" characters (see discussion in chapter 4), and Naevolus identifies his slave, abjectly, with the "low" Homeric character here, i.e., the "savage" Polyphemus. The slave—as Naevolus's property and, as such, a reflection of the character of his household—easily maps on to Naevolus himself, and this has the effect of pitting Naevolus-as-Polyphemus against the stingy patron-as-Ulysses. As we saw above, Ulysses reappears at the very end of Satire 9, where Naevolus once again conceptualizes him as someone against whom he can make no headway (this time referring to the inability of the Sirens to get through to Ulysses). Although it is difficult to say whether the two Homeric references in the poem were closely connected in Juvenal's mind, it is undeniable that Naevolus is made in each case to portray Ulysses as a legitimate target of complaint, and himself as unfairly oppressed. Braund (1988, 151) suggests that Juvenal may have construed Naevolus as a parody of a Cynic, and notes (247n70) that Ulysses often figured in Cynic discourse in both a positive and negative light. See also Juv. 15.13–26, where Juvenal again adverts to Ulysses' narration among the Phaeacians, this time to prepare his readers for his own narration of similarly incredible events (cannibalism among the Egyptians).

4. Virro, the Forgotten Target in Satires 9 and 5

If we are justified in construing Naevolus as a mirror of Juvenal the satirist, it becomes eminently clear that Juvenal has pulled off a quite extraordinary literary feat. For without being explicitly programmatic, the poem nevertheless becomes one the most programmatic works we have encountered in this entire book. What I mean by this is that once we understand how Juvenal has refracted the figure of the satirist through Naevolus, we can watch how he questions virtually all aspects of the satiric enterprise itself, often through self-conscious parody, and always, as we might expect, with an irony that precludes, finally, any stable conception of what satirists actually do.

It is hard to imagine, in fact, a better example than Satire 9 of the kind of literary gamesmanship that satire is capable of. To begin with, we might consider the supreme deception Juvenal has accomplished for nearly two millennia in making audiences believe that the "point" of Satire 9 is to "attack" Naevolus *tout court*. Juvenal the satirist constructs Naevolus as his target and although there appear to be touches of sympathy here and there, we are supposed to construe these as ironic and ultimately malicious. Indeed the portrait of Naevolus is so well drawn, so powerfully transgressive and so dramatically central to the narrative, that it seems natural to assume that the poem is intended as a satire on all the kinds of degraded people he represents. No doubt this is what Juvenal at some level hoped for as well, since it certainly makes for a "safe" reception of the poem. But it should be clear by now that such an analysis, if we cannot simply say it is incorrect, certainly raises more questions about satiric poetics than it answers. Most significant of all is the question of the satirist's target. Centuries of obsession about Naevolus have almost completely obscured the fact that the "real" target of the satire, formally speaking, is not Naevolus but his patron Virro.[35] As a character in the dramatic dialogue, Juvenal never once says anything to indicate that he intends to mock or criticize Naevolus. Laden with their own moral baggage, critics have routinely *assumed* that Juvenal cannot possibly approve of Naevolus, and that any *amicitia* he displays toward him must be feigned and ironized; but even this would not make Naevolus into a satirist's *target*, *especially* when the poem has already furnished one in the character of Virro.

35. See Courtney 1980, 424: "Juvenal does not make an overt attack on Naevolus, but represents himself as a detached listener who pretends to sympathise with him." For Courtney (and others) this poem marks a transition to a "new stylistic phase, from the *indignatio* of the earlier satires to the cooler manner of Book IV." But he also adds of Satire 9, "this is not to say that his moral indignation has decreased, but that he has found here a different way of expressing it. . . ." In other words, the poem is still, for him, ultimately a sincere attack on Naevolus's character. But see now Tennant 2003, who prefers to take the spotlight off of Naevolus and shine it on Virro. For him, the "real" target of the satire is the corrupt client-patron system that Virro represents.

What makes this poem so remarkable, then, is that Juvenal has called attention to all the moral and didactic ambiguities that, as we have seen, perennially plague satirical works. The effect is no doubt intended to be humorous, but the insight behind it is substantive: He has constructed a thoroughly "disreputable" character, but this character has a "legitimate" complaint against another thoroughly disreputable character, Virro. To repeat two questions we asked in chapter 3: "Where does the blame lie?" "With whom are we supposed to sympathize?" If Juvenal is supposed to disapprove of Naevolus, what does it mean that, at the same time, he unites with him in their disapproval of Virro? Juvenal is "attacking" Virro through Naevolus, but what does this mean for our assessment of Naevolus's character itself? The "blame" formally lies with Virro, and our "sympathies" by implication, then, lie with Juvenal as the author of the poem; but if Naevolus is also made to attack Virro from within the poem, are our sympathies also supposed to lie with him? If answered affirmatively, though, are we somehow condoning his behavior at the same time? None of these questions is intended to be answered but Juvenal certainly seems devilishly aware that he has forced his attentive readers to think about them at every turn.

The proposition that Juvenal is self-consciously drawing attention here to the complex dynamics and ambiguities of satire is further strengthened when we consider Satire 9 in the light of another satire that features Virro as its target, Satire 5. Some basic similarities between these two satires are occasionally noted:[36] Both satires concern the dysfunctional relationship between patron and *cliens*, and both are structured as protreptic addresses to subordinates who are angry at the treatment they have received from what appears to be the same person, Virro.[37] The two satires are also affiliated, however, by a more fundamental connection: While they both share a common target in the boorish, stingy, impotent Virro, the attack on him is effected obliquely through a friendlier sort of criticism of the poems' interlocutor. While Juvenal banters sympathetically with Naevolus in Satire 9, and warns him against expecting anything from Virro, in Satire 5 he similarly cautions Trebius from becoming too attached to Virro's dinner invitations. As he sums up at lines 12–13:

primo fige loco, quod tu discumbere iussus
mercedem solidam veterum capis officiorum.

Keep this in mind in the first place: that dinner invitation will
constitute your only tangible payment for all your previous services.

36. See, for example, Courtney 1980, 230.
37. The name is not common, and seems ascribable to only one known historical figure, S. Vibidius Virro, evidently a notoriously unsavory character during Tiberius's reign, who was expelled from the Senate in 17 CE for immoral behavior. See Syme 1970 [1949] 76–77; and Ferguson 1987, 244.

The bulk of the Satire consists of a vivid, humorous account of a typical banquet hosted by Virro, and for the most part reads like a straightforward enough *psogos* against a favorite character-type of the period.[38] For most of the poem, Juvenals rails indignantly at the way Virro treats his guests at the dinner party, but near the end, the focus shifts from Virro's reprehensible behavior to Trebius's complicity in the pathological client-patron relationship. Virro is hardly exonerated in the end, but his behavior is at least partially explained by the fact that Trebius (and people like him) behaves precisely as Virro wants him to. The poem ends with this astonishing passage:

> forsitan inpensae Virronem parcere credas.
> hoc agit, ut doleas; nam quae comoedia, mimus
> quis melior plorante gula ? ergo omnia fiunt
> si nescis, ut per lacrimas effundere bilem
> cogaris pressoque diu stridere molari.   160
> tu tibi liber homo et regis conuiua uideris
> captum te nidore suae putat ille culinae,
> nec male coniectat; quis enim tam nudus, ut illum
> bis ferat, Etruscum puero si contigit aurum
> uel nodus tantum et signum de paupere loro?   165
> spes bene cenandi uos decipit. 'ecce dabit iam
> semesum leporem atque aliquid de clunibus apri,
> ad nos iam ueniet minor altilis.' inde parato'
> intactoque omnes et stricto pane tacetis.
> ille sapit, qui te sic utitur. omnia ferre   170
> si potes, et debes. pulsandum uertice raso
> praebebis quandoque caput nec dura timebis
> flagra pati, his epulis et tali dignus amico.

You might imagine that Virro is intent on saving money. No—he does it deliberately, to pain you. After all, what comedy or farce is better than a whining gut? So, let me tell you, his entire intention is to make you vent your anger in tears and keep you gnashing and grinding your teeth. In your own eyes you are a free man and my Lord's guest. He reckons you're enslaved by the smell of his kitchen —and he's not far wrong. After all, how could anyone who in his childhood wore the Tuscan gold, or at least the symbolic knotted leather thong of the poor man, be so destitute as to put up with Himself more than once? It's the hope of dining well that ensnares you. "Look, any minute now he'll give us a half-eaten hare or a portion from the boar's haunch. Any minute now we'll get a scrappy

---

38. Cf., e.g. Shero 1923.

chicken." So you all wait there in silence, brandishing your bread at the ready, untouched. The man who treats you like this is shrewd. If there is nothing you can't put up with, then you deserve it all. Sooner or later, you'll be offering to have your head shaved and slapped, and you won't flinch from a harsh whipping. That's the kind of banquet you deserve, and that's the kind of friend. (5.156–73; trans. Braund, modified)

While we had been led to assume throughout the poem that Virro was in fact just a boorish cheapskate, the "blame" suddenly seems to shift to Trebius for playing along with Virro's games. Virro, it turns out, is not stupid, he is merely using people like Trebius to generate entertainment, and if Trebius does not like the way he is treated, he has only himself to blame (170) : *ille sapit, qui te sic utitur. omnia ferre* || *si potes, et debes*. Trebius's role here, in other words, is akin to Naevolus's in Satire 9: Juvenal presents himself as one who sympathizes with the *indignatio* of an abject friend, but qualifies his sympathies by exposing his friend's role in causing his own abjection. The poem ends with the image of Trebius acting like a performing buffoon, who deserves what he gets from Virro (171–73): . . . *pulsandum uertice raso* || *praebebis quandoque caput nec dura timebis* || *flagra pati, his epulis et tali dignus amico*).

There is an implicit inevitability to Trebius's fate that maps on strikingly to one of the central paradoxes of satire and mockery that we have articulated elsewhere in this study: How can there be satire if there is nothing to complain about? The *indignatio* and *ira* of a satirist is always presented as a "negative" force, and always implies a desire for things to be better than they are, but the poetry itself can only exist when the world is construed as incapable of amelioration. This is why, when a satirist *claims* to be moralizing, we can never be entirely sure what these claims amount to, for to imagine a world in which there is nothing to complain about is to imagine a world without satire. And what satirist *qua* satirist (that is, in his *role* as the composer of his satirical verse, not, for example, as a historical individual) would really want a world in which the things he once complained about are "corrected"?

Some thought such as this, at any rate, seems to lie behind the opening of this passage (156–60), quoted above, which begins to read like an analysis of all the components of satire itself. Virro begins as the poem's target, and remains so. As a fundamentally reprehensible figure, he is the ultimate inspiration for the poem, the object of *indignatio*. But suddenly we are offered a rare glimpse of the response a target knowingly expects to elicit from the people he offends: *dolor, lacrimae*, and *bilis*—all programmatically charged as hallmarks of satire. More revealing still is the reason why Virro is said to crave such responses: It makes for a fine comic performance. For him, the best comic show on earth is to watch a hungry client begging for food, then crying over it and about to burst with anger. Trebius has now become an abject figure, who plays an essential role in generating a comic performance, and as such his behavior replicates exactly that of prototypical satirist—angry, indignant, and morally self-righteous, but ultimately "frustrated" in his attempt to effect any change in his situation by his own "weakness" for *improbitas/ponêria*. Satire, in other words, will complain about people like Virro, but the satirist wants his *comoedia*, and he will have to rely on the Virro's of the world to produce it by mistreating the Naevoluses and Trebiuses of the world. Satire thus exists in an inescapable relationship of symbiotic codependency with its targets, each requiring the existence and role-playing of the other for there to be satirical comedy. To put the matter another way: The moment that Trebius might hypothetically take Juvenal's advice and refuse to attend banquets such as Virro's, is the moment when comedy ceases to exist; for, as Juvenal says, Virro understands that it is anger and indignation that makes people laugh, and if Virro no longer has a Trebius to rankle, Juvenal himself no longer has the *materia* and *res* for his satire.

In the lines immediately preceding the passage quoted above, lines 149–55, Juvenal, in fact, seems to go out of way to prepare his reader for associating Trebius with the procedures of satire. For here, Juvenal, in presenting his final example of the egregiously unequal treatment Trebius will receive at Virro's banquet, constructs a stark and revealing polarity with decidedly literary overtones:

> Virro sibi et reliquis Virronibus illa iubebit
> poma dari, quorum solo pascaris odore,
> qualia perpetuus Phaeacum autumnus habebat,
> credere quae possis subrepta sororibus Afris:
> tu scabie frueris mali, quod in aggere rodit
> qui tegitur parma et galea metuensque flagelli
> discit ab hirsuta iaculum torquere capella.

> For himself and the other Virros, Virro will order apples whose
> aroma on its own is a meal: the sort of apples that the everlasting
> fruit time of the Phaeacians used to produce, apples you could
> believe had been stolen from the African sisters [= the Hesperides].
> Your treat is a scabby apple—like the apple gnawed by the creature
> dressed up with shield and helmet on the Embankment, that in
> terror of the whip learns to hurl a javelin from the back of a shaggy
> she-goat. (5.149–55; trans. Braund)

The comparison of the fine fruits reserved for Virro's real friends to the fruits of the Phaeacians (alluding to Homer *Odyssey* 7) and of the apples guarded by the Hesperides (associated with the labors of Heracles)[39] seems calculated

---

39. For the literary and artistic background of this labor of Heracles, see Gantz 1993, 410–13.

to conjure up a distinctly heroic, epic world—high-brow, elevated, and poetically decorous. Homer and Odysseus function here, as we saw they do in Satire 9, as emblems of a world inaccessible to someone of Trebius's social, and by extension, literary, standing. Trebius and his ilk are likened by contrast to monkeys *performing* for rotten apples from the back of a hairy goat.[40] Not only that, but the particular performance he is given here is one of epic parody—the monkey is dressed up as a soldier and tosses a spear from the goat! The simian metaphor here, with its "low," bestial imagery of hair and goats, will recall our discussion of the Cercopes in chapter 2, those monkey-like creatures captured by Heracles, but released by him when their mockery of his hairy buttocks made him laugh. There is no need to imagine that Juvenal's monkey alludes in any *conscious* way to the Cercopes, but it is striking how similarly each functions as a paradigm of comic satire. In each case, comedy is ultimately generated by the *performance* of a "low" stance of beleaguerement, servitude, and abjection, which, in addition to ironic self-abasement, will also include mockery of its target. In the case of Trebius at the end of Satire 5, this relationship between "oppressed" mocker and "superior" target is evidently also analogized to a literary relationship imagined to hold between satirical genres and genres of a putative "legitimacy," such as epic. The monkey on the goat's back "performs" a mocking version of Iliadic epic, just as the satirist engages in epic parody and other forms of mockery, but neither, as Juvenal says, can ever aspire to anything other than the "rotten apple," a memento of the satirist's perennial state of comic abjection.[41]

Both Satires 5 and 9, then, begin as protreptic consolation poems to a beleaguered "friend" who feel unjustly oppressed by a miscreant patron, and as such Juvenal can be said to join forces with Trebius and Naevolus over against their common target Virro. But as we have seen, neither Trebius nor Naevolus is portrayed as particularly appealing, and Juvenal makes sure we see how ironic and comical this situation can become. Not only do we end up losing sight of the "real" target, Virro, as Juvenal shifts the focus to the fate of his harried addressees, but we confront the unsettling fact that both these socially marginal characters actually "do" exactly what Juvenal himself does in his role as

---

40. Cf. Freudenburg 2001, 275: "that monkey . . . forages for trash, and thus it bears a certain figurative resemblance to the satirist himself." (See next note.)

41. Cf. Freudenburg (2001, 274–77) on the ending of Satire 5. Freudenburg sees the monkey's performance as a parody of Lucilian satire, and the satirist's abjection at the end of the poem as emblematic of Juvenal's ultimate inability to live up to Lucilius's majestically unbridled satire. As Freudenburg argues, because Juvenal is unable to realize the Lucilian promise of Satire 1, both he and the reader end up feeling frustrated at the end of Satire 5 (i.e., the end of the first book). Juvenal, according to this reading, becomes a "companion in our frustration" (275) and as readers we leave the book as the guest leaves Virro's banquet, angry and hungry for more. I like Freudenburg's sense of the irony and slipperiness at the end of Satire 5, but am doubtful that Juvenal (or his readers—even Roman ones) would ever think that his "frustration" as a satirist was *actually* an unwelcome or negative posture, or that it marked him as somehow distinctly non-Lucilian.

a satirist: They represent themselves as unjustly oppressed by forces beyond their control, indignant at their current situation, and driven to complain about it. In a very real sense, as I have argued, in a supreme act of self-mockery (itself a common gesture of comic abjection), Juvenal essentially *becomes* Trebius and Naevolus, and through them continually ironizes his own moralizing pretenses throughout the poems. By creating such distinct and vivid characters as Trebius and Naevolus, Juvenal is able to distance himself sufficiently at the literal level from the "moral degradation" that each one represents, and to make a show, at least, of disapproving of their behavior. But "moralizing" turns out to be more complicated than might first appear, and any attentive reader might eventually wonder what it means when even morally reprehensible figures such as Trebius and Naevolus can be portrayed as feeling a "legitimate" or "moral" *indignatio* against the incorrigibly reprehensible Virro. The didactic, moralizing stance of the satirist suddenly becomes—paradoxically—a little less predictably "moral," at least in any stable, unproblematic sense of the term, for if a character as unsavory as Naevolus can display *indignatio,* what criteria in the end do we use to distinguish *his* causes from those of the satirist? Can we ever be sure that the satirist is a person of upright character simply by trusting in his own self-righteous claims? Juvenal's answer in both these poems seems to be, in fact, that one cannot; or rather that the moralizing tropes of satire, while essential, defining characteristics of the genre, exist solely for the purpose of generating comedy, not for actually trying to edify the audience in some vaguely paternalistic way. Juvenal may or may not have "really disapproved" of the reprehensible people who populate his satires, but there is every reason to think, as I have tried to show in this chapter, that he was far more interested in obfuscating, rather than clarifying, the content of his moral claims.[42]

42. In her recent study, Plaza 2006 (e.g., 235–56) is sympathetic to this approach, but in the end seems uncomfortable with the notion of Juvenal relinquishing his satirical "authority": ". . . while Juvenal's persona is occasionally ridiculed, his authority is not altogether destroyed, certainly not to the degree of making him the victim of his satires" (255). I remain unconvinced, in any case, by Plaza's statement (256) that "the overwhelming evidence is in favour of reading the persona's views as endorsed by the author," especially, as she proceeds herself to note, given the frequency with which these views are undercut by the poet himself.

7

Archilochus, Critias, and the Poetics
of Comic Abjection

Ancient Responses to Satiric Ponêria

Our study has taken us across a broad chronological sweep of classical antiquity and put us in contact with many types of satirical poetry, composed by poets of diverse temperaments for a variety of performative contexts. Yet despite the many contingencies of culture, occasion, language or literary form that make each poet idiosyncratic to his own time and place, we are now in a better position to appreciate some of the features that affiliate all of them as participants in a common poetic enterprise. Sometimes, as we have seen, poets showed themselves to be drawing self-consciously on traditional poetic structures and protocols that take them well beyond their own historical moment— we may think of Callimachus's relationship with Hipponax, for example, or Horace's professed admiration for Athenian Old Comedy. But even in cases where we can be less certain that they gave much thought to the specific antecedents or generic provenance of their chosen form of poetic mockery, or, as we saw in our discussion of Homer and Theocritus, where representations of mockery are embedded within genres not otherwise conceptualized as satirical, or even particularly comic—even these poets implicitly understood that successful mockery and satire was in large measure a function of broadly abstracted tropes and authorial postures. These hallmarks of satire, in turn, could serve as a framework which the poet could then fill out with all the localizing details that marked the poetry as unmistakably their own.

Of all the maneuvers of this sort that we have come to associate with poets of mockery and satire, perhaps the most fraught is the relationship they all seem to crave with a putative audience. All poetry can be said in one way or another to imply some sort of relationship with an audience, but satirical poetry, especially when it is written in the first-person, wants (or, more precisely, *claims* to want) that relationship to be particularly intimate, even urgent. All the emotional registers that such poetry represents, and the rhetoric that these gestures engender, imply a desire, sometimes an impassioned one, to bring an audience over to the poet's cause. Hence we find poetry that mocks and abuses continually suffused with moral self-righteousness and didacticism; the battle lines, and the various moral issues at stake, always seem clearly drawn at first. The poet is indignant and justified in his complaints, and the audience is assumed to be sympathetic and to take vicarious pleasure in the poet's aggression. But there can be little humor in straightforward indignation, certainly even less in serious didaxis. So it is no surprise to find that what seems clearly drawn at one moment in this type of poetry is soon blurred at another. Many things can happen to compromise the pretense of seriousness: The poet who once complained of his target's *ponêria* might suddenly seem *ponêros* himself;[1] but his claims of self-righteousness might easily fail to convince as his language becomes indecorous or his self-portrait increasingly unsavory, and so forth. The trick seems to be for the satirist to allow the audience to imagine that *some* people other than themselves will continue to regard him as an uncomplicated moralist, while they themselves remain free to laugh along with his posing, preening, and ultimate elusiveness. That is, the veneer of moral stability and self-righteousness is as important as the poet's insistence on undermining it, for, as we have seen in a number of cases already, this veneer is imagined to shield the poet from external criticism while he chips away at all its pretenses from within. Such, then, are some of the ironizing strategies which, we have observed, ensure that the fictions of poetic mockery remain comic.

But this analysis also inspires a new set of questions, to which we must turn in this chapter. If all poets of comic mockery and abuse really compose for several audiences at the same time, even, at times, playing the one off the other, and if we have been right to argue that all their earnest claims and transgressive maneuvers should be seen first and foremost as a function of, and largely subordinate to, larger poetic structures, how do we judge their poetic success? Was all the *aiskhrologia*, *ponêria*, vituperation, and self-mockery intended *in fact* to scandalize some portion of the audience? If that is the case, is the poet successful when he has succeeded, paradoxically, in alienating his audience, when even his pretense of didaxis and self-righteousness fails to protect? Or was he writing rather primarily for the "in-group" that has figured so prominently in a number of our earlier discussions—the kind of sophisticated, knowing audience who would understand poetic fictionality, and not succumb to the satire's insistent personal voice? To put the matter most simply: Has it taken us several millennia to appreciate what was "really" going on in ancient satirical poetry? Were ancient audiences incapable of the levels of sophistication we can bring to bear on it? Or

---

1. The most expansive, if somewhat over-glorified, appreciation of *ponêria* in classical Greek literature remains Whitman 1964, which focuses on the Aristophanic *ponêros*; see esp. 26–41. More recently, see Rosenbloom 2002, who argues for a narrower, decidedly negative meaning of *ponêria* in fifth-century Athens. He suggests that the term refers specifically to a newly emergent "leadership elite," composed of "wage-earners and the commercial-judicial elite," and resented by the *khrêstoi*. There may well be some truth to this claim, although it is worth remembering that the adjective *ponêros* would hardly have been considered a technical term, and a more generalized concept of *ponêria* can be often be detected even in the absence of the word itself.

would our conclusions about satire and mockery have been equally intelligible to ancient readers and critics of such poetry?

We will approach such questions here by considering how ancient readers reacted to the quintessential satirical poet of antiquity, Archilochus. In so many ways, Archilochus is ideally suited for this task: Not only is he our earliest extant bona fide example of iambic poetry (in the technical, generic sense of the term), which means we can trace his *Nachleben* across all of Greco-Roman literary culture as we know it, but he seems to have been well known and generally popular throughout. He composed poetry in non-iambic genres as well, and some of his finely wrought elegiac poems presented ancient audiences with a real dilemma if they happened to disapprove of his more obscene productions. Can one really admire a poet for only some of his poetry, after all, and repudiate the rest as scandalous?[2] Such a dilemma highlights the classic problem of the satirist's relationship with his audience: He claims to be morally indignant, but he portrays himself as abject and degraded, uses bad language and situates himself in a picaresque world of *ponêria* which he insists is real. The mind boggles: Is he trying to endear himself to his audience or alienate them? The question lurks not far beneath the surface of any satirist's work, but it is all the more inscrutable when a poet simultaneously represents a side of himself, as Archilochus does, that seems almost antithetical to the scandalous proclivities that characterize the rest of his work.

It is probably safe to say that of all the canonical classical authors, Archilochus's literary reputation was among the most peculiar: There were certainly many writers whose *kleos* varied according to the changing tastes of different historical periods or the idiosyncratic agenda of literary critics, but it is hard to think of anyone with as *consistently* ambivalent and deeply polarized a reputation as Archilochus. In virtually every period of antiquity, we can find critics who thought of him either as the pinnacle of literary excellence—with a stature second only to Homer himself—or the opposite, the paradigm of poor taste and immorality.[3] Others seemed to have enjoyed him as something of a guilty pleasure: They raved about his poetic excellences, but felt a little apologetic for the more controversial aspects of his poetry—the obscenities, the harsh mockery of poor Lycambes and his daughters, and so forth.[4] *These* critics es-

2. See Kantzios 2005.

3. See von Blumenthal 1922; Rankin 1977, 1–10; Lefkowitz 1981, 25–31; Bossi 1990, 31–34; and Clay 2004, 1–2.

4. See, e.g., Quintilian *IO* 10.1.60 (Tarditi Testim. 152), who alludes to critics who would regard anything resembling a fault in Archilochus as the result of a "fault in his subject matter":

> *summa in hoc vis elocutionis, cum validae tum breves vibrantesque sententiae, plurimum sanguinis atque nervorum, adeo ut videatur quibusdam, quod quoquam minor est, materiae esse non ingenii vitium.* ["In this poet we find the greatest force of delivery, opinions that are strong, terse and energetic, and a lot of vigor and pluck, to such a degree that some people, if they admit he is inferior to anyone, hold that this would be because of a fault of subject matter rather than poetic talent]."

sentially were seeking forgiveness for what they considered occasional lapses in an otherwise exquisite poet.

In our own time, we tend to think of all this ancient handwringing as rather naïve, if not laughable. We like to think that we have developed sophisticated theoretical methods by which we can explain all those things that troubled ancient readers. Most of us no longer worry quite so much about whether Archilochus's invective against his targets was autobiographical or not, and so whether it reflected some aspect of his actual personality and moral character. We speak, as we have throughout this study, in terms of *personae*, of *a priori* generic constraints, conceits, tropes, and so forth. In short, we try to take seriously the fictionality of fictional literary genres, even when confronting satirical authors who employ a subjective, putatively autobiographical, voice and so often insist that their fictions are actually *not* fictional at all. Much of Archilochus's poetry falls into this latter category, and we have developed our own ways of explaining what might lie behind his use of the subjective *ego* in his poems. We try to conceptualize this *ego* as something that had to be constructed by the poet like any of his other characters, and we regard as suspect the truth-value of every declarative statement he makes about himself.

It is worth asking, however, whether our own understanding of Archilochus, and other ancient poets like him, is significantly different from that of ancient audiences and readers. To what extent were ancient readers and critics able to understand what *we* believe Archilochus was doing when his poetry became transgressive, when he deployed obscene language, engaged in vituperative satire, or wrote about things considered vulgar or indecorous according to the social norms of the day.[5] More specifically, I would like here to revisit a question about Archilochus that rankled the ancients, and, in different guises, remains very much alive today,[6] namely what we are to make of a poet who consistently presents *himself* in as negative a light as the other aspects of his poetry. Satire is, as we have often noted in this study, a fundamentally comic

---

Somewhat later (fourth-century CE), the emperor Julian imagines that Archilochus incorporated fables in his poetry expressly to assure that people would take him seriously as a poet (*Or.* 7.207b-c = Tarditi Testim. 90): ἡδύσματα ταῦτα παρὰ τῆς ποιητικῆς Μούσης ἐδρέψατο, καὶ παρέθηκέ γε αὐτὸς τούτου χάριν, ὅπως μὴ σιλλογράφος τις, ἀλλὰ ποιητὴς νομισθείη ["Archilochus plucked these seasonings from his poetic Muse, and offered them up himself so that he not be considered a writer of lampoons, but rather a poet."] See also Plutarch, *De rect. rat. aud.* 45a-b (= Tarditi Testim. 142), where he notes that while some might blame Archilochus (among others) for his "content" (*hypothesis*), they should acknowledge that "idiosyncratic faculty" which makes good poets so appealing to audiences (ἕκαστός γε μὴν ἐπαινεῖται κατὰ τὸ ἴδιον τῆς δυνάμεως, ᾧ κινεῖν καὶ ἄγειν πέφυκεν).

5. I am aware, of course, that we cannot speak of all Greek and Roman readers as some sort of monolith. At least in the case of Archilochus, however, we have evidence about his reception for most periods of Classical antiquity (see von Blumenthal 1922), which allows us to form some idea of basic attitudes and interpretative trends surrounding his poetry.

6. See below, n. 42.

mode, despite its fondness for complaint, blame, and indignation, and portraying oneself in a negative light is just one of the time-honored strategies available to the satirist not only for amusing one's audience, but also for engaging them in a collusive relationship over against all the things he claims to be attacking. A hypothetical audience (that is, an audience imagined by the poet to exist, whether or not it is real) will naturally sympathize with a poet whose indignation is a function of his beleaguered state, and the irony that results from playing up this sense of beleaguerment assures the work's comic tone. When satire works, as I have argued throughout, we (the audience) end up both laughing at the poet because he has turned himself into a risible specimen of abjection, and also sympathizing with him, as we might with anyone who persuades us that he has been unjustly treated by the world. We manage to take the poet's stance of abjection with a grain of salt, whether it be his use of vulgar language, his claims, even boasts, of morally unappealing behavior or unsavory social status, or anything else that may leave an impression of self-loathing or inferiority. If we are at all temperamentally disposed to play along with the game, we laugh along with the poet, perhaps admire his artistry, and somehow manage to understand that the poetic "I" is something ontologically different from the historical, autobiographical "I."

Throughout history there have always been plenty of people happy enough to accept a poet's autobiographical claims as a reasonably accurate reflection of his life. And, as we have seen, even when edgy satirists do not seem to have suffered from people misunderstanding their work, they often like to imagine that they have, or that they would at some point in the future. In our own time, however, it is easy enough to find people who are truly attuned to what a satirist is doing, who never lose sight of the fact that satire is a *performance* of some sort and that whatever they choose to believe about the satirist as a result of that performance is mediated by genre, form, and occasion. When someone comes along who wants to censor a satirist they are often accused by the satirist's fans and devotees of failing to understand what is really going on with such performances, failing to appreciate what we have come to call a poetics of satire.[7] To put it simply, fans will tend to understand a satirist's stance of abjection ironically, while censors find it difficult *not* to take such a stance literally: What you hear or see is what you get, and the satirist who portrays himself

---

7. It is probable that Archilochus's troubles with audiences began even in his own lifetime in the seventh-century BCE. The famous Mnesiepes inscription from the third-century BCE (=Tarditi Testim. 4), seems to relate (this particular section of the inscription is unfortunately extremely fragmentary) how Archilochus (possibly after he introduced the cult of Dionysus to his native Paros) performed a poem that was immediately deemed to be scandalous (or "too iambic") (see E1 col. III.37–38: . . . ὡς κακῶς ἀκ|ου . . . || ἰαμβικώτερο[ν . . .). Evidently, there was an indictment of some sort, as a result of which the citizens were rendered impotent by an angry god (possibly Dionysus), lines 42–46. When they went to Delphi for help, they were told (lines 47–50) to honor Archilochus. See Brown 1997, 46–48; Clay 2001 and 2004, 16–23.

as disreputable is particularly threatening to anyone who believes that artists can influence the behavior of an audience. In short, while there may be no shortage in our own era of people who object to satire and satirists, there are just as many people—and not just academics and critics—who have come to understand what satirists do as a fundamentally fictional production, no matter how much the satirist may in fact draw on autobiographical details, and insist that his mimesis is true-to-life. Can we say the same thing for satire in antiquity? Was Archilochean satire doomed to be misunderstood as soon as it was taken outside of the small circle of *philoi* for whom it was apparently performed?[8]

1. Critias on Archilochean Abjection

The starting point for our discussion is a passage well-known to students of Archilochus, Critias's censorious judgment of Archilochus, as preserved in Aelian's *Varia Historica* (10.13):

αἰτιᾶται Κριτίας Ἀρχίλοχον, ὅτι κάκιστα ἑαυτὸν εἶπεν. εἰ γὰρ μή, φησίν, ἐκεῖνος τοιαύτην δόξαν ὑπὲρ ἑαυτοῦ εἰς τοὺς Ἕλληνας ἐξήνεγκεν, οὐκ ἂν ἐπυθόμεθα ἡμεῖς οὔτε ὅτι Ἐνιποῦς υἱὸς ἦν τῆς δούλης οὔθ' ὅτι καταλιπὼν Πάρον διὰ πενίαν καὶ ἀπορίαν ἦλθεν εἰς Θάσον οὔθ' ὅτι ἐλθὼν τοῖς ἐνταῦθα ἐχθρὸς ἐγένετο οὐδὲ μὴν ὅτι ὁμοίως τοὺς φίλους καὶ τοὺς ἐχθροὺς κακῶς ἔλεγε. πρὸς δὲ τούτοις, ἦ δ' ὅς, οὔτε ὅτι μοιχὸς ἦν, ἤδειμεν ἄν, εἰ μὴ παρ' αὐτοῦ μαθόντες, οὔτε ὅτι λάγνος καὶ ὑβριστής, καὶ τὸ ἔτι τούτων αἴσχιστον, ὅτι τὴν ἀσπίδα ἀπέβαλεν. οὐκ ἀγαθὸς ἄρα ἦν ὁ Ἀρχίλοχος μάρτυς ἑαυτῷ τοιοῦτον κλέος ἀπολιπὼν καὶ τοιαύτην ἑαυτῷ φήμην. ταῦτα οὐκ ἐγὼ Ἀρχίλοχον αἰτιῶμαι, ἀλλὰ Κριτίας. (Critias 88 B 44 DK= Ael. *VH* X 13)

Critias blames Archilochus because he spoke very badly about himself. "For if," he says, "that one had not disseminated such an opinion about himself among the Greeks, we would have learned neither that he was the son of Enipo, a slave woman, nor that he left Paros because of poverty and indigence and went to Thasos, nor that when he got there he became an enemy to the people living there; and we also wouldn't

8. For the notion that Archilochus's ideal audience—even for his strongest invective—were *philoi*, see, above pp. 26 n.37, 111 and 114. On the notion of an "in-group" (those who are sympathetic to the satirist, who can be said to "get it") and an "out-group" (a group just as often imagined rather than real, who are scandalized by the satirists' aggressive and transgressive proclivities), see above, pp. 117 n.1 and 244.

have learned that he spoke ill of friends and enemies alike. What's more, Critias says, we would not have known that he was an adulterer, if we had not learned it from him directly, nor that he was lecherous and arrogant, and what is really the height of shamefulness, that he threw away his shield. And so, Archilochus was not a good witness for himself when he left behind such a reputation and such talk about himself." I'm not the one blaming him for this, but Critias.

This testimonium is a real treasure, not only because it is so early (fifth-century BCE), but also because it calls attention, at least implicitly, to so many issues of ancient literary criticism. Many Archilochus scholars have grappled with this passage over the years, and the results have been fruitful: Its cultural background is reasonably well understood, as are the basic critical principles underlying it.[9] Critias was a prominent fifth-century politician and intellectual of a well-defined type: aristocratic, supercilious, conspiratorial, ultimately tyrannical in his politics and unbridled (if we can trust the evidence) in his personal life.[10] His was not a temperament to display weakness or to find anything funny about slumming it. However he behaved in his personal life, his public ethics were highly aristocratic, doubtless marked by the traditional values of the day— *andreia, sôphrosynê,* rhetorical eloquence, and so forth.[11] It should come as no surprise to us, therefore, that he would not endorse many of the character traits that satirists often claim for themselves; in the case of Archilochus, Aelian reports that Critias disapproved specifically of the poet's self-portrait as slavish, poor, vituperative, antagonistic, lecherous, arrogant, and, for the *coup de grâce,* as a military deserter.

The criticism seems straightforward and predictable enough, but a few peculiarities lurk not too far below the surface. First, Critias seems less concerned about the various behavioral pathologies that Archilochus claimed for himself in his poetry than he is about the mere fact that the poet drew attention to them in the first place. Critias, that is, censured Archilochus "because he spoke very ill of himself." What mattered was the poet's public face, not his actual behavior; this has long been recognized as another aristocratic value of sorts, and one that his contemporary Socrates famously argued against ("*seeming* to be good, rather than actually *being* good").[12] It is worth thinking

9. See von Blumenthal 1922, 1–8; Tarditi 1956; Rankin 1977, 10–18 (with further bibliography); Clay 2004, 2, 23; and Rotstein 2006.

10. The fragments relevant to Critias are collected in Diels-Kranz 88, 378–400. For discussion of Critias's politics, see Ostwald 1986, 461–90 (passim), and 541–43. Nestle 1903 is also still valuable, especially for its detailed treatment of Critias's literary fragments. See also now, Bultrighini 1999 and Ianucci 2002.

11. See Rotstein 2006, who argues that Critias, from his aristocratic perspective, inveighs against Archilochus as being an emblem of democratic ideology.

12. See Rankin 1975, 326–28.

through, however, what the exact nature of this censure is: Critias's opinion is usually taken as a repudiation of Archilochean satire, not terribly unlike Pindar's famous censure in *Pythian* 2.52–56:

ἐμὲ δὲ χρεὼν
φεύγειν δάκος ἀδινὸν κακαγοριᾶν.
εἶδον γὰρ ἑκὰς ἐὼν τὰ πόλλ᾽ ἐν ἀμαχανίᾳ
ψογερὸν Ἀρχίλοχον βαρυλόγοις ἔχθεσιν
πιαινόμενον·

. . . But I must flee the intense bite of slander. For I have seen from afar blaming (ψογερόν) Archilochus many times in abjection (ἐν ἀμαχανίᾳ) fattening himself on strong-worded hostilities.

Pindar contrasts his portrait of an Archilochus sunk in abjection (ἐν ἀμαχανίᾳ) and "fattening himself on strong-worded hostilities" (βαρυλόγοις ἔχθεσιν πιαινόμενον) with his own praise poetry, and his criticism seems as much leveled at Archilochean *poetry*—and indeed the entire genre of satire—as it is against the poet himself. Pindar's Archilochus is *psogeros*, an epithet he clearly intends to be pejorative. Critias, by contrast, hardly seems to object to Archilochean *psogoi* as a matter of principle, but only insofar as they reflect negatively on the poet himself: "For *if he had not disseminated such an opinion about himself among the Greeks*, we would have learned neither. . . ," etc.

We might then, however, want to ask Critias, "and what if we *had not* learned all this from Archilochus? What would your opinion of Archilochus and his satire then be?" Critias's answer, I suspect, would be that if Archilochus had never imputed such compromising details to himself, it would have been a lot easier for Critias to think of him as the sort of person he wanted him to be, namely, as someone who resembled an Athenian aristocrat. "Let him *be* as *lagnos* and *hybristês* as he wants," he might reply, "only let him not tell the world that he is—what we don't *know* about an author cannot be held against him." It seems implicit in this passage, in fact, that Critias sees no problem with the *aiskhrologia* or unelevated subject matter of satire, as long as the poet himself comes off unscathed.[13] It does seem significant that Critias singles out *this* quite specific and limited aspect of Archilochean satire for censure, while avoiding the broader criticism of satire we find in Pindar, and which we might rather expect of a high-brow Athenian such as Critias.

Critias's attitude here, therefore, seems to be a small, if incomplete, step toward understanding the literary mechanisms of satire: He understands the

---

13. As Cassio 1984, 62, has put it: "da nessun punto del testo si può ricavare che ci sia un'accusa diretta di Crizia ad Archiloco perché si era comportato male: l'accusa riguarda solo il fatto di aver detto lui in prima persona di essersi comportato male." *Contra*, Bossi 1990, 33n3.

notion that a poet could adopt stances, discourse, create fictions even, which no self-respecting Athenian *kaloskagathos* could sanction for himself, and *still remain* a respectable figure in real life. As such, Critias does seem to reveal here at least an inchoate awareness of genre, occasion, and fictionality. The fact that he cannot abide, on the other hand, poets claiming to *be* as abject as their subject matter and diction, does suggest that he does not really quite understand that when literary satirists go out of their way to portray themselves as disreputable people, they do so for predominantly literary, rather than autobiographical, purposes. Certainly Aelian seems to have recognized this blind spot of Critias's when he apologetically ends his account by saying that it was Critias, not Aelian himself, who was censuring Archilochus along these lines. Aelian, of course, had the benefit of nearly six centuries of subsequent satire and literary theorizing since Critias's time. It is quite possible that the reason he refuses to go along with Critias's censure of Archilochus is because he knew that Archilochus's abject self-presentation was not only a routine strategy of literary satire—not to be taken entirely literally—but an amusing one at that.

Some forty years ago, in a now-famous article that was well ahead of its time in its attempt to apply anthropological evidence to Archilochean poetry, Kenneth Dover proposed (Dover 1964) that certain aspects of preliterate song culture informed Archilochean poetry, among them being a poet's freedom to "assume any personality he liked" without fear that his audience would assume he was necessarily referring to his actual, "real" self. As Dover well observed, however, as such basically oral poets became more literate and they began to think of a posterity for their work, a new relationship between the poet's literary self-portrayal and his work would have to evolve. Dover has in mind that the poet himself would need to rethink, or perhaps be more cautious about, his unbridled literary self-portraits, not knowing how posterity would take them; I doubt, though, that Archilochus would be much concerned about this, given the fact that satirists themselves tend to revel in their abjection within the poetic space they construct.

Dover's remarks about the effects of literacy, however, do seem relevant to the question of audience reception of archaic lyric, and in our specific case, to the question of whether audiences of posterity were capable of understanding Archilochean satire "correctly" (by which I mean, capable of understanding the performative conditions and poetic dynamics that shaped it). For, as Archilochus became "literary" in subsequent generations—textually fixed—he also became classicized, and so routinely mentioned in the same breath as the other great classics, Homer and Hesiod. As audiences become increasingly distanced from any original performance context, the effect was particularly pronounced with satirical poetry, where so much often depends (as it certainly did in the case of Archilochean satire) on familiarity with individuals known to the local community and topical issues of the day. As Dover put it (1964, 210): "The community in which [the pre-literate poet] composes a song knows its context; other communities in which it is sung will not know or care who composed it, nor will they necessarily know or care what its original point and meaning were." While I am skeptical of Dover's inference from this that poets such as Archilochus, as they realized their works would be preserved in texts, began to worry about being understood by these "other communities" and so *reconceptualized* the very notion of their "poetic personality," it does makes sense to think that the greater an audience's distance from the poet's original performance community, the more difficult it will be for the audience to understand what the poet was actually up to. Classicizing, ironically perhaps, is an even greater obstacle to recovering or replicating some sort of notionally original poetic moment, since classicizing implies a movement away from localization and toward a more universal "applicability"—texts become classicized, that is, precisely for their ability to speak to more than one community and to more than one period of time.[14] In the case of Archilochus, it is reasonably clear from the testimonia about his ancient *Nachleben* that it was his well known affinities with Homeric epic that encouraged his classicization, not his *psogoi* against Lycambes and family, which displayed all the localizing hallmarks of family feud, gossip, and scandal that can make for great, lurid comedy but are less easily transferable to communities to which these characters have no direct ties.

It is not hard to understand, therefore, why Critias might have had so much trouble with a firmly classicized poet claiming attributes for himself that seem almost anti-universalizing, that is, so tied into the poet's here-and-now, and focused so often on the sort of ignoble qualities which are traditionally not supposed to be emulated by others. To appreciate such conceits fully, one almost has to deliberately resist the pull of classicizing and deliver oneself completely over to the particularizing fictions of satire. Athenian audiences would have been used to doing this when they watched Old Comedy; for here, as we have discussed earlier in this study, poets routinely found ways of speaking about themselves, whether formally in the parabases through the mouthpiece of their chorus-leaders, or more obliquely through their characters. Aristophanes' stances of abjection are well known, and some have already figured at length in earlier pages of this book: We may recall among others, for example, his feud with Cleon as mapped on to the agon between the Sausage-seller and the Paphlagonian in *Knights* (see above, pp. 78–89), his complaint in *Clouds* that the play's first production was misunderstood,[15] or that Eupolis stole ideas from his *Knights*,[16] and so on. Then there is Cratinus's *Pytinê*, produced the same year as *Clouds* in 423 BCE, a play in which the poet not only spoke of him-

14. See now Porter 2005.
15. Aristophanes *Clouds* 518–28. Discussion, in particular the relevance of this passage to the question of a second version of the play, in Dover 1968, lxxx–xcviii; Henderson 1993; and Rosen 1997.
16. See Storey 2003, 39–40

self in negative terms, but even (as it seems) cast himself as one of the *dramatis personae*.[17] A scholium on Aristophanes' *Knights* 400 (itself a passing dig at Cratinus) preserves the basic outline of the plot:

ὅπερ μοι δοκεῖ παροξυνθεὶς ἐκεῖνος, καίτοι τοῦ ἀγωνίζεσθαι
ἀποστὰς καὶ συγγράφειν, πάλιν γράφει δρᾶμα, τὴν Πυτίνην, εἰς
αὐτόν τε καὶ τὴν μέθην, οἰκονομίᾳ τε κεχρημένον τοιαύτῃ. τὴν
Κωμῳδίαν ὁ Κρατῖνος ἐπλάσατο αὐτοῦ εἶναι γυναῖκα καὶ
ἀφίστασθαι τοῦ συνοικεσίου τοῦ σὺν αὐτῷ θέλειν, καὶ
κακώσεως αὐτῷ δίκην λαγχάνειν, φίλους δὲ παρατύχοντας τοῦ
Κρατίνου δεῖσθαι μηδὲν προπετὲς ποιῆσαι, καὶ τῆς ἔχθρας
ἀνερωτᾶν τὴν αἰτίαν, τὴν δὲ μέμφεσθαι αὐτῷ ὅτι μὴ κωμῳδοίη
μηκέτι, σχολάζοι δὲ τῇ μέθῃ.
(Sch. Ar. *Kn.* 400 = Suda k 2216 = Kassel-Austin Testim. ii., p. 219)

It was in irritation at this, it seems, that even though he had retired from competition and writing, he wrote a play once again, the *Pytinê*, about himself and drunkenness, which employed the following outline: Cratinus pretended that Comedy was his wife, and wanted a divorce from him, and filed a lawsuit against him for mistreatment. But Cratinus's friends happened by and begged her not to do anything rash, and asked the reason for her hostility. She criticized the fact that he no longer wrote comedies, but spent his time in idle drunkenness.

I have written at length elsewhere about this play,[18] and will reiterate here only one point, that Cratinus's abject posture in this play, as indicated by the scholium quoted above, would have fit squarely within the long tradition of satirists, who at some point in their work eventually direct their satire at themselves.

One really wonders what Critias would have made of Cratinus's portrayal in *Pytinê*, or indeed what he would have been thinking the many times he must have sat in the Athenian theater watching comic actor and choruses represent their authors as losers of one sort or another, driven by their alleged beleaguerment to mockery, complaint, or indecorous and shameless self-promotion. We cannot answer this question, of course, but it is not difficult to believe that Critias conceptualized the poetic antics of an abject Cratinus very differently from Archilochus's self-representations. I say this for reasons that largely derive from Dover's observations in the article adduced above. For Critias, that is, the comic poets had not yet become classicized: They were still part of his

17. See also chapter 6, above, on Juvenal's self-identification with the reprobate Naevolus in *Sat.* 9.
18. Rosen 2000; see also Luppe 2000, Biles 2002, and Ruffel 2002.

own "local community," and it would have been fully evident to him that the comic theater was a marked space that offered considerable license for the poet to present himself with far more abandon than he might in real life. The comic playwrights and many of the characters of their plays would have been known to Critias, and he would have been able to gauge for himself whether these dramatic representations were accurate or not. It is far easier, I would suggest, to understand the *poetics* at work in satire when one can test the satirist's claims in his work against some sort of nonpoetic, nonfictionalized reality. Satirists, as we have repeatedly seen, invariably try to encourage audiences to take what they say at face value, but we tend to succumb to this literary *apatê* more readily the more remote we are from the original performative setting, and when the work and poet together have already achieved something of a classic status. Hence Critias's readiness to assume that Archilochus must always have been telling the truth about himself, even when that truth was unflattering.

Critias was hardly unusual among ancient writers in his tendency to take at face value the claims that Archilochus (and other classicized poets) made about himself in his poetry. The extensive testimonia about Archilochus rarely, if ever, offer what we might regard as a nuanced or sophisticated reading of his "psogeric" side, and the same is basically true for Hipponax, whose mocking invectives were repeatedly assimilated into biography.[19] Only the elder Pliny (*NH* 36.12) was bold enough to question the veracity of parts of Hipponax's vita by what we might call fact-checking (calling "false" the claim that Hipponax's *psogoi* against the sculptor Bupalus and his brother Athenis drove them to suicide),[20] but even so, he had no particular literary insights to offer as explanation for how such stories developed to begin with. Like so many ancient critics, Critias subscribed to the basic principle that a writer's work is a function of his character, and vice versa, in a kind of inescapable critical loop. Scholars have long recognized that this principle guides so many ancient vitae, and it is easy to see how subjective poetry gave rise to particularly imaginative narratives—once a poet uses an "I" in his work, after all, the vita essentially writes itself.[21]

19. See Degani 1984, 19–83; Brown 1997, 84–85.

20. Pliny *NH* 36.12 (= Degani Testim. 8); Pliny notes that Bupalus and his brother continued to produce sculptures in neighboring islands after they supposedly had committed suicide.

21. Lefkowitz 1981, viii–ix, and passim, notes that the tendency in antiquity for audiences to create biography from *any* poetry was strong to begin with, whether or not it was subjective. The principle was well articulated already by the fifth century, as Aristophanes' famous parodies of it attest. One thinks, e.g., of the ways in which Aristophanes portrays Euripides in *Acharn.*, *Thesmo.*, or (with Aeschylus, too) *Frogs*, where Euripides is made to look and behave as one might (parodically) infer from his own poetry. According to Aristophanes' comic version of the poetry-is-the-man principle, there was a one-to-one correspondence between anything a poet represented in his work and his own character; and so, it goes without saying that Euripides would be, by turns, effeminate, intellectually fraught, and abject, and Aeschylus, by contrast, would be robust, taciturn, and irascible when provoked.

But Critias was interested far more in *evaluating* the *vita* of Archilochus than in generating one of his own, and in this respect, I think, his testimony is especially valuable. For there is a philosophical dimension—ethical and ontological—to his concerns here, however inchoate, which anticipates in revealing ways Plato's famous discussion of mimesis in his *Republic*. Critias was related to Plato through his mother—his mother Perictione and Critias were first cousins[22]—and he appears as a character in several Platonic dialogues. One may indeed wonder, therefore, whether Plato was working out in the *Republic*, now with greater rigor, ideas about mimesis that had found their way to him through family circles. Whether or not that was the case, however, a consideration in the next section of Plato's views on mimesis, will shed considerable light on the protoliterary theory that informed Critias's censure of Archilochus, and, in turn, on the question of how ancient satirists were received by their ancient readers.

2. Plato on the Poetic Representation of Bad People and Things

Plato's discussion of poetic mimesis in *Republic* 2 and 3 is wide-ranging and complex, but the broad outline will be very familiar to anyone with even a passing interest in the history of literary criticism: The larger topic of these books is the proper education of the Guardians in the hypothetically just and rational state, and in this context Plato famously banishes some of the most valued poetry of the day for the potential threat it poses to the moral integrity of the citizenry. Beginning at 392c, Socrates narrows his concerns by considering the differences between the two basic types of narrative, what he calls, at 392d, "simple" narration (*haplê diêgêsis*) and narration "through imitation/ representation" (*dia mimêseôs*). In the first type of narration, the author will speak as a narrator of events happening to others. In the second, the author will take on the voice of the characters he is representing. He offers examples from Homer, a master of both styles but notoriously fond of narrative "through representation," especially in his speeches. Tragedy and comedy, as Socrates goes on to say (394 b–c), are pure representation, and the more worrisome to him for it. Although it is not obvious from Socrates' discussion in 394–95 exactly what he fears his guardians might *do* that would count as "narrative through representation,"[23] it is clear what bothers him:

τὰ δὲ ἀνελεύθερα μήτε ποιεῖν μήτε δεινοὺς εἶναι μιμήσασθαι,
μηδὲ ἄλλο μηδὲν τῶν αἰσχρῶν, ἵνα μὴ ἐκ τῆς μιμήσεως τοῦ εἶναι

---

22. For genealogical details, see Nails 2002, 108–11.
23. It does not seem very likely, for example, that he envisions his guardians suddenly deciding to become actors!

ἀπολαύσωσιν. ἢ οὐκ ᾔσθησαι ὅτι αἱ μιμήσεις, ἐὰν ἐκ νέων πόρρω
διατελέσωσιν, εἰς ἔθη τε καὶ φύσιν καθίστανται καὶ κατὰ σῶμα
καὶ φωνὰς καὶ κατὰ τὴν διάνοιαν·

. . . they should neither do, nor be skilled at representing anything un-
becoming a free man, or any other shameful thing, in case they make
the leap from representation to reality. Or haven't you noticed that if
representations continue beyond childhood, they become ingrained in
one's habits and naturalized in a person's body, speech and thought?"
(395c-d; trans. Waterfield 1993)

The kind of representation that Socrates proceeds to forbid, then, involves
precisely the type of characters that comic poets of all stripes routinely represented, whether through actors on the stage, or worse still no doubt, through
their own voice in the nondramatic genres. As Socrates says at 395d, not only
must good men not imitate women (since this would clearly compromise their
manhood), especially cantankerous, unruly, or lovesick women,[24] but, as he
adds at 395e–396a, they should avoid representing ". . . bad men who are cow-
ards . . . who use abusive speech [κακηγοροῦντας] and make fun of [κωμῳ-
δοῦντας] and use foul language [αἰσχρολογοῦντας] against each other when
they're drunk, or even when they're sober, or other things of this sort that such
men do both in speech and action when they sin against themselves and others [ἁμαρτάνουσιν εἰς αὑτούς]."[25]

Although Socrates is speaking here in the most general terms, the passage
reads like a veritable catalogue of Archilochean poetry, and one that would be
entirely familiar to Critias, who also mentions Archilochus's abuse of others
and *himself*, and was especially scandalized by Archilochus's apparent admis-
sion of cowardice.[26] Critias may never mention the word "mimesis," but the
Platonic formulation in this passage makes it quite clear that Critias must have
had something like this on his mind when he censured Archilochus: When
Archilochus takes on "bad" attributes in his poetry *in propria persona*, Critias

24. οὐ δὴ ἐπιτρέψομεν, ἦν δ' ἐγώ, ὧν φαμὲν κήδεσθαι καὶ δεῖν αὐτοὺς ἄνδρας ἀγαθοὺς
γενέσθαι, γυναῖκα μιμεῖσθαι ἄνδρας ὄντας, ἢ νέαν ἢ πρεσβυτέραν, ἢ ἀνδρὶ λοιδορουμένην
ἢ πρὸς θεοὺς ἐρίζουσάν τε καὶ μεγαλαυχουμένην, οἰομένην εὐδαίμονα εἶναι, ἢ ἐν
συμφοραῖς τε καὶ πένθεσιν καὶ θρήνοις ἐχομένην· κάμνουσαν δὲ ἢ ἐρῶσαν ἢ ὠδίνουσαν,
πολλοῦ καὶ δεήσομεν.

25. οὐδέ γε ἄνδρας κακούς, ὡς ἔοικεν, δειλούς τε καὶ τὰ ἐναντία πράττοντας ὧν
νυνδὴ εἴπομεν, κακηγοροῦντάς τε καὶ κωμῳδοῦντας ἀλλήλους καὶ αἰσχρολογοῦντας,
μεθύοντας ἢ καὶ νήφοντας, ἢ καὶ ἄλλα ὅσα οἱ τοιοῦτοι καὶ ἐν λόγοις καὶ ἐν ἔργοις
ἁμαρτάνουσιν εἰς αὑτούς τε καὶ εἰς ἄλλους.

26. See Archil. fr. 5W.

would say, our first instinct is to assume that the poet's character either *is* similarly "bad," or is in danger of *becoming* so as a result of playing out such a role.

But even though *we* might see an Archilochus lurking behind the kind of representations Plato's Socrates here repudiates, would Plato himself have? What are we to make of the fact that elsewhere Plato seems to speak of Archilochus with the greatest admiration?[27] Would he have repudiated Archilochean poetry here, as indeed he does most of the great tragedians and a good deal of Homer too, only to remain consistent with his philosophical agenda for his new, experimental state? Was it only the iambographic Archilochus he would have had trouble with, while the political, more "elegiac," Archilochus could be salvaged? Was Plato really incapable of distinguishing between a representation and the thing represented, or understanding that poetry had something to offer an audience beside moral paradigms? These are famously complicated questions that we cannot address adequately here, but for our purposes it is worth noting that Plato did not seem entirely comfortable dismissing the mimesis of baseness *tout court*. From a moral, philosophical perspective, he says at 396e, any self-respecting decent person will be ashamed to assimilate his character to any of the debased examples Socrates had provided "not only because he is *untrained* [ἀγύμναστος] in representing this type of person, but also because he finds it distasteful to mould and conform himself to an inferior stamp, which his mind finds contemptible." But to this he adds a tag: "unless it's for the sake of *joking* ["play," or "jest"; ὅτι μὴ παιδιᾶς χάριν.]"[28] But what does this really mean? And what does Socrates mean by saying that people should avoid representing base characters because they are "untrained" at it? How would one go about, we might ask, *getting* training in some sort of proper method of such a mimesis, and what would it mean to have it?

Stephen Halliwell (2002, 83) has recently commented on this passage, and aptly describes this section as a "cautious concession to comedy…phrased almost as an afterthought." He concludes from this "that we have here a marginal acknowledgement that role playing can sometimes be separated from the psychological internalization that is otherwise treated as an entailment

---

27. Twice in the *Ion* Plato refers to Archilochus in the same breath as Homer and Hesiod (531a2 and 532a6), and at *Rep.* 365c5, he calls him σοφώτατος.

28. ὅταν δὲ γίγνηται κατά τινα ἑαυτοῦ ἀνάξιον, οὐκ ἐθελήσειν σπουδῇ ἀπεικάζειν ἑαυτὸν τῷ χείρονι, εἰ μὴ ἄρα κατὰ βραχύ, ὅταν τι χρηστὸν ποιῇ, ἀλλ᾽ αἰσχυνεῖσθαι, ἅμα μὲν ἀγύμναστος ὢν τοῦ μιμεῖσθαι τοὺς τοιούτους, ἅμα δὲ καὶ δυσχεραίνων αὑτὸν ἐκμάττειν τε καὶ ἐνιστάναι εἰς τοὺς τῶν κακιόνων τύπους, ἀτιμάζων τῇ διανοίᾳ, ὅτι μὴ παιδιᾶς χάριν. [However, when he comes across a degrading character [lit.: "unworthy of himself"], he won't be prepared to assimilate himself seriously to this inferior person, except on the few occasions when this character does something good. He'd be ashamed to do so, not only because he's untrained in representing this type of person, but also because he finds it distasteful to mould and conform himself to an inferior stamp, which his mind finds contemptible, unless it's for the sake of joking/play. (trans. Waterfield, modified)]

of engagement with the mimetic mode."[29] "Marginal" this certainly is, and Plato is not, to be sure, focusing on theories of literature at the moment, but the passage does seem to open a small window to a set of attitudes about comic and satirical poetry that is worth exploring a little further. To begin with, Plato does seem in fact to acknowledge here that comic role-playing is something of a *technê*, something one can be trained, and acquire expertise, in. But this raises many other questions: Exactly what does such skill consist of for Plato? Does it refer to the deployment of certain kinds of diction? Is it a performative skill, such as an ability to act or recite in a manner particularly appropriate to such poetry? Is it, for example, a question of comic timing, to use a term of our own day? It is difficult to say for sure, but if we combine this notion of expertise in taking on comically compromised roles with Plato's benign attitude toward "jesting/play" (παιδιά), we may infer here an acknowledgement that the behavior of a truly professional comic poet operates in a zone informed by generic and performative protocols quite distinct from those of prosaic everyday reality.

The implication of this is that if everyone could properly *understand* what role-playing actually is—that it is a distinctly poetic/fictionalizing gesture which ought to have no bearing on the subject assuming it—then the topic would presumably not even interest Plato. Plato's belief that it is extremely difficult for anyone *not* to succumb to the influence of debased roles without the proper training, seems to acknowledge just how few people could actually understand how comedy—even the unbridled, aischrologic, and vituperative kinds—really worked. But the important point here is that, even though Plato may have repudiated comic role-playing for his ideal polis, he seems not to have been interested in repudiating the work of *comic poets themselves*, nor did he assume that every comic who engaged in a mimesis of debased characters was himself necessarily doomed to being himself similarly debased. Critias seems to have assumed that people would make this assumption, which is why he took Archilochus to task for portraying himself in a negative light, and Plato would presumably have been nervous about how such portrayals might have influenced naïve people in the audience, who did not understand the dynamics of such poetry. But it seems unlikely that Plato would have worried as much about Archilochus—a professional, experienced poet—assimilating himself to compromising roles, as he would about his fledgling guardians, were they to do the same thing without the proper training in poetics, and without suitable aptitude for it. This may explain, in fact, why Plato is virtually silent about

29. Cf. Ferrari 1989, 119: "[T]he phrase seems to make room for a satirical kind of imitation, in which the good could attend to or enact the actual voices of the bad while yet remaining disengaged—not treating them as role-models—and 'laughing them down' in the manner we have seen Socrates wish the young would adopt in the face of unworthy Homeric sentiments." I infer from this formulation that Socrates would concede to such a person an ability to make aesthetic judgments about the imitation of bad things, independent of moral judgments.

the *iambic* Archilochus in his writings: I suspect that for Plato the aischrologic Archilochus was *himself* no more a problem than Homer and the tragedians, even when they all represented people behaving in problematic ways. While Plato may have worried about how such representations would influence *an audience*, his admiration for them *as poets* never seemed to diminish.

This much seems borne out by *Republic* 398a–b:

ἄνδρα δή, ὡς ἔοικε, δυνάμενον ὑπὸ σοφίας παντοδαπὸν γίγνεσθαι καὶ μιμεῖσθαι πάντα χρήματα, εἰ ἡμῖν ἀφίκοιτο εἰς τὴν πόλιν αὐτός τε καὶ τὰ ποιήματα βουλόμενος ἐπιδείξασθαι, προσκυνοῖμεν ἂν αὐτὸν ὡς ἱερὸν καὶ θαυμαστὸν καὶ ἡδύν, εἴποιμεν δ᾽ ἂν ὅτι οὐκ ἔστιν τοιοῦτος ἀνὴρ ἐν τῇ πόλει παρ᾽ ἡμῖν οὔτε θέμις ἐγγενέσθαι, ἀποπέμποιμέν τε εἰς ἄλλην πόλιν μύρον κατὰ τῆς κεφαλῆς καταχέαντες καὶ ἐρίῳ στέψαντες, αὐτοὶ δ᾽ ἂν τῷ αὐστηροτέρῳ καὶ ἀηδεστέρῳ ποιητῇ χρώμεθα καὶ μυθολόγῳ ὠφελίας ἕνεκα, ὅς ἡμῖν τὴν τοῦ ἐπιεικοῦς λέξιν μιμοῖτο καὶ τὰ λεγόμενα λέγοι ἐν ἐκείνοις τοῖς τύποις οἷς κατ᾽ ἀρχὰς ἐνομοθετησάμεθα, ὅτε τοὺς στρατιώτας ἐπεχειροῦμεν παιδεύειν.

So it follows that were a man who was clever enough to be able to assume all kinds of forms and to represent everything in the world to come in person to our community and want to show off his compositions, we'd treat him as an object of reverence and awe, and as a source of pleasure, and we'd prostrate ourselves before him; but we'd tell him that not only is there no one like him in our community, it is also not permitted for anyone like him to live among us, and we'd send him elsewhere, once we had anointed his head with myrrh and given him a chaplet of wool. Left to ourselves, however, with benefit as our goal, we would employ harsher, less entertaining poets and story-tellers, to speak in the style of a good man and to keep in their stories to the principles we originally established as lawful, when our task was the education of our militia. (trans. Waterfield)

Plato acknowledges in this passage, it seems, that he finds some poetry "entertaining" and "pleasing" even if he disapproves of its moral content;[30] we may infer from such a concession, as well, that he would at least find it *possible* for some people to enjoy poetry of "bad content" and remain morally unscathed. This is a dichotomy—pleasure vs. benefit—that remains only inchoate

---

30. See Ferrari 1989, 119: "The qualification is of special relevance to anyone attempting to configure Plato's own literary practice with Socrates' prescriptions in this work. After all, the *Republic* itself boasts in its opening book a lengthy and direct 'imitation' of Thrasymachus, an unworthy character acting unworthily." Blondell 2002, 239 makes a similar point.

in the *Republic*, only to be taken up in earnest by theorists in subsequent centuries; but it raises questions about Plato's understanding of poets and poetics relevant to our immediate concerns in this chapter about how ancient audiences might have conceptualized satirical genres of poetry.[31]

Plato here seems to entertain the possibility that there can be good poetry with bad content; the goodness of such poetry is a function of the poet's *sophia* —his trained ability to represent things in a way that audiences will find pleasurable, regardless of the effect on their behavior. It is a poet's *sophia*, then, that Plato is rewarding when he says that the citizens should treat such a person with religious reverence and wonder. The paradox is no doubt intended by Plato to be slightly comical—lavishing a poet with honors while banishing him from the city—but it has the effect of emphasizing just how aware Plato was that poetry operates in a very distinct, highly marked space. It is interesting, in fact, to see how Plato's hypothetical poets come from a space *outside* the city, conceptualized as an alien force bringing an *epideixis*—the product of *sophia*—to a place where, he claims, no one like that lives (οὐκ ἔστιν τοιοῦτος ἀνὴρ ἐν τῇ πόλει παρ' ἡμῖν). It is as if Plato goes out of his way *not* to blame the person who engages in mimesis, no matter what the content of his poetry might be. A poet might well give an *epideixis* of indecent, aischrologic satire, and its moral value—its "benefit" (ὠφελία)—might be considered indisputably negative by all, but even Plato, it seems, could assess whether it was good *aiskhrologia* (causing pleasure, regardless of moral value), or bad (in the sense that it was nonpleasurable, not entertaining, not well-executed, and so forth).[32]

---

31. See Nehamas 1999, 279–99, a chapter entitled "Plato and the Mass Media," who urges us (persuasively, I think) to regard Plato's critique of poetry as a critique of its status as a popular medium, not so much as a "fine art." His fears about poetry, in other words, are almost exclusively concerned with the perils of widespread dissemination across a broad democratic audience whose interpretive abilities will vary. I doubt Nehamas is correct to say (1999, 289) that "[n]othing in Plato's time answered to our concept of the fine arts, especially to the idea that the arts are a province of a small and enlightened part of the population" (Aristophanes' *Frogs* alone, e.g., offers ample evidence for some sort of elevated literary connoisseurship in fifth-century Athens; cf. also the parabasis to *Clouds*, 510–626); but even if Plato were to acknowledge explicitly that some people were perfectly capable of appreciating problematic poetry without any dire psychological effect, Plato would surely have far less interest in them, as Nehamas's argument implies, than in the vast majority, who would tend to take public poetry as "transparent" representations of reality (288–90).

32. At *Laws* 816d-e, where Plato takes up the question of comic performance specifically, he shows himself to be rather less open-minded than he seems to be in the *Republic*, yet still willing to acknowledge that even the basest forms of comedy have some pedagogical utility: "For it is impossible to learn serious matters without the comic . . . if one wants to be a wise man" (ἄνευ γὰρ γελοίων τὰ σπουδαῖα . . . μαθεῖν μὲν οὐ δυνατόν, εἰ μέλλει τι φρόνιμος ἔσεσθαι). But this, in turn, poses a real dilemma for Plato, in that virtuous men, he says, should not imitate both bad and good, lest they end up "doing or saying funny (*geloia*) things out of ignorance" (τοῦ μή ποτε δι' ἄγνοιαν δρᾶν ἢ λέγειν ὅσα γελοῖα). His solution is to consign comic performances to "slaves and paid foreigners," from which a Greek audience will be able to learn the difference between the comic and the serious. For discussion and survey of early bibliography on this passage, see Mader 1977, 47–52.

This passage serves as our earliest explicit articulation of a tension between two approaches to aesthetic evaluation, which we would construe as a tension between form and content, even if Plato himself did not quite have the vocabulary to put it this way.[33] Plato was well aware that one could make an argument for the quality of poetry using several criteria, that at least part of the pleasure people take in poetry often has little to do with the actual words, and when it does, the words need not represent good things for us to take pleasure in them. Indeed, it is precisely because Plato realized that poetry can so directly appeal to the visual and aural senses,[34] unmediated by the rational mind, that he worried so much about its content. This explains why Plato had no trouble privileging moral utility (*ôphelia*) over all other criteria, at least for the purposes of establishing his new state. Like Plato, Critias too might be described as in the know about how comedy, including self-mockery, worked, but also like Plato, he assumed that most people would not have such literary sensitivity: Most would fuse form with content, and so unwittingly assume that comic representations of base things were both real and somehow protreptic, a call to action. But whereas Plato was most worried about the social implications of such a response to poetry, Critias seems to have been more irritated that Archilochus himself would be misunderstood by most people who heard his self-mockery. He does not, in any case, censure him for inculcating bad morals in his audiences. His complaint is rather that they will laugh at the comically abject poet, but also believe that this is what he actually was; and this, Critias implies, would be doing a disservice to a fellow aristocrat, who should not allow himself to be characterized in such a way. As we might put it, Critias perhaps felt that *he* could appreciate the irony of satire, but this was a privilege—an aesthetic insight—that few others shared.

Was it really true, however, that only relatively few in Critias's time and beyond could fully appreciate satire, and more specifically, could understand comic abjection and satirical irony? To judge from the intense debates about poetic evaluation spawned by Plato's aesthetics in subsequent centuries, the answer is likely to be a qualified "no." Aristotle's position on comedy is not especially well documented in the surviving works,[35] but it is reasonably clear that he had little interest in anything but the gentlest forms, and that for him,

---

33. On the various ways of expressing this dichotomy in ancient Greek literary theory, see Porter 1995, with further bibliography. The terms *dianoia* (for "meaning" or "content") and *lexis* (for "language" or "style") were frequently used, although Porter's essay brings out the full complexity (and often, confusion) of the debate over these concepts, especially in the hands of Hellenistic theorists.

34. Indeed, in other contexts Plato worried about people who put too much stock in sensible phenomena; see *Rep.* 475d, where he refers to "sight-lovers" (*philotheamones*) and sound-lovers (*philêkooi*). For discussion, see Irwin 1995, 264–66.

35. See, e.g., Janko 1984 and Golden 1992.

vituperative satire was a mark of boorishness and ill-breeding.[36] Although less obsessed with the moral utility of poetry than Plato, at root he too had little patience for the obviously frivolous or gratuitously transgressive, and, perhaps, less of a sense of humor than Plato. But thanks, in particular, to recent work in the area of Hellenistic aesthetics, it is clear that a strong reaction to Plato's moralizing calculus set in early.

3. Hellenistic Critics on the Poetic Representation of Baseness

The famous third-century BCE intellectual Eratosthenes is said (in remarks preserved by Strabo, early first-century CE) to have repudiated the notion that poetry was a kind of moral philosophy, and to have maintained instead that poetry should be evaluated strictly by its ability to "move the soul" (or, as we might say, "stir the emotions," or simply "entertain").[37] The term he used for this was ψυχαγωγία:

> ποιητὴν γὰρ ἔφη πάντα στοχάζεσθαι ψυχαγωγίας, οὐ διδασκαλίας. τοὐναντίον δ᾽ οἱ παλαιοὶ φιλοσοφίαν τινὰ λέγουσι πρώτην τὴν ποιητικήν, εἰσάγουσαν εἰς τὸν βίον ἡμᾶς ἐκ νέων καὶ διδάσκουσαν ἤθη καὶ πάθη καὶ πράξεις μεθ᾽ ἡδονῆς· οἱ δ᾽ ἡμέτεροι καὶ μόνον ποιητὴν ἔφασαν εἶναι τὸν σοφόν. διὰ τοῦτο καὶ τοὺς παῖδας αἱ τῶν Ἑλλήνων πόλεις πρώτιστα διὰ τῆς ποιητικῆς παιδεύουσιν, οὐ ψυχαγωγίας χάριν δήπουθεν ψιλῆς, ἀλλὰ σωφρονισμοῦ·

> . . .τοῦτο μὲν δὴ ὀρθῶς ἂν λέγοις, ὦ Ἐρατόσθενες· ἐκεῖνα δ᾽ οὐκ ὀρθῶς, ἀφαιρούμενος αὐτὸν τὴν τοσαύτην πολυμάθειαν καὶ τὴν ποιητικὴν γραώδη μυθολογίαν ἀποφαίνων,ᾗ δέδοται πλάττειν, φησίν, ὃ ἂν αὐτῇ φαίνηται ψυχαγωγίας οἰκεῖον.

For Eratosthenes says that every poet aims to entertain (*psykhagôgia*), not to teach (*didaskalia*). But the ancients claimed, by contrast, that poetry is a kind of 'first philosophy' (*prôtê philosophia*), which leads us along in life from our youth and teaches us in a pleasant way about character, emotions, and action; and those in our camp say also that only the wise man is a poet. For this reason, then, Greek cities educate their children at first through poetry, certainly not for the sake of simple entertainment, but rather for moral edification.

---

36. On Aristotle's notion of the "liberal jest" see discussion in Freudenburg 1993, 52–72; on Aristotle's term *geloion*, see also Held 1984, 163–64; Halliwell 2002, 219–20; Cullyer 2006; and Rosen 2006.

37. Geus 2002, 266, is skeptical that we can extrapolate much of a poetic theory from this passage.

. . . On that point [that it is absurd to look to Homer for instruction in all the arts], Eratosthenes, you may be correct. But you're not right to take away from him his great erudition (*polymathiê*), asserting that poetry is a sort of story-telling we associate with old women, which has been allowed to 'shape,' as you put it, whatever seems appropriate for entertainment [*psykhagôgia*]. (Strabo 1. 3)

This was certainly a radical departure from the Platonic stance, and the ramifications of such a position occupied literary theorists—sometimes with deep passion—for centuries after. But was this only a debate among intellectuals? What about "normal" audiences for poetry? When they read or saw performances of satirical poetry, did they think in such analytical terms, and attempt to distinguish the bad content from the good form, or vice versa? Trying to gauge audience reception in antiquity is always difficult, since we rarely have direct access to matters of corporate psychology, but there is one intriguing passage from a papyrus fragment of the first-century BCE theorist Philodemus, which not only addresses the specific problem of how one evaluates *comic* poetry, but in doing so claims to describe how earlier periods of Greek history responded to problematic satirical (here, specifically iambographic) poetry.

ἀλλ᾽ ἐξ᾽ ὅτου τὸν Ἀρχίλοχον ἐθαύμαζε καὶ τὸν Ἱππώνακτα καὶ τὸν Σημωνίδην, καὶ τῶν παρ᾽ Ὁμήρῳ καὶ Εὐρειπίδει καὶ τοῖς ἄλλοις ποιηταῖς ἔνια πονηροῖς προσώποις περικείμενα καὶ περὶ πονηρῶν πραγμάτων γεγραμμένα καὶ κατεγέλα χρηστοῖς περικείμενα, καὶ περὶ χρηστῶν ἀκούουσα πραγμάτων οὕτως ἐπέπειστο, καὶ ποιητὴν μὲν ἀγαθὸν ὑπελάμβανε τὸν ἐξεργασάμενον, ὡς ἔφην, ὁποῖόν ποτ᾽ ἂν διανόημα λάβῃ παρ᾽ ἑτέρων ἢ αὐτὸς προθῆται, τάχα δὲ ἄνθρωπον πονηρὸν καὶ τόνδ᾽ ἐνέγκαντα διονοήματα χρηστά, μὴ καλλωπίσαντα δ᾽ οὕτω . . .
(Philodemus, *P. Herc.* 1074 fr. f col. iii 1–12 = Archil. Testim. 128 Tarditi = Hipponax Testim. 48 Dg.)

But ever since [Greece] used to admire Archilochus, Hipponax, Semonides, and some of the things in Homer, Euripides and the other poets that have to do with bad [*ponêrois*] characters and that were written about bad actions, and [sc. ever since Greece] used to mock [*kategela*] things that had to do with good characters, even when it [Greece] heard about good actions [that is, in poetry], it had been persuaded in this way [that is, to enjoy poetry of the bad and ridicule poetry of the good], and thought that a good poet was the one who worked out, as I said, whatever meaning he took from others or proposed on his own, and probably [supposed] even this one to be a bad person who conveyed good meanings but without making them aesthetically attractive. . . .

The absence of a full context makes it difficult to extrapolate exactly what larger point Philodemus is making (in particular, whether he is endorsing the behavior of earlier Greeks,[38] or repudiating them as views of his opponents), but the assumptions he makes about early Greek audiences are revealing: to an implied question, "How could anyone find anything to admire in poetry that depicts bad things?" he responded by citing the cultural habits of a bygone era. Poetry of comic abuse and satire, which relied on the mimesis of bad characters and events (and which would include depictions of the poet himself), were popular in Greece, the argument goes, precisely because they provided what audiences evidently wanted; they had certain expectations from the genre, and judged the poet by his ability to deliver the goods. Comic genres were supposed to depict scoundrels and buffoons, shady dealings, scandalous exploits, and abject narrators. Such, at any rate, is my understanding of the idea behind the sentence claiming that Greece "thought that a good poet was the one who worked out…whatever meaning he took from others or proposed on his own." The poet who "takes from others" seems to describe a poet working self-consciously within a specific poetic tradition; and the one who "proposes something on his own" is that same poet innovating within the parameters of that tradition. When Philodemus says that the early Greeks used to "mock things that had to do with good characters," he seems to mean not so much that the Greeks were scornful of all morality, but that they would have felt it generically inappropriate, in the case of comic genres, for a poet to focus on (so as to endorse) "good characters and actions." How, after all, could Archilochus rail against Lycambes and his daughters with sexual innuendo and obscenity, or Hipponax accuse his rival Bupalus of incest, if they presented themselves as, say, mild-mannered gentlemen writing poetry about "nice" people? In the case of Homer and Euripides—Philodemus's other, non-comic, examples here—the point is surely that audiences wanted their Thersiteses, their Iruses, their Phaedras and their Medeas to be as unsavory as ever, and they were not about to be worried whether these characters were bad or not. What counted was how the poetry was "worked out" (*exergasamenon*), that is, crafted so as to foreground, perhaps, rather than to obscure, the badness of its mimesis. For the early Greeks, according to this view, good form always trumped any concerns about morality in the evaluation of poetry.[39]

38. Daly (1963) seems to miss at least part of the point of this passage when he says that Philodemus here "described a change of attitude toward the iambic poets and toward poets in general." He translates the imperfect ἐθαύμαζε as "[Hellas] *has come to* admire," but the verb seems rather to refer to an earlier age in the history of Greek poetry.

39. I thank one of the referees of this book for helping me to see, however, that the passage not only describes the position that poetic form should trump moral content, but is in fact critical

It is likely that Philodemus himself recounts this position for the purpose of refining or even repudiating it, since other fragments suggest a belief that the morality of a poem was not entirely irrelevant to the question of its value. But there is a difference, as he makes clear, between the mere fact of moral content and its utility or benefit. Unlike Plato, who privileged *to ôphelimon* in poetry over everything else, Philodemus would much prefer a "fine" poem with no benefit to a lesser poem with much benefit.[40] Philodemus may not have been quite as cavalier about the moral content of an Archilochus as he implies that Greece once was, but there is little doubt that he could keep questions of morality and utility separate from questions of poetic accomplishment. The point of his remarks about the reception of problematic poetry by earlier Greek audiences may be to contrast a time when people were capable of keeping these critical realms (morality and poetic value) separate, to conditions of his own day, when audiences— or at least some professional critics—found it increasingly difficult to do so.

It is impossible to know on the basis of what evidence Philodemus makes his pronouncements about Greek audiences of an earlier age, although it is reasonable to assume that his feel for past Greek culture was not wholesale fantasy. Philodemus's remarks do seem to suggest that many, perhaps even most, ancient audiences, were capable of reasonably nuanced and complex evaluation of comic and satirical poetry, even if they were never called upon to articulate it, or lacked the technical means of a professional critic like Critias or Philodemus to do so. The Critias fragment shows well enough how problematic the representation of "badness" was in early Greece, especially when that badness was appropriated by the poet himself. The inference we can draw from Philodemus that most audiences understood and enjoyed it for what it was—fictional or semi-fictional comedy—seems reasonably sound.[41]

---

of it. The idea in the last line that early Greeks might have considered a (morally) "good" poet, who purveyed "good" things in his work, a "bad" person simply because his poetry was not entertaining, seems an unsettling irony to the commentator.

40. See Philodemus *On Poems* 5, cols. xxxii 9–17, with discussion, and translation, in Asmis 1995, 154: "[too much emphasis on a poem's benefit] expels with the rod many wholly beautiful poems, some of which have a content that is not beneficial . . . and prefers many lesser poems, as many as contain beneficial or more beneficial [thoughts]."

41. Having said this, it is noteworthy that virtually none of the ancient testimonia about Archilochus shows any active appreciation of the poet specifically as a satirist or "comedian." Many ancient writers would praise him effusively, sometimes (as with Quintilian, above n. 4) even singling out his "vigor" or "energy," but almost without fail their praise was offered *in spite of* a recognition that at least some of his poetry was also scandalous. It is likely, however, that the evidence of these testimonia is skewed: Like so many other authors who survive from antiquity, these are largely members of an aristocratic élite, who are not likely to go out of their way to admit that they enjoyed poetry that reveled in *aiskhrologia* (such diction would not be considered *aiskhra* if they were not supposed to scandalize a social "norm") and "low" topics. Philodemus seems to imply that a more balanced and nuanced account of how ancient audiences responded to "scandalous" literature could be written if we had a more representative sample of ancient opinions about it.

What might we conclude from all this about Philodemus's attitude specifically toward a satirist's abject self-presentation? I suspect that he would take a more tolerant stance toward Archilochus than Critias did several centuries earlier, but that in the end, they would have agreed on several fundamental points. Philodemus would almost certainly have initially evaluated Archilochean poetry—even the most self-incriminating, degrading parts—in terms of its poetic qualities and been less disturbed by its representations of baseness, but if he were to imagine Archilochus in front of him, he might well take him to task, as Critias did, for assuming degrading roles in his poetry—not because he felt Archilochean poetry would put his very soul at risk and serve as a bad moral paradigm for his audiences, as Plato might say, but rather because it might potentially damage his *kleos*. There is, after all, a paradox inherent in satirical poetry written in the poet's own voice: The poetic medium may be by definition fictional, but its subjective "I" continually proclaims the opposite, i.e., that what it says as actually true. So although a sophisticated listener might think he can see through such claims, the poet continually works hard, as we have often seen in this study, to prevent even an aficionado such as this from being able to delineate clearly the line between a fictionalized and a genuinely autobiographical abjection. Critias seems to have been sensitive to this paradox, whether or not he could have articulated it as such: He must have known that Archilochus probably was not in reality as base as he often claimed to be, but he could not escape the persuasive spell of the poet's autobiographical posturing. Ironically, Critias's annoyance at Archilochus is ultimately a testimony to the poet's success as a satirist: Archilochus has written poetry that is convincing enough to be confused with real-life and so "tricked" Critias into equating poetic reality with autobiographical reality.

The answer to our initial question—did ancient audiences understand a poetics of abjection when they encountered satirical poetry?—turns out to be no less complicated than it remains today. To begin at the most general level, we can say that some people clearly did, while others did not, understand that satire functioned like any other poetic genre, following compositional and performative protocols, and fulfilling audience expectations in a realm ontologically distinct from real life. Even those who did, however, were often confounded by the autobiographical "I," especially when it cultivated a stance of baseness and abjection. Some people no doubt did not care whether the poet degraded himself by such posturing, as long as the result was comical and entertaining; Philodemus may have been in this category. Others, such as Plato, were perfectly capable of seeing the humor of such self-representations, and probably did not think a professional like Archilochus ran much *personal* psychological risk in composing this sort of poetry. A Platonist, however, would be concerned for the psychological vulnerability of the *audience*, not the poet, and would fear that they might too readily attempt to replicate in their own lives whatever negative things they found in satirical poetry. Critias, as we have

seen, falls somewhere in the middle: He seems to have understood that Archilochus's negative self-portrait was fictional, but worried about what *others*
would do with it, and what effect this might have on the poet's reputation.
Critias's attitude was characteristic of an aristocrat who, on the one hand,
thought he was capable enough *himself* of seeing through Archilochus's fictional personae, but assumed that the rest of the world could not. So while he
seemed to have had a basic understanding of poetic discourse, he had a blind
spot (as many people still do today) when it came to a critical appreciation of
scandalously self-compromising poetry in particular. There, as often happens,
the very power of the poet's personal voice, and his insistence on the reality of
his self-portraits and the drama in which he casts himself, prove too hard to
resist.[42] It seems not to have occurred to Critias that if Archilochus were to
have written a different sort of poetry, as he implies in the Aelian passage, and
in so doing were to recast himself in his poetry as ever the genteel aristocrat,
instead of the scurrilous rake, there would be little left that anyone would recognize as comic satire.

It may well be that satire is the riskiest genre a poet can work in. Certainly
this is a favorite trope of satirists throughout history, as we have seen throughout our study, and they might be right: Irony, after all—surely satire's most
conspicuous hallmark—is notoriously difficult for an audience to assess, and
good satirists, fond as they are of maintaining an elusive subjectivity, are not
about to offer them much help. Clearly, satire is not for the faint-hearted:

---

42. The problem can be especially acute when the actual lives of comic artists happen also to
run parallel to the events that figure in their works. With ancient poets we rarely have any reliable,
or particularly detailed information, about the poets' lives to which we could compare to the autobiographical details that emerge from their work. But many examples can be adduced from our
own era of comic artists whose lives we can track as they were portrayed both within their works
and independently of it. Needless to say, numerous interpretative problems arise in such cases. To
cite merely one example, in the 1950's and '60's the American comedian Lenny Bruce seemed to
have lived out the kind of life that he constantly worked into his nightclub acts—irreverent, comically blasphemous, edgy, obscene, satirically vituperative, and fueled by drugs and alcohol; except
for the fact that he was not performing in verse forms, he was every bit a Hipponax or Aristophanes
redivivus. When faced with a case such as this, where "art imitates life" (or vice versa), one can feel
pulled inexorably toward the conclusion that, in fact, we must take at face value everything such an
artist says about himself (and, by extension, what he complains about) in his work. Stronger souls,
however, might be able to entertain the possibility that the two biographies operate according to
quite dissimilar dynamics and goals, even as they appear to run along parallel lines. Lenny Bruce's
performance of comic mockery as part of an act, in other words, will have served rather different
ends than the comic mockery he might perform in his real life. It is interesting, however, that in his
particular case, toward the end of his life even he seemed to confuse the two worlds. Constantly
called upon to defend himself against criminal charges of obscenity, he worked his growing obsession with constitutional law into his nightclub act, sometimes reading long passages from law codes
and offering commentary on his legal troubles. As critics have pointed out, as the sense of comic
irony and triumphant indignation was increasingly overshadowed by what appeared to be uninflected
bitterness and paranoia, these rants lost much of their value as comedy. See now Nachman 2003,
418–24 and Kercher 2006, 389–424.

Mockery, jest, and insult can be dangerous enough speech acts in everyday life, often with very real consequences, and turning them into poetry is no guarantee that they will be received as any less toxic. The *parodos* of Aristophanes' *Frogs*, in fact, a passage that we encountered at the beginning of our study, made precisely this point, when the chorus urges anyone in the audience who fails to appreciate the difference between comic mockery and everyday abuse simply to withdraw from the proceedings:

κωμῳδηθεὶς ἐν ταῖς πατρίοις τελεταῖς ταῖς τοῦ Διονύσου.
τούτοις αὐδῶ καὖθις ἐπαυδῶ καὖθις τὸ τρίτον μάλ᾽ ἐπαυδῶ
ἐξίστασθαι μύσταισι χοροῖς· ὑμεῖς δ᾽ ἀνεγείρετε μολπὴν
καὶ παννυχίδας τὰς ἡμετέρας αἳ τῇδε πρέπουσιν ἑορτῇ.

. . . on the grounds that he has been satirized (*kômôidêtheis*) in our
   ancestral celebrations of Dionysus.
To such as these, I say it once, twice, and even a third time, that
they should stand back from our mystic dances. Now everyone wake
   up our song
and our all-night dances, which are fitting for this festival.
   (*Frogs* 368–71)

Still, they say, even those who remain—the poetically initiated who understand the dynamics of satire—will need to proceed with boldness (ἀνδρείως):[43]

χώρει νυν πᾶς ἀνδρείως
εἰς τοὺς εὐανθεῖς κόλπους
λειμώνων ἐγκρούων
   κἀπισκώπτων
καὶ παίζων καὶ χλευάζων

Now let each one come forth boldly
into the flowery folds
of the meadows, dancing,
and mocking
and joking and taunting . . . . (*Frogs* 372–77)

We only have to consider Archilochus's checkered reputation across the centuries to see how erratically and unpredictably audiences can respond to satirical poetry. But this ultimately only means that satire has accomplished what it set out to do.

___

43. On *andreia* as a metaphor for comic mockery and satire, see Rosen and Sluiter 2003, 13–20.

BIBLIOGRAPHY

Acosta-Hughes, B. 2002. *Polyeideia: The Iambi of Callimachus and the Archaic Iambic Tradition*. Berkeley: University of California Press.

Adams, J. N. 1982. *The Latin Sexual Vocabulary*. Baltimore: The Johns Hopkins University Press.

Adrados, F. R. 1975. *Festival, Comedy and Tragedy: The Greek Origins of Theatre*. Trans. C. Holme. Leiden: E. J. Brill.

Aellen, C. 1994. *À la Recherche de l'ordre cosmique: Forme et fonction des personnifications dans la céramique italiote*. Zürich: Akanthus.

Anderson, W. S. 1964. "Anger in Juvenal and Seneca." *California Publications in Classical Philology* 19:127–96. (= Anderson 1982, 293–61).

———. 1982. *Essays on Roman Satire*. Princeton: Princeton University Press.

Arnott, W. G. 1972. "Parody and Ambiguity in Euripides' *Cyclops*." In *Antidosis: Festschrift fur Walter Kraus zum 70. Geburtstag*, ed. R. Hanslick, A. Lesky and H. Schwalb, 21–30. Vienna: Hermann Böhlaus.

———. 1996. *Alexis: The Fragments: A Commentary*. Cambridge: Cambridge University Press.

Asmis, E. 1995. "Philodemus on Censorship, Moral Utility, and Formalism in Poetry." In *Philodemus and Poetry: Poetic Theory and Practice in Lucretius, Philodemus and Horace*, ed. D. Obbink. New York: Oxford University Press. 148–77.

Austin, N. 1983. "Odysseus and the Cyclops: Who Is Who?" in C. Rubino, and C. Shelmerdine, edd. *Approaches to Homer*. 3–37 Austin:University of Texas Press.

Barchiesi, A. 2001. "Horace and Iambos: The Poet as Literary Historian." In *Iambic Ideas: Essays on a Poetic Tradition from Archaic Greece to the Late Roman Empire*, ed. A. Cavarzere, A. Aloni and A. Barchiesi.. Lanham, Md.: Rowman & Littlefield. 141–64.

Bakhtin, M. M. 1984a. *Rabelais and His World*. Trans. H. Iswolsky. Bloomington: Indiana University Press.

———. 1984b. *Problems of Dostoevsky's Poetics*. Trans. C. Emerson. Minneapolis: University of Minnesota Press.

Bartol, K. 1992. "Where Was Iambic Poetry Performed? Some Evidence from the Fourth Century B.C." *Classical Quarterly*, n.s., 42: 65–71.

————. 1993. *Greek Elegy and Iambus: Studies in Ancient Literary Sources*. Poznan: A. Mickiewicz University Press.

Basson, A. F., and Dominik, W. J. 2003. *Literature, Art, History: Studies on Classical Antiquity and Tradition. In Honour of W. J. Henderson*. Frankfurt am Main: Peter Lang.

Bell, C. 1992. *Ritual Theory, Ritual Practice*. Oxford: Oxford University Press.

Bellandi, F. 1973. "Poetica dell' *indignatio* e *sublime* satirico in Giovenale." *Annali della Scuola Normale Superiore di Pisa*, 3rd ser., 3.1: 53–94.

————. 1974. "Naevolus cliens." *Maia: Rivista di Litterature Classiche* 26: 279–99.

————. 1980. *Etica diatribica e protesta sociale nelle satire di Giovenale* (Opuscula Philologa 2). Bologna: Pàtron.

Bernabé, A. *Poetarum Epicorum Graecorum : Testimonia et Fragmenta*. 2 vols. Leipzig: Teubner, 1987.

Bernstein, M. A. 1992. *Bitter Carnival: Ressentiment and the Abject Hero*. Princeton: Princeton University Press.

Biles, Z. P. 2002. "Intertextual Biography in the Rivalry of Cratinus and Aristophanes." *American Journal of Philology* 123: 169–204.

Bing, P. 1988. *The Well-Read Muse: Present and Past in Callimachus and the Hellenistic Poets* (Hypomnemata 90). Gottingen: Vandenhoeck & Ruprecht.

Blondell, R. 2002. *The Play of Character in Plato's Dialogues*. Cambridge: Cambridge University Press.

Bogel, F. V. 2001. *The Difference Satire Makes: Rhetoric and Reading from Jonson to Byron*. Ithaca, N.Y.: Cornell University Press.

Bossi, F. 1990. *Studi su Archiloco*. Bari: Adriatica Editrice.

Bowie, A. M. 1993. *Aristophanes: Myth, Ritual and Comedy*. Cambridge: Cambridge University Press.

————. 2003. "Fate May Harm Me, I Have Dined Today: Near-eastern Royal Banquets and Greek Symposia in Herodotus." *Pallas* 61: 99–109.

Bowie, E. 1996. "Frame and Framed in Theocritus Poems 6 and 7." In *Theocritus* (Hellenistica Groningana 2), ed. M. A. Harder, R. F. Regtuit and G. C. Wakker, 91–100. Groningen: Egbert Forsten.

————. 2001. "Early Greek Iambic Poetry: The Importance of Narrative." In *Iambic Ideas: Essays on a Poetic Tradition from Archaic Greece to the Late Roman Empire*, ed. A. Cavarzere, A. Aloni and A. Barchiesi, 1–28. Lanham, Md.: Rowman & Littlefield.

————. 2002. "Ionian *Iambos* and Attic *Komoidia*: Father and Daughter, or Just Cousins?" In *The Language of Greek Comedy*, ed. A. Willi, 33–50. Oxford: Oxford University Press.

Branham, B. 1989. *Unruly Eloquence: Lucian and the Comedy of Traditions*. Cambridge: Harvard University Press.

Braund, S. 1982. "Anger and Indifference in Juvenal." Review of *Etica diatribica e protesta sociale nelle satire di Giovenale* (Opuscula Philologa 2), by F. Bellandi. *Classical Review*, n.s., 32: 169–70.

Braund, S. 1988. *Beyond Anger: A Study of Juvenal's Third Book of Satires*. Cambridge: Cambridge University Press.

———. 1996. *Juvenal: Satires Book 1*. Cambridge: Cambridge University Press.

———. 2004. "*Libertas* or *Licentia*? Freedom and Criticism in Roman Satire." In *Free Speech in Classical* Antiquity, ed. I. Sluiter and R. M. Rosen, 409–28. Leiden: E. J. Brill.

Bremmer, J. 1983. "Scapegoat Rituals in Ancient Greece." *Harvard Studies in Classical Philology* 87: 299–320.

Brillante, C. 1990. "Myth and History: History and the Historical Interpretation of Myth." In *Approaches to Greek Myth*, ed. L. Edmunds, 93–138. Baltimore: The Johns Hopkins University Press.

Brink, C. O. 1962. "Horace and Varro" in *Varron* (Fondation Hardt 9), ed. O. Reverdin, 173–206. Geneva.

Brock, S. 1971. *The Syriac Version of the Pseudo-Nonnos Mythological Scholia*. Cambridge: Cambridge University Press.

Brown, C. 1997. "Iambos." In *A Companion to the Greek Lyric Poets*, ed. D. E. Gerber, 13–88. Leiden: E. J. Brill.

Bultrighini, U. 1999. *Maledettta Democrazia: Studi su Crizia*. Chieta Scalo.

Burkert, W. 1979. *Structure and History in Greek Mythology and Ritual*. Berkeley: University of California Press.

———. 1983. *Homo Necans: The Anthropology of Ancient Greek Sacrificial Ritual and Myth*. Berkeley: University of California Press.

Cairns, D. L. 2003. "Ethics, Ethology, Terminology: Iliadic Anger and the Cross-cultural Study of Emotion." In *Ancient Anger: Perspectives from Homer to Galen* (Yale Classical Studies 32), eds. S. Braund and G. Most, 11–49. Cambridge: Cambridge University Press.

Carey, C. 1986. "Archilochus and Lycambes." *Classical Quarterly*, n.s., 36: 60–67.

Carrière, J.-C. 1979. *Le carnaval et la politique*. Paris: Les Belles Lettres.

Cassio, A. C. 1984. "L'accusa di Crizia e le più antiche valutazioni di Archiloco." In *Lirica greca da Archiloco a Elitis: Studi in onore di Filippo Maria Pontani*, 61–65. Padova: Liviana.

Clay, D. 1998. "The Theory of the Literary Persona in Antiquity." *Materiali e discussioni per l'analisi dei testi classici* 40: 9–40.

———. 2001. "The Scandal of Dionysos on Paros (The Mnesiepes Inscription E1 III)." *Prometheus* 27.2: 97–112.

———. 2004. *Archilochos Heros: The Cult of Poets in the Greek Polis*. Washington, D.C.: Harvard University Center for Hellenic Studies.

Clay, J. S. 1989. *The Politics of Olympus: Form and Meaning in the Major Homeric Hymns*. Princeton: Princeton University Press.

Clayman, D. 1980. *Callimachus' Iambi*. (*Mnemosyne* Supplement 59). Leiden: E. J. Brill.

Coffey, M. 1989. *Roman Satire*. (2nd ed.) Bristol: Bristol Classical Press.

Cook, E. F. 1995. *The Odyssey in Athens: Myths of Cultural Origins*. Ithaca and London: Cornell University Press.

————. 1999. "Active and Passive Heroics in the *Odyssey*." *Classical World* 93: 149–67.

Corbeill, A. 1996. *Controlling Laughter: Political Humor in the Late Roman Republic*. Princeton: Princeton University Press.

————. 2002. "Ciceronian Invective." In *Brill's Companion to Cicero: Oratory and Rhetoric*, ed. J. M. May. 23–48. Leiden: E. J. Brill.

Cornford. F. 1993. *The Origin of Attic Comedy*. [1st ed. 1934]. Ann Arbor: University of Michigan Press.

Cottone, R. S. 2005. *Aristofane e la poetica dell' ingiuria. Per una introduzione alla λοιδορία comica*. Rome: Carocci.

Courtney, E. 1980. *A Commentary on the Satires of Juvenal*. London: Athlone.

Cozzoli, A. T. 1996. "II I giambo e il nuovo ἰαμβίζειν di Callimaco." *Eikasmos* 7: 129–47.

Crusius, O. 1883. *Analecta critica ad paroemiographos Graecos*. Leipzig: B. G. Teubner.

Csapo, E. 2005. *Theories of Mythology*. Oxford: Blackwell.

Cucchiarelli, A. 2001. *La satira e il poeta. Orazio tra epodi e sermones*. Pisa: Giardini.

Culler, J. 1975. *Structuralist Poetics: Structuralism, Linguistics, and the Study of Literature*. Ithaca, N.Y.: Cornell University Press.

Cullyer, H. 2006. "*Agroikia* and Pleasure in Aristotle," in Sluiter and Rosen 2006, 181–217.

Dale, A. M. 1963. "Notes on Euripides: *Helena* 1441–50." *Maia: Rivista di Litterature Classiche* 15: 310–13.

Daly, L. 1963. Review of *Hipónax de Éfeso I: Fragmentos dos Iambos*, by W. Medeiros. *American Journal of Philology* 84: 438–41.

Dane, J. *The Critical Mythology of Irony*. Athens: University of Georgia Press.

Davis, M. 1988. *Epicorum Graecorum fragmenta*. Göttingen: Vandenhoek and Ruprecht.

Dawson, C. M. 1950. "The *Iambi* of Callimachus: A Hellenistic Poet's Experimental Laboratory." *Yale Classical Studies* 11: 1–168.

de Jong, I. J. F. 1987a. *Narrators and Focalizers: The Presentation of the Story in the Iliad*. Amsterdam: B. R. Grüner.

————. 1987b. "The Voice of Anonymity: *tis*-Speeches in the *Iliad*." *Eranos* 85: 69–84.

————. 2001. *A Narratological Commentary on the* Odyssey. Cambridge: Cambridge University Press.

Degani, E. 1984. *Studi su Ipponatte*. Bari: Adriatica Editrice.

————. 1991. *Hipponax: Testimonia et Fragmenta*. (2nd ed.) Leipzig: B. G. Teubner.

Delatte, A. 1955. *Le Cycéon: Breuvage rituel des Mystères d'Éleusis*. Paris: Les Belles Lettres.

Depew, M. 1992. "*Iambeion kaleitai nun*: Genre, Occasion, and Imitation in Callimachus frr. 191 and 203 Pf." *Transactions of the American Philological Association* 122: 313–30.

Detienne, M. 1973. *Les maîtres de vérité dans la Grèce archaïque* (2nd ed.). Paris: F. Maspero.

————. 1979. *Dionysus Slain*. Trans. M. Muellner and L. Muellner. Baltimore: The Johns Hopkins University Press.

Devereux, G. 1983. *Baubo: La vulve mythique*. Paris: Jean-Cyrille Godefroy.

Dexter, M. R. and Mair, V. H. 2005. "Apotropaia and Fecundity in Eurasian Myth and Iconography: Erotic Female Display Figures."In *Proceedings of the Sixteenth Annual UCLA Indo-European Conference* (Los Angeles, November 5–6, 2004) (Journal of Indo-European Studies Monograph Series), ed. K. Jones-Bley et al. 97–121.Washington, D.C.: Institute for the Study of Man.

di Nola, A. 1974. *Antropologia religiosa: Introduzione al problema e campioni di ricerca*. Florence: Vallecchi.

Dickie, M. W. 1981. "The Disavowal of *Invidia* in Roman Iamb and Satire." *Papers of the Liverpool Latin Seminar* 3: 183–208.

Diels, H., ed. 1901. *Poetarum Philosophorum Fragmenta*. Berlin: Weidmann.

————. 1907. "Arcana Cerealia." In *Miscellanea di archeologia, storia, e filologia dedicata al Prof. A. Salinas*, 3–14. Palermo: Virzi.

Dodds, E.R. 1960. *Euripides:* Bacchae (2nd ed.). Oxford: Clarendon Press.

Dougherty, C. 2001. *The Raft of Odysseus: The Ethnographic Imagination of Homer's Odyssey*. Oxford: Oxford University Press.

Dover, K. J. 1964. "The Poetry of Archilochus." In *Archiloque* (Fondation Hardt 10), ed. J. Pouilloux et al., 183–222. Geneva: Fondation Hardt.

————. 1968. *Aristophanes Clouds*. Oxford: Oxford University Press.

Dowden, K. 1992. *The Uses of Greek Mythology*. London-New York: Routledge.

Dumezil, G. 1943. *Servius et la Fortune: Essai sur la fonction sociale de louange et de blâme et sur les elements indo-européens du* cens romain. Paris: Gallimard.

Dunand, F. 1984. "Une 'pseudo-Baubo' du Musée de Besançon." In *Hommages à Lucien Lerat* (Annales littéraires de l'Université de Besançon 294), ed. H. Walter. Paris: Les Belles Lettres, 263–68.

Easterling, P. E. 1988. "Tragedy and Ritual: 'Cry "Woe, Woe," but May the Good Prevail'." *Métis* 3: 87–109.

Ebert, J. 1969. "Die Gestalt des Thersites in der *Ilias*." *Philologus* 113: 159–75.

Edmunds, L. 1987. *Cleon, Knights, and Aristophanes' Politics*. Lanham, New York: University Press of America.

————. 1990. *Approaches to Greek Myth*. Baltimore: The Johns Hopkins University Press.

Ercolani, A. 2002. "Sprechende Namen und politische Funktion der Verspottung am Beispiel der *Acharner*"in, E. Ercolani, *Spoudaiogeloion: Form und Funktion der Verspottung in der aristophanischen Komödie*. (Beiträge zum antiken Drama und seiner Rezeption 11). Stuttgart and Weimar: J. B. Metzler. 225–54.

Falivene, M. R. 1993. "Callimaco serio-comico: il primo *Giambo* (fr. 191 Pf.)." In *Tradizione e innovazione nella cultura greca da Omero all'Età Ellenistica: Scritti in onore di Bruno Gentili*, Vol. 3 *Letteratura Ellenistica*, ed. R. Pretagostini, 911–25. Rome: Gruppo Editoriale Internazionale.

Farioli, M. 2001. *Mundus alter: Utopie e distopie nella commedia greca antica*. Milan: Vita e Pensiero.

Fehr, B. 1990. "Entertainers at the Symposion: The *Akletoi* in the Archaic Period," in *Sympotica. A Symposium on the Symposion*, ed. O. Murray. 185–95, Oxford: Oxford University Press.

Ferguson, J. 1987. *A Prosopography to the Poems of Juvenal.* Brussels: Latomus.

Ferrari, F. 1988. "*P. Berol.* Inv. 13270: I Canti di Elefantina." *Studi classici e orientali* 38: 181–227.

Ferrari, G. R. F. 1989. "Plato and Poetry." In *The Cambridge History of Literary Criticism*, Vol. 1, *Classical Criticism*, ed., G. A. Kennedy, 92–148. Cambridge: Cambridge University Press.

Kirkpatrick, J. and Dunn, F., 2002. "Heracles, Cercopes, and Paracomedy." *Transactions of the American Philological Association* 132:29–61.

Flashar, H. 1994. "Aristoteles, das Lachen und die Alte Komödie." In *Laughter Down the Centuries* Vol. 1 (Annales Universitatis Turkuensis 208), ed S. Jäkel and A. Timonen, 59–70. Turku: Turun yliopisto, 1994–.

Fluck, H. 1931. *Skurrile Riten in griechischen Kulten.* Ph.D. diss., University of Freiburg. Endingen: Emil Wild.

Foley, H. P., 1993. "Oedipus as Pharmakos." In *Nomodeiktes: Greek Studies in Honor of Martin Ostwald*, ed. R. M. Rosen and J. Farrell, 525–38. Ann Arbor: University of Michigan Press.

———., ed. 1994. *The Homeric Hymn to Demeter: Translation, Commentary and Interpretive Essays.* Princeton: Princeton University Press.

Ford, A., 1992. *Homer: The Poetry of the Past.* Ithaca and London: Cornell University Press.

Fowler, A. 1982. *Kinds of Literature: An Introduction to the Theory of Genres and Modes.* Cambridge: Harvard University Press.

Fraenkel, E. 1957. *Horace.* Oxford: Oxford University Press.

Freidenberg, O. 1930. "Tersit." *Japheticeskii Sbornik* 6: 231–53.

Freud, S. 1960. *Jokes and their Relation to the Unconscious.* [Originally published 1912]. Trans. by J. Strachey. New York: W. W. Norton.

Freudenburg, K. 1993. *The Walking Muse: Horace on the Theory of Satire.* Princeton: Princeton University Press.

———. 2001. *Satires of Rome. Threatening Poses from Lucilius to Juvenal.* Cambridge: Cambridge University Press.

Friedländer, L. 1895. *D. Junius Juvenalis Saturarum Libri V.* Leipzig: Hirzel.

Friedrich, R. 1987. "Heroic Man and *Polymetis:* Odysseus in the *Cyclopeia.*" *Greek, Roman and Byzantine Studies* 28: 121–33.

———. 1991. "The Hybris of Odysseus." *Journal of Hellenic Studies* 111: 1–28.

———. 1996. "Everything to Do with Dionysos? Ritualism, the Dionysiac, and the Tragic." In *Tragedy and the Tragic*, ed. M. Silk, 257–83. Oxford: Oxford University Press.

Gagarin, M. 1981. *Drakon and Early Athenian Homicide Law.* New Haven: Yale University Press.

Gantz, T. 1993. *Early Greek Myth: A Guide to Literary and Artistic Sources.* Baltimore: The Johns Hopkins University Press.

Geertz, C. 1973. *The Interpretation of Cultures.* New York: Basic Books.

Geffcken, J. 1911. "Studien zur griechischen Satire." *Neue Jahrbücher für das klassische Altertum* 27: 393–411, 469–93.

Gelzer, T. 1991. "Feste Strukturen in der Komödien des Aristophanes." In *Aristophane* (Fondation Hardt 38), ed. J. M. Bremer and E. W. Handley, 51–96. Geneva: Fondation Hardt.

Gentili, B. 1988. *Poetry and its Public in Ancient Greece : From Homer to the Fifth Century* (trans. A. T. Cole). Baltimore: The Johns Hopkins University Press.

Gerber, D. 1997. *A Companion to the Greek Lyric Poets*. Leiden: E. J. Brill.

Geus, K. 2002. *Eratosthenes von Kyrene. (Müncher Beiträge zur Papyrusforschung und antiken Rechtsgeschichte* 92). Munich: C. H. Beck.

Girard, R. 1986. *The Scapegoat*. Trans. Y. Freccero. Baltimore: The Johns Hopkins University Press.

Glenn, J. 1971. "The Polyphemus Folktale and Homer's *Kyklopeia*." *Transactions of the American Philological Association* 102: 133–85.

Goffmann, E. 1974. *Frame Analysis: An Essay on the Organization of Experience*. New York: Harper and Row.

Golden, L. 1992. "Aristotle on the Pleasure of Comedy." In *Essays on Aristotle's Poetics*, ed. A. O. Rorty. 379–86. Princeton: Princeton University Press.

Gow, A. S. F., ed. 1950. *Theocritus*. 2 vols. Cambridge: Cambridge University Press.

Graf, F. 1974. *Eleusis und die orphische Dichtung Athens in vorhellenistischer Zeit*. Berlin: De Gruyter.

———. 1993. *Greek Mythology: An Introduction*. Trans. Thomas Marier. Baltimore: The Johns Hopkins University Press.

Griffin, D. 1994. *Satire: A Critical Reintroduction*. Lexington: University Press of Kentucky.

Hackman, O. 1904. *Die Polyphemsage in der Volksuberlieferung*. Helsinki: Frenckellska.

Halliwell, S. 1984. "Ancient Interpretations of ὀνομαστί κωμῳδεῖν in Aristophanes." *Classical Quarterly*, n.s., 34: 83–88.

———. 1987. *The Poetics of Aristotle: Translation and Commentary*. Chapel Hill: University of North Carolina Press.

———. 1991. "The Uses of Laughter in Greek Culture." *Classical Quarterly* 41:279–96.

———. 2002. *The Aesthetics of Mimesis: Ancient Texts and Modern Problems*. Princeton: Princeton University Press.

———. 2004. "Aischrology, Shame and Comedy." In *Free Speech in Classical Antiquity*, ed. I. Sluiter and R. M. Rosen, 115–44. Leiden: E. J. Brill.

Heath, M. 1990. "Aristophanes and His Rivals," *Greece and Rome* 37: 143–58.

Held, G. F. 1984. "*Spoudaios* and Teleology in the *Poetics*." *Transactions of the American Philological Association* 114: 159–76.

Heldmann, K. 1987. "Die Wesenbestimmung der Horazischen Satire durch die Komödie." *Antike und Abendland* 33: 133–39.

Henderson, J. 1991. *The Maculate Muse: Obscene Language in Old Comedy*. [1st ed. 1975]. Oxford: Oxford University Press.

———. 1993. "Problems in Greek Literary History: The Case of Aristophanes' Clouds." In *Nomodeiktes: Greek Studies in Honor of Martin Ostwald*, ed. R. M. Rosen and J. Farrell, 591–601. Ann Arbor: University of Michigan Press.

————. 1993. Preface to Francis Cornford, *The Origin of Attic Comedy*. [1st ed. 1934]. Ann Arbor: University of Michigan Press, xi–xxvii.

Hendrickson, G. L. 1900. "Horace, Serm. 1.4: A Protest and a Programme." *American Journal of Philology* 21: 121–42.

Heubeck, A., and Hoekstra, A.. 1989. *A Commentary on Homer's* Odyssey. Vol. 2, *Books IX-XVI*. Oxford: Clarendon Press.

Highet, G. 1954. *Juvenal the Satirist*. Oxford: Oxford University Press.

Holland, G. R. 1884. *De Polyphemo et Galatea*. (*Leipziger Studien zur classischen Philologie*, vol. 7). Leipzig: Hirzel.

Hordern, J. H. 1999. "The *Cyclops* of Philoxenus." *Classical Quarterly*, n.s., 49: 445–55.

————. 2004. "*Cyclopea*: Philoxenus, Theocritus, Callimachus, Bion." *Classical Quarterly*, n.s., 54: 285–92.

Hubbard, T. K. 1991. *The Mask of Comedy Aristophanes and the Intertextual Parabasis*. Ithaca-London: Cornell University Press.

Hunt, R. 1981. "Satiric Elements in Hesiod's *Works and Days*."*Helios* 8: 29–40.

Hunter, R. L. 1983. *Eubulus: the Fragments*. Cambridge: Cambridge University Press.

————.1985. "Horace on Friendship and Free Speech." *Hermes* 113: 480–90.

————. 1997. "(B)ionic man: Callimachus' Iambic Programme." *Proceedings of the Cambridge Philological Society* 43: 4 1–52.

————. 1999. *Theocritus: A Selection*. Cambridge: Cambridge University Press.

Hutcheon, L. 1994. *Irony's Edge: The Theory and Politics of Irony*. New York: Routledge.

Hynes, W. J., and Doty, W. G., eds. 1993. *Mythical Trickster Figures: Contours, Contexts and Criticisms*. Tuscaloosa: University of Alabama Press.

Ianucci, A. 2002. *La parola e l'Azione: I Frammenti Simposiali di Crizia*. Bologna: Edizioni Nautilus.

Iddeng, J. W. 2000. "Juvenal, Satire, and the Persona Theory." *Symbolae Osloenses* 75: 107–29.

Irwin T. 1995. *Plato's* Ethics. Oxford: Oxford University Press.

Jameson, F. 1972. *The Prison-House of Language: A Critical Account of Structuralism and Russian Formalism*. Princeton: Princeton University Press.

Janko, R. 1984. *Aristotle on Comedy: Towards a Reconstruction of Poetics II*. Berkeley: University of California Press.

Jensen, B. F. 1981–1982. "Crime, Vice and Retribution in Juvenal's *Satires*." *Classica et Mediaevalia* 33: 155–68.

Jörgensen, o. 1904. "Das Auftreten der Götter in den Büchern i—m der *Odyssee*." *Hermes* 39:357–82.

Kantzios, I. 2005. *The Trajectory of Archaic Greek Trimeters*. (Mnemosyne Supplement, 265). Leiden: E. J. Brill.

Kauffmann-Samaras, A. 1981. "Amazones" in *Lexicon Iconographicum Mythologiae Classicae* 1.1.596–601. Zurich: Artemis.

Karaghiorga-Stathacopoulou, T. 1986. "Baubo." *Lexicon Iconographicum Mythologiae Classicae* 3.1: 87–90; 3.2: 67–68. Zurich: Artemis.

Kassel, R. and Austin, C. 1983–. *Poetae Comici Graeci*. Berlin and New York: Walter de Gruyter.

Kercher, S. E. 2006. *Revel with a Cause: Liberal Satire in Postwar America*. Chicago: University of Chicago Press.

Kerkhecker, A. 1999. *Callimachus' Book of Iambi*. Oxford: Oxford University Press.

Kernan, A. 1959. *The Cankered Muse: Satire of the English Renaissance*. New Haven: Yale University Press.

Kirk, G. S. 1970. *Myth. Its Meaning and Functions in Ancient and Other Cultures*. Cambridge and Berkeley: Cambridge University Press and University of California Press.

Kirkpatrick, J. and Dunn F. 2002. "Heracles, Cercopes, and Paracomedy." *Transactions of the American Philological Association*. 132: 29–61.

Kleinknecht, H. 1937. *Die Gebetsparodie in der Antike*. Stuttgart: Kohlhammer.

Köhnken, A. 1996. "Theokrits Polyphemgedichte." In *Theocritus* (Hellenistica Groningana 2), ed. M. A. Harder, R. F. Regtuit, and G. C. Wakker, 171–84. Groningen: Egbert Forsten.

Konstan, D. 1981. "An Anthropology of Euripides' *Cyclops*." *Ramus* 10: 87–103.

———. 1998. "The Dynamics of Imitation: Callimachus' First Iambic." In *Genre in Hellenistic Poetry* (Hellenistica Groningana 3), ed. M. A. Harder, R. F. Regtuit and G. C. Wakker, 133–42. Groningen: Egbert Forsten.

Korus, K. 1991. *Die griechische Satire: Die theoretischen Grundlagen und ihre Anwendung auf Homers Epik*. Warsaw: Jagiellonian University Press.

Kossatz-Deissmann, A., 1981, "Achilleus" in *Lexicon Iconographicum Mythologiae Classicae* 1,1.161–71 Zurich:Artemis.

Koster, S. 1980. *Die Invektive in der griechischen und römischen Literatur*. (Beiträge zur klassischen Philologie 99). Meisenheim am Glan: Hain.

Kovacs, D. 1994. *Euripides:* Cyclops, Alcestis, Medea. Loeb Classical Library 12. Cambridge: Harvard University Press.

Kugelmeier, C. 1996. *Reflexe früher und zeitgenössicher Lyrik in der Alten attischen Komödie*. Stuttgart: B. G. Teubner.

Kullmann, W. 1960. *Die Quellen der Ilias*. Munich.

Lada-Richards, I. 1999. *Initiating Dionysus: Ritual and Theatre in Aristophanes'* Frogs. Oxford: Oxford University Press.

Lasserre, F. 1979. "Iambische Dichtung und antike Theorien über den Iambos bei Aristoteles." *Acta Philologica Aenipontana* 4: 59–61.

Lattimore, R. 1951. *The Iliad of Homer*. Chicago: University of Chicago Press.

———. 1965. *The Odyssey of Homer*. New York: Harper and Row.

Lefkowitz, M. R. 1981. *The Lives of the Greek Poets*. Baltimore: The Johns Hopkins University Press.

Lehnus, L., ed. 1989. *Bibliografia Callimachea: 1489–1988* (Pubblicazioni del Darficlet 123). Genova: Università degli Studi di Genova, Dipartimento di Archeologia, Filologia Classica e loro Tradizioni.

Lelli, E. 1996. "La figure del rovo nel *Giambo* IV di Callimaco." *Rivista di Cultura Classica e Medioevale* 38: 311–18.

Leo, F. 1889. "Varro und die Satire." *Hermes* 24: 66–84.

Leonhardt, J. 1991. *Phalloslied und Dithyrambos: Aristoteles über den Ursprung des griech-*

ischen Dramas (Abhandlungender Heidelberger Akademie der Wissenschaften, Philosophisch-historische Klasse 4). Heidelberg: C. Winter.

Limon, J. 2000. *Stand-up Comedy in Theory, or, Abjection in America*. Durham, N.C.: Duke University Press.

Lobel, E. 1941. *The Oxyrhynchus Papyri, vol. 18*. London: Egypt Exploration Fund.

López Eire, A. 2003. "Tragedy and Satyr-drama: Linguistic Criteria." In *Shards from Kolonos: Studies in Sophoclean Fragments*, ed. A. H. Sommerstein. 387–412. Bari: Levante Editori.

Lorenz, K. 1966. *On Aggression*. Trans. Marjorie Kerr Wilson. New York: Harcourt, Brace, and World.

Lowry, E. R., Jr. 1991. *Thersites: A Study in Comic Shame*. New York: Garland.

Luppe, W. 2000. "The Rivalry between Aristophanes and Kratinos." In *The Rivals of Aristophanes: Studies in Athenian Old Comedy*, ed. D. Harvey and J. Wilkins, 15–20. London: Duckworth.

Mader, M. 1977. *Das Problem des Lachens und der Komödie bei Platon*. Stuttgart: Kohlhammer.

Mankin, D. 1995. *Horace:* Epodes. Cambridge: Cambridge University Press.

Manuwald, B. 1990. "Der Kyklop als Dichter: Bemerkungen zu Theokrit, Eid. 11." In *Beiträge zur hellenistischen Literatur und ihrer Rezeption in Rom (Palingenesia 28)*, ed. P. Steinmetz, 77–91. Stuttgart: F. Steiner.

Marks, J. 2005. "The Ongoing *neikos*: Thersites, Odysseus and Achilleus." *American Journal of Philology* 126: 1–31.

Martin, R. P. 1989. *The Language of Heroes: Speech and Performance in the* Iliad. Ithaca, N.Y.: Cornell University Press.

Martyn, J. 1979. "Juvenal's Wit." *Grazer Beiträge* 8: 219–38.

Mason, H. A. 1962. "Is Juvenal a Classic?" *Arion* 1: 8–44; 2: 39–79.

Masson, O. 1962. *Les Fragments du Poète Hipponax*. Paris: C. Klincksieck.

Mastromarco, G. 2002. "*Onomastì Komoideín* e *spoudaiogeloion* ." In *Spoudaiogeloion: Form und Funktion der Verspottung in der aristophanischen Komödie*, ed. A. Ercolani. (*Beiträge zum antiken Drama und seiner Rezeption* 11). 205–23. Stuttgart and Weimar: J. B. Metzler.

Mayer, R. 1994. *Horace:* Epistles *Book 1*. Cambridge: Cambridge University Press.

MacDowell, D. M. 1995. *Aristophanes and Athens: An Introduction to the Plays*. Oxford: Oxford University Press.

Meuli, K. 1975. "Die gefesselten Götter." In *Gesammelte Schriften*, ed. T. Gelzer 2 vols. Basel and Stuttgart: Schwabe.

Miller, P. A. 1994. *Lyric Texts and Lyric Consciousness: The Birth of a Genre from Archaic Greece to Augustan Rome*. London and New York: Routledge.

———. 1998. "The Bodily Grotesque in Roman Satire: Images of Sterility." *Arethusa* 31: 257–83.

Miralles, C., and Pòrtulas, J.. 1983. *Archilochus and the Iambic Poetry*. Rome: Edizioni dell'Ateneo.

———1988. *The Poetry of Hipponax*. Rome: Edizioni dell' Ateneo.

Mondi, R. 1983. "The Homeric Cyclopes. Folktale, Tradition, and Theme." *Transactions of the American Philological Association* 113: 17–38.

Morelli, G. 2001. *Teatro attico e pittura vascolare: Una tragedia di Cheremone nella ceramica italiota* (*Spudasmata* 84). Hildesheim: Georg Olms.

Moulinier, L. 1952. *Le pur et l'impur dans la pensée de Grecs: D' Homère à Aristote.* Paris: C. Klincksieck.

Müller, C. W. 1992. "Aristophanes und Horaz. Zu einem Verlaufsschema von Selbstbehauptung und Selbstgewissheit zweier Klassiker." *Hermes* 120: 129–41.

Murnaghan, S. 1994. Review of *Reciprocity and Ritual: Homer and Tragedy in the Developing City-State*, by R. Seaford. *American Journal of Philology* 117: 316–19.

Nachman, G. 2003. *Seriously Funny: The Rebel Comedians of the 1950s and 1960s.* New York: Pantheon Books.

Nagy, G. 1979. *The Best of the Achaeans: Concepts of the Hero in Archaic Greek Poetry.* Baltimore: The Johns Hopkins University Press.

———. 1991. *Pindar's Homer: The Lyric Possession of an Epic Past.* Baltimore: The Johns Hopkins University Press.

———. 1996. *Homeric Questions.* Austin: University of Texas Press.

———. 2004. "Transmission of Archaic Greek Sympotic Songs: from Lesbos to Alexandria." *Critical Inquiry* 31.1: 26–48.

Nails, D. 2002. *The People of Plato: A Prosopography of Plato and Other Socratics.* Indianapolis, Ind.: Hackett.

Nauck, A., ed. 1889, *Tragicorum Graecorum Fragmenta.* Vol. 1 (2nd ed.). Leipzig: Teubner.

Nehamas, A. 1999. *Virtues of Authenticity: Essays on Plato and Socrates.* Princeton: Princeton University Press.

Nesselrath, H.-G. 1990. *Die attische Mittlere Komödie: Ihre Stellung in der antiken Literaturkritik und Literaturgeschichte.* Berlin: Walter de Gruyter.

Nestle, W. 1903. "Kritias: Eine Studie." *Neue Jahrbücher für das klassische Altertum* 11: 81–107, 178–99.

Newton, R. M. 1983. "Poor Polyphemus: Emotional Ambivalence in *Odyssey* 9 and 17." *Classical World* 76: 137–42.

Nünlist, R. 1998. *Poetologische Bildersprache in der frühgriechischen Dichtung* (Beiträge zur Altertumskunde 101). Stuttgart-Leipzig: B. G. Teubner.

O'Higgins, L. 2003. *Women and Humor in Classical Greece.* Cambridge: Cambridge University Press.

O'Sullivan, J. N. 1987. "Observations on the *Kyklopeia.*" *Symbolae Osloenses* 62: 5–24.

Obbink, D., ed. 1995. *Philodemus and Poetry: Poetic Theory and Practice in Lucretius, Philodemus and Horace.* Oxford: Oxford University Press.

Olender, M. 1990. "Aspects of Baubo: Ancient Texts and Contexts." Trans. R. Lamberton. In *Before Sexuality: The Construction of Erotic Experience in the Ancient Greek World*, ed. D. M. Halperin, J. J. Winkler, and F. I. Zeitlin, 83–113. Princeton: Princeton University Press.

Olson, S. D. 1995. *Blood and Iron: Stories and Storytelling in Homer's* Odyssey. Leiden: E. J. Brill.

———. 1998. *Aristophanes: Peace.* Oxford: Clarendon.

———. 2002. *Aristophanes: Acharnians.* Oxford: Clarendon.

Ostwald, M. 1986. *From Popular Sovereignty to the Sovereignty of Law: Law, Society and Politics in Fifth-Century Athens*. Berkeley: University of California Press.

Padgett, J. M., Comstock, M. B., Herrmann, J. J., and Vermeule, C. C. 1993. *Vase Painting in Italy: Red-Figure and Related Works in the Museum of Fine Arts, Boston*. Boston: Museum of Fine Arts Press.

Page, D. L. 1973. *Folktales in Homer's Odyssey*. Cambridge: Harvard University Press.

Parker, R. 1983. *Pollution and Purification in Early Greek Religion*. Oxford: Clarendon.

Paton, J. M. 1908. "The Death of Thersites on an Apulian Amphora in the Boston Museum of Fine Arts."*American Journal of Archaeology* 12: 406–16.

Paul, G. 1991. "Symposia and Deipna in Plutarch's *Lives* and in Other Historical Writings." In *Dining in a Classical Context*, ed. W. J. Slater, 157–69. Ann Arbor: University of Michigan Press.

Pellizer, E. 1983. "Della zuffa simpotica." In *Poesia e simposio nella Grecia antica: Guida storica e critica*, ed. M. Vetta, 29–41. Rome: Laterza. Also in *Oinêra Teukhê: Studi Triestini di poesia conviviale*, ed. K. Fabian, E. Pellizer, and G. Tedeschi, 31–41. Alessandria: Edizioni Dell' Orso, 1991.

Peradotto, J. 1990. *Man in the Middle Voice: Name and Narration in the* Odyssey Princeton: Princeton University Press.

Pfeiffer, R., ed. 1949–1953. *Callimachus*. 2 vols. Oxford: Clarendon.

Pfisterer-Haas, S. 1989. *Darstellungen alter Frauen in der griechischen Kunst* (European University Studies, Series 38, vol. 21). Frankfurt am Main: Peter Lang.

Philippson, P. 1947. "Die vorhomerische und die homerische Gestalt des Odysseus" *Museum Helveticum* 4:7–22.

Plaza, M. 2006. *The Function of Humour in Roman Verse Satire: Laughing and Lying*. Oxford: Oxford University Press.

Podlecki, A. 1961. "Guest-gifts and Nobodies in *Odyssey* 9." Phoenix 15: 125–33.

Popper, K. R. 1959. *The Logic of Scientific Discovery* New York: Basic Books.

———. 1965. *Conjectures and Refutations. The Growth of Scientific Knowledge* (2nd ed.).New York: Basic Books.

Porter, J. I. 1995. "Content and Form in Philodemus: The History of an Evasion." In *Philodemus and Poetry: Poetic Theory and Practice in Lucretius, Philodemus and Horace*, ed. D. Obbink, 97–147. Oxford: Oxford University Press.

———. 2005. "What Is 'Classical' about Classical Antiquity?—Eight Propositions." *Arion* 13: 27–61.

Puelma Piwonka, M. 1949. *Lucilius und Kallimachos: Zur Geschichte einer Gattung der hellenistisch-römischen Poesie*. Frankfurt am Main: Vittorio Klostermann.

Rankin, H. D. 1972. "Thersites the Malcontent: A Discussion." *Symbolae Osloenses* 47: 32–60.

———. 1975. "ΜΟΙΧΟΣ, ΛΑΓΝΟΣ ΚΑΙ ΥΒΡΙΣΤΗΣ: Critias and his Judgement of Archilochos." *Grazer Beiträge* 3: 324–34.

———. 1977. *Archilochus of Paros*. Park Ridge, N.J.: Noyes.

Rau, P. 1967. *Paratragodia: Untersuchungen einer komischen Form des Aristophanes*. Munich: Beck.

Reckford, K. 1987. *Aristophanes' Old-and-New Comedy*. Chapel Hill: University of North Carolina Press.

Reinhardt, K. 1948. *Von Werken und Formen: Vorträge und Aufsätze*. Godesberg: H. Küpper.

Ribbeck, O. 1865. *Der echte und der unechte Juvenal: eine kritische Untersuchung*. Berlin: I. Guttentag.

Richardson, N. J. 1974. *The Homeric Hymn to Demeter*. Oxford: Oxford University Press.

Richlin, A. 1992. *The Garden of Priapus: Sexuality and Aggression in Roman Humor* 2nd ed. Oxford: Oxford University Press.

Riu, X. 1999. *Dionysism and Comedy*. Lanham, Md.: Rowman and Littlefield.

Röhrich, L. 1962. "Die mittel-alterlichen Redaktionen des Polyphem-Marchens (AT 1137) und ihr Verhältnis zur ausserhomerischen Tradition." *Fabula* 5: 48–7l.

Roscher, W. H. 1884–1937. *Ausführliches Lexicon der griechischen und romischen Mythologie*. 6 vols. Leipzig: B. G. Teubner.

Rose, G. P. 1969. "The Unfriendly Phaeacians. " *Transactions of the American Philological Association* 100: 387–406.

Rosen, R. M. 1984. "The Ionian at Aristophanes' *Peace* 46." *Greek, Roman and Byzantine Studies* 25: 389–96.

———. 1987. "Hipponax Fr. 48Dg. and the Eleusinian Kykeon." *American Journal of Philology* 108: 416–26.

———. 1988. *Old Comedy and the Iambographic Tradition*. Atlanta: Scholars Press.

———. 1990. "Hipponax and the Homeric Odysseus." *Eikasmos* 1: 11–25.

———. 1995. "Plato Comicus and the Evolution of Greek Comedy." In *Beyond Comedy: Tradition and Diversity in Greek Comedy*, ed. G. Dobrov, 119–37. Atlanta: Scholars Press.

———. 1997. "Performance and Textuality in Aristophanes' *Clouds*." *Yale Journal of Criticism* 10: 397–421.

———. 2000. "Cratinus' *Pytine* and the Construction of the Comic Self." In *The Rivals of Aristophanes: Studies in Athenian Old Comedy*, ed. D. Harvey and J. Wilkins, 23–39. London: Duckworth.

———, and Marks, D. R. 1999. "Comedies of Transgression in Gangsta Rap and Ancient Classical Poetry." *New Literary History* 30: 897–928.

———, and Baines, V. 2002. "'I Am Whatever You Say I Am': Satiric Program in Juvenal and Eminem," *Classical and Modern Literature* 22.2: 103–27.

———. 2003. "The Death of Thersites and the Sympotic Performance of Iambic Mockery." *Pallas* 61: 121–36.

———, and Sluiter, I., eds. 2003. *Andreia. Studies in Manliness and Courage in Classical Antiquity*. Leiden: E. J. Brill.

———, and Sluiter, I., eds., 2006. *City Countryside and the Spatial Organization of Value in Classical Antiquity*. Leiden: E. J. Brill.

———. 2006. "Comic Aischrology and the Urbanization of *Agroikia*," in Rosen and Sluiter 2006, 218–38.

Rosenbloom, D. 2002. "From *Ponêros* to *Pharmakos*: Theater, Social Drama, and Revolution in Athens, 428–404 BCE." *Classical Antiquity* 21.2: 283–346.

Rösler, W. 1980. *Dichter und Gruppe: Eine Untersuchung zu den Bedingungen und sur historischen Funktion früher Lyrik am Beispiel Alkaios*. Munich: W. Fink.

————. 1985. "Persona reale o persona poetica? L'interpretazione dell' 'io' nella lirica greca arcaica." *Quaderni Urbinati di cultura Classica*, n.s., 19: 131–44.

————. 1986. "Michail Bachtin und die Karnevalskultur im antiken Griechenland." *Quaderni Urbinati di Cultura Classica*, n.s., 23: 25–44.

————. 1993. "Über Aischrologie im archaischen und klassischen Griechenland." In *Karnevaleske Phänomene in antiken und nachantiken Kulturen und Literaturen. Statten und Formen der Kommunikation im Altertum I* (Bochumer Altertumswissenschaftliches Colloquium 13), ed. S. Döpp, 75–97. Trier: Wissenschaftlicher Verlag Trier.

Rosmarin, A. 1985. *The Power of Genre*. Minneapolis: University of Minnesota Press.

Rotstein, A. 2006. "Critias' Invective against Archilochus," *Classical Philology* (forthcoming).

————. 2007. *The Idea of Iambos from Archilochus to Aristotle*. Oxford: Oxford University Press (forthcoming).

Rudd, N. 1966. *The Satires of Horace*. Cambridge: Cambridge University Press.

————. 1976. *Lines of Enquiry: Studies in Latin Poetry*. Cambridge: Cambridge University Press.

Ruffell, I. 2002. "A Total Write-Off: Aristophanes, Kratinos and the Rhetoric of Comic Competition." *Classical Quarterly*, n.s., 52: 138–63.

Russo, J., Fernandez-Galiano, M., Heubeck, A. 1992. *A Commentary on Homer's Odyssey. Vol. 3. Books XVII–XXIV*. Oxford: Clarendon Press.

Rusten, J. 1977. "*Wasps* 1360–1369: Philokleon's ΤΟΘΑΣΜΟΣ." *Harvard Studies in Classical Philology* 81: 157–61.

Scarpi, P. 1976. *Letture sulla religione classica: L'Inno omerico a Demeter (elementi per una tipologia del mito)*. (Università di Padova: Facoltà di lettere e filosofia 56). Florence: L. S. Olschki.

Schein, S. L. 1970. "Odysseus and Polyphemus in the *Odyssey*." *Greek, Roman and Byzantine Studies* 11: 73–83.

Schmidt, E. A. 1990. *Notwehrdichtung: Moderns Jambik von Chénier bis Borchardt (mit einer Skizze zur antiken Jambik)*. Munich: Fink.

Schmidt, M. 2002. "La ceramica di Taranto." *Atti del 41: Convegno di studi sulla Magna Grecia*. Taranto : Istituto per la storia e l'archeologia della Magna Grecia. 343–64.

————. 2003. "Schreibende Vasenmaler in Unteritalien." In *Griechische Keramik im kulturellen Kontext: Akten des internationalen Vasen-Symposium in Kiel vom 24–28.09.2001*, ed B. Schmaltz and M. Söldner, 171–74. Münster: Scriptorium.

————. 2005. "Livello culturale di singoli pittori: Dalla erudizione individuale all' automatismo artigianale." In *La céramique apulienne : Bilan et perspectives : Actes de la table ronde, Centre Jean Bérard, 30 Novembre-2 Décembre 2000*. Ed. M. Denoyelle, E. Lippolis, M. Mazzei, C. Pouzadoux. (Collection du Centre Jean Bérard 21). 201–6. Naples: L'Arte Tipographica.

Schröter, R. 1950. *Die Aristie als Grundform homerischer Dichtung*. Ph.D. diss., University of Marburg. Marburg: University of Marburg Press.

Scodel, R. 1987. "Horace, Lucilius, and Callimachean Polemic." *Harvard Studies in Classical Philology* 91: 199–215.

Seaford, R. 1982. "The Date of Euripides' *Cyclops*." *Journal of Hellenic Studies* 102: 161–72.

———. 1984. *Euripides' Cyclops*. Oxford: Oxford University Press.

———. 1994. *Reciprocity and Ritual: Homer and Tragedy in the Developing City-State*. Oxford: Oxford University Press.

———. 1996. "Something to Do with Dionysos—Tragedy and the Dionysiac: Response to Friedrich." In *Tragedy and the Tragic: Greek Theater and Beyond*, ed. M. S. Silk, 284–94. Oxford: Oxford University Press.

Segal, C. P. 1961. "The Character and Cults of Dionysus and the Unity of The *Frogs*," *Harvard Studies in Classical Philology*, 65: 207–42.

———. 1977. "Thematic Coherence and Levels of Style in Theocritus' Bucolic Idylls." *Wiener Studien* 90: 35–68.

———. 1983. "Greek Myth as a Semiotic and Structural System and the Problem of Tragedy." *Arethusa* 16: 173–98. Repr., C. Segal, *Interpreting Greek Tragedy: Myth, Poetry, Text*. 1986. Ithaca and London: Cornell University Press, 48–74.

———. 1994. *Singers, Heroes, and Gods in the* Odyssey. Ithaca, N.Y.: Cornell University Press.

Seidel, M. 1979. *Satiric Inheritance: Rabelais to Sterne*. Princeton: Princeton University Press.

Seidensticker, B. 1978. "Archilochus and Odysseus," *Greek, Roman and Byzantine Studies* 19: 5–22.

Shero, L. 1923. "The *Cena* in Roman Satire." *Classical Philology* 18: 126–43.

Sifakis, G. 1971. *Parabasis and Animal Choruses*. London: Athlone.

Silk, M. S. 1993. "Aristophanic Paratragedy." In *Tragedy, Comedy, and the Polis*, ed. A. H. Sommerstein, et al., 477–504. Bari: Levante Editori.

Sommerstein, A. H. 1981. *Aristophanes: Knights*. Warminster: Aris and Phillips.

———. 1982. *Aristophanes: Clouds*. Warminster: Aris and Phillips.

———. 1996. *Aristophanes: Frogs*. Warminster: Aris and Phillips.

———. 2001. *Aristophanes: Wealth*. Warminster: Aris and Phillips.

Spina, L. 2001. *L'oratorio scriteriato: Per una storia letteraria e politica di Tersite*. Naples: Loffredo.

Stanford, W. B. 1963. *The Ulysses Theme: A Study in the Adaptability of a Traditional Hero*. 2nd ed. Oxford: Basil Blackwell.

Stark, I. 1993. "Soziale Wurzein der Griechischen Komödie?" *Archiv für Kulturgeschichte* 75: 251–56.

———. 1995. "Who Laughs at Whom in Greek Comedy." In *Laughter Down the Centuries*, ed. S. Jäkel and A. Timonen, vol. 2, 99–116. Turku: Turun Yliopisto.

———. 2004. *Die hämische Muse: Spott als soziale und mentale Kontrolle in der griechischen Komödie*. Munich: C. H. Beck.

Steinhausen, J. 1910. *KOMOIDOUMENOI: De grammaticorum veterum studiis ad homines in comoedia attica irrisos pertinentibus*. Bonn: Karl George.

Steinrück, M. 2000. *Iambos. Studien zum Publikum einer Gattung in der frühgriechischen Literatur*. (*Spudasmata* 79). Hildesheim: Olms.

Stocker, C. W. 1835. *The Satires of Juvenal and Persius*. London: Longman.

Stoessl, F. 1976. "Das Liebesgedicht des Archilochos (P. Colon. 7511), seine literarische Form und seine Zeugnis über Leben und Sitten im Paros des 7. Jh. a.C." *Rheinisches Museum* 119: 242–66.

Storey, I. C. 2003. *Eupolis, Poet of Old Comedy*. Oxford: Oxford University Press.

Syme, R. 1970. "Personal Names in *Annals* I–VI." In R. Syme, *Ten Studies in Tacitus*. Oxford: Oxford University Press. Originally published in *Journal of Roman Studies* 39 (1949): 6–18.

Tarditi, G. 1956. "La nuova epigrafe archilochea e la tradizione biografica del poeta." *La Parola del Passato* 47: 122–39.

———. 1978. "Le muse povere (Call. *Ia*. I, fr. 191,92–93 Pf.)." In *Studi in onore di Anthos Ardizzoni*, ed. E. Livrea and G. A. Privitera, 1015–21. Rome: Edizioni dell' Ateneo & Bizzarri.

Tennant, P. 2003. "Queering the Patron's Pitch: the Real Satirical Target of Juvenal's Ninth Satire." In Basson and Dominick 2003, 123–32.

Thalmann, W. G. 1984. *Conventions of Form and Thought in Early Greek Poetry*. Baltimore: The Johns Hopkins University Press.

———. 1988. "Thersites: Comedy, Scapegoats, and Heroic Ideology in the *Iliad*." *Transactions of the American Philological Association* 118: 1–28.

Trendall, A. D., and A. Cambitoglou. 1982. *The Red-Figured Vases of Apulia*. Oxford: Oxford University Press.

Turner, V. 1977. *The Ritual Process: Structure and Anti-Structure*. Ithaca, N.Y.: Cornell University Press.

Usener, H. 1897. "Der Stoff des griechischen Epos, *Sitzungsberichte der kaiserlichen Akademie der Wissenschaften in Wien (Philosophisch-Historische Klasse)*" 137: 42–63.

Ussher, R. G. 1978. *Euripides:* Cyclops. Rome: Edizioni dell' Ateneo & Bizzarri.

Van Rooy, C. A. 1965. *Studies in Classical Satire and Related Literary Theory*. Leiden: E. J. Brill.

Vernant, J.-P. 1990 [1972]. *Myth and Society in Ancient Greece*. Trans. Janet Lloyd. New York: Zone Books.

Versnel, H. S. 1990. "What's Sauce for the Goose Is Sauce for the Gander: Myth and Ritual, Old and New." In Edmunds 1990, 25–90.

Voelke, P. 2003. "Drame satyrique et comédie: À propos de quelques fragments sophocléens." In *Shards from Kolonos: Studies in Sophoclean Fragments*, ed. A.H. Sommerstein. 329–51. Bari: Levante.

Volk, K. 2002. *The Poetics of Latin Didactic: Lucretius, Vergil, Ovid, Manilius*. Oxford: Oxford University Press.

von Blumenthal, A. 1922. *Die Schätzung des Archilochos im Altertume*. Stuttgart: Kohlhammer.

von Möllendorff, P. 1995. *Grundlagen einer Ästhetik der Alten Komödie: Untersuchungen zu Aristophanes und Michail Bachtin* (Classica Monacensia 9). Tübingen: Gunter Narr.

Waterfield, R. 1993. *Plato: Republic*. Oxford: Oxford University Press.

Watson, L. C. 2003. *A Commentary on Horace's* Epodes. Oxford: Oxford University Press.

Wetzel, W. 1965. *De Euripidis Fabula Satyrica Quae Cyclops Inscribitur, Cum Homerico Comparata Exemplo*. Wiesbaden: O. Harrassowitz.

Webster, T. B. L. 1970. *Studies in Later Greek Comedy*. 2nd ed. Manchester: University of Manchester Press.

West, M. L. 1974. *Studies in Greek Elegy and Iambus*. Berlin and New York: De Gruyter.

———. 1981. "Melos, Iambos, Elegie und Epigramm." In *Neues Handbuch der Literaturwissenschaft: Griechische Literatur*, ed. E. Vogt, 73–142. Wiesbaden: Akademische Verlagsgesellschaft Athenaion.

———. 1994. *Greek Lyric Poetry*. Oxford: Oxford University Press.

Westermann, A. 1843. *Mythographoi: Scriptores Poeticae Historiae Graeci*. Brunswick: Georgius Westermann.

Whitman, C. H. 1964. *Aristophanes and the Comic Hero*. Cambridge, MA: Harvard University Press.

Wiechers, A. 1961. *Aesop in Delphi*. Meisenheim am Glan: Hain.

Willi, A. 2003. *The Languages of Aristophanes: Aspects of Linguistic Variation in Classical Attic Greek*. Oxford: Oxford University Press.

Woodford, S. 1992. "Kerkopes" in *Lexicon Iconographicum Mythologiae Classicae* 6.1: 32–25. Zurich: Artemis.

Zancani Montuoro, P., and U. Zanotti-Bianco. 1954. *Heraion alla Foce del Sele* II. Rome: Libreria dello Stato, 185–91.

Zimmermann, K. 1997. "Thersites" in *Lexicon Iconographicum Mythologiae Classicae* 8.1, Supplement, 1207–09. Zurich: Artemis.

72: 138 n. 49, 18.95–100: 138,
18.111: 139, 19.13: 231, 20.287–
319: 86 n. 33, 22.79–88: 169 n. 89,
22.287: 86 n. 33
Homeric Hymn to Demeter 202: 53,
202–3: 53, 242–49: 47–8, 305ff.:
60 n. 43, 305–13: 61 n. 45, 453–
56: 61 n. 45
Homeric Hymn to Hermes 55–58: 112
Horace
   Epist. 1.19.23–25: 188 n. 27
   Epod. 6.11–14: 184
   Serm. 1.4: 6 n. 5, 208–9, 1.4.1–7: 5–
   6, 7, 1.4.5: 7–8 n. 10, 6 n. 2,
   1.4.39: 10, 10 n. 14, 1.4.41–42: 46
   n. 9, 1.4.78–105: 21 n. 31, 1.4.81–
   91: 228, 1.5.30: 74 n. 14, 1.9: 229
   n. 25, 1.10: 6, 2.1: 227, 2.1.1: 46
   n. 9, 2.3: 229 n. 25, 2.4: 229 n. 25,
   2.7: 229 n. 25, 4.26–31: 230 n. 28,
   4.78: 230 n. 28

Julian *Or.* 7.207b–c: 246 n. 4
Juvenal 1.30: 46 n. 9, 77, 1.79–80: 10
   n. 14, 1.85–86: 225 n. 34, 1.132–
   34: 9, 1.147–51: 9 n. 13, 1.165–68:
   228, 2: 89, 4.106: 230, 5.12–13:
   237, 5.149–55: 240, 5.156–73:
   238–39, 7.50–51: 9–10, 7.53: 10,
   7.53–62: 233, 7.59–62: 10, 7.66–
   71: 10, 234, 9: 210–17, 9.1–2:
   225–26, 9.9–11: 226–27, 9.27–33:
   10, 9.27–40: 231–32, 9.33–37:
   231, 9.63: 229, 9.63–65: 235 n. 34,
   9.130–33: 229 n. 25, 9.132–38:
   232, 9.137–47: 234, 9.147–50:
   227–28, 15.13–26: 235 n. 34

Lucian
   Dial. Mort. 30 119 n. 3
   Ver. Hist. 20: 119 n. 3
Lucilius 1022–23: 13 n. 15

P.Oxy. 1800 fr. 2 ii.32–63: 99, 2174:
   154 n. 70

Persius 1.107–10: 228
Pherecrates fr. 165 KA: 104
Philochorus=*FGrH* 328 F 103: 55
   n. 27
Philodemus
   fr. = *P.Herc.* 1074 fr. f col. iii 1–12=
   Archil. Testim. 128 Tarditi =
   Hipponax Testim. 48 Dg.: 263–64
   On Poems 5, cols. xxxii 9–17: 265
   n. 40
Philoxenus fr. 5, 818 *PMG* 158 n. 77
Photius *Bibl.* 279, 534a3–4 Bekker: 100
   n. 56
Pindar
   Nem. 8.32–33: 71 n. 9, 8.50–51: 71
   n. 9
   Pyth. 2.52–56: 71 n. 8, 250, 2.55–56:
   99 n.54, 118 n. 2, 121 n. 9
Plato
   Ion 531a2: 257 n. 27, 532a6: 257
   n. 27
   Laws 816d–e: 260 n. 32
   Rep. 365c5: 257 n. 27, 377–99: 33
   n. 51, 392c: 255, 395c–d: 255–56,
   395e–396a: 256, 398a–b: 259,
   475d: 261 n. 33, 620c: 73 n. 12
   Symp. 215a5–222b7: 226 n. 17
Platon Fr. 95–97 K-A: 58 n. 35
Pliny *NH* 36.12: 254
Plutarch
   De Rect. Rat. Aud. 45a–b: 246 n. 4
   Lyc. 12.6: 115
   Mor. 60c: 59 n. 39
Proclus *Chrestomathia* p.67.25–26
   Bernabé: 93f.
Propertius 3.11.15: 94 n.42
Pseudo-Nonnus scholia to Gregory of
   Nazianzus 39: 58

Quintilian 10.1.60: 245 n. 4, 10.1.93:
   208–9 n. 2
Quintus Smyrnaeus 1.538–722: 94
   n. 42, 1.723–47: 94–96, 1.747–49:
   94 n. 43, 1.750–54: 96, 1.767–69:
   97–98, 1.774–78: 97–98

Cyclops, *see also*, Oedipus and the
Cyclopes and Polyphemus
as comic figures, 143

Damoetas and Daphnis, 167–69
Demeter, 47
and Iambe, 44, 47–57, 59–60, 91
Demodocus, 123, 125
Dikê, 121
Diomedes, on the Boston
Thersitoktonos vase, 105, 109–110
Dionysius I of Syracuse, 155–58
Dionysus, 27–29, 31

Eleusis, 30, 47, 49
mysteries at 52, 56, 60–61
Ennius, 207
Epic, 126, 240–41
and comic, 90, 114
Epos, 90, 95–96, 126 n. 20
Eratosthenes, 262
Erynnis, on the Boston Thersitoktonos
Vase, 107
Euripides, 141–59, 264

Fictionality, 22
Freud, 32–33

Galatea, 157–59, 166–69
Geertz, 32 n. 47
Geloion, 37–39, 89–90 n. 35, 90
Genital humor, 62, 65
Genre, 14 f., 55, 61, 14 n. 19, 126, 207,
208 n. 1, 246
and myth, 54, 56
conceived inductively or
deductively, 13–14 nn. 17–18
Gephyrismos, 30
Greek literature, and satirical poets 46
n. 9
Greek vase painting
Boston MFA 03.804, *see*, Boston
Thersitoktonos Vase
Boston Thersitoktonos Vase, 104–116
Getty Museum 81.AE.189, 63

Heracles,
and Cercopes, 44–46, 57 f., 103
reception of Cercopes story,
57–58
Hermes, on the Boston Thersitoktonos
Vase, 105, 109
Hesiod, 126 n.20
Hipponax, 4, 11–12, 59, 66, 70, 104
n. 65, 127 n. 24, 152, 154–55, 166
n. 85, 171, 229, 232, 254, 264
and Callimachus, 172f., 243
and "Hipponactean," 175 n. 3, 176 f.
Homer, 37–38, 68, 70, 72, 77, 78
n. 24, 111, 123 f., 142, 170–71,
231, 264
and psogic discourse, 119–120
Homeric scenes as embedded
mockery, 75–76
sympathy for the Cyclopes, 159
Horace, 3, 7–8, 175
and Greek iambography, 4, 184
and Old Comedy, 7, 209, 243

Iambe, 44–57, 59–60
Iambic poetry, 51, 61, 63, 66, 128, 166,
180
Iambos, 51–53, 174–75, 206 n. 53
Irony, 51, 180, 219
and Odysseus 136
Irus, see, Odysseus and Irus

Juvenal, 3–4, 8–11, 89, 209 f.,
principle of satire 77, 80

Kômôidein onomasti, *see*, mockery, of
individuals by name
Kykeôn, 49, 52, 60

Laughter, 15, 20, 40, 60, 61, 65–66,
139 n. 51
and sexual obscenity, 49, 91
as currency, 59
in epic combat, 142
Lucian, 9 n. 12
Lucilius, 6, 7, 207, 209